Shopping Towns Europe

Shopping Towns Europe

Commercial Collectivity and the Architecture of the Shopping Centre, 1945–1975

Edited by Janina Gosseye and Tom Avermaete

BLOOMSBURY VISUAL ARTS
LONDON • NEW YORK • OXFORD • NEW DELHI • SYDNEY

BLOOMSBURY VISUAL ARTS
Bloomsbury Publishing Plc
50 Bedford Square, London, WC1B 3DP, UK
1385 Broadway, New York, NY 10018, USA

BLOOMSBURY, BLOOMSBURY VISUAL ARTS and the Diana logo are trademarks
of Bloomsbury Publishing Plc

First published in Great Britain 2017
Paperback Edition published 2020

Copyright © Janina Gosseye and Tom Avermaete, 2017, 2020

Janina Gosseye and Tom Avermaete have asserted their right under the Copyright,
Designs and Patents Act, 1988, to be identified as Editors of this work.

Cover design: Sanne Dijkstra
Cover image © Kestone-France/Gamma-Keystone via Getty Images

All rights reserved. No part of this publication may be reproduced or transmitted
in any form or by any means, electronic or mechanical, including photocopying,
recording, or any information storage or retrieval system, without prior
permission in writing from the publishers.

Bloomsbury Publishing Plc does not have any control over, or responsibility for, any third-party
websites referred to or in this book. All internet addresses given in this book were correct at the time
of going to press. The author and publisher regret any inconvenience caused if addresses have changed
or sites have ceased to exist, but can accept no responsibility for any such changes.

A catalogue record for this book is available from the British Library.

A catalog record for this book is available from the Library of Congress.

ISBN: HB: 978-1-4742-6737-3
        PB: 978-1-3501-5445-2
        ePDF: 978-1-4742-6738-0
        eBook: 978-1-4742-6740-3

Typeset by Integra Software Services Pvt. Ltd.

To find out more about our authors and books visit www.bloomsbury.com
and sign up for our newsletters.

Contents

Notes on contributors   vii

Shopping towns Europe, 1945–1975 *Janina Gosseye and Tom Avermaete*   1

Part 1 Urbanism harnessing the consumption-juggernaut: Shopping centres and urban (re)development

1. Shopping à *l'américaine*   Kenny Cupers   25
2. The 1960s shopping centre grid of Helsinki: A framework for future development   *Juhana Lahti*   38
3. Shopping centres as catalysts for new multifunctional urban centralities: The case of two shopping centres around Brussels   *Yannick Vanhaelen and Géry Leloutre*   51
4. The Lijnbaan in Rotterdam: A sound urban form against city disruption   *Dirk van den Heuvel*   65
5. Displays of modernity: The urban restructuring of post-1963 Skopje   *Jasna Mariotti*   78

Part 2 Constructing consumer-citizens: Shopping centres shaping commercial collectivity

6. Miracles and ruins, citizens and shoppers: Frankfurt 1963   *Inderbir Singh Riar*   95
7. Collectivity in the prison of plenty: The French commercial centres by Claude Parent, 1967–1971   *Tom Avermaete*   110

8	Hello, consumer! Skärholmen Centre from the Million Programme to the mall *Jennifer Mack*	122
9	Milton Keynes' Centre: The apotheosis of the British post-war consensus or, the apostle of neo-liberalism? *Janina Gosseye*	138
10	Shopping as a part of a political agenda: The emergence and development of the shopping centre in socialist Croatia, 1960–1980 *Sanja Matijević Barčot and Ana Grgić*	155
11	Unico Prezzo Italiano: Corporate consumption and retail architecture in post-war Italy *Daniele Vadala'*	168

Part 3 Shifting forms of shopping: Between dense and tall and the low-slung (suburban) shopping mall

12	The creation of civic identity in post-war corporate architecture: Marcel Breuer's Bijenkorf in Rotterdam, 1953–1957 *Evangelia Tsilika*	183
13	The shopping centre comes to Germany: Frankfurt's Main-Taunus-Zentrum at the crossroads of mass-motorization and retail economics *Steffen de Rudder*	196
14	Built for mass consumption: Shopping centres in West Germany's boom years *Olaf Gisbertz*	210
15	The drive to modernize: Remodelling Birmingham city centre, 1945–1965 *Jo Lintonbon*	222
16	Malls and commercial planning policies in a compact city: The case of Barcelona *Nadia Fava and Manuel Guàrdia*	238
	Index	251

Notes on contributors

Tom Avermaete is Professor at ETH Zürich, where he holds the Chair of the History and Theory of Urban Design. Avermaete has a special research interest in the post-war public realm and the architecture of the city in Western and non-Western contexts. He is the author of *Another Modern: The Post-War Architecture and Urbanism of Candilis-Josic-Woods* (2005) and *Casablanca, Chandigarh: A Report on Modernization* (2014, with Maristella Casciato). Avermaete has also edited numerous books, including *Acculturating the Shopping Centre* (2018, with Janina Gosseye), and is a member of the editorial team of *OASE Architectural Journal* and the advisory board of the *Architectural Theory Review,* among others.

Kenny Cupers is Associate Professor in the History and Theory of Architecture and Urbanism at the University of Basel. His research projects centre on questions of human and material agency, the epistemology and geopolitics of modernism, and design as a technique of social intervention. Cupers is the author of *The Social Project: Housing Postwar France* (2014), winner of the SAH Spiro Kostof Award amongst other prizes. Other publications include *Use Matters: An Alternative History of Architecture* (2013) and *Spaces of Uncertainty* (2002, with Markus Miessen).

Steffen de Rudder is Professor at the Bauhaus University in Weimar, where he teaches urban design and history. He was Guest Professor of Urban History at Anhalt University in Dessau, Adjunct Professor for Urban and Architectural History at University Erfurt, DAAD Fellow at the Academy of Architecture in Amsterdam, Assistant Professor at Bauhaus University Weimar and Adjunct Professor at Humboldt University in Berlin. Before starting his academic career, Professor de Rudder worked as an architect and urban planner in Berlin. He received his PhD from Bauhaus University Weimar and graduated from the Technical University Berlin. His research focuses on the history of post-war modern architecture and urbanism.

Nadia Fava holds a doctorate in architecture from the Polytechnic University of Catalonia, and is currently a Lecturer in Urban Planning at the University of Girona. Her research focuses on urban history and planning, mainly on urban evolution, tourism and city retailing in the 19th, 20th and 21st centuries. Her work has been published in international peer-reviewed journals, including the *Journal of Urban History* (2016) and *Town Planning Review* (2015).

Olaf Gisbertz is Assistant Professor at the Institute for Building History at TU Braunschweig. Professor Gisbertz has curated several exhibitions and organised a number of conferences and roundtables on post-war architecture. He has also authored and edited numerous publications on this subject, including *Bauen für die Massenkultur: Stadt- und Kongresshallen der 1960er und 1970er Jahre* (2015). Since 2014, Professor Gisbertz has been the Director of the Building Research + Communication + Conservation Centre at TU Braunschweig.

Janina Gosseye is a Senior Research Associate at ETH Zürich and an Honorary Senior Fellow of the University of Queensland School of Architecture. Her research is situated at the nexus of architectural theory, urban planning and social and political history. Gosseye has edited and authored several books, including *Acculturating the Shopping Centre* (2018, with Tom Avermaete) and *Speaking of Buildings: Oral History in Architectural Research* (2019, with Naomi Stead and Deborah van der Plaat). Her research has also been published in leading journals, including *the Journal of Architecture, the Journal of Urban History and Planning Perspectives*. In 2018, she was made an Honorary Member of the Australian Institute of Architects (AIA).

Ana Grgić completed her PhD at the University of Zagreb's Faculty of Architecture in 2011. After working in an architectural office she started her academic career with a research project on the 'Architecture of Split 1945-2000' at the Faculty of Civil Engineering, Architecture and Geodesy in Split, Croatia. Currently an Assistant Professor, Grgić teaches architecture and urban design courses and also organises international workshops. Grgić has edited several publications, taken part in architectural and urban design competitions, and participated in international scientific conferences related to her research interest in spatial and landscape planning and public space.

Manuel Guàrdia holds a doctorate in architecture and is a Lecturer in Architectural History, Urban History and Urban Planning at the Polytechnic University of Catalonia. His research focuses on urban history and urban planning; mainly on the long-term evolution of space structures and city supply. He has edited several books, including: *Atlas Histórico de Ciudades Europeas* (1994–1996), *La Revolución del Agua en Barcelona. De la Ciudad Preindustrial a la Métropoli Moderna, 1867–1967* (2011), and *Making Cities through Market Halls. Europe, 19th and 20th Centuries* (2015).

Juhana Lahti is an Art Historian and holds a PhD from the University of Helsinki (2006). Lahti is currently the Head of Research/Director of Collections at the Museum of Finnish Architecture (MFA) in Helsinki. His research and publications focus on the history of modern architecture and planning, especially in the post-Second World War period; he is also interested in questions related to digital paradigm shifts in culture. Lahti previously worked in different positions at the MFA, the University of Helsinki and the Finnish Foundation for the Visual Arts in New York City.

Géry Leloutre holds a degree in Architecture from ISA Victor Horta in Brussels and in Urban Planning and Design from KULeuven. He recently completed his doctoral thesis, jointly with the Free University of Brussels and the IUAV in Venice, on the modus operandi of city building in Brussels in the mid-20th century. From 2006 to 2008, Leloutre was Editor in Chief of the *Brussels Review of Urbanism BrU* and in 2007, he founded his own practice, 'Karbon, Architecture et Urbanisme'. Through his teaching at the ULB Architecture Faculty and his design practice, Leloutre continues to expand his research on Brussels and urban planning.

Jo Lintonbon is an architect and a Lecturer at Sheffield School of Architecture, the University of Sheffield, UK. She studied architecture at Cambridge and Sheffield and completed her PhD in 2002 on the historical development of shop typologies and the role of commercial architecture in transforming the high street. Her ongoing research interests are focused on the cultural and economic processes that continue to shape the built environment and address social practices and everyday architecture, heritage and identity, and the architectural transformation of existing buildings and spaces through conservation-led regeneration.

Jennifer Mack is a Postdoctoral Fellow at Uppsala University and researcher at KTH Royal Institute of Technology. She combines ethnography, history, and formal analysis to study social change and the built environment, with current projects on the design of large-scale mosques and churches, the politics of landscape in allotment gardens, and the Swedish town centre (*centrum*). Her forthcoming book investigates the 'segregated' Swedish town of Södertälje since the 1960s through her notion of 'urban design from below'.

Jasna Mariotti studied Architecture at the Faculty of Architecture in Skopje and obtained a Masters Degree in Architecture, Urbanism and Building Sciences from TU Delft in 2007. In 2014 she completed a PhD on post-socialist cities and their urban transformations at the Faculty of Architecture, University of Ljubljana. She currently works at the School of Planning, Architecture and Civil Engineering at Queen's University Belfast. Before moving to Belfast, Mariotti was Assistant Professor in Urban Design at the Faculty of Architecture in Skopje and worked as an architect and urban designer at West 8 in Rotterdam.

Sanja Matijević Barčot is an architect and Postdoctoral Research Assistant at the University of Split, Faculty of Civil Engineering, Architecture and Geodesy. She received her PhD in History and Theory of Architecture and Historic Preservation from the University of Zagreb in 2014. For her doctoral dissertation she investigated how socialist housing strategies determined the conditions of architectural production and shaped the architecture of Split in the period between 1945 and 1968. Her research interests include modern architecture and culture in Croatia, the legacy of socialist housing strategies and politics of urban planning after the Second World War.

Evangelia Tsilika is an architect and independent researcher. She studied architecture at Aristotle University of Thessaloniki (1997), did her postgraduate studies at the Harvard Graduate School of Design (1999) and completed her doctorate at the National Technical University of Athens in 2008. She has lectured on architectural design and theory at several universities and institutions. She has worked both in New York and Athens, where she is currently involved in public projects as Head of the Department of Ports' Building Infrastructure at the Ministry of Mercantile Marine. The chapter that she has authored in this book is part of her comprehensive study of Marcel Breuer's architecture.

Inderbir Singh Riar is Associate Professor in the Azrieli School of Architecture & Urbanism at Carleton University (Canada). His research currently explores how the post-war metropolis was imagined as producing ideal citizenries. This work includes a study on Toulouse-Le Mirail, the French new town, undertaken in collaboration with the Paris-based photographer Mark Lyon and supported by the Graham Foundation for Advanced Studies in the Fine Arts. In 2013, he was selected for the Japan Foundation Invitation Program for Curators. Trained as an architect, Riar completed his PhD at Columbia University with the dissertation 'Expo 67, or the Architecture of Late Modernity' (2014).

Daniele Vadala' obtained his Masters in Architecture from the University Mediterranea of Reggio Calabria (2001) and a PhD in Building Engineering and Renovation Projects at University of Messina (2010). He is currently a Lecturer in Contemporary Architectural History at the University of Catania, and has previously collaborated with the Pontifical University San Bonaventura in Rome for work in the field of environmental and landscape protection. His research interests lay at the crossroads between contemporary practice and architectural history, with a specific focus on cultural landscapes and adaptive infrastructures.

Dirk van den Heuvel is Associate Professor at TU Delft and Head of the Jaap Bakema Study Centre at Het Nieuwe Instituut, Rotterdam. Van den Heuvel curated various exhibitions, including the Dutch national pavilion at the Venice Biennale 2014, 'Open: A Bakema Celebration'. His book publications include: *Jaap Bakema and the Open Society* (2016), *Architecture and the Welfare State* (2015, with Mark Swenarton and Tom Avermaete), *Team 10: In Search of a Utopia of the Present 1953-1981* (2005, with Max Risselada) and *Alison and Peter Smithson: From the House of the Future to a House of Today* (2004, with Max Risselada).

Yannick Vanhaelen graduated in architecture from the Université Libre de Bruxelles (ULB). After his studies, he worked in the architectural practices of NL Architects in the Netherlands and 51N4E in Belgium, where he was project leader for the elaboration of a territorial vision for the Brussels Capital Region in 2040. In 2013 he co-founded the office DEV-space. Vanhaelen is currently a PhD researcher at the Laboratory on Urbanism, Infrastructure and Ecologies (LoUIsE) of the ULB Architecture Faculty. His PhD, for which he obtained a grant from the Belgian National Fund for Scientific Research, focuses on the urban and mobility impacts of large cultural infrastructures in the metropolitan area of Brussels.

Shopping towns Europe, 1945–1975
Janina Gosseye and Tom Avermaete

The shopping center is one of the few new building types created in our time…. Because shopping centers represent groupings of structures and because of the underlying cooperative spirit involved, the need for environmental planning for this building type is obvious. Where this need has been fully understood shopping centers have taken on the characteristics of urban organisms serving a multitude of human needs and activities, thus justifying the designation: shopping towns.[1]

With these words, Viennese émigré architect Victor Gruen and American economist Larry Smith opened their 1960 landmark publication *Shopping Towns USA: The Planning of Shopping Centers*, which aimed to 'further the understanding and use of good planning principles [in shopping centre design]'. Of the eight shopping centres shown in the book's introduction, three were located in Europe: the Lijnbaan in Rotterdam, Vällingby Centrum near Stockholm and Harlow's New Town Centre near London. Gruen and Smith, however, did not discuss these European examples in great detail, limiting themselves '… to a discussion of shopping centers in the United States' in spite of being 'fully aware of the significant contributions towards the planning of shopping facilities … which are being made today in shopping centers in other parts of the world'. *Shopping Towns Europe* is thus a foil to *Shopping Towns USA*, differing from it in two key ways. Firstly, while *Shopping Towns USA* did '… not attempt to be a history of shopping center development',[2] *Shopping Towns Europe* – published more than half a century later – does offer a historical account of shopping centres in the three decades following the Second World War. Secondly, and more importantly, contrary to Gruen and Smith's work, the focus of this publication is on Europe, not the United States.

In Europe, shopping centres emerged and became an everyday phenomenon roughly between the early 1950s and the mid-1970s. In this period the incomes of large sections of the population increased, class differences and social conflict decreased and new forms of cultural differentiation emerged. It was the heyday of the European welfare state. Since the late 1990s, the European welfare state has gained increasing recognition in architectural history, albeit mainly through the lens of state-driven

---

[1] Victor Gruen and Larry Smith, *Shopping Towns USA: The Planning of Shopping Centers* (New York/Amsterdam/London: Reinhold Publishing Corporation, 1960), 11.
[2] Ibid., 11–12.

initiatives in the realm of housing and 'community building'. This has resulted in the production of a particular set of histories that portray the emergence of post-war 'modernity' as intimately entangled with state-driven action.[3] Although highly relevant, these accounts only partially explain the modernity that people experienced on an everyday basis in post-war Europe. As the work of the Regulation School has demonstrated,[4] the European welfare state was a contract between the public sector, the private sector and civic society. Apart from the state (and often in close cooperation with it), civic society and the private sector contributed greatly to the introduction of the modern in the built environment. Civic organizations, for instance, instructed citizens in 'good' design for their homes,[5] while the private sector developed a vast range of new household products,[6] created 'modern' spaces for production, such as offices, factories and distribution centres, and also articulated novel spaces for consumption, including the shopping centre. Although the private sector was an important actor in establishing new relations between modernity and the built environment, the role that corporate and commercial modernism played in reforming post-war Europe is still astonishingly understudied. While some research has been conducted into the expansion of supermarkets and offices,[7] the typology of the

---

[3]Tom Avermaete, *Another Modern: The Postwar Architecture and Urbanism of Candilis–Josic–Woods* (Rotterdam: NAi Publishers, 2005); Elke Beyer, Anke Hagemann and Michael Zinganel (eds.), *Holidays after the Fall: Seaside Architecture and Urbanism in Bulgaria and Croatia* (Berlin: Jovis, 2013); Nicholas Bullock, *Building the Post-war World: Modern Architecture and Reconstruction in Britain* (London/New York: Routledge, 2002); Kenny Cupers, *The Social Project: Housing Post-war France* (Minneapolis: University of Minnesota Press, 2014); Janina Gosseye, Hilde Heynen (eds.), André Loeckx and Leen Van Molle, *Architectuur voor Vrijetijdscultuur* (Leuven: LannooCampus, 2011); Christoph Grafe, *People's Palaces: Architecture, Culture and Democracy in Post-war Western Europe* (Amsterdam: Architectura & Natura, 2014); Helena Mattsson and Sven-Olov Wallenstein (eds.), *Swedish Modernism: Architecture, Consumption and the Welfare State* (London: Black Dog Publishing, 2010); Gérard Monnier and Richard Klein (eds.), *Les Annéés Zup: Architectures de la Croissance (1960–1973)* (Paris: Picard, 2002); Michael Ryckewaert, *Building the Economic Backbone of the Belgian Welfare State: Infrastructure, Planning and Architecture 1945–1973* (Rotterdam: 010 Publishers, 2011); Andrew Saint, *Towards a Social Architecture: The Role of School-building in Post-war England* (New Haven, CT: Yale University, 1987); Greg Stevenson, *Palaces for the People: Prefabs in Post-war Britain* (London: B.T. Batsford Ltd, 2003); Karina Van Herck and Tom Avermaete (eds.), *Wonen in Welvaart: Woningbouw en Wooncultuur in Vlaanderen, 1948–1973* (Rotterdam: 010/Antwerp: VAi & CVAa, 2006); Cor Wagenaar (ed.), *Happy: Cities and Public Happiness in Post-war Europe* (Rotterdam: NAi Publishers, 2004).

[4]The Regulation School is a group of writers in political economy and economics whose origins can be traced to France in the early 1970s. Their work focuses on how historically specific systems of capital accumulation are 'regularized' or stabilized, often with the aid of state intervention.

[5]This has been well documented in Belgium by Fredie Floré, *Lessen in Goed Wonen: Woonvoorlichting in België, 1945–1958* (Leuven: Leuven University Press, 2010) and Els De Vos, *Hoe zouden we graag wonen? Woonvertogen in Vlaanderen tijdens de jaren zestig en zeventig* (Leuven: Leuven University Press, 2012).

[6]While Beatriz Colomina, Annemarie Brennan and Jeannie Kim – through the history of the ballpoint pen, TV dinners, … – document how technological innovation permeated American life in every aspect and at every scale in their edited book *Cold War Hothouses: Inventing Postwar Culture, from Cockpit to Playboy* (New York: Princeton Architectural Press, 2004), Victoria De Grazia eloquently demonstrates how these novel products contributed to the formation of an American consumption society, which took Europe's bourgeois civilization by storm in the twentieth century: *Irresistible Empire: America's Advance through 20th Century Europe* (Cambridge, MA/London: The Belknap Press of Harvard University Press, 2005).

[7]See Sibylle Brändli, *Der Supermarkt im Kopf: Konsumkultur und Wohlstand in der Schweiz nach 1945* (Wien: Böhlau, 2000); Emanuela Scarpellini, 'Shopping American-Style: The Arrival of the Supermarket in Postwar Italy', *Enterprise & Society* 5, no. 4 (2004): 625–668; Babette Sluijter, *Kijken is grijpen: Zelfbedieningswinkels, Technische Dynamiek en Boodschappen doen in Nederland na 1945*, doctoral thesis (Eindhoven, 2007); Gideon Haigh, *The Office: A Hardworking History* (Melbourne: The Miegunyah Press, 2012); Juriaan Meel, *The European Office: Office Design and National Context* (Rotterdam: 010 Publishers, 2000); Dennis Doxtater, *Architecture, Ritual Practice and Co-Determination in the Swedish Office* (Aldershot: Avebury, 1994); Siri Blakstad, *The Scandinavian Office Building 1900–1980* (Trondheim: Trondheim University, 1997); Gert Staal, *Between Dictate and Design: The Architecture of Office Buildings* (Rotterdam: 010 Publishers, 1987).

shopping centre has remained largely and conspicuously absent from European architectural history. This historiographical dearth has skewed our understanding of the relation between architecture and modernity. As canonical accounts of post-war architecture and urban planning in Europe commonly depict modernity as a condition that emerged mainly (or even solely) from state initiatives underpinned by strong ideological motivations, for many modernity has become synonymous to emancipatory initiatives in the realm of public housing and government-funded architecture for health, education and leisure. This however only shows one side of the coin. Apart from public authorities, a suite of private actors (sometimes in close collaboration with public stakeholders) defined a different sort of modernity; a modernity that was not experienced through novel dwelling practices or government-funded spaces for health, education or leisure, but rather through spaces imbued with the tantalizing logic of mass consumption. It is this multiplicity of actors and simultaneity of processes of modernization, along with the coexistence of various notions of the modern, that established the very condition of modernity in post-war Europe.

Shopping Towns Europe thus sets out to redress the historiographical imbalance as it widens the perspective beyond state-driven initiatives and engages with commercial modernity. Complementing European accounts on welfare state architecture and American scholarship on the post-war spaces of consumption,[8] this book demonstrates the profound impact that the shopping centre has had on everyday life in post-war Europe, focusing particularly on how this typology's omnipresent 'other' modernity was paired with an alternative definition of the collective realm, both rhetorically and spatially. In contrast to state-led modernization, which often idealized the collective realm and defined it as a weighty contract between society and the individual, the collectivity of the shopping centre was described in terms of necessity, and (above all) in terms of leisureliness. This alternative definition of the collective realm is also legible in the novel spaces that were created within the shopping centre: from parking lots and plazas to malls and arcades.

Spanning the continent from Finland to Spain and Belgium to Croatia, also including the UK, the sixteen chapters included in *Shopping Towns Europe* are subdivided into three parts. Part 1, 'Urbanism harnessing the consumption-juggernaut: Shopping centres and urban (re)development', connects the emergence of shopping centres in post-war Europe to urban reconstruction efforts and highlights their (often) pivotal role in urban expansion schemes. Part 2, 'Constructing consumer-citizens: Shopping centres shaping commercial collectivity', iterates how shopping centres' novel modern environments were designed to elicit specific (desirable) modern behaviours. They not only enticed visitors to consume, but also encouraged human association, civic education and even cultural formation. Part 3, 'Shifting forms of shopping: Between dense and tall and the low-slung (suburban) shopping

---

[8]David Smiley, *Pedestrian Modern: Shopping and American Architecture, 1925–1956* (Minneapolis: University of Minnesota Press, 2013); Richard Longstreth, *City Center to Regional Mall: Architecture, the Automobile, and Retailing in Los Angeles, 1920–1950* (Cambridge, MA: MIT Press, 1997); Richard Longstreth, *The Drive-In, the Supermarket, and the Transformation of Commercial Space in Los Angeles, 1914–1941* (Cambridge, MA: MIT Press, 1999); Richard Longstreth, *The American Department Store Transformed, 1920–1960* (New Haven: Yale University Press, 2010); Vicki Howard, *From Main Street to Mall: The Rise and Fall of the American Department Store* (Philadelphia: University of Pennsylvania Press, 2015); Jeffrey Hardwick, *Mall Maker: Victor Gruen, Architect of an American Dream* (Philadelphia: University of Pennsylvania Press, 2004).

mall', explores the typological variations that emerged and coexisted in post-war Europe as a result of continuing urban versus ex-urban shopping debates.

Urbanism harnessing the consumption-juggernaut: Shopping centres and urban (re)development

Victor Gruen is often called the father of the shopping centre.[9] An immigrant from Austria who fled the Nazis in 1938, Gruen arrived in the United States just in time to witness the onset of drastic urban transformations. Starting from the 1940s, the construction of hundreds of thousands of new houses, many of which were underwritten by federally financed mortgage insurance, along with the rapid increase in car ownership and federally funded highway construction facilitated the American 'white flight'. For the first time, a powerful interaction between segregation laws and race differences, which were expressed in socioeconomic terms, enabled the white middle classes to abandon inner cities in favour of suburban living. This resulted in an explosive expansion of outlying areas, which were almost exclusively residential and lacking in collective amenity.

Gruen conceived of the shopping centre as a means to redress America's unfettered sprawl. He envisaged the shopping centre to become a 'suburban crystallization' point or 'satellite downtown' that – once several were realized – could develop into a network of nodes, which would not only structure decentralization but also safeguard the commercial viability of the (traditional) city centre.[10] These regional centres, he wrote, '… will by no means decrease the importance of the downtown business district but they will alleviate the unbearable traffic and parking conditions in the downtown area, thus improving shopping conditions'.[11]

Gruen's most famous shopping centre was Southdale. Built in 1956, it was the first enclosed shopping centre in America – a prototype of the suburban shopping centre type that in twenty short years would come to dominate American retailing. Gathering seventy-two shops and two anchor department stores under one roof, with air conditioning for the summer and heating for the winter, Southdale shopping centre was a sensation – hailed by consumers and exalted by reporters.[12] The early plans for Southdale shopping centre, however, differed significantly from the solitary, climate-controlled commercial container plunked down in Edina, just outside of Minneapolis. Gruen had originally placed the shopping centre at the heart of a tidy 463-acre development, complete with apartment buildings, houses, schools, a medical centre, a park and a lake. He saw Southdale shopping centre as a vehicle to build collectivity in the suburb – a means to foster a shared sense of community. Gruen's grand plans for Southdale were however never realized. No parks or schools or apartments were built, only a big box

---

[9] Alex Wall, *Victor Gruen: From Urban Shop to New City* (Barcelona: Actar, 2005); Hardwick, *Mall Maker*.
[10] Timothy Mennel, 'Victor Gruen and the Construction of Cold War Utopias', *Journal of Planning History* 3, no. 2 (May 2004): 116–150.
[11] Smiley, *Pedestrian Modern*, 191; Mennel, 'Victor Gruen and the Construction of Cold War Utopias', 137.
[12] Hardwick, *Mall Maker*, 145–147.

in a sea of parking. His nearly utopian socialist dream was built by American capitalists who, with the aid of the American Congress, turned it into a paradise of the liberal economy.[13]

Gruen soon became painfully aware that his dream was slipping away and in 1968, left the United States, gravely disillusioned. He retired from Victor Gruen Associates, the practice he had set up in Los Angeles seventeen years earlier, and returned to Vienna. That same year, he was invited to give a talk in Brussels for the occasion of the Congress on Commerce and Urban Planning. There he noted: 'To me it seems unnecessary, illogical and tragic, that Europe and other regions should repeat the mistakes made in the United States rather than to make use of the new concepts which have arisen from our own shortcomings and our search for better methods.'[14] Gruen's criticism resonated with European proponents of the shopping centre, many of whom had travelled to the United States by the scores on study tours that were organized by federal and local administrations as well as by retailing, planning and design expert organizations. One of the key lessons that these European experts took away from observing declining downtowns in the United States was the need to include the city centres in their reflection. However, not only did North America serve as a source for inspiration, certain European countries also became shopping centre destinations, most notably Sweden.[15]

Consumerism found its way to Sweden earlier than to most other European countries. While most parts of the continent only transitioned from crisis to golden age after the Second World War, the economic boom in Sweden started in the mid-1930s and overlapped with the Keynesian politics formulated by the Social Democratic finance minister Ernst Wigforss. He saw consumption as a driving force in society and attributed it a key role in the country's development. As a result, the logic of consumption became firmly embedded in Swedish mid-century architecture and planning.[16] It is then not surprising that one of Europe's pioneering shopping centres was built in Sweden in 1955. Designed by British émigré architect Ralph Erskine, 'Shopping' in Luleå was to create an enjoyable environment for everyone all year round, irrespective of weather conditions, which were very harsh at times, given its location in the northernmost part of Sweden. It offered not only bountiful merchandise and goods, but also entertainment and social spaces, making the shopping centre a natural meeting point for everyone in the city – a city within a city.[17] Opening one year prior to Gruen's Southdale, 'Shopping' in Luleå lays

---

[13]In 1954, Congress – in an attempt to stimulate investment in manufacturing – made a radical change in the tax rules governing depreciation. It launched a programme called 'accelerated depreciation', which allowed developers to rapidly write off construction of new business buildings and even claim losses against unrelated income. The depreciation deductions were so large that in the first few years after a shopping centre was built, it was almost certainly losing money, at least on paper, as it ensured enormous tax benefits and allowed shopping centre developers to recoup the cost of the investment in a fraction of time. Shopping centres thus became lucrative tax shelters for investors, leading to a 'bonanza' for developers. See Malcolm Gladwell, 'The Terrazzo Jungle', *New Yorker*, 15 March 2004, http://www.newyorker.com/magazine/2004/03/15/the-terrazzo-jungle, accessed 21 April 2016.
[14]Cited in Günter Schütze, 'Internationaler Kongress "Handel und Städtebau" in Brüssel', *Der Aufbau* 21, no. 2 (May 1967): 10–12.
[15]In 'The Janus-Faced Shopping Center: The Low Countries in Search of a Fitting Shopping Paradigm', published in the *Journal of Urban History* (2016), Janina Gosseye describes the various 'shopping centre excursions' (to both North America and Europe) undertaken by architects, planners and politicians from the Low Countries in an attempt to successfully integrate (or translate) the suburban shopping centre paradigm in (to) Belgium and the Netherlands.
[16]Mattsson and Olov-Wallenstein, *Swedish Modernism*.
[17]Helena Mattsson, 'Where the Motorways Meet: Architecture and Corporatism in Sweden 1968', in *Architecture and the Welfare State*, eds. Mark Swenarton, Tom Avermaete and Dirk van den Heuvel (London: Routledge, 2014), 159.

claim to being 'the world's first interior shopping center ever built'.[18] However, Sweden's best-known shopping centre, which Gruen and Smith also featured in their 1960 publication *Shopping Towns USA*, had opened one year earlier, in 1954. Vällingby Centrum was a large all-pedestrian open-air shopping centre composed of a collection of low-slung rectangular buildings, one or two storeys high. Apart from shops, these buildings housed the town hall, library, youth centre and also a cinema. Vällingby Centrum was situated at the heart of Vällingby, a new town located fifteen kilometres northwest of Stockholm. Its combination of commercial spaces with administrative, cultural and social venues was believed to add to the appeal of the new town by recreating an imaginary of urban centrality and conviviality, similar to (and prefiguring) Gruen's plans for Southdale.

The aptitude of shopping centres to function as the heart of new towns became generally accepted among politicians and urban planners. It significantly aided the typology's advance through post-war

Figure I.1 Interior of Luleå shopping centre in Sweden, designed by Ralph Erskine, 1955.
Source: Photograph by Sune Sundahl, Wikimedia Commons.

[18]Christopher, 'A Mid-Century Shopping Centre in Northern Sweden', *Ultraswank*, 16 January 2012, http://www.ultraswank.net/stores/a-mid-century-shopping-centre-in-northern-sweden/, accessed 21 April 2016.

Shopping towns Europe, 1945–1975

Figure I.2 Vällingby Centrum in Sweden, 1957.
Source: Lennart af Petersens, Stockholm City Museum.

Europe. During the war, many buildings had been damaged or destroyed[19] which, combined with depression era slowdowns, led to overcrowding and congestion. New towns were to take the pressure away from congested centres by rehousing people in new, freshly built, fully planned towns that were self-sufficient and provided for the community. Kenny Cupers' chapter 'Shopping à l'américaine' chronicles the story of France, where in 1965 Charles de Gaulle launched the *villes nouvelles* (or 'new towns') programme. Designed to decentralize Paris and entice regional economic development, it relied on shopping centres to imbue these *villes nouvelles* with a much-needed sense of centrality. By forging new relationships between private commercial development and centralized state planning,

---

[19] Jeffry M. Diefendorf, 'Urban Reconstruction in Europe after World War II', *Urban Studies* 26 (1989): 128–143; John R. Pendlebury, Erdem Erten and P.J. Larkham, *Alternative Visions of Post-war Reconstruction: Creating the Modern Townscape* (London: Routledge, 2015).

Cupers argues that these French new-town shopping centres offered an unparalleled terrain of experimentation, which encouraged architects to not only look at examples from across the Atlantic, but also at 'local', national patterns of consumption. Recounting the case of Évry, a new town approximately twenty-five kilometres south of Paris, Cupers illustrates how these opposing (public versus private) demands and varying references resulted in a true form of transculturation. Apart from examples in the United States, Juhana Lahti similarly cites various European points of reference (including Vällinbgy Centrum in Sweden) for the development of shopping centres in Finland in his chapter 'The 1960s shopping centre grid of Helsinki'. Focusing on three key examples – Munkkivuori, Puotinharju (Puhos) and Tapiola – he demonstrates how post-war Finnish shopping centres, much like the examples from France and Sweden, aspired to become the 'urban' heart of new housing settlements around the Finnish capital. Commonly arranged around a pedestrian street or inner court and surrounded by parking areas and bus stations, each of them was located close to housing areas where a stop along a 'fast tramline', connecting the new settlement to Helsinki's city centre, was envisioned. Munkkivuori, Puotinharju (Puhos) and Tapiola were among the thirty-eight shopping centres that were opened in greater Helsinki between 1959 and 1968. The majority of these had been designated in a shopping centre grid produced by the Helsinki's Regional Planning Association in 1961, the same year that the Ministry of the Interior commissioned a regional plan for Helsinki and its surrounding municipalities. The development of shopping centres in and around the Finnish capital was thus closely tied to the planning of the city's urban growth.

This was also the case in Brussels, as the chapter 'Shopping centres as catalyst for new multifunctional urban centralities' illustrates. Yannick Vanhaelen and Géry Leloutre refute the common assumption that the post-war development of shopping centres around Brussels was the result of a liberal *laissez-faire* policy. Instead, they put forward the hypothesis that even though – contrary to the example of Helsinki – no overall regional plan was produced, shopping centres constructed in the Belgian Capital Region during the 1960s and 1970s served as catalysts for the development of new multifunctional centralities aimed at structuring suburbanization around Brussels. Unravelling the histories of Woluwe shopping centre and Westland shopping centre, Vanhaelen and Leloutre demonstrate how these commercial entities were designed as components of large, mixed-use suburban cores – one to the east of Brussels and one to the west – which apart from retail included housing, offices and a range of public spaces. Similarly to the example of the new town of Évry in the Paris periphery, these mixed-use urban cores around Brussels were co-produced by both public and private actors. As a core element of new urban development, the European shopping centre appears not as a figure of non-interventionist policy, but rather as the site of intentional collaborations, where the contract between the three partners of the European welfare state – government, civic society and the private sector – was continuously negotiated and renegotiated.

Apart from urban expansion and decentralization the shopping centre also became a tool for urban regeneration. Numerous European cities were heavily damaged during the Second World War. The case of Rotterdam is particularly poignant, albeit with a silver lining. To force the Netherlands into early capitulation, the German forces launched an airstrike on Rotterdam on 14 May 1940, destroying more than 11,000 buildings, killing more than 1,000 people and rendering 80,000 homeless. The architectural office of Jo van den Broek and Jaap Bakema was commissioned to design a new centrality on the wreckage of this fragmented urbanity. It conceived of a linear open-air shopping typology with a department store on either end, which Dirk van den Heuvel analyses in his chapter 'The Lijnbaan in Rotterdam'. Opening in 1953, the construction of the Lijnbaan paralleled that of numerous open-air shopping malls across the United States that were bookended by department stores – a type that became known as the 'dumb-bell mall', referring to the shape of handheld weights.[20] However, contrary to the American examples, the Lijnbaan was not a suburban but a decisively urban figure which, van den Heuvel explains, was designed as part of a large, mixed-use urban project that apart from commercial, public and cultural spaces also included a series of high-rise housing slabs along its western edge. Qualified by Lewis Mumford as a 'sound urban form that could be adapted anywhere',[21] the Lijnbaan became a canonical figure in the history of modern architecture and exemplary for numerous urban regeneration projects in which the shopping centre played a key role.

One of these projects was the reconstruction of the city of Skopje, which is the subject of Jasna Mariotti's chapter 'Displays of modernity'. On 26 July 1963, Skopje was struck by a devastating earthquake, which reduced the majority of its urban fabric to rubble. The office of van den Broek and Bakema was both directly and indirectly involved in the city's reconstruction. In 1964, it was among the eight teams invited to submit a proposal for the city's redevelopment. Although their bid was not successful – Kenzo Tange from Japan together with the team of Miscevic and Wenzler from Zagreb were given the commission – the concepts and ideas that they expressed in their earlier Lijnbaan project did permeate parts of the subsequent design. Following the guidelines set out in the 'Ninth Project', as the master plan by Tange, Miscevic and Wenzler was called, a series of large-scale competitions was organized for different sites in the city, including one for a new City Trade Centre in 1967. This competition was won by Živko Popovski, a young Macedonian architect who had previously worked in the office of van den Broek and Bakema in Rotterdam. His design, a horizontal linear structure, which apart from commercial units also included various public and administrative functions and a series of vertical housing towers, clearly drew upon his experience garnered in the Netherlands. Like the Lijnbaan, it stitched the fragmented urban tissue of the central part of Skopje together through an internal network of streets that connected adjacent public spaces. Both van den Heuvel and Mariotti point out how the shopping centre as a reconstruction project was believed to spatially and symbolically insert the civic values of an open society in the confines of an existing urban condition.

Constructing consumer-citizens: Shopping centres shaping commercial collectivity

In her acclaimed book *Irresistible Empire: America's Advance through 20th Century Europe,* Victoria de Grazia chronicles the journey many European countries took after the end of the Second World War '… from the ruins of the bourgeois regime of consumption to the jerry-built foundations of what… [became]

---

[20]Cynthia Overbeck Bix, *Spending Spree: The History of American Shopping* (Minneapolis: Twenty-First Century Books, 2014), 49.
[21]Lewis Mumford, 'The Sky Line. A Walk through Rotterdam', *The New Yorker*, 12 October 1957, 174, cited in Dirk van den Heuvel's chapter in this book.

known as "the mass consumer society"'.[22] Unravelling this journey, de Grazia highlights how in post-war years the European vision of the social citizen became entangled with the American notion of the sovereign consumer as European nations attempted to harness the behemoth of consumerism to forge a new, classless society. The result: the emergence of the 'consumer-citizen'. In Italy, for instance, article 2 of the new constitution that was put into effect on 1 January 1948 asserted: 'it is the duty of the Republic to remove all economic and social obstacles that, by limiting the freedom and equality of citizens, prevent the full development of the individual and the participation of all workers in the political, economic and social organisation of the country'.[23] That same year the Christian Democrat Ludwig Erhard, who was on his way of becoming the German Federal Republic's first minister of economic affairs, reasoned that the 'modern day economy' would be 'neither a free-market system of liberalized buccaneering' nor a 'free interplay of forces', but 'a socially committed market economy conferring the deserved rewards on achievement'.[24] This 'socially committed market economy' or *Soziale Marktwirtschaft* was to chart a third way between capitalism and a planned economy; the design of shopping centres in West Germany – as elsewhere in Europe – was to embody it. Given that individual consumers were a force inimical to totalitarianism, shopping centres were deemed the ideal locales to redefine the relationship between the individual and the collective. Here, many believed, a modern community would rise from the rubble of the war like a phoenix from the ashes, while eschewing the all-too extreme versions that such a community could adopt. In his chapter 'Miracles and ruins, citizens and shoppers: Frankfurt 1963', Inderbir Singh Riar details how these aspirations were incorporated in the Frankfurt-Römerberg design by the office of Candilis–Josic–Woods. In 1963 the city of Frankfurt organized an architecture competition to regenerate the mediaeval Römerberg district, which had been levelled by Allied bombing on 22 March 1944. Meandering between the cathedral, the town hall and the Old St Nicholas Church, Candilis–Josic–Woods proposed a 'web' consisting of three stacked decks that contained a mix of functions, including offices, socio-cultural venues, housing, generous car-parking (on two underground levels) and, importantly, shops. This 'web' not only sought to reconstruct a piece of historical urban tissue, but also responded to new urban realities and practices characteristic of the post-war period, including mass retail and automotive mobility.[25] It was expected, as Riar illustrates in his chapter, that this 'web' would help citizens emerge from the dark shadows of the past; acclimatize them to the good fortune of the present and, by crafting 'consumer-citizens' who were both socially committed and culturally educated, build a new consumer society for the future.

Also in France consumer-citizens, famously labelled 'the children of Marx and Coca-Cola' by Jean Luc Godard, were given a paramount role in the modernization of society.[26] Shopping centres became one of their main arenas and opened up a vast new field of creative experimentation for architects. In 1963, one year prior to entering the Frankfurt-Römerberg competition, the partnership

---

[22]de Grazia, *Irresistible Empire*, 337.
[23]Ibid., 339.
[24]Erhard to Christian Democratic Union Party Congress, 28 August 1948, cited in de Grazia, *Irresistible Empire*, 339–340.
[25]Avermaete, *Another Modern*, 306–315.
[26]Rebecca Pulju, *Women and Mass Consumer Society in Postwar France* (Cambridge: Cambridge University Press, 2013).

of Candilis–Josic–Woods was, for instance, commissioned to design an enormous shopping centre for the new town of Toulouse-Le Mirail in the south of France.[27] Presaging their Frankfurt-Römerberg bid, they responded to this programme with a 'web' that wove together different practices and programmes into a continuous patch of urban tissue. Raised on a platform, the complex was based on a five-by-five metre structural grid with technical cores and open spaces regulating the pattern of the design. This resulted in an intricate complex of retail spaces with different heights and sizes. Permeated with the time-logic of mass consumption and tailored to both pedestrian and vehicular traffic – cleverly keeping both separate through grade separation – it created a new public domain for the consumer society. Similar aspirations can be identified in the *centres commerciaux* that Claude Parent designed in France in the late 1960s. In his chapter 'Collectivity in the prison of the plenty', Tom Avermaete describes how Parent, when commissioned to design four shopping centres for the retail chain Goulet-Turpin, proposed an alternative spatial conception which he believed to be more in tune with the new reality of mass consumption and mass production: the *fonction oblique*. It dispensed of the idea that architecture was composed of horizontal and vertical planes, instead introducing the

Figure I.3 Toulouse-le-Mirail shopping centre, 1970.
Source: Centre d'archives d'architecture du XXe siècle, Fonds Georges Candilis, 236 Ifa.

---

[27]Avermaete, *Another Modern*, 271–279.

inclined surface to generate a new-fangled experience of space. By dislocating the traditional spatial definitions of the horizontal and the vertical, this oblique architecture, Avermaete suggests, provoked the possibility for a new articulation of the social realm, which could accommodate a new collective of consumer-citizens.

The interaction between the collective and the individual – both in political and in commercial terms – became a key concern in the design of post-war shopping centres that often functioned as physical testing grounds of Europe's third way. The question 'how to create "consumer-citizens"' – a perfect blend of 'socialist' and 'capitalist' concepts of man – was often placed at the centre of the debate. These consumer-citizens, many believed, held the key to the formation of a new, modern post-war society that was devoid of totalitarian overtones. Some critics were quite optimistic and saw the consumer first and foremost as a citizen 'to the extent that he was autonomous and self-determined, and that his autonomy depended on his rational capacities, on his ability firstly to know and define his own needs … and secondly to pursue them rationally'.[28] Others, however, challenged the very possibility of a consumer-citizen and predicated that consumer capitalism created false needs that lulled citizens into complacency. These leftist writers, including Theodor Adorno and Max Horkheimer, saw consumption as a tool of 'mass deception',[29] wielded by capitalists consolidating their reigns. The consumer, they argued, was nothing more than a dupe in the hands of capitalist markets – a slave to his own desires.[30] Simply put, these debates revolved around what some saw as the inherent opposition between the active, rational citizen who was both socially and politically engaged, and the passive, witless consumer – a needy ninny – unable to distinguish his 'true' needs from his 'false' wants. It is precisely this antagonism that Jennifer Mack challenges in 'Hello, consumer! Skärholmen Centre from the Million Programme to the mall'. Mack's chapter focuses on Skärholmen Centre, the nucleus of a new town on the outskirts of Stockholm, which was festively opened on 8 September 1968. Built on an alliance between commerce and civic functions – a pact that had been embedded in Swedish architecture and urbanism since the mid-1930s – it developed overtly and proudly as both a centrum and a shopping centre. Its inauguration, however, unleashed a debate over the apparent conflict between Social Democratic agendas and the economic variables that shaped Swedish town centres, as Skärholmen's planners were accused of replacing citizens with apathetic consumers. Unravelling its history, Mack's chapter documents how Skärholmen Centre, a space that was depicted by many as overly commercial, paradoxically (even ironically) became a locus of political action. Not the broad offer of consumables but rather the abrupt encounter with the logics of mass consumption provoked autonomous reactions from the inhabitants of Skärholmen and produced a generation of 'critical consumers' – true 'consumer-citizens'.

The architects, planners and politicians involved in the development of the Centre, a large new shopping centre to be built at the heart of the new town of Milton Keynes, were equally hopeful that this

---

[28] Don Slater, *Consumer Culture and Modernity* (Cambridge: Polity Press, 2008), 54.
[29] Max Horkheimer and Theodor Adorno formulated the notion of mass consumption as 'mass deception' as early as 1944 in their book *Dialektik der Aufklärung* (The Dialectic of Enlightenment).
[30] Slater, *Consumer Culture and Modernity*, 61. See also: Donica Belisle, *Retail Nation: Department Stores and the Making of Modern Canada* (Vancouver/Toronto: UBC Press, 2011), 5.

massive commercial complex would double as a civic centre. Officially opened on 25 September 1979, it was one in a long line of shopping centres located at the heart of new towns that were developed in the UK following the 1946 New Towns Act. In many of these new towns, the concept of the 'town centre' (or 'civic centre') was conflated with that of the 'shopping centre', thus intimately intertwining the public sphere with private interests. Early examples in Britain included Cumbernauld in Scotland (1955), located approximately twenty-five kilometres north-east of Glasgow, and Harlow (1955) and Stevenage (1958), both to the north of London. Similarly to their contemporary Swedish counterparts such as Vällingby and Farsta, these early hybrid centres at the heart of British new towns were often hailed as successful examples of post-war urban planning. In 1959 *Town and Country Planning*, for instance, commended 'the new all-pedestrian town centre of Stevenage' as '... one of the boldest planning and architectural experiments of recent years', stating that 'it is indeed already more than an experiment; it is an achievement'.[31] One year later, *The Builder* confirmed: '... the town centre [of Stevenage] ... has existed long enough to prove the undoubted success of an all-pedestrian centre and shopping precinct'.[32] However, much like it had happened in Sweden, striking the right balance between 'shopping centre' and 'civic centre' became a more precarious exercise in later decades. Just like Skärholmen Centre, Milton Keynes' Centre also accrued significant criticism. Constructed at a turning point from modernism to post-modernism, at a time when Margaret Thatcher's neo-liberal regime was busily undermining (what it saw as) profligate government spending, the Centre's ambiguous position in-between became a point of contention. In her chapter on 'Milton Keynes' Centre', Janina Gosseye unstitches the threads of this dissension. She illustrates how its architects aspired to craft elevated consumer-citizens through the shopping centre's design – its lusciously green arcades, its generous 'public' squares, its inspiring artworks and so on – but were ultimately criticized for failing to do so, or for relying on bygone architectural concepts in their endeavour. However, by wrapping the building in a post-modern jacket of mirror glazing, Gosseye suggests that the architects did hint at the glazed superficiality of Milton Keynes' commodified urban life and ultimately confessed to the civic-centre simulacrum that Milton Keynes' (shopping) Centre offered its new town residents.

As a founding member of the Non-Aligned Movement striking the right balance between 'consumer' and 'citizen', 'shopping centre' and 'civic centre' was an even more precarious exercise for post-war Yugoslavia – one that its President, Josip Broz Tito, navigated with aplomb. Acknowledging the power of consumerism as a new opiate for the people, but simultaneously denouncing capitalism, he issued a State Decree in the early 1960s, stipulating that a national retail network was to be established with the financial support of socially owned trading companies and public funds. In their chapter 'Shopping as part of a political agenda', Sanja Matijević Barčot and Ana Grgić study how this Decree played out in Croatia – a country that up until 1991 was an integral part of Yugoslavia. Here, two commercial models popularized between the early 1960s and the late 1970s: the department store on the one hand and the 'peri-urban' shopping centre, which was often located at the heart of new state-financed housing developments, on the other. As part of a governmental agenda and freed from the dictate of profitability,

---

[31] T. Hampson, 'The Stevenage Town Centre', *Town and Country Planning* 27 (1959): 13.
[32] 'Stevenage Town Centre', *The Builder* 198 (15 January 1960): 127.

Figure I.4 Stevenage Town Centre, 1966.
Source: Collectie Het Nieuwe Instituut/Van Eesteren archive/EEST 10.8.

Barčot and Grgić describe how these shopping facilities were to define a novel type of public space in post-war Yugoslavia, the popularity of which was to express the superiority of the country's non-aligned path to modernity.

Contrary to Barčot and Grgić's story, Daniele Vadala's chapter discusses the de-politicization of a commercial model that had emerged under (and had strong ties to) Italy's fascist regime: the downtown department store. Responding to the new constitution that was put into effect on 1 January 1948, the Italian department store was reinvented (and thereby slightly 're-politicized') in post-war years to create democratic spaces of consumption where the collective of consumer-citizens – Italy's emerging middle-classes – could meet. Tracing the history of La Rinascente-Upim, Vadala's chapter evidences the lead role that this private company played in introducing this novel type of commercial collectivity to Italy. It opened stores not only in major Italian city centres, but also at the heart of smaller towns, where these buildings performed a civic function which, Vadala' claims, was underscored by their architectural design. Blending urban and rural motifs, the neorealist architecture of the La Rinascente-Upim department stores walked a fine line between tradition and modernity, and succeeded in combining mass consumption with a sense of place – commercial values and civic culture. Vadala's chapter underscores, once again, the strong complicity between private and public actors, between market and state, in the definition of new collective spaces for the European city. In the post-war period, the swift modernization that many European countries were experiencing, which rapidly transformed traditional and rural societies into industrialized and urban ones came with the need to redefine notions of collectivity and individuality. The shopping centre and its programme of mass consumption offered not only a contact zone for the negotiation between different societal actors (market, state, civic society) but also a real-life testing ground for new definitions of the collective and the citizen.

Shifting forms of shopping: Between dense and tall and the low-slung (suburban) shopping mall

The term 'shopping centre' is frequently used rather loosely. Since the mid-twentieth century, a long list of definitions has been proffered by a wide variety of authors, including architects, geographers, planners, developers and economists, to qualify precisely what constitutes a 'shopping centre'. In 1951, Geoffrey Baker and Bruno Funaro, for instance, described the shopping centre as: '… a compound of the department store, the rural general store, the downtown shopping block and a traditional street market … usually … under single ownership, a dominating fact which … show[s] itself through a certain architectural unity which ties the stores together'.[33] In 1960 Gruen and Smith, in turn, offered a more free characterization in the opening pages of *Shopping Towns USA*. 'The shopping centre', they wrote, '… represents one of the rare instances in which a number of individual enterprises, in banding together, are ready to submit to certain overall rules in order to further their common welfare.'[34] The definition offered by the Urban Land Institute in 1977 aptly combined Baker and Funaro and Gruen and Smith's suggestions, defining the shopping centre as '[a] group of architecturally unified commercial establishments built on a site which is planned, developed, owned and managed as an operating unit related in its location, size, and type of shops to the trade area that the unit serves.'[35]

The plasticity of these definitions of course allowed great variation, and in post-war Europe the shopping centre concept accordingly assumed many forms, which were often strongly informed by its location: urban versus peri-urban. Contrary to the United States, where between 1945 and 1975

---

[33] Geoffrey Baker and Bruno Funaro, *Shopping Centres: Design and Operation* (New York: Reinhold Publishing Corporation, 1951), 4.
[34] Gruen and Smith, *Shopping Towns USA*, 11.
[35] Urban Land Institute, *Shopping Center Development Handbook* (Washington, DC: Urban Land Institute, 1977), 1.

most shopping centres were built in peri-urban contexts, some of the earliest commercial complexes developed in Europe after the Second World War were constructed at the heart of established, war-torn urban centres.[36] In an attempt to re-establish precincts that had been heavily damaged during the war, new, architecturally coherent commercial facilities (which were commonly pedestrianized) were built, which fit the definition of a 'shopping centre'.[37] The Frankfurt Römerberg plan developed by the architects trio Candilis–Josic–Woods, discussed in the chapter by Inderbir Singh Riar, offers an excellent example; as does the project proposed by the office of van den Broek and Bakema for the reconstruction of Rotterdam, which is the subject of Dirk van den Heuvel's contribution. Both designs are, however, radically different in form. While Candilis–Josic–Woods proposed a 'web' of three stacked decks, van den Broek and Bakema's Lijnbaan assumed the form of an inner-city dumb-bell mall, bookended by two department stores. One of these department stores, the Bijenkorf, is the subject of Evangelia Tsilika's chapter 'The creation of civic identity in post-war corporate architecture'. Designed by Marcel Breuer, the Bijenkorf (or 'beehive') combined commercial and business functions, with leisure facilities and cultural amenities to create an ever-busy nucleus of activity. It was, Tsilika contends, therefore not a 'typical' iteration of the department store, but a new interpretation of this nineteenth-century concept, adapted to inner-city post-war Rotterdam.

In post-war years, also two distinct peri-urban shopping-centre-types developed in Europe. The first is the shopping centre located at, and defining, the heart of satellite cities or new towns. Several such shopping centres, which were believed to introduce a sense of centrality and urbanity, are discussed in this book: Évry in France (chapter by Kenny Cupers), Munkkivuori, Puotinharju and Tapiola in Finland (chapter by Juhana Lahti), Skärholmen in Sweden (chapter by Jennifer Mack) and Milton Keynes in the UK (chapter by Janina Gosseye). The other peri-urban type that found its way to Europe was the *bona fide* American regional shopping centre: a lone big box with no urban aspirations, commonly built at the junction of major motorways and surrounded by abundant parking lots. The first such peri-urban shopping centre to open in Britain was Brent Cross in 1976. Located at a major traffic intersection, it not only followed the American planning pattern, but also adopted the typical dumb-bell plan formula, running east to west, parallel to the North Circular Road, with the two largest stores at either end. The first of this type to open on the continent was the Main Taunus Zentrum near Frankfurt, which is the subject of Steffen de Rudder's chapter 'The shopping centre comes to Germany'. Discussing various

---

[36]By the mid-1950s, three main types of shopping centres had been identified: neighbourhood centres, community centres and regional centres. The distinction between these three types was informed by the size of the centre, together with related function, tenant mix and catchment area. Broadly speaking, neighbourhood and community centres served local residential populations and predominantly featured convenience stores, while regional centres provided a much wider range of goods and services and were generally located close to major road intersections in order to serve a larger catchment population. See Clifford M. Guy, 'Classifications of Retail Stores and Shopping Centres: Some Methodological Issues', *GeoJournal* 45 (1998): 255–264. More detailed descriptions of these three types can be found in John Dawson, *Shopping Centre Development* (London/New York: Longman, 1983), 17–26. In his book, Dawson argues for an extension of this traditional three-tier classification, arguing that due to the American shopping centre's 'movement towards the development of downtown centres', questions must be posed regarding the comprehensiveness of the existing taxonomy.

[37]In Britain, examples of such post-war regeneration projects can be found in Coventry, Plymouth and Southampton. See R.L. Davies and D.J. Bennison, *British Town Centre Shopping Schemes: A Statistical Digest* (Reading: Unit for Retail Planning Information, 1979), 192.

Figure I.5 Brent Cross Shopping Centre in Britain, 1976.
Source: Graham Wood/Stringer, Hulton Archive.

aspects of its design, including location, accessibility, influences and architecture, de Rudder examines to what extent this shopping centre resembled its American ancestors and how (or if) it was adapted to West German society.

Ironically, even before the Main Taunus shopping centre opened on 2 May 1964, debates began on how the development of such peri-urban American-inspired commercial centres could be prevented in the future. In the mid-1960s, the scene in Germany seemed set for the rapid growth of big-box regional shopping centres. Only six months after the Main Taunus Zentrum opened, another free-standing, car-oriented consumer-leviathan landed in Bochum: the Ruhrpark Zentrum. These two developments led to proposals for a further eighty-one such shopping centres to be built in the country over the following ten years. However, in 1966 developers, faced with increasing opposition from regional planning authorities, quickly cancelled all such speculative plans. Nonetheless, despite the dramatic halt in the expansion of this type of out-of-town centres, peri-urban shopping centres that were integrated in existing urban fabrics (of smaller towns) or used in city expansion plans did continue to grow and in 1972, sixteen were operational in Germany.[38] Olaf Gisbertz discusses several such cases in his chapter 'Built for mass consumption'. This German trend was representative of what happened in most parts of Europe. Given European land use planners' objections to American-style regional centres, developers sought alternative avenues and, as a result, many shopping centres were integrated in existing urban areas as part of a controlled provision of decentralized retailing within (growing) cities and towns. Also in Britain, the fact that only one of these 'American' big-box shopping centres (Brent Cross) was built in the period under investigation in this book – actually just beyond the period under investigation – was in a large measure due to negative attitudes towards such large-scale out-of-town retail developments.[39]

Around the mid-1960s, like a pendulum, the shopping centre returned to the historic European downtown, where it became an important 'tool' for urban revitalization. In this period many European city centres experienced social and spatial decay owing to the suburban flight of (mostly) well-to-do families with children and to structural underinvestment in both the development and the maintenance of the historic urban fabric. Against this background, the shopping centre was called upon for its (assumed) capability to renew the city and re-establish urban vitality. Also, commonly set up as public–private partnerships, these inner-city shopping centre schemes attempted to lure private investors back to the city. In the UK this (re)turn to the city first manifested itself in Birmingham where the Bull Ring shopping centre, designed by architects Sydney Greenwood and T.J. Hirst, opened in 1964.[40] In 'The drive to modernise', Jo Lintonbon unravels the history of this commercial complex, which was 'complex' in every way. A pioneer in its field, the Bull Ring not only had to overcome the complexities of dealing with the existing urban fabric while ensuring optimal car accessibility to the centre, but – as a public–private enterprise – also had to balance the civic and commercial aspirations for the site while ensuring optimal returns for all retailers in the centre, which were incidentally spread across five levels.

Shortly after the Bull Ring opened, the Elephant and Castle scheme in London (1965), the Merrion shopping centre in Leeds (1965) and the first of the town centre Arndale schemes in Doncaster (1968) followed suit. Like the Bull Ring, these were the forerunners of a subsequent decade of plans preoccupied with town centre revitalization and environmental improvement.[41] A famous example – or perhaps rather 'infamous' example, as large parts of the old city were demolished to enable its construction – of such a commercial revitalization project in the Netherlands is Hoog Catharijne in Utrecht. Officially opened on 24 September 1973, this shopping centre is generally considered a *magnum opus* of Dutch urban renewal. Apart from shopping, it included a large office complex and featured several elevated pedestrian walkways that connected various city functions, including the train station. As such, Hoog Catharijne was believed to create a completely novel urban core, befitting a modern (consumer) society. The lavish interior, which also accommodated roof gardens with an

---

[38] G. Shaw, *Retail Development and Structural Change in West Germany* (Corbridge, Northumberland: Retail and Planning Associates, 1978), 37, cited in Dawson, *Shopping Centre Development*, 25–26.
[39] Dawson, *Shopping Centre Development*, 26.
[40] Davies and Bennison, *British Town Centre Shopping Schemes*, 192.
[41] Ibid.

Figure I.6 The Clarentuin with olive trees in Hoog Catharijne, 1973.
Source: Collectie Het Nieuwe Instituut/Wiekart archive/WiekfL25.

aviary, an art gallery and even a small theatre, was believed to insert a sense of modern urbanity in the very heart of the historical city. As Dutch critic J. Petri noted: 'Whereas in most cases the exploding metropolis is accompanied by a relative decline of the city centre ... at present Utrecht stands a good chance of becoming ... the modern, expansive sub-city of the Randstad Holland.'[42] Contrary to early post-war inner-city redevelopment schemes – such as the Frankfurt-Römerberg plan and the Lijnbaan in Rotterdam – which were open-air, largely horizontal and at times a bit diffuse, the 1960s and 1970s revitalization schemes, such as the Bull Ring and Hoog Catharijne, were predominantly enclosed, high-density and multi-level complexes. Their goal was not to reconstruct the city but to endow it with a new, modern urbanity from within.

---

[42]H. Cammen, Len Klerk, Gerhard Dekker, P.P. Witsen and Michael O'Loughlin, *The Selfmade Land: Culture and Evolution of Urban and Regional Planning in the Netherlands* (Houten: Spectrum, 2012), 25.

In their chapter 'Malls and commercial planning policies in a compact city', Nadia Fava and Manel Guardia illustrate how also in post-Franco Spain the shopping centre became part and parcel of a programme for 'commercial renewal' of the historical city, albeit with a bit of delay. Fava and Guardia illustrate how the norms and forms of the shopping centres in the city of Barcelona resonated with the dominant modes and models of contemporary urban renewal. The design principles of shopping centres and the discourse on urban renewal went hand in hand, focusing alternatively on issues of public space, infrastructure and the 'compact city'. In Spain, just as in other parts of Europe, the shopping centre thus became entrusted with the challenging task of re-energizing the urban condition. Politicians, planners, architects and citizens all placed great faith in the capacity of the shopping centre to modernize the historical city.

Unravelling

The saga of the shopping centre that is relayed in the pages of this book strongly challenges the current canonical image of post-war European architecture, urbanism and planning. The various chapters illustrate that architectural modernity in Europe was not only a matter of state-led initiatives in the realm of housing, leisure and culture, but was also strongly indebted to joint public–private commercial developments. For many European citizens the shopping centre exemplified the quintessential everyday modern living environment. It was not restricted to particular sites but was ubiquitous – a pervasive modernity. In Europe, the shopping centre not only adopted the identity of the lone capitalist wolf that lurked at the intersection of major traffic corridors, but frequently also became the civic 'core' of suburban precincts, satellite cities and new towns, and often even assumed the appearance of the 'urban patch' as it ventured into the very heart of established historical cities. In all of these different loci, the shopping centre, in the various guises that it assumed, was not only part and parcel of urban development – engaging alternatively with practices and discourses of urban reconstruction, urban expansion, urban planning and urban renewal – but also introduced a modernity that would be intensely experienced and practised by large numbers of European citizens. The shopping centre thus offered Europeans a new reality that reshaped their values, perceptions and desires and, most importantly, set the stage for the radical redefinition of their collective and personal identities. In 1970, in his seminal study *La Société de Consommation: Ses Mythes, ses Structures*, French philosopher Jean Baudrillard critically pegged the shopping centre as 'a sort of summit of the urban process, a true social laboratory and melting pot where "the collectivity" reinforces its cohesion, as in feasts and performances'.[43] In this convergence between collective identity and consumption lies not only one of the main features of post-war culture, but also the importance of the architecture of the European shopping centre.

---

[43] Jean Baudrillard, *La Société de Consommation: Ses Mythes, ses Structures* (Paris: Denoel, 1970), 265. The original text reads: 'une sorte de sommet de ce procès urbain, un véritable laboratoire et creuset social, où "la collectivité" (Durkheim, dans *Les Formes Élémentaires de la Vie Religieuse*) renforce sa cohésion, comme dans les fêtes et les spectacles.' The translation in *The Consumer Society* reads: 'a kind of pinnacle of this urban process, a positive laboratory and social testing ground, where, as Durkheim writes in *The Elementary Forms of Religious Life*, the collectivity reinforces its cohesion, as in feasts and spectacles.' Jean Baudrillard, *The Consumer Society, Myths and Structures* (London: Sage Publications, 1998), 166.

However, the saga of the post-war European shopping centre was all but eternal. The foundations of the invigorating European welfare state regime, which had been instrumental in harnessing capitalism's consumption-juggernaut, started to shake in 1972 when the so-called Club of Rome published their influential book *The Limits to Growth* and finally began to crumble when Margaret Thatcher was elected British prime minister in 1979.[44] In 1975, in between these two defining events, the European Economic Community (the predecessor of the European Union) voted its first resolution for consumer protection.[45] As the power equilibrium between public sector, private sector and civic society began to shift, it became clear that citizens would no longer be capable of acting as autonomous consumers. Abandoned to the whims of corporate capitalism, they were increasingly seen as vulnerable subjects that needed to be protected. The salad days of welfare state ideals and commercial interests merrily going hand in hand were over. The ties were unravelled. Previously a prime physical manifestation of the welfare contract (or consensus) between state and market, the shopping centre now increasingly became the exclusive domain of private developers and its design was more often than not reduced to a formulaic collection of stores with little to no ambitions of influencing urban conditions and communal activities.

In some European countries the changing character of the shopping centre sparked criticism vis-à-vis both new and existing commercial developments. In the Swedish case of Skärholmen, which strongly expressed the ideology of individual liberation through consumption, architecture became a target in the general questioning of the Swedish model of the welfare state. Similarly, in the new town of Milton Keynes the built form of the shopping centre came to be considered as the ultimate expression of the failure of the British post-war welfare state. Also in the Dutch public debate the architecture of shopping centres like Hoog Catharijne was heavily criticized for its incapacity to engender the urbanity that its designers had promised. Writing about the Utrecht shopping centre in 1972, a Dutch journalist concluded: 'The heart of the city is dead.'[46] The final *coup de grâce* came from the father of the shopping centre himself. In 1978, less than two decades after his propagation of the shopping centre as an urban organism,[47] Victor Gruen gave a keynote address entitled 'Shopping Centres, Why, Where, How?' at the Annual European Conference of the International Council of Shopping Centers in London. In his talk, Gruen forever closed the chapter on the particular character of the post-war European shopping centre by typecasting its most recent manifestations as expressions 'of the effort of substituting naturally and organically grown mixtures of various urban expressions by an artificial and therefore sterile order'.[48] The three-decade saga of *Shopping Towns Europe* had reached its end.

---

[44]Donella H. Meadows, et al., *The Limits to Growth: A Report for the Club of Rome's Project on the Predicament of Mankind* (New York: Universe Books, 1972); Aditya Chakrabortty, 'The Welfare State, 1942–2013, Obituary', *The Guardian*, 8 January 2013, http://www.theguardian.com/commentisfree/2013/jan/08/welfare-state-1942-2013-obituary, accessed 7 May 2016.

[45]The Council Resolution of 14 April 1975 on a preliminary programme of the European Economic Community for a consumer protection and information policy constituted the formal inauguration of consumer protection policy at EU level.

[46]'Hoog Catharijne: 'Modern Winkel – en Werk Hart (1973)', Het Utrechts Archief, http://www.hetutrechtsarchief.nl/educatie/basis-onderwijs/onderwerpen/hoog-catharijne, accessed 7 May 2016.

[47]Victor Gruen, *The Heart of Our Cities, The Urban Crisis: Diagnosis and Cure* (London: Thames and Hudson, 1964).

[48]Victor Gruen, 'Shopping Centres, Why, Where, How?', Third Annual European Conference of the International Council of Shopping Centres, Hilton Hotel London, 28 February 1978: 1–18. VGC Box 32, Loose, 12, cited in: Paul Edwards, 'Reimagining the Shopping Mall: European Invention of the "American" Consumer Space', *U.S. Studies Online: The BAAS Postgraduate Journal* 7 (Spring 2005), http://www.baas.ac.uk/issue-7-spring-2005-article-1/#65, accessed 8 May 2016.

Part 1

Urbanism harnessing the consumption-juggernaut: Shopping centres and urban (re)development

Chapter 1

Shopping à *l'américaine*
Kenny Cupers

When Parly 2, a prestigious shopping centre at a major highway intersection on the western outskirts of Paris, opened its doors on 4 November 1969, it was the first of its kind in France. Both champions and critics saw the project as an unabashedly American import and a watershed in the development of suburban France. With over one hundred boutiques, a supermarket, a cinema, bars and restaurants and the first suburban outposts of the Parisian department stores Printemps and BHV, the project offered a second, interiorized city that competed directly with the existing city. In fact, its brand name was simply to be 'Paris 2', but due to political opposition over the use of the French capital's name it was amended

Figure 1.1 Rendering of Parly 2, commercial brochure, late 1960s.
Source: Archives nationales, France, CAC199110585/011.

to 'Parly 2', in reference to the nearby forest of Marly.[1] Customers from all over the capital flocked to the gleaming temple of consumption, which was laid out over two floors around an interior street and surrounded by vast parking lots. Similar shopping centres emerged around Paris and across Europe in the early 1970s.

French architects and planners at this time were engaged in the country's largest state-led planning project: the construction of modern new towns (*villes nouvelles*) to decentralize Paris and spur regional economic development.[2] Since the Second World War, the capital had undergone rapid suburban growth, particularly in the form of large housing estates, called *grands ensembles*. Often located far from public transport connections, these estates were almost immediately criticized for their lack of urban amenities. The new towns – an ambitious national programme launched by Charles De Gaulle in 1965 and in full force during the 1970s – promised to remedy the suburban blues of these so-called 'dormitory estates' by creating new, vibrant urban centres in the periphery. These would be interconnected by a new regional express train network converging in downtown Paris. What seems to have kept these planners awake at night, perhaps more than anything else, was the threat of privately developed shopping centres such as Parly 2. The planning team of the new town of Évry, for example, emphasized that its new centre was to be 'an embryo of an Urban Heart' and would thus avoid, as if that was otherwise its natural fate, 'the American-style shopping centre, anti-urban by its very nature, with its desolate facades and sea of parking space'.[3] Defined against the pervasive influence of American culture in post-war France, their ambition was to recreate a 'Latin' form of urbanity. Planners at this time regularly used the term 'Latin' to refer to an urban imaginary constructed around urban density, social and functional mixing and an active street life during the day and at night.[4] Why then did the final result look exactly like the much-loathed American suburban dumb-bell malls – at least from the angle represented by this contemporary photograph? (see Figure 1.2).

This chapter examines how the development of suburban shopping shaped the design of France's new towns in the late 1960s and 1970s. Counter to contemporaneous impressions and dominant historical interpretation, suburban shopping in France, paradigmatic as it is of the country's explosive suburbanization in the post-war decades, was more than just an American import. In her landmark study, *Irresistible Empire: America's Advance through Twentieth-Century Europe*, Victoria de Grazia has cast the shopping mall as an example of the Americanization of post-war Europe.[5] More recent historical scholarship, however, suggests that particular national cultures of consumption and longer term historical change were as important as the so-called 'transfer' of American models and expertise in

---

[1] Camille Meyer-Léotard, *Si Parly m'était conté …: Epopée d'une Ville à la Campagne* (Paris: Textuel, 2010), 26.

[2] See Pierre Merlin, *Les Villes Nouvelles en France* (Paris: PUF, 1991); Kenny Cupers, *The Social Project: Housing Postwar France* (Minneapolis: University of Minnesota Press, 2014), chapter 5.

[3] '… éviter le shopping-center à l'américaine, anti-urbain par nature avec ses façades désolantes et sa marée de parkings.' Source: 'Pour une expérience pilote d'action sur l'environnement urbain: La ville nouvelle d'Évry et la mis en oeuvre d'une politique de l'environnement, 1970', III.1. Source: 19780319/001, Centre d'Archives Contemporaines, Archives Nationales, France.

[4] Cupers, *The Social Project*, 234.

[5] Victoria De Grazia, *Irresistible Empire: America's Advance Through Twentieth-Century Europe* (Cambridge, MA: Belknap Press of Harvard University Press, 2005).

Figure 1.2 The commercial centre of Évry.
Source: Photograph by Kenny Cupers, 2008.

the modernization of European retail practices.[6] Following this line of inquiry, I argue that the architecture of suburban shopping is to be understood not as the transparent sign of an American-imposed modernity that spread to Europe across the networks of the Cold War, but as a form of transculturation. In other words, the types and forms of suburban shopping in France developed from specific routes of circulation, translation and appropriation, across the Atlantic and within Europe. European retail entrepreneurs and commercial distributors looked eagerly to the United States, and while some indeed attempted to implement American models, these were necessarily adapted to national regulatory and cultural conditions. The modernization of retail and distribution along these lines in France prompted architects and planners to not only imagine new experiences and forms of shopping, but also to forge new relationships between private commercial development and centralized state planning. The new towns offered an unparalleled terrain of experimentation in exactly this sense.

Hypermarkets and dumb-bell malls

Until the 1960s, commercial retail in France was still predominantly located in the historic core of cities. For any suburban housewife in the Paris region, shopping, apart from everyday necessities, required a commute to the *grands boulevards* in the heart of the city. The first self-service supermarkets emerged in French suburbs during the 1950s, but they were relatively small in number and size. Some of these supermarkets were inserted in the neighbourhood centres of mass housing estates such

---

[6]Ralph Jessen and Lydia Langer, *Transformations of Retailing in Europe after 1945* (London: Ashgate, 2012).

as Sarcelles, while others were privately developed; but in any case, they remained small and, with only a few parking spaces and lack of public transport connections, catered to a very local clientele. During the 1960s then, a veritable revolution in suburban retail took place with the emergence of two particular types of development – each of which with a distinct pedigree, commercial rationale and architectural form.

The first is the *hypermarché* (hypermarket) or superstore, a suburban retail type first developed, at least in France, by Carrefour.[7] This pioneering company was the result of a collaboration between two families, represented by Marcel Fournier on the one hand and the brothers Denis and Jacques Defforey on the other. The former were owners of two dry goods stores (*magasins de nouveautés*), the latter food wholesalers, which explains the unique character of the hypermarket: the combination of food and non-food items, including textiles and home decoration, at discounted prices under one roof. The first Carrefour hypermarket opened in Saint-Geneviève-des-Bois, in the southern suburbs of Paris, on 15 June 1963. At 2,400 m², the megastore was four times the size of the average French supermarket of its time. The building was designed and built by Francis Bouygues, a young entrepreneur. It was essentially a large hall, made with a prefab steel structure and organized in isles. Vegetables, meats and fish were organized in specialized sections at the outer walls of the hall. Customers could look into the meat preparation space from the store, a novelty at the time. Another novelty was the snack bar at the centre of the store.[8] The 'Carrefour grand magasin', as it was called, was open from 10 am to 10 pm, including Sunday morning and Monday afternoon, upsetting the regular opening hours of French retail at the time. The store was located at a considerable distance from Paris' inner city, in a municipality that counted just 18,000 inhabitants. But thanks to the store's 400 parking spaces and its own discount gas station, it was able to draw customers from a much larger area than commercial experts then deemed viable. Despite their scepticism, the store was immediately overrun by customers and was a huge financial success.

Carrefour's subsequent retail project at Vénissieux, in the suburbs of Lyon, was even more exemplary for the new hypermarket type. Opened in 1966, the vast store had a commercial surface of 10,000 m² and 2,000 parking spaces. With this second leap in size, the store was geared towards a customer catchment area of 200,000–300,000 inhabitants.[9] Compared to supermarkets, this signalled more than just a shift in scale. Filled with an unprecedented array of foods, clothing, household appliances and furniture at prices up to 20 or 30 per cent below usual retail offerings, the hypermarket was the first exclusively suburban 'machine for selling', for which customers drove considerable distance in order to buy in large quantities. The hypermarket was a motor of development in and of itself, fuelling the rapid suburbanization of post-war France.

---

[7]On the history of the hypermarket, see Jean-Marc Villermet, *Naissance de l'Hypermarché* (Paris: Armand Colin, 1991); Christian Lhermie, *Carrefour ou l'Invention de l'Hypermarché* (Paris: Vuibert, 2003); Jacques Marseille (ed.), *La Révolution Commerciale en France: Du 'Bon Marché' à l'Hypermarché* (Paris: Le Monde-Editions,1997); René Péron, *La Fin des Vitrines: Des Temples de la Consommation aux Usines à Vendre* (Paris: Cachan/Editions de l'ENS, 1993); Solange Jungers, 'L'Invention de l'Hypermarché', in *Les Années ZUP: Architectures de la Croissance 1960–1973*, eds. Gérard Monnier and Richard Klein (Paris: Picard, 2002).
[8]Lhermie, *Carrefour*, 28.
[9]Ibid., 4.

When the term 'hypermarché' was coined by Jacques Pictet in *Libre Service Actualité*, dated May 1968, the Carrefour stores had already become a formula, quickly emulated by competitors such as Auchan or Euromarché.[10] In 1970, there were already over fifty hypermarkets across France; and in 1973 more than 200.[11] During the following decades, hypermarkets continued to proliferate and they have continued to fundamentally reshape French retail and distribution systems. The suburban consumers of the baby-boom generation made them an immediate and long-lasting success. To limit investment and offer cut-throat prices, the hypermarkets were often not more than expediently built hangars. Their location, near existing and future highway infrastructure, was most crucial to their success; the hypermarket was a product of suburbia in that the highway was its mainspring.

Historians and commentators have alternately described the hypermarket as a European invention and a direct import from the United States. Most recently, research has shown that – contrary to the still dominant assumption that the hypermarket was invented by Carrefour in France – it was in fact first developed in Belgium by the company GB. Their first three 'discount department stores' as they were called, opened in 1961 in Bruges, Auderghem and Anderlecht, and were widely publicized.[12] Pictet even wrote an article in *Libre-Service Actualité* that year, and considering that business directors at the time were closely connected through international associations and networks, Fournier and the Defforeys were undoubtedly aware of GB's projects.[13] Nevertheless, both in France and Belgium at this time, the new superstores were not seen as inventions, but simply as American imports. The principle of self-service was indeed first launched in the United States, by Clarence Saunders in 1916. In France, the first self-service store, which was a mere 40 m² in size, opened only in 1948, after a group of leading French retailers made a study trip to the United States.[14] The supermarket, and its underlying idea of discount pricing – selling more at a lower profit margin – was also an American invention, picked up and further developed by Edouard Leclerc in France after the Second World War.[15] Although GB's stores were more indebted to the department store and Carrefour's to the supermarket, both relied on similar sales methods, in particular as proselytized by Bernard Trujillo, then the world's leading retail guru.[16] During the 1950s, Trujillo, a Colombian from a wealthy background, had become famous for the seminars he organized at the National Cash Register in Dayton, Ohio – the number one producer of cash registering machines. His seminars were enthralling, and his predictions lauded as prophecies. Among his well-known slogans were 'shop windows are the stores' coffins', 'pile high, but sell low' and 'no parking, no business'.[17]

---

[10] Jacques Pictet, article of 1 May 1968 in *Libre-Service Actualités*. Cited in: ibid., 36.
[11] Ibid., 40.
[12] Jean-Pierre Grimmeau, 'A Forgotten Anniversary: The First European Hypermarkets Open in Brussels in 1961', *Brussels Studies* 67 (10 June 2013): 1–10.
[13] Ibid., 5.
[14] Lhermie, *Carrefour*, 6.
[15] Ibid., 7.
[16] See Villermet, *Naissance de l'Hypermarché*, 125–129.
[17] Lhermie, *Carrefour*, 24.

Over the years, an entire generation of European businessmen attended Trujillo's seminars – signalling his formidable impact on European retail development. Fournier met Trujillo in 1962.[18] Yet the men behind Carrefour did not simply follow his dictums. Trujillo was highly sceptical of the idea to mix food and non-food items in discount stores, due to his understanding of American consumer behaviour and retail systems. Most supermarkets in the United States at this time sold only foods, and were distinct from chain stores specializing in particular products. Although Meijer's, a Midwestern supermarket chain, established a series of very large supermarkets that offered additional dry goods in the 1960s, the hypermarket idea became widely adopted in the United States only during the 1980s.[19] In short, Carrefour's novelty was in scaling up the supermarket idea while adding textiles, furniture and other non-food products and services. Yet rather than seeing innovation as either imported or located in a particular location – and therefore either foreign or autochthonous – it is better understood as a trans-local and transcultural phenomenon. The development of suburban shopping in France relied on American models and Belgian precedents as much as it did on existing national distribution systems and a particular entrepreneurial culture.

The second type of development, the 'regional commercial centre' (*centre commercial régional*), was equally successful in the late 1960s, but its success was nevertheless short-lived.[20] Parly 2, one of the first such shopping centres in France, and the many similar developments that followed might seem at first glance more authentically 'American'. They followed a well-trodden architectural and retail model: the dumb-bell mall. This type of organization consisted of two department stores or supermarkets at the ends of an interior 'street' lined with a variety of smaller boutiques. In the American suburbs, the first generation of shopping centres were structured around open-air streets, but from the mid-1950s onwards, they were usually fully enclosed and came to be called 'malls'. The Austro-American architect and urban planner Victor Gruen was instrumental to this shift, and his designs, such as the Southdale Center near Minneapolis, were widely emulated across the United States and beyond.[21]

Parly 2's developers Robert de Balkany and Jean-Louis Solal, who had met while they were studying in the United States, explicitly engaged American-based design and commercial expertise. Solal was in fact directly inspired by Gruen's Southdale Center, whose organization over two floors corresponded to Solal's desire for an increased density in the face of limited available terrains.[22] As their economic consultant, the developers hired Larry Smith, co-author with Gruen of *Shopping Towns USA,* a bible for commercial developers.[23] Even the design of Parly 2 was by an American architect, Lathrop Douglass, who had by the late 1960s already designed more than seventy shopping centres in the United States

---

[18] Ibid., 23.
[19] Hervé Paturle, *Marcel Fournier l'Hyperman* (Paris: La Martinière, 2005), 240–241.
[20] Large shopping centres such as Parly 2 eventually lost against the hypermarkets in the following decades. See Péron, *La Fin des Vitrines*.
[21] See Jeffrey M. Hardwick, *Mall Maker: Victor Gruen, Architect of an American Dream* (Philadelphia: University of Pennsylvania Press, 2003).
[22] Meyer-Léotard, *Si Parly m'était conté*, 29.
[23] Victor Gruen and Larry Smith, *Shopping Towns USA: The Planning of Shopping Centers* (New York: Reinhold, 1960).

and Europe.[24] Despite this imported expertise, the architectural result differed significantly from the standard dumb-bell malls proliferating in American suburbia at the time. Parly 2 and many of the projects following it, including Vélizy 2 and Rosny 2, were multifunctional complexes that often also included housing, offices and a variety of other urban amenities, such a cinema or a hotel.[25] In fact, Parly 2 was first and foremost a large-scale housing development, a middle-class, private alternative to the *grands ensembles*.[26] In their combinations of functions and amenities therefore, they resembled not just American malls but also the new French urban centres that were being designed by new town planners at this time, such as Évry and Cergy-Pointoise.

Even though the hypermarket and the shopping mall emerged in France at about the same time, through mechanisms of transatlantic exchange, they were characterized not only by a different pedigree but also by a different commercial logic and target audience. Hypermarkets catered to the lower end of the market, attracting price-conscious suburban shoppers eager to buy at discounted prices in a rather bare-bones environment. Shopping centres were more capital-intensive and promised spectacle and diversity, including upscale fashion boutiques and department stores for customers who would otherwise shop in the city centre. Yet despite these different markets, they often entered into competition with one another; both required the same lots of land near highway exits in metropolitan suburbs promising a large mass of customers. And, perhaps most importantly, both constituted a formidable challenge for planners and policymakers in such a uniquely centralized state planning apparatus as that of France.

A touch of soul

The success and proliferation of suburban shopping vexed new town planners and policymakers as much as it fascinated them. The hypermarkets and shopping centres popping up at the outskirts of Paris and other large cities during the 1960s generated exactly the kind of crowds they imagined for the new urban centres currently underway. Yet they had no control over these developments, their location or their architecture. Most new town planners were critical of hypermarkets and shopping malls, following the critiques of many French intellectuals who denounced them as tasteless American imports destroying the French way of life and as the emblems a new mode of capitalism. For the sociologist Jean Baudrillard, Parly 2's most famous commentator, the shopping centre signalled the advent of new society of mass consumption – so vehemently critiqued around and after May 1968. In his 1970 book *The Society of Consumption*, Baudrillard even included an image of one of Parly 2's luxuriously decorated atriums, captioned with the phrase: 'On these beaches without paving stones, the class A and non-class A people will come to get tanned in the sun of commodities.'[27] This was an ironic allusion to that famous catchphrase of 1968, 'Under the paving stones, the beach'.

---

[24]See Jean-Louis Solal, 'Le Centre Commercial Région de Parly 2', *Urbanisme* 108–109 (May–June 1968); 'Centre Commercial Régional de Parly 2,' *Urbanisme* 114 (June 1969).
[25]See 19910585/011, Centre d'Archives Contemporaines, Archives Nationales, France.
[26]See Meyer-Léotard, *Si Parly m'était conté*.
[27]'Sur ces plages sans pavés, les A et les non-A viendront bronzer au soleil de la marchandise.' Source: Jean Baudrillard, *La Société de Consommation: Ses Mythes, Ses Structures* (Paris: S.G.P.P., 1970), 27.

For new town planners, however, the solution was not to overturn mass consumer culture altogether but to channel it in a new direction. Their approach was perfectly summarized in the words of Prime Minister Chaban-Delmas, when he proclaimed that France needed 'to master the society of consumption by bestowing it with a touch of soul'.[28] As such, the new architecture of suburban shopping became a key source of inspiration for the new urban centres of the French new towns. In the country's postwar suburbs, which were increasingly criticized for their soullessness, the shopping centres and hypermarkets guaranteed the crowds and thus the kind of liveliness reminiscent of that of a traditional city. Yet instead of accepting the idea that such private commercial developments had their own logic and that this suburban car-oriented logic might actually befit a new generation of consumers, they set themselves the task of harnessing what they saw as 'wild' and 'anti-urban' private commercial developments in coordinated urban projects. Even though today we might call these 'public–private partnerships', their design and financing was still tightly controlled by state planning agencies.

The design for the centre of the new town of Évry, in the south-eastern suburbs of Paris, was exemplary of this ambition.[29] Together with Cergy-Pontoise, Évry was the first of Paris's new towns to be further developed after the launch of the national programme in 1965. After an initial working group was charged to develop the general outlines of the plan, the planning responsibilities were handed over in 1969 to a multidisciplinary team consisting of urbanists, engineers, sociologists, geographers and architects.[30] This planning team established a large-scale urban plan for the new town. From the outset, planners were acutely aware of development pressure in the suburban region surrounding the new town, and in particular of plans for hypermarkets and commercial centres. André Lalande, who led the planning team, has recounted that 'there were some good hypermarkets around, and we were certain there would be one at one or two kilometres from the [new] centre, hence the permanent worry we had to build [our] commercial centre as soon as possible'. The biggest perceived risk in his opinion was the construction of a 40,000 m² Carrefour, 'which would have been catastrophic'.[31]

But suburban shopping was not only a threat to Évry's planners; it was also a crucial opportunity. The Parisian department store Printemps had announced its plans to expand business by opening new suburban locations, firstly at Parly 2 and then across suburban Paris. The news was received as revolutionary in a country so uniquely focused on inner-city Paris.[32] For the planners of Évry, the department store was a perfect magnet to draw large crowds to the future urban centre. Since such a department store would constitute a unique pole of attraction to suburbanites otherwise forced to travel into Paris, they preferred it over a hypermarket. Yet this preference also demonstrates the class-bias of

---

[28]'Il s'agit de maîtriser la société de consommation en lui apportant un supplément d'âme!' Source: Jacques Chaban-Delmas quoted in: ibid., 298.

[29]See Cupers, *The Social Project,* chapter 6.

[30]The Mission d'Étude, a multidisciplinary urbanism workshop to develop the basic plan for the new town, was created in 1966, the actual planning agency EPA (or *Etablissement Public d'Aménagement*) in 1969.

[31]'Il n'y avait plus qu'un risque, c'est qu'il se construise un Carrefour de 40,000 m² sur le terrain de M. Bouygues, ce qui aurait été la catastrophe. Il était donc grand temps que le centre commercial arrive.' André Lalande, cited in: 'Journée d'Études du 17 Octobre 1973 sur les Centres Urbains', 52. Source: 19840342/334, Centre d'Archives Contemporaines, Archives Nationales, France.

[32]Meyer-Léotard, *Si Parly m'était conté.*

Figure 1.3 Aerial photograph of the new urban centre of Évry, circa 1975.
Source: Fonds Le Couteur. Service interministériel des Archives de France/Cité de l'architecture et du patrimoine/Archives d'architecture du XXe siècle.

many planners, intent on attracting middle-class inhabitants to the new towns. For a shopping centre project such as Parly 2, economic studies had already shown that the nearby highway intersection at Grigny, about five miles away, would be an ideal location.[33] But having a privately developed shopping centre so close by would severely endanger the viability of Évry's new urban centre. In other words, shopping was not just an element in the programmatic mix for the project; it was quite literally a matter of life or death.

Although new town planners were convinced they needed to attract upscale retail companies like those gathered at Parly 2, they strongly disapproved of the urban and architectural form such developments took. They were particularly critical of the enclosed nature of these 'cities within a city' and the sprawling parking lots that cut them off from the surrounding area.[34] From the beginning, the

---

[33] See 'Journée d'études du 17 octobre 1973 sur les centres urbains', 32–33. Source: 19840342/334, Centre d'Archives Contemporaines, Archives Nationales, France.
[34] See Presentation by Mottez about Évry, in: ibid.

new towns for Paris had been planned around a new express commuter rail network, the RER (*Réseau express régional*). For the new centre of Évry, this meant tying the urban plan directly to this new public transport link. The RER line was diverted several kilometres west from its existing path along the Seine in order to pass right through the middle of the new town. The question for planners then was how to combine this public planning strategy with a suburban shopping centre, since the latter was usually located near the highway.

Not surprisingly, the negotiations between state planners and the private developers they were attempting to engage were difficult and lengthy. Ultimately, it was a conflict between two different pools of expertise and hence, two different forms of rationality. The developers relied on economic and marketing studies such as those by Larry Smith & Co. Such studies were in part based on axioms like Trujillo's 'no parking no business' and in part on economic location theory, which allowed to calculate profitability through action radii and the demographic characteristics of target populations.[35] The result was a fixed model: an isolated, internally integrated shopping mall with easy car access and plenty of parking space. French state planners on the other hand held the fundamental belief that the state was the bearer of an overarching rationality and should thus guide the 'uncoordinated' actions of different actors in the market. Moreover, the planners had lofty social ambitions: they were intent on creating new urban environments that would integrate myriad urban activities and people from different classes in order to provide a much-needed sense of urbanity in the often-dreary suburbs around the capital. Whether or not they were aware of the discussions about the 'urban core' within CIAM two decades earlier is unclear. Their ambitions derived not from any dogmatic or theoretical position but rather from the critiques of France's state-led suburbanization that had been percolating inside the very institutions of the state during the late 1960s – in particular those revolving around Henri Lefebvre's idea of the 'right to the city'.[36]

The final design for Évry's urban centre embodies these conflicting approaches: developers' demand to incorporate American models of suburban shopping on the one hand, and planners' desire for intense urban integration on the other hand. For its design, the planning team of Évry had hired Jean Le Couteur, a Beaux-Arts trained architect who had a long-standing relationship with the centralized state apparatus. Le Couteur divided the urban centre into two distinct parts. One part was coined the 'regional commercial centre' – adapted from the model of the American-style dumb-bell mall, despite planners' aversion, with a department store and a hypermarket on each end. The other part contained all non-commercial or civic functions and was baptized the 'Agora'. Right underneath both parts would run the new RER line.

Despite this seemingly simple division, the design was an extraordinary hybrid. Three sides of the centre were surrounded by vast planes of asphalt despite planners' efforts to hide parking spaces underneath the complex or have it stacked in multi-storey structures. From one angle, Évry's new centre thus looked just like any suburban shopping centre. Yet, at the same time, Le Couteur's design facilitated

---

[35]Paul Claval and R.J. Johnston, *Geography since the Second World War: An International Survey* (London: Croon Helm, 1984).
[36]Cupers, *The Social Project*, 204–210.

an astounding degree of integration of functions and activities that made it a truly urban centre. This included cafés, bars and restaurants, a bowling hall, a nightclub, a cinema, a skating ring, a sports hall and a swimming pool, a theatre, a library, an information centre, a family care centre, a centre for maternal and child protection, a kindergarten, a meeting centre, an ecumenical church, a broadcasting studio, a national employment agency, creative workshop spaces, a police station and of course a panoply of shops and department stores. These programmatic elements were aggregated over several floors, unified by massive plinth, underneath which parking and public transport was organized. When the centre opened in 1975, the new inhabitants of Évry and its surrounding suburbs were treated to the most unlikely combination of commercial functions, public activities and social programmes. These were not literally found under one roof, but were nevertheless all connected via interior walkways that came together in a double-height central atrium, which was meant to serve as the main public square of the complex. Despite the functional imbrication, some elements of the programme (the swimming pool, the skating rink and the sports hall most expressively) were formally articulated as distinct sculptural volumes.

The significance of this project is difficult to grasp without adjusting the lens we usually employ to evaluate the historical role of architecture in the transformation of the built environment at large. The design of Évry's urban centre was not the result of individual genius or architectural 'influence', but of negotiation and compromise. Its unique complexity was the result of exterior forces, such as the rise and popularity of privately developed suburban shopping centres, as much as the ambitions of modern architects and planners. Designs such as these should not be read as signs of an architectural avant-garde influencing daily building practice, but rather as creative attempts to marry private commercial development with modernist state-led planning. The resulting forms and spaces speak of an architectural agency embedded in a complex mix of private and public interests and a multitude of actors and ideas. They embody a transcultural modernity, influenced by American practices that were translated, appropriated and sometimes misunderstood, but in any case creatively transformed in their adaptation to French suburban conditions.

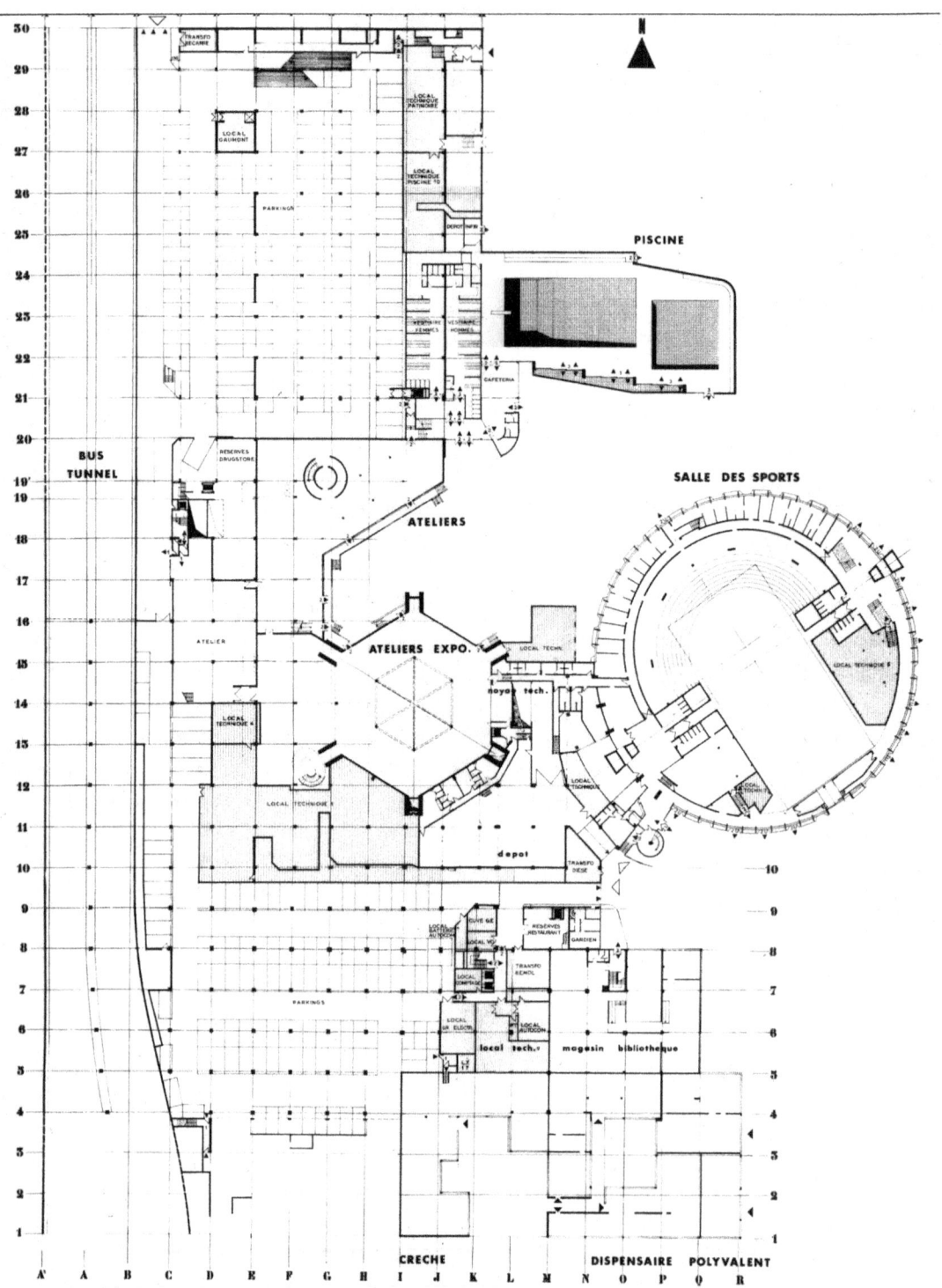

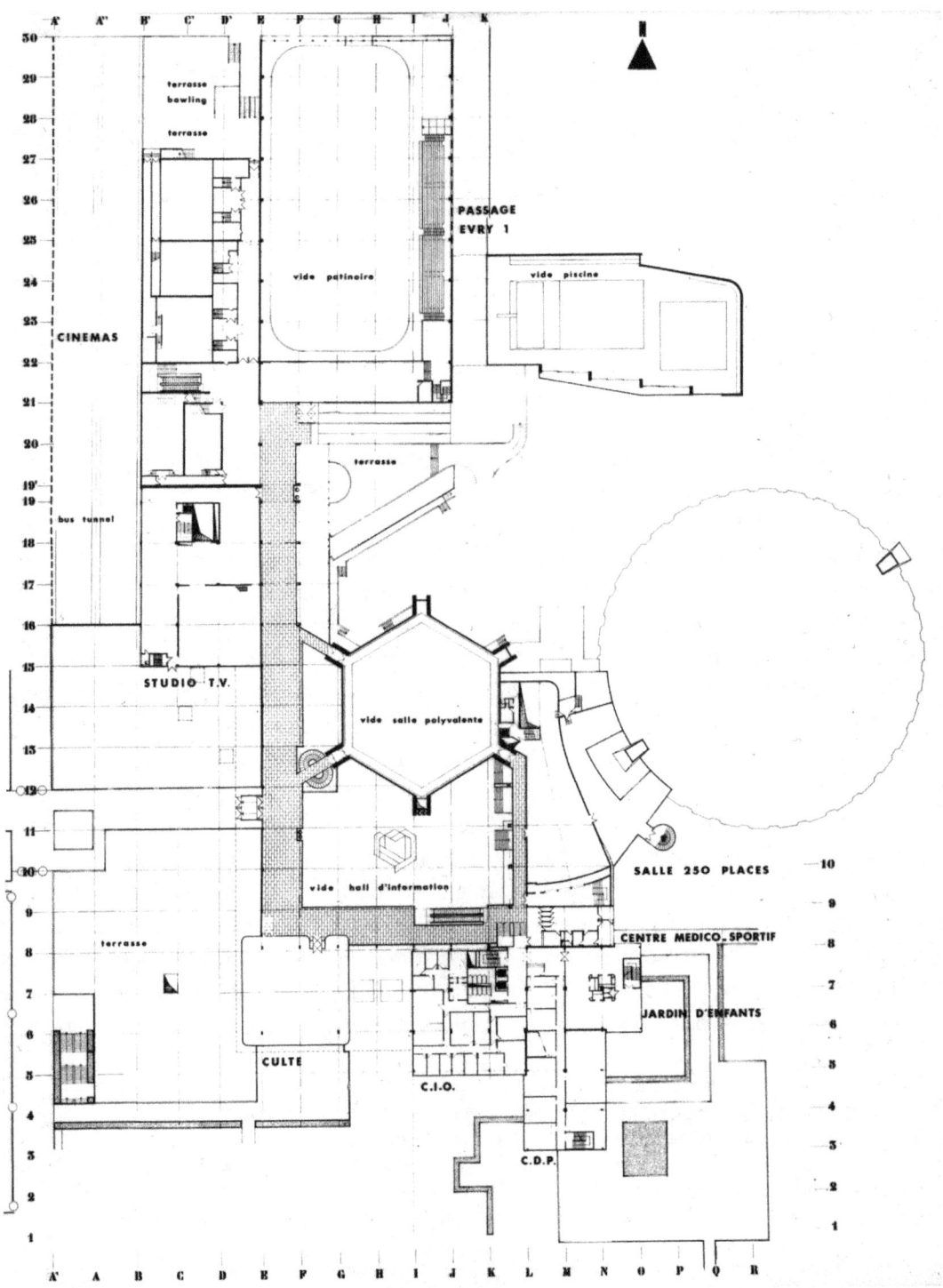

Figure 1.4 Plans of the Agora of Évry. The shopping centre is attached to the left of this complex.
Source: Fonds Le Couteur. Service interministériel des Archives de France/Cité de l'architecture et du patrimoine/Archives d'architecture du XXe siècle.

Chapter 2

The 1960s shopping centre grid of Helsinki: A framework for future development
Juhana Lahti

Introduction

The shopping centre concept arrived in Finland in the mid-1950s, when the first shopping centre opened in Helsinki in 1956.[1] In the following four years, five other shopping centres opened,[2] but it was not until the 1960s that shopping centre development in the country started in earnest. Since 1946 the Helsinki Regional Planning Association had been developing plans for Helsinki's future urbanization, and in 1961 it introduced a plan for a shopping centre grid, the primary purpose of which was to guide the planning of shopping centres in the greater Helsinki region. This plan was created in collaboration with the Helsinki Regional Planning Committee, a subsidiary of the Helsinki Chamber of Commerce, which was founded in 1954. Both the head of Helsinki City Planning and the director of the Helsinki Regional Planning Association were members of the Helsinki Regional Planning Committee, as were several representatives of the Finnish economy and of Finland's central firms; the Committee thus quickly became the primary forum for the discussion of 'commercial' planning in the Helsinki region.

The new Building Act that was drafted by the Ministry of Interior and approved in 1958 – the previous Town Planning Act dated back to 1932 – also played an important role in the development of Helsinki's shopping centre grid, as it (for the first time) acknowledged the concept of a master plan and a regional plan.[3] This new legislation thus supported collaboration between the City of Helsinki and its surrounding municipalities.[4] It was then no coincidence that the first map by the Regional Planning Association that shows the shopping centre grid is dated 1961, the same year that the Ministry of the Interior commissioned a regional plan for Helsinki and its surrounding municipalities.[5] This chapter examines

---

[1] Erätori in Herttoniemi by architect Eliel Muoniovaara.

[2] See Sari Saresto, Anne Salminen and Mira Vierto, *Ostari – lähiön sydän*. Rakennushistoriallinen selvitys. Helsingin kaupunginmuseon tutkimuksia ja raportteja 2/2004 (Helsinki: Helsinki City Museum, 2004).

[3] Juhana Lahti, 'The Helsinki Suburbs Tapiola and Vantaanpuisto: Post-War Planning by the Architect Aarne Ervi', *Planning Perspectives* 23 (April 2008): 151.

[4] Helsinki Master Plan proposal 1953–1960; Helsinki Master Plan proposal 1970; Helsinki Regional Planning Association 'Skeleton plan' 1968.

[5] The growing popularity of the car also played an important role in the development of shopping centres in the Helsinki Region and had a major influence on the Finns' shopping behaviour. During the 1960s, the region's modern road network was built to accommodate increasing car ownership. While in the early 1960s there were around 160,000 private cars in the country, by the end of the decade this number had risen to 643,000. Uusimaa province alone, in which Helsinki is located, counted 156,000 cars by the end of 1969. See *The Statistical Yearbook of Finland* (Helsinki: Central Statistical Office/Statistics Finland, 1970), 224.

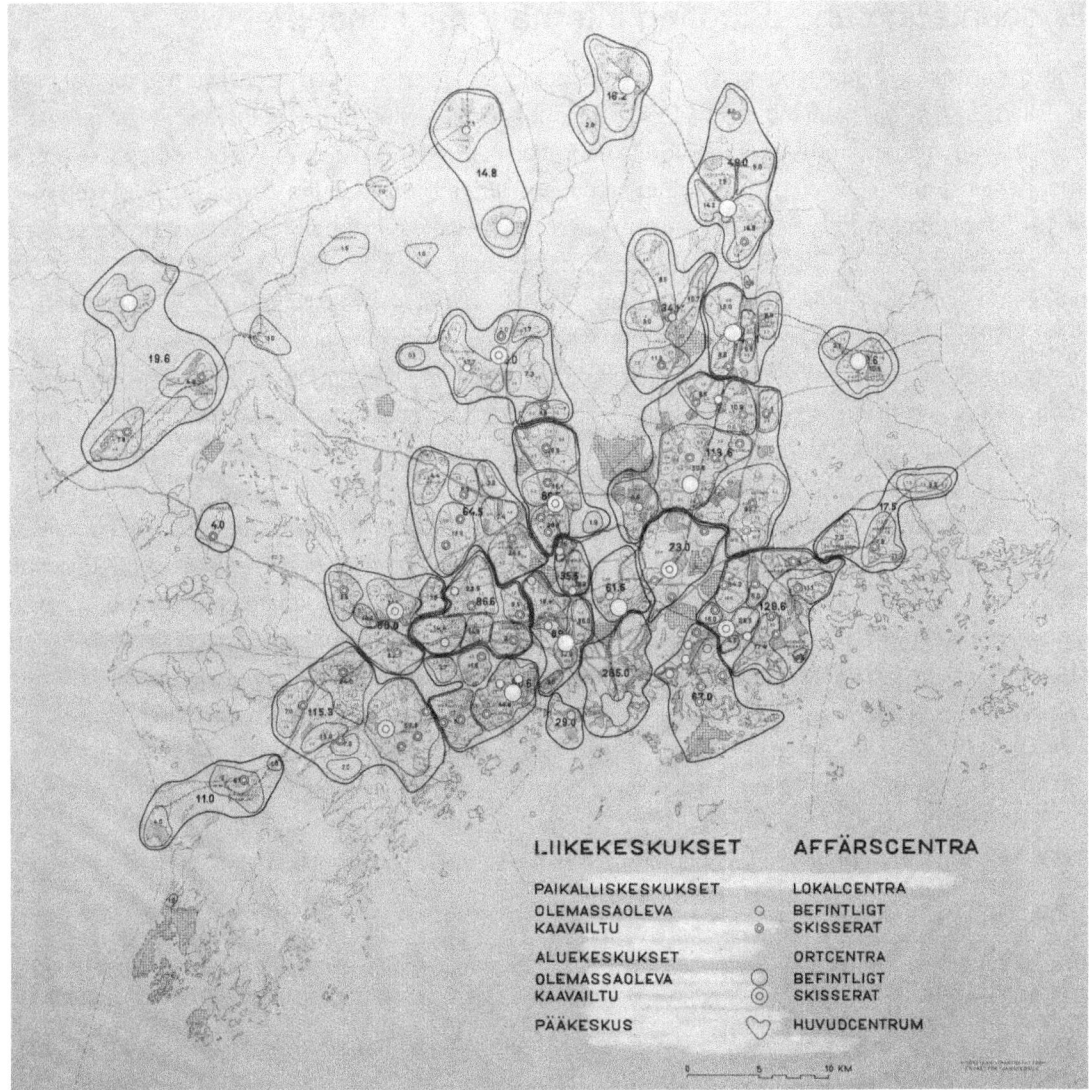

Figure 2.1 Helsinki shopping centre grid by the Helsinki Regional Planning Association, 1961. The legend on the (far) right of the map translates as: SHOPPING CENTRES (*AFFÄRSCENTRA*), with below it: local centres (*lokalcentra*), existing (*befintligt*), planned (*skisserat*); regional centres (*ortcentra*), existing (*befintligt*), planned (*skisserat*), and city centre (*huvudcentrum*).
Source: National Archives of Finland.

how the development of shopping centres in Helsinki were closely bound to the city's urban growth and the construction of its modern suburbs,[6] as it traces the development of Helsinki's shopping centre grid and analyses the design of the first 'regional' shopping centres in the area.

---

[6]This chapter relies on sources from the archives of Helsinki Chamber of Commerce, Housing Foundation and Helsinki Regional Planning Association, held in the National Archives of Finland, as well as from the collections of Museum of Finnish Architecture.

Encountering and adapting international concepts

Both the shopping centre typology and the neighbourhood-unit planning model assumed pivotal roles in Finland's post-war planning theory. First developed in the United States in the early twentieth century, these concepts found their way to Finland after the Second World War, where they played an important role in the planning of suburban areas, and strongly affected the development of Helsinki.[7] In 1947 Professor Otto-Iivari Meurman published an influential textbook on town planning entitled *Asemakaavaoppi*, which discussed the concept of decentralization and the notion of the 'core'.[8] It not only introduced the neighbourhood-unit concept to Finland, but also highlighted the benefits of zoning and traffic segregation as planning instruments capable of supporting hierarchy. In *Asemakaavaoppi*, Meurman did however not yet discuss shopping centres. The shopping centre concept only arrived in Finland during the 1950s, when designers and developers across the Western world had already devised a classification for the type, which ranged from small neighbourhood centres to large regional centres. This classification was based on the scale of the shopping centre as well as on its potential geographical 'reach'.[9] However, when the Helsinki Chamber of Commerce introduced this classification in Finland in 1962, it neglected to adjust the 'taxonomy' to the Finnish circumstances.[10] This was not unusual as the influence of the Anglo-Saxon world on Finland increased perceptibly after the war. Finnish architects were familiar with Eero Saarinen's and Robert Swanson's design for Willow Run (1943) as well as with Victor Gruen's designs of the following decade. Morris Ketchum's book *Shops and Stores* was widely read[11] and Victor Gruen's *Shopping Towns USA*[12] arrived in the library of the Finnish Architects Association in 1960.[13]

Studies of Swedish shopping centres were equally influential in introducing the new typology in Finland. Vällingby centre (1954) in particular was widely recognized and praised.[14] In 1957, Swedish researcher Arne Sjöberg described shopping centres in Europe as different from the American shopping

---

[7] The neighbourhood-unit concept was introduced to Finnish planning discussions through British and Scandinavian sources. In Otto-Iivari Meurman's textbook *Asemakaavaoppi* 1947, the County of London plan 1943 is presented, but the source is a Swedish article by O. Danneskiold-Samsoe in *Byggmästaren*.

[8] Meurman refers to the German concept of *Kernbildung*. Otto-I. Meurman, *Asemakaavaoppi* (Helsinki: Otava, 1947), 60, 75; Lahti, 'The Helsinki Suburbs Tapiola and Vantaanpuisto', 151.

[9] Shopping centre classifications: In 1957 Arne Sjöberg made the following classification: neighbourhood centres (*närhetscentra*), community or district centres (*distriktscentra*), suburban or outlying central city centres (*förortscentra*) and regional centres (*regionala centra*). See Aarne Sjöberg, *Shoppingcentra i USA och Sverige* (Stockholm: Grosshandels Utredningsinstitut, 1957), 10–15. This classification was based on E.J. Kelley, *Shopping Centres: Locating Controlled Regional Centres* (Saugatuck, CT: The Eno Foundation for Highway Traffic Control, 1956). In 1960, Victor Gruen also defined a classification in his *Shopping Towns USA: The Planning of Shopping Centres* (New York: Reinhold, 1960), 272, 278–279. Five years later, the Stockholm Chamber of Commerce also introduced a classification into D neighbourhood, C district, B area and A regional centres in *Swedish Shopping Centres. Experiments and Achievements* (Stockholm: Stockholm Chamber of Commerce, 1965, 1961), 12, 18.

[10] Annual report *Helsingin kauppakamari v. 1962*, 37–38. Archives of the Helsinki Chamber of Commerce.

[11] Morris Ketchum, *Shops and Stores* (New York: Reinhold, 1957).

[12] Gruen, *Shopping Towns USA*.

[13] *Arkkitehtiuutiset*, 19 August 1960, 15–16.

[14] See David Pass, *Vällingby and Farsta – From Idea to Reality: The New Community Development Process in Stockholm* (Cambridge, MA: MIT Press, 1973).

centre.[15] These differences, Sjöberg explained, related to both the use of cars and the selection of shops.[16] However, in a brochure by the Stockholm Chamber of Commerce the inspiration for Swedish development was said to have come from the Anglo-Saxon world: first from the experiences in Great Britain and later, after private cars popularized, from the United States.[17] Close connections between Finnish and Swedish architects, as well as between the Chambers of Commerce of Helsinki and Stockholm aided the exchange of topical ideas regarding the development of shopping centres.

Travels, congresses and meetings

After the Second World War, Finnish architects and other experts involved in shopping centre planning commonly travelled to other Scandinavian countries and occasionally to the United States. One of the most active travellers was Aarne Ervi, who took numerous photographs during his trips.[18] In 1947 he travelled to the United States, where he drove by car from New York to Los Angeles. During this journey he visited the latest shopping centre developments, including Wilshire Boulevard and Grenshaw Boulevard in Los Angeles. Ervi also published an article on his journey in the Finnish architectural review *Arkkitehti* in 1948, which explained the term and concept of the 'shopping centre' through a comparison with the department store. Ervi illustrated this text with an image of 'a shopping centre plan near Boston', but failed to mention that this was the Beverly Shopping Centre by Ketchum, Gina & Sharp, which was presented in *Architectural Forum* in June the previous year.[19] This was likely the first time that the shopping centre was discussed as a term and concept in a Finnish publication.[20] Seven years later, in 1955, Ervi visited several shopping centres in Sweden and Denmark and in 1956 went to de Lijnbaan in Rotterdam.[21]

In 1954, the Regional Planning Committee also undertook a trip to Stockholm and Göteborg.[22] It is not known precisely which places they visited, but Vällingby was undoubtedly on the list.[23] Seven years later, the Committee arranged another trip to Stockholm, Göteborg and Copenhagen, the main goal of which was to visit shopping centres.[24] Otto Flodin, Director of the Regional Planning Association, was among the participants. In 1968, both Flodin and Ervi, who at the time was the Head of the Helsinki

---

[15] Sjöberg, *Shoppingcentra i USA och Sverige*, 20.
[16] Ibid., 24.
[17] *Swedish Shopping Centres. Experiments and Achievements*, 5.
[18] Linda Leskinen, 'Aarne Ervi's Trip to the United States of America in 1947', in *Aarne Ervi: tilaa ihmiselle/Architect Aarne Ervi 1910–1977*, eds. Eriika Johansson, Juhana Lahti and Kristiina Paatero (Helsinki: Museum of Finnish Architecture, 2010), 81.
[19] Aarne Ervi, 'Matkavaikutelmia U.S.A:sta ja sen arkkitehtuurista', *Arkkitehti* 7–8 (1948): 87–90.
[20] Further on in the same issue, Ervi also presented the Bullock´s Department Store in Pasadena by Walter Wurdeman and Welton Beckett. Aarne Ervi, 'Tavaratalo Bullock´s', *Arkkitehti* 7–8 (1948): 102–104.
[21] Photos from travels. Collections of Aarne Ervi. Museum of Finnish Architecture.
[22] Annual report *Helsingin kauppakamari v. 1954*, 29–31. Archives of the Helsinki Chamber of Commerce.
[23] Programme of the journey. Helsingin aluesuunnitelmaliitto. Aluesuunnitteluvaliokunnan matka Ruotsiin 12–16.5.1954. Collection of the Helsinki Regional Planning Association. National Archives of Finland.
[24] Stockholm: Farsta, Hagsätra, Högdalen; Göteborg: Kortedala, Biskopsgården; Copenhagen: Lyngby, Sorgenfri, Naerum, Karlsruhe. Annual report *Helsingin kauppakamari v. 1961*, 27–28. Archives of the Helsinki Chamber of Commerce.

City Planning Department, participated in the Committee's visit to Stockholm.[25] Other professionals also travelled abroad in pursuit of shopping centre experience and to establish contacts with foreign shopping centre experts.[26] In May 1961, architect Erkki Karvinen participated in a shopping centre conference in Oslo; in 1966, Ahti Haukkavaara, a member of the Helsinki Chamber of Commerce, participated in the Distribution and Town Planning conference in Brussels;[27] and during the 1960s, the Director of the Housing Foundation and developer of Tapiola, Heikki von Hertzen maintained contact with Clarence Stein, Morris Ketchum and Victor Gruen as well as shopping centre developer James Rouse who was specialized in 'regional enclosed malls'.[28]

Helsinki expands to a region

Between the late 1950s and the end of the 1960s Finland experienced extensive urbanization. In this decade planning legislation, municipal administration and the organization of urban planning increased significantly. In the early twentieth century Helsinki started to expand beyond its municipal borders[29] and after the Second World War large areas were incorporated in the city as several small municipalities vanished. Helsinki quintupled in area into '(greater) Helsinki', covering over 160 square kilometres and its population grew from 276,000 to 341,000. Instead of a traditional mono-centric city, Helsinki thus transformed into a modern polycentric region composed of several smaller suburbs.

In 1956, when the idea of regional shopping centres was still vague, architect Otto Flodin, Director of the Regional Planning Association, identified four possible locations for the development of such regional centres.[30] One of them was Tapiola. Around that time, the City of Helsinki asked the Regional Planning Committee's opinion in relation to a forthcoming master plan; the Committee proposed shopping centres as a solution to organize commercial services.[31] And so, in 1961 the Helsinki Regional Planning Association introduced a grid of regional shopping centres, which resulted from collaborations between the Regional Planning Committee and various municipal planning organizations. In February 1963, Flodin announced to the National Planning Council that the Regional Planning Committee had defined the possible location and size of planned shopping centres in Helsinki and its surroundings,[32] and in a

---

[25] Annual report *Helsingin kauppakamari v. 1968*, 30–31. Archives of the Helsinki Chamber of Commerce.

[26] Oslo: Lambertseter, Veitveld; Stockholm: Vällingby, Farsta. Annual report *Helsingin kauppakamari v. 1961*, 28. Archives of the Helsinki Chamber of Commerce.

[27] Ahti Haukkavaara, *Elinkeinoekspansio pääkaupunkiseudulla 1960-luvulla*, (Helsinki: 2006), 48.

[28] Heikki von Hertzen's correspondence and a brochure by Rouse Company: *A New Standard of Retail Merchandising in the Houston Marketplace: Almeda Mall, Northwest Mall*. Archives of the Housing Foundation. Espoo City Museum.

[29] The city of Helsinki was founded in 1550 and it became the capital in 1812. In 1917, Finland got independency. Before that it was an autonomous part of Russian empire.

[30] Vantaa, Kerava, Håkansböle, Tapiola: Otto Flodin. Helsingin aluesuunnittelun nykyvaihe -selostus valtuuskunnan kokouksessa 16.5.1956. Collection of the Helsinki Regional Planning Association. National Archives of Finland.

[31] Annual report *Helsingin kauppakamari v. 1958*, 61–63. Archives of the Helsinki Chamber of Commerce.

[32] Otto Flodin. Helsingin ja sen lähivaikutusalueen muodostaman suuryhdyskunnan kehittämisestä. Valtakunnansuunnitteluneuvostolle 7.2.1963 annettu selostus. Collection of the Helsinki Regional Planning Association. National Archives of Finland.

1965 article in *Arkkitehti* he referred to Helsinki's metropolitan region as 'the smallest of its kind in the world'.[33] Although he referred to an area formed by the ten constituting municipalities,[34] he expected Helsinki to remain the only true urban centre in this area.

The first regional shopping centres

The first 'regional' shopping centres in 'greater Helsinki', Tapiontori shopping centre in Tapiola and Munkkivuori shopping centre, paved the way for future developments, such as the Puotinharju shopping centre (Puhos) and Heikintori shopping centre in Tapiola. These projects were the most ambitious in terms of architectural design and in their collaborative use of resources to adapt the regional shopping centre to local circumstances. Munkkivuori was the result of a collaboration between Helsinki City, the Chamber of Commerce and four central firms; Tapiola was a project of the Housing Foundation outside the city's borders, and Puotinharju was developed by a joint stock company founded and owned by the three central firms: Elanto, Kesko and SOK. In Puotinharju, however, the City and the Chamber of Commerce were no longer involved as clearly as in Munkkivuori; although the City did prepare the urban plans and the Committee conducted surveys.

Munkkivuori

The preparatory planning for Munkkivuori shopping centre started in 1954.[35] In 1955 the Regional Planning Committee studied the sizing of the shopping centres in Helsinki and in the case of Munkkivuori stated that it should be constructed in phases following a comprehensive plan.[36] The following year the central firms requested a more detailed study from the Committee. This study, which referenced Swedish examples, predicted that the planned Munkkivuori shopping centre had a very good chance of developing into the largest commercial centre in the Helsinki region.[37] That same year, the Helsinki City Real Estate Department enquired if the Helsinki Chamber of Commerce could take care of the planning and construction of the centre. The Chamber responded that this kind of activity was not in their interest, but that they were in favour of a collaboration between the different interest groups, which included several Finnish firms.[38] The Regional Planning Committee subsequently arranged a discussion that focused (amongst other things) on the adaptability of shopping centres to the circumstances in Helsinki,[39] and early in 1957 founded a sub-committee to take care of the planning of the centre. Besides the Chamber of Commerce, this sub-committee included the firms Kesko, OTK, SOK and

---

[33]Otto Flodin, 'Helsingin metropolitanalue pienimpiä maailmassa', *Arkkitehti* 7 (1965): 186–188.
[34]Helsinki city, Helsinki rural commune, Espoo rural commune/market town, Kauniainen market town, Kerava Market town, as well as the rural communes of Kirkkonummi, Järvenpää, Nurmijärvi, Vihti, Tuusula (and Sipoo).
[35]Annual report *Helsingin kauppakamari v. 1954*, 33–35. Archives of the Helsinki Chamber of Commerce.
[36]Ibid., 37–38.
[37]Annual report *Helsingin kauppakamari v. 1956*, 38. Archives of the Helsinki Chamber of Commerce.
[38]Ibid., 40–41.
[39]Ibid., 42.

Figure 2.2 Munkkivuori shopping centre under construction in Western Helsinki.
Source: Heikki Havas, Museum of Finnish Architecture.

Tukkukauppojen Oy.[40] Since the objective was to design the first 'true' shopping centre in Finland, the Committee decided to organize an open architectural competition in 1957. A total of fifty-four entries were submitted following the competition brief, which stated that – in line with international trends – the shopping centre needed to be designed for pedestrians.[41] Many of the submissions suggested a market-square kind of an approach and arranged the buildings around an open courtyard. The jury however deemed narrower pedestrian streets a better solution.[42] The competition brief furthermore stipulated that apart from a shopping centre, the complex also needed to include office spaces for Helsinki City, apartments and a cinema theatre. None of these auxiliary functions were however ever realized.

Architect Antero Pernaja won the competition with Juhani Kivikoski, Nils-Henrik Sandell, and Pertti Pernaja. The second and the third prize were both awarded to proposals by Viljo Revell and his

---

[40]Annual report *Helsingin kauppakamari v. 1957*, 47–48. Archives of the Helsinki Chamber of Commerce.
[41]'Pohjois-Munkkiniemen ostoskeskuksen suunnittelukilpailu', *Arkkitehti* 11–12 (1957): 27–37, 27.
[42]Competition records. Pohjois-Munkkinimen ostoskeskuksen arkkitehtuurikilpailun pöytäkirja. Competition Archive. Museum of Finnish Architecture.

assistants. Suggesting that developing a shopping centre adapted to Finnish conditions required multi-faceted research and that international models could not be applied as such,[43] the jury commended the submitted designs for presenting solutions whose size and shape suited the needs of Finnish businesses. In this frame of mind, the competition brief had also extended the shopping centre's traffic question beyond private transportation (parking spaces) and emphasized the need for the integration of public transport stations (bus, metro and fast tram line) in the complex. The Munkkivuori shopping centre competition was in this sense very region-focused and future-oriented. It not only introduced the modern shopping centre concept in Finland but also sought to combine architectural and economical questions with urban planning. After winning the competition, Pernaja further developed his competition design with his colleagues and construction on the first four buildings started in 1959. Although several small (local) 'shopping centres' had been in operation in Helsinki since 1956, when Munkkivuori opened seven months after construction started, it became the first 'regional' shopping centre in 'greater Helsinki'. The second phase of construction was implemented in 1962 when the western wing of the building complex was added. At this point, an entrance for the metro was constructed in the basement, which still awaits the arrival of the metro today. The city of Helsinki played an active role in the development of Munkkivuori shopping centre, and continued to do so in the next regional centre built in Helsinki; Puotinharju.

Puotinharju (Puhos)

In November 1958, the Head of Helsinki City Planning Väinö Tuukkanen presented preliminary plans for a new regional shopping centre East of Helsinki to the Regional Planning Committee.[44] The city had asked the Committee to advise on this new centre, which was widely considered the Finnish counterpart of Vällingby and Farsta in Stockholm, as it was destined to become the first large-scale centre in Finland, which also included housing areas. Although the nearest housing areas were planned for a population of less than 10,000, the centre was designed to serve a 'local' customer-base of 55,000 and a potential regional customer-base of 200,000. The Committee accordingly proposed that it was to have a footprint of 21,000 square metres and 2,400 parking spaces.[45] Puotinharju shopping centre was designed by architect Erkki Karvinen[46] in collaboration with his assistants, Antero Roivola and Jussi Saarelainen, both architecture students. It was built between 1964 and 1965 with the financial support of a joint stock company, which was founded by three central firms – Elanto, Kesko and SOK – especially for this purpose.[47] The original building, a two-storey fan-shaped complex, was penetrated by four open corridors departing radially from the open yard towards the housing area

---

[43]'Pohjois-Munkkiniemen ostoskeskuksen suunnittelukilpailu', 27.
[44]Annual report *Helsingin kauppakamari v. 1958*, 64. Archives of the Helsinki Chamber of Commerce.
[45]Annual report *Helsingin kauppakamari v. 1960*, 34–35. Archives of the Helsinki Chamber of Commerce.
[46]During the 1960s Karvinen became the leading shopping centre architect in Finland. He designed a total of eleven shopping centres in Helsinki and Vantaa during his career. Eight of them were built around Helsinki by the end of the 1960s.
[47]All the main positions of the administrative board were divided between representatives of the three major store chains in Finland (chair Elanto, vice chair Kesko, deputy landlord SOK). *Helsinki-lehti* 6/1965, 12.2.1965.

Figure 2.3 Puotinharju shopping centre in Eastern Helsinki in its original condition.
Source: Simo Rista, Museum of Finnish Architecture.

in the north-west,[48] effectively dividing the shopping centre into five segments. The complex was all concrete construction and the concave walls on the façades facing the housing areas were cast in 'spray concrete', a technique then used in tunnel construction.[49] Service traffic was located in a tunnel under the shopping centre, which was deemed to have cultural potential as outdoor concerts in the central yard were listed among the envisioned future activities. When Puotinharju opened, it was the largest shopping centre in Finland, providing 6,429 square metres of shopping area and parking spaces for circa hundred cars. From its inception, the centre was expected to triple in size, and accordingly planned in stages to reach 21,000 square metres by the 1970s. It was expected it would then include a small department store and parking spaces for 2,400 cars.[50] Some twenty-five years later, when the shopping centre was finally extended in two phases – one happened in 1987

---

[48]Erkki Karvinen, 'Einkaufszentrum in Helsinki – Puotinharju/Finland', *Architektur und Wohnform*, heft 8 (1965): 434–437; Erkki Karvinen, 'Einkaufszentrum in Helsinki-Puotinharju', *Bauwelt* 18 (1966): 1377.
[49]Sari et al., *Ostari – lähiön sydän*, 82.
[50]Annual report *Helsingin kauppakamari v. 1960*, 34–35. Archives of the Helsinki Chamber of Commerce; *Suomen Sosiaalidemokraatti* 26.2.1965.

and another one in 1990 – the original idea had been altered radically, even though Karvinen's office was responsible for these extensions.

Tapiola

In 1951, a group of public utility organizations[51] established Asuntosäätiö (The Housing Foundation) to manage the establishment of a new town West of Helsinki. Lawyer Heikki von Hertzen, the Executive Director of Väestöliitto (The Family Welfare Federation), led this project. Architect Otto-Iivari Meurman drew the first plans for the entire area in the mid-1940s and in 1952 five Finnish architects were commissioned to design the first housing neighbourhood following the modernistic plan that Meurman had set out. One of them was Aarne Ervi, who two years later won the competition for Tapiola's new town

Figure 2.4 The entrance to Tapiola centre in Espoo (Tapiontori shopping centre and Central tower) on a winter evening. *Source:* Eero Troberg, Museum of Finnish Architecture.

---

[51]Väestöliitto (The Family Welfare Federation), Mannerheimin lastensuojeluliitto (The Mannerheim League for Child Welfare), Suomen ammattiyhdistysten Keskusliitto SAK (The Confederation of Finnish Trade Unions), Suomen Siviili- ja Asevelvollisuusinvalidien Keskusliitto (The Finnish Association of Disabled Veterans and Servicemen), Virkamiesliitto (The Society of Civil Servants) and Vuokralaisten Keskusliitto (The Central Association of Tenants).

Figure 2.5 The first indoor/enclosed shopping centre in Finland (Heikintori in Tapiola).
Source: Aarne Ervi, Museum of Finnish Architecture.

centre together with Olli Kuusi and Tapani Nironen. In the studies that the Regional Planning Committee made between 1955 and 1956 for the dimensioning of shopping centres, Tapiola was the first outside the city of Helsinki.[52] By that time, the Housing Foundation had already proposed the development of a shopping centre at the heart of the new town, which was to serve 30,000 customers. The Committee deemed this figure overly optimistic, as the planned population for Tapiola only amounted to 15,000 and the major roads leading to Helsinki were relatively far from the 'garden city', as the new town became known.[53] Nonetheless, a competition for a centre for Tapiola had already been announced in 1953 and by 26 April 1954, seventeen entries had been submitted.[54]

Ervi's winning entry placed the offices in a tower block and the shops in a U-shaped shopping centre at the core of the development. The first part of Ervi's design was completed in the early 1960s

---

[52] Annual report *Helsingin kauppakamari v. 1956*, 35–36. Archives of the Helsinki Chamber of Commerce.

[53] Asuntosäätiön hallituksen pöytäkirjat, liite 50/56. Kauppakamarin lausunto Tapiola citysta 9.3.1956. Archives of the Housing Foundation. Espoo City Museum.

[54] Competition records. Archives of the Housing Foundation. Espoo City Museum; Competition Archive. Museum of Finnish Architecture.

when the office tower and the pedestrian shopping centre were finished.[55] Tapiontori was constructed in three phases between 1959 and 1961. In the first stage, a single and two-storey building in a U-shaped plan served as a local shopping centre for the housing areas under construction while a thirteen-storey office block stood as the landmark of the Tapiola centre in the suburban topography.[56] In the next stage, towards the end of the decade, Ervi enlarged the centre in collaboration with Pertti Solla as project architect. Following this design, another office block was built and Finland's first enclosed regional shopping mall, Heikintori, was realized between 1967 and 1968.[57] The three-storey, 12,000 square metre Heikintori, the second of the shopping centre buildings, was located on the axis of the pedestrian street which penetrated the centre area. Following Swedish examples, store spaces in Heikintori were owned by the shopkeepers and private companies, while in Tapiontori they were owned by a company of the Housing Foundation and were rented to the shopkeepers. Tapiontori thus adopted the Scandinavian tradition of cooperation as the form of retail trade in the modern shopping centre under the guidance of the foundation.

Conclusion: The future of 1968

During the 1960s, a total of thirty-eight centres were opened in greater Helsinki and its bordering municipalities, Espoo, Kauniainen and (what is today known as) Vantaa. All three shopping centres discussed in this chapter were built between 1959 and 1968 and were located close to the housing areas where a forthcoming station of a 'fast tramline' railroad connection to the Helsinki city centre was envisioned. All of them were also arranged around a pedestrian street or area, with surrounding parking areas and bus stations.[58] In 1968, after these three shopping centres had been built, the Helsinki Regional Planning Association finally published its preliminary regional plan, which proposed a system of regional centres, eight of them located in Helsinki – Puotila and Malmi in Helsinki, Tapiola, Leppävaara, Kivenlahti and Muurala (Espoon keskus) in Espoo – and two in surrounding municipalities: Tikkurila and Koivukylä.[59] Four others were located in four surrounding municipalities; in reality these more or less corresponded to the existing centres of villages and towns.[60] With two exceptions – Munkkivuori and Southern

---

[55] Aarne Ervi, 'Tapiolan Keskusta', *Arkkitehti* 12 (1961): 192–199.

[56] 'These complexes (Shopping Centres) were conceived not just as concentrations of business, but as a landmarks on the metropolitan periphery, functioning much like recreation centres and public and religious institutions as a focus for human interaction and as a definer of place.' Source: Richard Longstreth, 'The Diffusion of the Community Shopping Centre Concept during the Interwar Decades', *Journal of the Society of Architecture Historians* 56, no. 3 (1997): 270.

[57] Juhana Lahti, 'Tapionraitti – the Backbone of the Pedestrian Precinct', in *Tapiola – Life and Architecture*, eds. Timo Tuomi, Kristiina Lehtimäki and Kristiina Paatero (Espoo: City of Espoo/Helsinki: Building Information Ltd, 2003), 64.

[58] 'The shopping center is conventionally defined as a group of commercial establishments under a single ownership, planned, developed, and managed as a single unit, with off-street parking provided, and related to the area it serves in the size and type of its stores. Wholly planned and controlled, it differs thus from an ordinary retail street or district where independently owned stores are simply concentrated.' Source: Meredith Clausen, 'Northgate Regional Shopping Centre – Paradigm for the Provinces', *Journal of the Society of Architecture Historians* 43 (May 1984): 146.

[59] *Runkokaava* (Helsinki: Helsingin seutukaavaliitto, 1968).

[60] Kirkkonummi and Masala (in Kirkkonummi), Lohja, Vihti, Nurmijärvi and Rajamäki (in Nurmijärvi), Hyvinkää, Kerava, Järvenpää, Hyrylä (in Tuusula) and Nikkilä (in Sipoo).

Vantaa – the regional centres were approximately the same as presented in the 1961 shopping centre grid (see Figure 2.1). Prepared in collaboration with the Helsinki Regional Planning Committee, this grid had guided the development of shopping centres throughout the 1960s, and the majority of the regional and local shopping centres realized between 1961 and 1968 were then also situated according to what was presented in the new regional plan. However, when the outline of the regional plan was finally published in 1968, the grid had already started to evolve, and the purpose of this document – to guide future development – was challenged as soon as it saw daylight. At the end of the 1960s, a new type of shopping centre had started to emerge; the enclosed shopping mall. Heikintori, which opened in Tapiola in 1968 was one of its first exponents. This development was obviously well suited to Finland's northern climate, but was also informed by the rise of living standards. Heikontori, however, was still located at the heart of a new town, contrary to the enclosed shopping centres that were built during the 1970s, which were located close to traffic routes. In the latter half of the 1980s, another shift occurred as the enclosed shopping centres came to the central areas of Finnish cities.

In spite of the prominent role that shopping centres played in Finnish planning during the 1960s and 1970s, their designers have – save for a few exceptions – been relegated to the margins of Finnish architectural history. Toivo Korhonen and Erkki Karvinen, who specialized in shopping centre design, have not been a part of the canon of Finnish architecture and aside from the Tapiola centre, which was a part of a larger community plan, Finnish shopping centres as a building type only gained recognition around the turn of the twenty-first century. This lack of interest has allowed several of the early shopping centres in the Helsinki to be demolished. Vuosaari shopping centre (1967) by Viljo Revell was destroyed in 2003; Erkki Karvinen's Maunula (1962) and Myllypuro (1965) shopping centres were torn down recently; and most early post-war shopping centres have fallen victim to their own success, and have been continuously redeveloped since they were first erected.

Chapter 3

Shopping centres as catalysts for new multifunctional urban centralities: The case of two shopping centres around Brussels

Yannick Vanhaelen and Géry Leloutre

The shopping centres that developed in the periphery of Brussels during the 1960s and 1970s are among the oldest and biggest in Belgium. Thus far, however, they have been sparsely discussed in the context of Brussels' urban history. Scholarship on this period has been primarily concerned with the transformation of Brussels into a tertiary international centre, through the adaption of its road infrastructure and the radical transformation of its urban fabric, which is often discussed in terms of the destruction of the city's built heritage and considered responsible for the decreasing quality of urban life and the exodus of the middle class to the periphery.[1] Whenever the development of Brussels' peripheral shopping centres has been addressed, these have commonly been described as merely isolated realizations that result from a liberal *laissez-faire* policy, which has made both commercial forces and the car 'king' and contributed to the erosion of the city.[2]

Contesting these negative assessments, this chapter puts forward the hypothesis that shopping centres in the Belgian Capital Region have served as catalysts for the development of new multifunctional centralities, aimed at structuring urbanization around Brussels. These developments can be seen as the

---

[1] Among the key contributions to the documentation of the post-war transformation of Brussels, are G. Abeels et al., *Pierres et Rues. Bruxelles: Croissance Urbaine 1780–1980: Exposition* (Bruxelles: La société, 1982); J. Aron, *Le Tournant de l'Urbanisme Bruxellois, 1958–1978* (Bruxelles: Fond. Joseph Jacquemotte, 1978); C. Billen and J.M. Duvosquel (eds.), *Bruxelles* (Bruxelles: Mercator, 2000); M. Culot (ed.), *Bruxelles: Architectures de 1950 à Aujourd'hui* (Bruxelles: A.A.M., 2011); T. Demey, *Bruxelles: Chronique d'une Capitale en Chantier*, vol. 2 (Bruxelles: Paul Legrain/CFC19, 1992); R. Schoonbrodt, *Voir et Dire la Ville* (Bruxelles: A.A.M., 2007); M. Hubert, 'Expo '58 and "the Car as King": What Future for Brussels's Major Urban Road Infrastructure?', *Brussels Studies* no. 22 (2008); M. Ryckewaert, *Building the Economic Backbone of the Belgian Welfare State: Infrastructure, Planning and Architecture 1945–1973* (Rotterdam: 010, 2011).

[2] In *Commerce et Négoce*, two Brussels historians describe commercial evolution in the periphery. C. Billen describes the general context: 'Soon these structures (supermarkets) will be located in the periphery, along major road axis, accompanying the inhabitants of Brussels in their disaffection of the dense city.' In C. Billen, 'Jalons pour une Histoire du Commerce à Bruxelles', in Région de Bruxelles-Capitale, *Commerce et Négoce* (Sprimont: Mardaga, 2003), 29. S. Jaumain limits himself only to the dimension of car mobility: 'The two shopping centres are located ... in the city periphery, where contrary to the urban centre, it is still possible to build large parkings ...'. In S. Jaumain, 'Heurs et Malheurs des Grands Magasins Bruxellois', in Région de Bruxelles-Capitale, *Commerce et Negocé* (Sprimont: Mardaga, 2003), 98.

result of a loose form of coproduction between different public and private actors such as governmental bodies, urban planners, distribution companies and real estate developers. Acting across different scales, these actors shared common notions of modernist city planning theories as well as an interest in building new types of urban multifunctional districts. As such, these new commercial centres responded to a different rationale and vision: from managing the suburbanization of the capital city to supporting the growth of the national economy, improving housing conditions in the Brussels' agglomeration and promoting novel urbanization models. This chapter first elucidates the development policy pursued in the post-war period by the commercial operator responsible for the first large shopping centres in Belgium, and then focuses on two case study shopping centres in the Brussels area, describing not only their design but also clarifying their contribution to the processes of city-making in Belgium during the 1960s and 1970s.

From the importation of American distribution models …

The development of shopping centres in Brussels was the result of a two-stepped implementation of American distribution models by the GB group, a conglomerate of Belgian department stores.[3] While supermarkets existed in Brussels since 1957, the GB group was the first to implement the specific American combination of peripheral self-service shops with large car parks in Belgium and in 1961 was the first in Europe to develop what later became known as the 'hypermarket' – a self-service shop combining both food and non-food products in an accessible peripheral location with parking for hundreds of cars – a term coined in France in 1968.[4] In 1961 two hypermarkets opened in the Brussels' agglomeration; one in Auderghem on 15 September 1961 and one in Anderlecht on 14 October 1961. Even though these were mere commercial boxes of 9,100 and 7,950 square metres respectively, they represented the first step in the implementation of new distribution models in Belgium, which eventually led to the development of Brussels' first shopping centres.

Hypermarkets were developed first, as they were cheaper and quicker to build and could generate revenues during the lengthy and costly studies needed for a shopping centre.[5] In 1959, in preparation of the shopping centres' development, the GB group had acquired well-situated sites at the edge of Brussels' urbanization and at the intersection of important radial and ring roads, anticipating the realization of the national highway development plan.[6] After establishing the first two hypermarkets in

---

[3] In 1959, an Antwerp-based department store company, Le Grand Bazar d'Anvers, together with the Jewel Tea Company of Chicago founded the SA Supermarché GB. The following year, they joined two other department stores, the Brussels-based Bon Marché and Le Grand Bazar de Liège, to establish the SA SuperBazar. In 1969, the two companies officially merged and became GB Entreprises. In 1973 GB Entreprises merged with l'Innovation, and became the GB-Inno-BM SA, the largest Belgian retail conglomerate. In 1987 it was rebranded the GIB Group, a name it retained until 2002, when it was acquired by Carrefour, its French concurrent. In this chapter, we will refer to this evolving conglomerate as the GB group.

[4] For the history of the first European hypermarkets, see J.P. Grimmeau, 'A Forgotten Anniversary: The First European Hypermarkets Open in Brussels in 1961', *Brussels Studies* no. 67 (2013).

[5] In M. Cauwe, 'Genèse du Libre-service et des Hypermarché en Belgique'(1981), GIB Archives, deposited at ULB Archive Department, archive box 25Z-202.

[6] A plan of motorways integrated at the European level was made public in the brochure 'Bruxelles, Carrefour de l'Occident', which was published in 1956 by the Fonds des Routes of the Belgian Ministry of Public Works.

1961, the GB Group, in association with real estate company Devimo,[7] developed the first two shopping centres of Brussels: the Woluwe Shopping Centre in Woluwe-Saint-Lambert opened in September 1968 and had a surface area of 31,000 square metres, and the Westland Shopping Centre opened in Anderlecht in August 1972 and covered 35,000 square metres. These hypermarkets and shopping centres shared the same symmetrical composition: on either side of Brussels – one in the east and one in the west – with the shopping centres a few kilometres north of the hypermarkets at the intersection of large radial and ring roads (see Figure 3.1).

This pioneering work was the result of intensive exchanges with and visits to the United States by Maurice Cauwe, who in 1974 became President of the GB group.[8] From 1957 on, Cauwe participated in the (now famous) Modern Merchandising Methods Seminars with Bernardo Trujillo[9] and visited an extensive selection of Shopping Centres across the American continent. Cauwe thus quickly became a protagonist in the dissemination of mass distribution methods in Belgium and Europe. He was the chairman of the Association of Large Enterprise of Distribution in Belgium (AGED),[10] and of the Urbanism and Trade International Association (URBANICOM).[11] He also spearheaded the Shopping Centres US and Europe missions in 1960 and 1961 for the Belgium Service for the Advancement of Productivity (Office Belge pour l'Accroissement de la Productivité),[12] the reports of which influenced the construction of the first shopping centre in Belgium, which opened in August 1968 in the municipality of Genk.[13]

---

[7]To develop their shopping centres, the GB Group joined with the Galeries Anspach, the Bon Marché and the Innovation, the three main luxury shops of Brussels and created a common real estate company, Devimo. This was an expression of a 'collective interest formula', proposed by M. Cauwe to regulate competition and share profits of these peripheral developments between all partners, even if they were not all present in the shopping centres with their own brand. See AGED, 'Considération sur les Perspectives et Disciplines d'Action Nécessaires Découlant de la Création dans nos Grandes Agglomérations de Grands Centres Commerciaux Périphériques'(1967), GIB Archives, 25Z-193.

[8]M. Cauwe (1905–1985), Solvay engineer, started his career at Innovation, and subsequently joined Le Grand Bazar d'Anvers of which he became director in 1941. From 1948 on he visited the United States regularly and ended his career as President of the GIB Group. See Grimmeau, 'A Forgotten Anniversary'.

[9]B. Trujillo (1920–1971) is commonly considered the 'pope of modern distribution'. He organized the Modern Merchandising Methods (MMM) seminars in Dayton for the National Cash Register Company (NCR), which were organized between 1956 and 170 and attended by approximately 11,000 businessmen from all over the world. In E. Thil, *Les Inventeurs du Commerce Moderne* (Paris: Arthaud, 1966).

[10]The AGED organized several missions to the United States. In 1952 this organization considered the American market conditions to be twenty-five to thirty years ahead. See N. Coupain, *Distributie in België* (Brussels: Lannoo Campus, 2005), 28.

[11]Founded in Brussels in 1966, the International Association Urbanicom is still active to this date and organized its 14th congress in Brussels in October 2014.

[12]'I believe it is necessary to adequately inform public authorities and the distribution sector of the American evolution. To this end, I will contact the Belgium Service for the Enhancement of Productivity and suggest organising a study mission on shopping centres and American distribution. The Service accepts and entrusts me with its presidency.' In Cauwe, 'Genèse du Libre-service et des Hypermarché en Belgique', 6.

[13]See J. Gosseye, 'Collectivity and the Post-War European Shopping Centre', *Lusofona Journal of Architecture and Education* no. 8–9 (2014): 245–264.

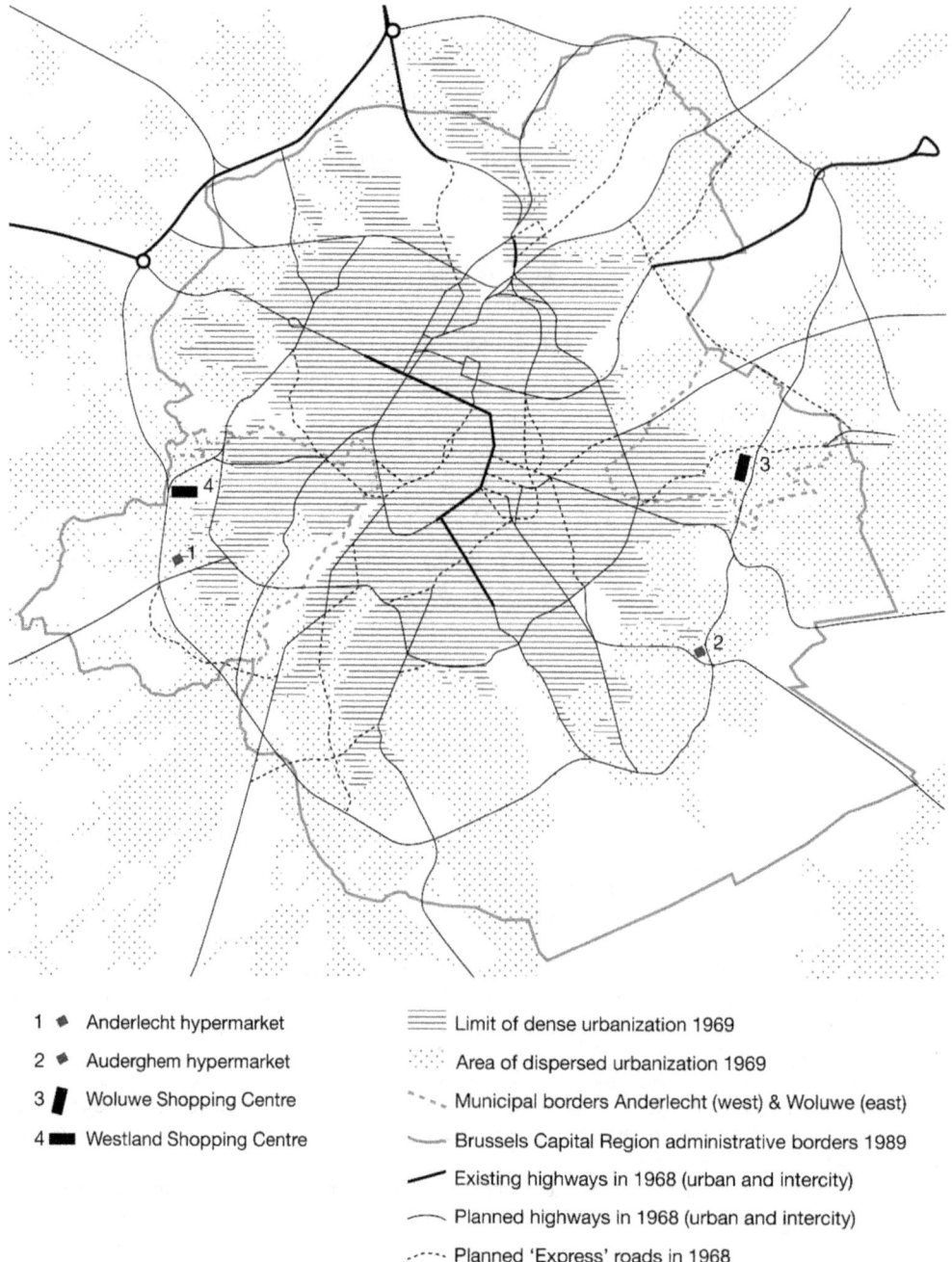

1	●	Anderlecht hypermarket
2	●	Auderghem hypermarket
3	▮	Woluwe Shopping Centre
4	▬	Westland Shopping Centre

≡ Limit of dense urbanization 1969
⋯ Area of dispersed urbanization 1969
‐ ‐ Municipal borders Anderlecht (west) & Woluwe (east)
— Brussels Capital Region administrative borders 1989
— Existing highways in 1968 (urban and intercity)
— Planned highways in 1968 (urban and intercity)
⋯⋯ Planned 'Express' roads in 1968

Figure 3.1 Map indicating the location of hypermarkets (Anderlecht–1 and Auderghem–2) and shopping centres (Woluwe Shopping Centre–3 and Westland Shopping Centre–4) referenced in the text. In the context of the planned highways as in 1968 and of Brussels' urbanization.
Source: Map developed by the authors on the basis of (1) 'Map (1968) Carte de Service de Bruxelles Capitale 1/20.000e' Ministere des Travaux Publics, administration des routes. In City Archives Woluwe-Saint-Lambert box 'Routes et Parkings', and (2) 'Map (1969) L'Agglomeration de Bruxelles- Edition 21/25.000e' Institut Geographique Militaire, Bruxelles 1975.

... To a proactive stance on urban issues

The American shopping centre's ability to generate profit and renew existing business models clearly fascinated Cauwe,[14] but what interested him most was the effect of increasing motorization on the American urban environment and the lifestyle of its population. According to Cauwe, it was only a matter of time before the growth of car ownership in Belgium would lead to similar results: rapid suburbanization, the exodus from city centres leading to their subsequent decay, problems of accessibility and congestion in and around city centres with a negative impact on business activity and the emergence of new consumer behaviours based on the extensive use of the automobile.[15] If the shopping centre was part of the solution for him, as it answered suburbanites' shopping needs (thus relieving the pressure on the city centre), he was very critical of the degeneration of American cities and the lack of intervention by public authorities. To avoid a similar downfall in Belgium, he advised for a double action to be taken by both the public and private sector. The first action was the so-called 'peripheral action'. It aimed to create new satellite centralities, fully equipped with public administrations and services, cultural and sportive centres and, of course, shopping centres. The second action was directed towards intensive urban renovation of city centres to enhance their accessibility and attractiveness and maintain their built heritage.[16]

Beyond commercial considerations, the development of the shopping centre typology was therefore also motivated by the willingness to take a positive attitude towards urban and societal evolutions – 'a question of social philosophy and urbanism' as Jean-Pierre De Bodt, the first administrator of the Woluwé and Westland shopping centres, put it.[17] To this end, the GB Group distanced itself from the American concept of the shopping centre and relied on the Swedish precedents of 'integrated shopping centres', which Cauwe referred to frequently.[18] An important point of reference was Vällingby, a satellite town of Stockholm (1957). Cauwe visited Vällingby in 1961,[19] which was incidentally the same year that Lewis Mumford praised this urban development in his renowned book *The City in History*.[20] In Vällingby, the shopping centre was part of a public–private joint venture at the heart of the new town, which included

---

[14]In his report to the Grand Bazar from his 1956 trip to the United States, Cauwe analyses the different typologies of distribution and advocates for the need to create a study group for the development of shopping centres in Belgium. In M. Cauwe, 'Les U.S.A. en 1956 – Discount houses, Downtown, Shopping Centers, Quick service, etc… – Rapport de Voyage aux Etats-Unis, Janvier 1956' (1956), GIB Archives, 25Z-806.

[15]M. Cauwe, 'Causerie Faite au Rotary Club d'Anvers Escaut par Monsieur Maurice Cauwe, Administrateur-Directeur Général du Grand Bazar d'Anvers, le Mardi 16 Septembre 1958' (1958), GIB Archives, 25Z-193.

[16]M. Cauwe, 'Commerce et Urbanisme', Extrait de la 'R.U.M.', no. 10 (1966), GIB Archives, 25Z-782. Both the diagnosis and proposed solutions are very close to what Victor Gruen promoted in his 1964 book: V. Gruen, *The Heart of Our Cities: The Urban Crisis: Diagnosis and Cure* (New York: Simon and Schuster, 1964).

[17]Interview with J.P. de Bodt, In 'Le Westland Shopping Center', *Distribution d'Aujourd'hui* (October 1972): 40–49, GIB Archives, 25Z-486.

[18]The first occurrence was in his 1958 *causerie*. In his 1972 interview, J.P. de Bodt similarly refers to Sweden, referencing the country's advanced shopping centre development, stating: 'We are going towards the Swedish models, which are the antithesis of American models.' See ibid.

[19]He was leading the 'Shopping Centre Europe' Mission of the Belgium Service for the Enhancement of Productivity, GIB Archives, 25Z-862.

[20]Lewis Mumford, *The City in History: Its Origins, Its Transformations, and Its Prospects* (London: Secker & Warburg, 1961). In Belgium, Vällingby was presented in the popular Belgian architectural journal *La Maison*, at the end of 1957. See E. Guerin, 'Vällingby, un Nouveau Centre Suburbain Suédois', *La Maison* (13 October 1957): 316–319.

housing, social, cultural and civic services and leisure activities. Nevertheless, even though the GB Group explicitly referred to the Swedish mixed-use developments as a model to strive for, it only took responsibility for the commercial aspect and left the development of the surrounding neighbourhood to the public authorities, with variable success as this chapter will demonstrate.

Woluwe shopping centre: from the east ...

The shopping centre as the trigger for a new municipal core

In July 1963, roughly two years after the opening of Auderghem and Anderlecht hypermarkets, Devimo presented a preliminary design by architect Marcel Blomme to the municipality of Woluwé-Saint-Lambert for 'the creation of a luxury shopping centre in the Woluwe valley'. This shopping centre was located at the intersection of the Boulevard de la Woluwe and the Avenue Paul Hymans, both planned to become important parts of the new road network. The municipal council reacted positively to Devimo's proposal, noting that such a shopping centre could constitute a 'nice architectural ensemble' that needed to be 'studied for its perfect integration in the neighbourhood'.[21] In December 1963, the municipality entrusted the Brussels-based urban planners of the Groupe Tekhné[22] with the realization of a master plan for the Woluwe valley, which took the envisaged construction of the shopping centre into account, and which constituted a concrete example of the peripheral action proposed by Cauwe. Indeed, the Groupe Tekhné saw the development of the Woluwe valley as the opportunity to convert Woluwé-Saint-Lambert into a full-fledged residential 'city', complete with commercial, economic, cultural, leisure, social and civic activities. To this end, the Tekhné master plan advocated for the centralization of all those activities in a specific district of the Woluwe valley, planned to become the 'heart of the city – an agora at the scale of our time'.[23]

The shopping centre as a component of the urban centre

While Devimo saw the shopping centre as an independent mono-functional development, the municipality grasped it as an opportunity to achieve a larger and more holistic plan. It aimed to create an urban heart for Woluwe, which combined shopping, leisure, culture as well as social and civic activities. The master plan therefore associated the shopping centre with a civic centre, reminiscent of the 'core' concept, which was first proposed at the 1958 CIAM Congress.[24] Similarly to Victor Gruen's vision of

---

[21]Correspondence dated 19 August 1963 from the municipality to Devimo refers to the presentation of M. de Bodt and M. Blomme to the City Urbanism Commission, which took place on 10 July 1963. In GIB Archives, 25Z-493.

[22]At the time, the Groupe Tekhné was renowned for its plan for the renovation of Brussels' city centre, envisioning its radical adaptation to the needs of a modern city. Gathered around Ernest Scaillon, the Tekhné Group was composed of former members of the Office des Cités Africaines, an official research office entrusted with the design of cities in Belgian Congo after the Second World War. Tekhné based their work on the Athens Charter precepts and rigorously applied the neighbourhood unit concept to organize the city.

[23]In: Tekhné 'Etudes Préliminaires – Secteur de la Woluwe, Plan Particulier d'Aménagement' (1965), 12, City Archives Woluwe-Saint-Lambert, unnumbered archive folder 'Boulevard de la Woluwe'.

[24]J. Tyrwhitt, J.L. Sert and E.N. Rogers (eds.), *The Heart of the City: Towards the Humanisation of Urban Life* (London: Lund, 1952).

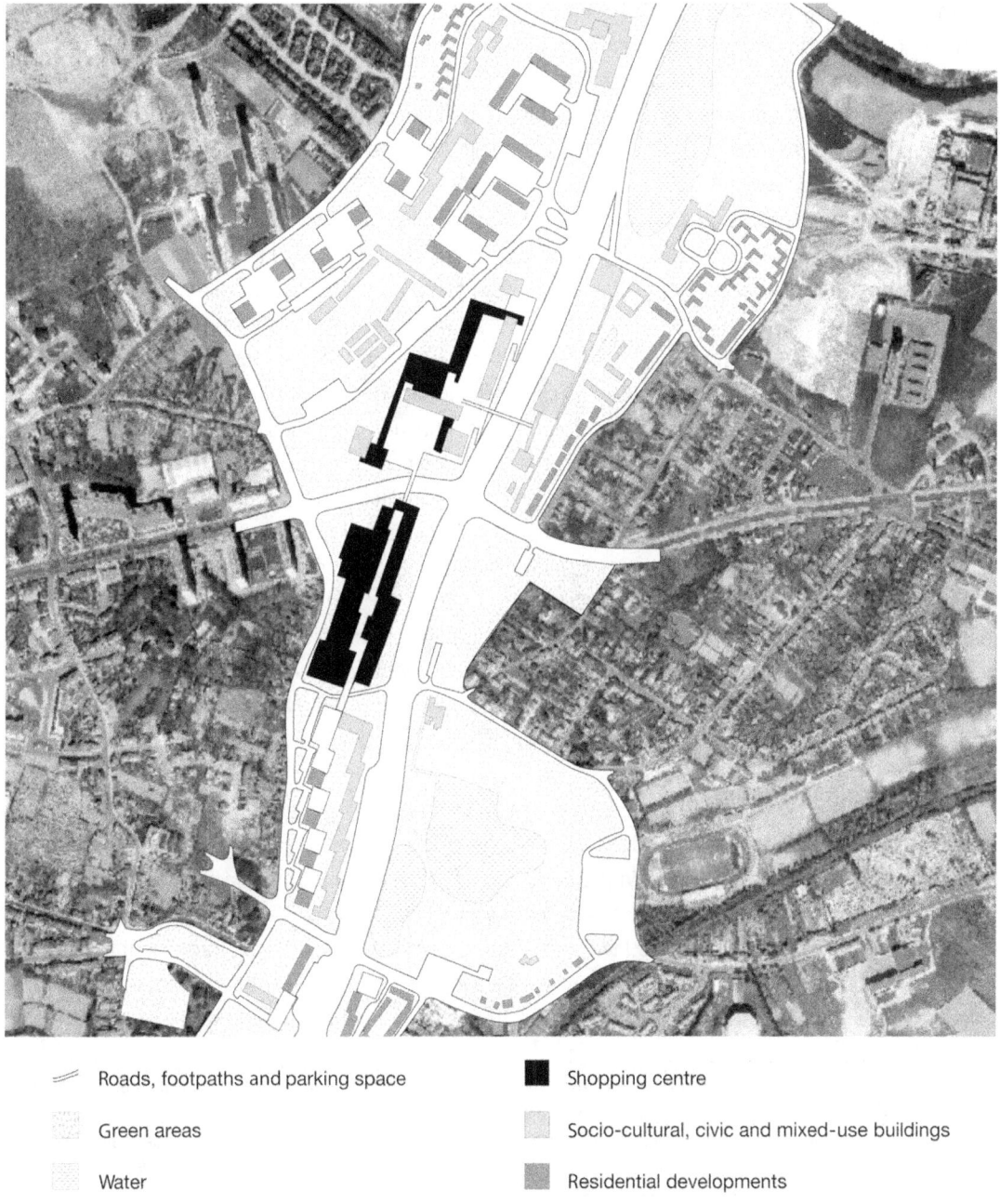

- Roads, footpaths and parking space
- Green areas
- Water
- Shopping centre
- Socio-cultural, civic and mixed-use buildings
- Residential developments

Figure 3.2 Collage of Tekhné's 1966 master plan for the Woluwé Valley superimposed on an aerial photograph of the context from 1971. Woluwé Shopping Centre is in the middle with the pedestrian system running in its middle and connecting it to the civic centre on the other side of the Avenue Paul Hymans.
Source: Map developed by the author on the basis of (in the background) an aerial photograph dating back to May 1971, sourced from BruCiel, Bruxelles Developpement Urbain, Direction Etudes et Planification, 2014: Archives of the Ministère des Travaux Publics de l'Etat Belge (service de Topographie et de Photogrammétrie); with in the foreground an image from Tekhné (1966) 'Plan Particulier d'Aménagement de la Vallée de la Woluwe, Plan Masse, 1/2.000e', in City Archives. Woluwé-Saint-Lambert, unnumbered archive folder 'Boulevard de la Woluwe'.

the shopping centre, the core was characterized by a desire to create a qualitative urban environment, adapted to the needs of modern society.

Forming the new urban centre of Woluwe, the shopping centre and the civic core were articulated on both sides of the Avenue P. Hymans along the Boulevard de la Woluwe. On the northern side, the mixed-use urban core was organized around a public space and included a civic centre, a cultural centre, offices, commercial programmes and high-rise residential developments, all ingredients of a 'centre of community life' as defined by J.L. Sert in *The Heart of the City*.[25] On the southern side, the shopping centre was organized around a 235 metres long central walkway, accompanied by a composition of mixed-use developments. While both the civic centre and the shopping centre were free-standing elements separated by the Avenue, they were connected by a pedestrian walkway on the first floor, thus effectively introducing grade separation – a distinctly modernist approach. Tekhné took its cue from the preliminary design of Blomme, which envisaged the shopping walkway as an open-air street on the first floor, reserving the ground floor for car parking. Taking this concept to the urban level, Tekhné designed its master plan around an elevated pedestrian spine, parallel to the boulevard, which integrated the shopping in the future city core, and connected it to both the future development of the U.C.L. University Hospital and the Parc Malou on the other side of the Boulevard.

The master plan was however never officially adopted and therefore never completely realized. The pedestrian walkways, connecting the shopping centre to the adjacent developments, disappeared in subsequent versions of the shopping centre's design, transforming the street-like elongated central walkway into a more common, enclosed, air-conditioned shopping mall. This evolution in the design coincided with both the enlargement of the design team – Copeland, Novak & Israël from New York became consulting architects[26] – and the arrival of Sears, Roebuck & Co[27] into Devimo's capital to finance the project.[28]

Nevertheless, while the shopping centre's design was altered significantly and most of the public facilities envisaged in Tekhné's master plan were never completed, the neighbourhood around the shopping centre still witnessed the implementation of novel urbanization models, albeit outside of the perimeter and independently from Tekhné's master plan. Etrimo,[29] one of the main residential real estate actors in Brussels, erected two twelve-storey apartment buildings alongside the shopping centre and later initiated a second residential operation behind the complex. Composed of similar apartment buildings, this operation necessitated the demolition of an existing row of typical Belgian

---

[25] J.L. Sert, 'Centres of Community Life', in *The Heart of the City: Towards the Humanisation of Urban Life*, eds. J. Tyrwhitt, J.L. Sert and E.N. Rogers (London: Lund Humphries, 1952), 3-16.

[26] Legend has it that the (typical) Belgian weather condition they experienced on their first site visit made them add a roof to the design. See P. Iserbyt, 'Histoire des Centres Commerciaux à Bruxelles', http://www.adt-ato.brussels/sites/default/files/3-Pierre_Iserbyt.pdf, accessed 6 September 2015.

[27] Sears, Roebuck & Co was a prominent developer of shopping malls in the United States. See R. Longstreth, 'Sears, Roebuck and the Remaking of the Department Store, 1924–42', *Journal of the Society of Architectural Historians* 65, no. 2 (2006): 238–279. Three years earlier, Sears had acquired the Galeries Anspach, one of the founding partners of Devimo. See S. Jaumain, 'Heurs et Malheurs des Grands Magasins Bruxellois', 98.

[28] Interview with J.P. de Bodt, In 'Le Westland Shopping Center'.

[29] Etrimo used to develop mass middle-class housing by repeating the same residential typology: a high-rise apartment set in a private landscaped park. Beyond economical considerations, Etrimo aimed to improve and promote new housing standards for the middle class: a qualitative modern housing set in a green and breathable environment.

Figure 3.3 Photograph of the Woluwe Shopping Centre taken in 1974, with the Boulevard de la Woluwe in the foreground and high-rise apartments developed by Etrimo in the background.
Source: Photograph of 1974. BruCiel, Régie des Bâtiments, 2014; Archives of the Ministère des Travaux Publics de l'Etat Belge (Service de Topographie et de Photogrammétrie).

single-family terraced houses. The presence of the shopping centre was used as the main argument for their demolition, stating the need to adapt the urban identity of the neighbourhood to this new commercial building.[30]

... to the west: Westland shopping centre

The shopping centre as the crowning point of a peripheral urban centrality rationale

If the story of the Woluwe is an example of a municipality reacting *a posteriori* to an initiative by private stakeholders, the narrative of the development of the Westland Shopping Centre in Anderlecht,

---

[30] Administrative files linked to the elaboration of the PPA n°53, adopted by the Central Government in July 1970, Archive of the Ministry of the Brussels-Capital Region, Bruxelles Developpement, Direction Urbanisme.

on the western side of Brussels, is the paradigm of a municipality adopting a proactive approach. Its socialist mayor, René Bracops, firmly supported urban development through planning, sustained by a systematic policy of real estate acquisition.[31] The municipality of Anderlecht was eager to attract new pioneering commercial developments after the successful integration of a SuperBazar in a new housing development in 1961, with the financial aid of the municipality. In an internal study, Anderlecht's Chief City Planner Jozef Janssens pinpointed the SuperBazar as 'an important milestone' in his vision for Anderlecht as the 'sub-capital of the west'.[32] Considering the characteristics of Anderlecht and taking into account the planned road infrastructure works and projected demographic evolutions, Janssens stated that Anderlecht had the potential to become – at the very least – a new complete peripheral urban centre and – at best – the sub-capital of the western region of Brussels. To this end, he consistently developed a vision for the west-side of Anderlecht, centred around the provision of housing (high-rise residential buildings, the majority of which were developed by Etrimo and its competitor Amelinckx), the optimization of Anderlecht's accessibility (in relation to the planned highways), the creation of various urban amenities (including a park system connecting the new developments) as well as the consolidation of commercial activities with high power of attraction. In his study, Janssens also made a clear reference to Vällingby, which he used to extrapolate the optimum ratio of commercial activities and parking space per inhabitant for the specifications of this 'sub-capital of the west' vision.[33]

Following their own rationale, Devimo had reserved a vacant lot of seventeen hectares in the Broeck valley for the development of their second shopping centre. This location, at a mere two kilometres from their Anderlecht SuperBazar and the core of Janssens' 'sub-capital of the west', was promising due to its direct connection, via a new radial road along the Broeck river (the Boulevard Sylvain Dupuis), to the planned Ring of Brussels and to the already existing intermediary Ring.

The shopping centre as the plinth of a new urban habitat

The interest of both parties to establish a shopping centre in Anderlecht was evident. It responded to Janssens' eagerness to attract luxurious shops in his municipality, giving it a more regional stature, while its optimal accessibility and the ongoing nearby urban developments suited Devimo's needs for a large consumer base in the west of Brussels. Moreover, Janssens was well aware of Devimo's shopping centre model. As a regular consultant to Etrimo, he drafted the design of the residential development in front of the Woluwe shopping centre.[34] The municipality and Devimo thus eagerly began collaborating on a joint master plan for the entire seventeen hectares site that became known as the plan 'Vallée du Broeck'. The resultant initial master plan foresaw not only a shopping centre, but also a residential

---

[31] The municipal authorities repeatedly published a portfolio of current and upcoming projects, strongly orientating discourse towards the creation of green spaces and collective facilities. See G. Messin, *Anderlecht, Commune d'Avant-Garde* (Bruxelles: Art et Technique, 1956); G. Messin and J.F. Janssens, *Stedenbouw in Actie: Groen Anderlecht* (Anderlecht: Commune d'Anderlecht, 1963); K. Grunewald and A. Souffriau, *Anderlecht 1971/76* (Bruxelles: s.l., Dereume, 1976).
[32] J. Janssens, 'Etude concernant Anderlecht' (circa 1963), in Janssens personal archives, deposited at the ULB Faculty of Architecture Archive Department, Folder 4.5, 21.
[33] Ibid.
[34] Janssens personal archives, box 'Projets d'Autres Communes', Folder 'Woluwe St. Lambert. PPA rue Saint Lambert, rue des Floralies'.

development for 2,500 inhabitants. Covering the entire site, the shopping centre was envisioned as the plinth on which several residential buildings would be built.[35] This vertical segregation was however not implemented. Technical difficulties and the longer construction time that this design required made Devimo and the municipality turn towards a more realistic, 'typical' solution.[36]

From vertical to horizontal integration

In the final design, the two programmes – shopping and housing – were separated in two distinct zones and their density was increased to compensate for the loss in square metres. The shopping centre became a two-storey mall, the first in Belgium, while the residential buildings similarly grew in height. If a vertical integration was unrealistic, the master plan nevertheless strove to maintain – to a certain extent – the integration of the shopping centre in the new development. Taking advantage of the height difference between the two sides of the site, located on either side of the valley, a common ground was created for the residential development at the level of the first floor of the shopping centre. A set of pedestrian walkways connected the shopping centre to the adjacent developments and bridged the vehicular traffic of both the shopping parking and the Boulevard Sylvain Dupuis. Unlike in Woluwé where such walkways were foreseen but never implemented, the pedestrian flyovers in Anderlecht became a successful element, enhancing the integration of the shopping centre and the housing blocs at a local scale.[37] On a larger scale, these pedestrian walkways connect the 'Vallée du Broeck' development to the larger park system that weaves together the different neighbourhoods of Anderlecht and connects several large-scale cultural and civic facilities that the municipality distributed throughout the various districts. The plan that was adopted in 1969 unambiguously defined this pedestrian path as well as its explicit connection to the city fabric; orienting it towards the skyline of the Saint-Guidon Church, where the historical heart of the municipality lies (see Figure 3.4).

The Westland shopping centre was built quickly after the final plan was approved in 1971. When it opened in 1972, only three out of the thirteen planned residential buildings had been constructed. One year later, in 1973, the economic crisis brought the project to a halt until 1989, when the newly founded Brussels-Capital Region[38] was looking to take some pressure off of the administrative centre of the city by decentralizing offices in its territory. Janssens seized this opportunity to propose an administrative sub-centrality around the Westland.[39] The municipality consequently amended the plan that was

---

[35]As described by Janssens in 'Plan Particulier d'Aménagement "Vallée du Broeck" Plan Modificatif Phase 2 Rapport technique' (undated), in Janssens personal archives, box 'Anderlecht', Folder 'Projet de Plan Particulier d'Aménagement: Vallée du Broeck'. No sketches of this preliminary design were found in Janssens' archives or in the City archives of Anderlecht.
[36]Ibid.
[37]Several sources indicate that the pedestrian system that connects the shopping to the residential developments is often used for leisurely activities, while the shopping itself is compared to 'a village in the city'. See C. Vanhoenacker, 'Le Westland a 40 Ans', *Le Soir,* 20 October 2012.
[38]Starting in the early twentieth century, the division of Belgium into specific linguistic territories led to the establishment of a federal state in 1980, when the Flemish and the Walloon regions were demarcated. In 1989, the delineation of the bilingual (French/Flemish) Brussels-Capital Region followed. These regions became responsible for urbanism and land planning within their territory.
[39]To this end, he sent a letter to the Minister-President of the Region, pleading for the Region's approval of the revised 'Vallée du Broeck' plan. In: Janssens personal archives, Folder 4.12.

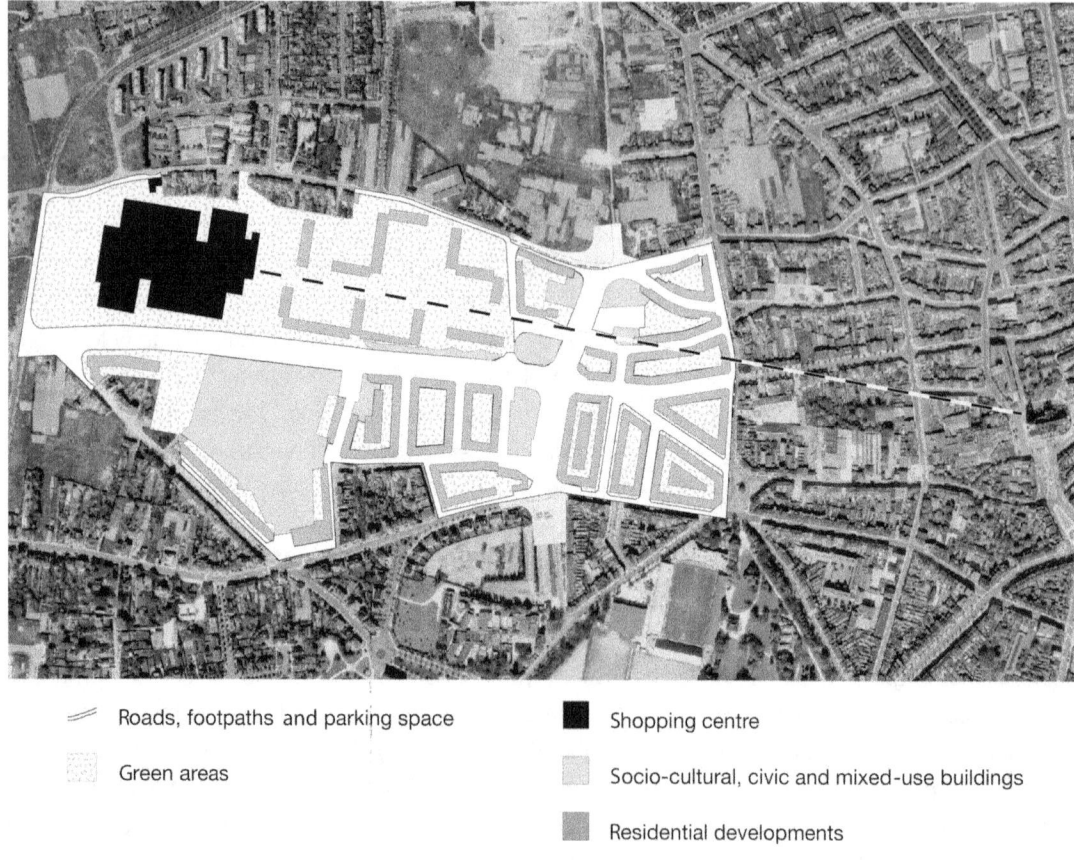

- Roads, footpaths and parking space
- Green areas
- Shopping centre
- Socio-cultural, civic and mixed-use buildings
- Residential developments

Figure 3.4 Collage of the 1969 'Vallée du Broeck' master plan superimposed on an aerial photograph from 1971. Westland Shopping Centre is on the left. The pedestrian axis towards the skyline of the Saint-Guidon Church is marked by a dashed line.
Source: Background image: aerial photograph of May 1971, from BruCiel, Bruxelles Développement Urbain, Direction Etudes et Planification, 2014; Archives of the Ministère des Travaux Publics de l'Etat Belge (service de Topographie et de Photogrammétrie). Foreground image: (1969) 'Plan Particulier d'Aménagement 'Vallée du Broeck', Plan Masse, 1/2.000e', in archives of the Ministère de la Région de Bruxelles-Capitale, box 'PPAS 166209'. Concepteur du site BruCiel.

approved in 1971 and several office buildings were built. The west-side of Anderlecht thus obtained a complete mix of urban functions, coherent with the new urban peripheral centrality rationale and the desire of Devimo to be inscribed in a mixed-use environment.

The implantation of the shopping centre in Anderlecht and the development of a peripheral urban centre for Brussels were also coherent with the urban logic underpinning the design of the ring road around the capital. The chief engineer of the Road Administration, Henry Hondermarcq, had envisioned the ring as a 'hybrid' infrastructure 'with an urbanization agenda'.[40] It not only aspired to improve traffic conditions, but also to support residential expansion and stimulate the economic development of the

---

[40] Ryckewaert, *Building the Economic Backbone of the Belgian Welfare State*, 201.

Figure 3.5 View of the Westland Shopping Centre, circa. 1972. The pedestrian walkways have already been realized, and await the advent of the adjacent residential developments. In the background is the peripheral suburb of Dilbeek.
Source: GIB Archives, deposited at the ULB Archives department, archive box 25Z-486, photograph named on the back 'Inno Shopping Centre Westland (BXL. W.) avec Galeries Anspachs Sears'.

capital. It was therefore designed not only for through-traffic and international connections, but also to provide a link between the city's suburbs.[41] As a result, the ring included a large number of access points where a set of facilities with regional impact, such as shopping centres and hospitals, could be realized.

Conclusion

The analysis of material from both the GB Group and the city archives presented in this chapter demonstrates that the post-war shopping centres developed around Brussels were integrated parts of larger urbanization plans that aimed at the creation of new peripheral urban centralities. Both examples show that the shopping centre was seen as one component of a programmatic mix that included housing,

---

[41]Ibid., 180.

commerce, offices and, in Woluwe, also civic and cultural functions. The case studies furthermore demonstrate that both public administrations and private developers saw these programmatic components as necessary ingredients for the successful creation of a new kind of urban core.

This analysis thus challenges the common and often all-too-narrow reading of such developments as mere figments of a liberal *laissez-faire* policy driven by the automobile industry. The designs of both case studies demonstrate a clear commitment to a detailed articulation between pedestrian and mechanical traffics across scales as they aspire to create mixed-use urban districts that function on both the local and the regional level. Furthermore, the beneficial integration of diverging interests across administrative levels from both public and private actors highlighted in this chapter, hints at a collective form of city-making. While a comprehensive master plan was defined for each case, different actors were responsible for its realization. This form of city-making should be seen as a loose form coproduction, in which both public and private actors promoted novel urbanization models that shaped these specific peripheral urban landscapes. While this intricate link between the different actors explains the rapid development of post-war shopping centres and their urban environments around Brussels, the fragmented actions of individual actors also partly explains the relative shortcomings of these master plans with regard to the integration of their different components and their legibility in the urban landscape. The shopping centres were, as this chapter has demonstrated, commonly completed first, while other operations were delayed, sometimes for decades. With such differences in goals and timing, one can understand that economic conditions as well as urban and architectural concepts were bound to be reinterpreted, leading to urban settings that have more in common with a sometimes awkward aggregation of components rather than a comprehensive urban development. Nevertheless, in all instances, the subsequent changes were in line with the initial programme and ambition.

The integration of both shopping centres in their respective (sub)urban environments was achieved mainly through the creation of a pedestrian network that weaved these mixed-use complexes together. Although less comprehensive in form than Vällingby, these pedestrian networks are an indication that the shopping centres were considered a collective space and part of the public realm, by both private and public bodies. The shopping centre's mall was usually set in the centre of this pedestrian network, at the heart of the modern urban core, embedded in the surrounding city fabric, while its proximity to national highways guaranteed its integration in regional and nationwide networks, in line with the State's agenda to manage suburbanization around Brussels through peripheral centralities and support economical development with its infrastructures.

Chapter 4

The Lijnbaan in Rotterdam: A sound urban form against city disruption
Dirk van den Heuvel

On 14 May 1940, in the early days of the Second World War, the city centre of Rotterdam was annihilated by German airstrikes to break the Dutch resistance to the Nazi invasion. The following day, after threats of bombing other cities as well, the Netherlands surrendered. In hindsight the death toll of about 1,150 people seems relatively low when seen in relation to the total devastation of the inner city of Rotterdam and its adjacent quarters. Over 11,000 buildings were demolished and about 80,000 people rendered homeless. When the war ended after five years of German occupation, the country was faced with the task of rebuilding not only its economy and institutions but also the city of Rotterdam. This would become one of its major feats. In his study on the reconstruction of Rotterdam, Dutch architectural historian Cor Wagenaar posits: '[t]he destruction of the Rotterdam inner city symbolically marked the radical end of Dutch society of the interwar period. In what way the social classes and economic structure would change was hard to foresee, yet, that they would change was a fact of life'.[1] Rather than reconstructing the city according to its historical pattern, the Rotterdam city council and its planners chose to redevelop the city centre following a completely new urban layout, the so-called Basisplan by Cornelis van Traa, the chief urban planner of the city.[2] When the initial results became visible, including the first phase of the Lijnbaan shopping centre, which was designed by the office of van den Broek and Bakema and completed in 1953, Rotterdam was hailed as a most audacious and successful example of post-war reconstruction in Europe.

In one of the many pieces he wrote for *The New Yorker,* American historian Lewis Mumford opened his eleven-page *hommage* by stating that '[e]veryone says Rotterdam is the one city in Europe that has turned the disasters of war and occupation into triumph. For once everyone is right'.[3] In *The City in History*, Mumford's overview and assessment of urban development throughout the ages

---

[1] Original quote: 'De verwoesting van de Rotterdamse binnenstad lijkt symbolisch voor het radicale einde van de Nederlandse samenleving van het interbellum. Hoe de sociale verhoudingen en de economische structuur zouden veranderen was niet te voorzien, dat ze zouden veranderen stond vast.' Source: Cor Wagenaar, *Welvaartsstad in Wording. De Wederopbouw van Rotterdam 1940–1952* (Rotterdam: NAi Uitgevers, 1992), 91.
[2] A first, more traditional scheme was proposed by W.G. Witteveen during the war years. Due to political pressure from the German authorities and a loss of support from Rotterdam entrepeneurs, Witteveen was forced to leave office in 1944. See Wagenaar, *Welvaartsstad in Wording*, chapters 4 and 5.
[3] 'The Sky Line. A Walk through Rotterdam', *The New Yorker*, 12 October 1957, 174.

Figure 4.1 Aerial photo of the Lijnbaan ensemble under construction and its environs, in the top right corner the town hall, post office and exchange building which survived the war, below the two department stores at the Binnenwegplein, just above them the remains of the Coolsingel hospital, centre and left of centre the low-rise shopping street.
Source: Photo by Aviodrome, collection Gemeente Archief Rotterdam.

published in 1961, he characterized Rotterdam's reconstruction as 'civic resurgence' 'through terror to triumph'.[4] The supreme embodiment of this post-war triumph was the brand new Lijnbaan. Comparing it favourably with Park Avenue in New York, Mumford situated the Lijnbaan in the grand tradition of historic inner city shopping streets and nineteenth-century arcades and argued that it belonged to the high ranks of exemplary cosmopolitan shopping places, such as the city of Venice, Rue de Rivoli in Paris and Rockefeller Plaza in Manhattan, that together make up a global, collective memory of urban spaces. Mumford praised the Lijnbaan for its intimate scale, the decision to pedestrianize the street and ban car traffic, and ultimately for its universalist qualities: a 'sound urban form that could be adapted anywhere'.[5]

Mumford's laudatory assessment of the Lijnbaan was representative of the general appreciation in the world of architecture and led to its inclusion in various historical overviews of the post-war period.

---

[4]Lewis Mumford, *The City in History* (New York: Harcourt, Brace & World, 1961), plates 62 and 63.
[5]Ibid., 182.

In their 1976 publication *Architettura Contemporanea*, Italian historians Manfredo Tafuri and Francesco Dal Co, for instance, called the Lijnbaan a 'true heart of the metropolis'.[6] Nonetheless, from the late 1970s onwards the postmodern critique of modern architecture and its rationalist city planning methods, compounded with a change of shops (small-scale and upmarket boutiques were replaced by loud and common jeans stores and hamburger restaurants), led to a shift in the appreciation of the Lijnbaan. Throughout the 1980s and 1990s, the Lijnbaan became notorious for frequent robberies. In this period various schemes were proposed to counter the downward trend of dilapidation and vandalism. One of these was a most ambitious scheme presented in 1988 by the British architect Derek Walker, who had previously been involved in the development of the main shopping centre in the English new town of Milton Keynes. Proposing to add a high-tech glass roof and an extra shopping gallery on the first floor, Walker's scheme envisaged to transform this post-war icon into a more generic shopping mall. This was one of the reasons why it elicited protest. Added to the lack of money needed for such a complete overhaul (estimates amounted to 200 million Dutch guilders), redevelopment was halted in summer 1990.[7] Yet, despite the overall dilapidation, the Lijnbaan remained a popular destination among shoppers, albeit for a lower class target group of consumers. A series of more modest upgrades of shop fronts, interiors and public spaces followed suit while piecemeal redevelopment of the wider area of the Rotterdam inner city introduced new shopping formulas, one of which was the much debated underground passage with a sunken plaza designed by Jon Jerde in postmodernist style.[8] Since the 1990s a profound reconsideration of the cultural value of the legacy of post-war architecture has taken place. In the Netherlands, as elsewhere, this has engendered a growing – albeit still hesitant – appreciation for post-war built heritage,[9] and has resulted in the listing of the central part of the Lijnbaan as a national monument in 2010.[10]

Against this background of shifting appreciation, this chapter investigates how to understand the very nature of the Lijnbaan as a monument, and examines what kind of interaction can be observed between the collective urban memory of overcoming the trauma of war as embodied by the material presence of the architecture of the Lijnbaan and the disruptive changes in fashion, lifestyle and shopping culture. Two seminal developments in twentieth-century architecture are intertwined in the Lijnbaan in an exemplary manner: one is the transformation, even deconstruction of the closed urban block and the other is the history of modern urban planning, more specifically the unfolding of the CIAM discourse on how modern architecture might accommodate the new spirit of a democratic, egalitarian society and its

---

[6]Manfredo Tafuri and Francesco Dal Co, *Modern Architecture* (Milan: Electa, 1986, original Italian edition 1976), 344.

[7]There is an endless stream of Dutch publications (including Rotterdam newspapers) discussing the Lijnbaan through the years. For this particular moment, see Herman Moscoviter, 'Lijnbaanplannen aan Zijden Draad', *Het Vrije Volk*, 12 January 1990, 11; 'Zonder de Gemeente kan 't niet', *Het Vrije Volk, Economie*, 11 July 1990, 2.

[8]Frances Anderton (ed.), *You Are Here. The Jerde Partnership International* (London: Phaidon Press, 1999), 156–161.

[9]For an early documentation of post-war built heritage in Rotterdam, see Anne-Mie Devolder and Hélène Damen (eds.), *Rotterdam Architecture 1945–1970* (Rotterdam: 010 Publishers, 1992); Martin Aarts (ed.), *Vijftig jaar Wederopbouw Rotterdam. Een Geschiedenis van Toekomstvisies* (Rotterdam: Uitgeverij 010, 1995).

[10]Based on various reports, a.o.: Crimson Architectural Historians, *De Lijnbaan, Cultuurhistorische Verkenning van het Lijnbaan Ensemble* (Rotterdam, December 2004); Urban Fabric, Steenhuis, *De Lijnbaan. Cultuurhistorisch Kader voor Transformatie* (Schiedam, 2007); Rijksdienst voor Archeologie, Cultuurlandschap en Monumenten, *Cultuurhistorische Waardestelling Lijnbaan-ensemble Rotterdam* (Zeist, 2008).

citizens. To do so new universalist urban concepts were proposed, such as 'core', 'heart of the city' and 'civic centre'.[11] Surprisingly, the architects and planners of the Lijnbaan never seemed to have imagined that this shopping centre for the middle classes would embody this new era, although they presented it as such post-factum. Yet, a careful retracing of the history of the Lijnbaan demonstrates how its 'sound urban form', as Mumford called it, represented the new era of a changed economic structure and its social classes.

The Lijnbaan as the outcome of city disruption

Today, the Lijnbaan is a pedestrianized shopping street running north–south just west of the erased historical inner city. Its name derives from the rather inconspicuous Lijnbaanstraat, a street that was situated here before, and was part of the expansion of Rotterdam's historical centre just outside the perimeter of its former fortifications, the so-called Stadsvest. This area began to urbanize in the seventeenth century when pleasure gardens and nurseries were developed on the site. During the nineteenth century, the nurseries and pleasure gardens were incrementally replaced by industry and housing. The Dutch word 'lijnbaan' accordingly refers to the former presence of a ropeyard. By the end of the nineteenth century, new cultural buildings of the period, such as the neo-classicist city theatre designed by Jan Verheul (1884–1887), were built in the area.[12] Together with large parts of the neighbourhood, this theatre was also eradicated by the German airstrikes.

When maps dating back to before the Second World War are compared with city plans drawn after the war, it immediately becomes apparent how the city centre shifted from its original inner city location to the west. This shift was already initiated in the early twentieth century, when the water of the western leg of the Stadsvest was filled to create the new Coolsingel avenue along which a brand new town hall by Henri Evers (1911–1920) and post office by Kees Bremer (1915–1922) were built. Just before the Second World War erupted, the modernist Exchange Building by Frits Staal (1936–1940) was added to this ensemble.[13] All three monumental buildings survived the war and together with the Coolsingel became the focal point of Van Traa's Basisplan. West of the Coolsingel a series of new city blocks were proposed, which were to house about 6.5 kilometres of the planned 12 kilometres of shop fronts for the whole inner city.[14] The blocks followed a regular grid, modulated only slightly to fit the former street pattern. This rationalized block typology included public inner courts, which serviced the shops thus leaving the public in the shopping streets undisturbed. In contrast to the new shopping district, the triangle of the historical city was to be dominated by monumental traffic ways to accommodate massive

---

[11] J. Tyrwhitt, J.L. Sert and E.N. Rogers (eds.), *The Heart of the City: Towards the Humanisation of Urban Life* (London: Lund Humphries, 1952), with contributions by Jaap Bakema: 'Relationship between Men and Things', 67–68, and the Rotterdam CIAM group 'Opbouw', 116–117; For a discussion of the notion of core and Bakema's ideas, see Leonardo Zuccaro Marchi, *The Heart of the City. Continuity and Complexity of an Urban Design Concept*, dissertation TU Delft, 2013.
[12] For nineteenth-century Rotterdam and its planning, see Hetty E.M. Berens, *W.N. Rose 1801–1877. Stedenbouw, Civiele Techniek en Architectuur* (Rotterdam: NAi Uitgevers, 2001).
[13] Dolf Broekhuizen (ed.), *Stadhuis Rotterdam. Honderd jaar een Baken in de Stad* (Rotterdam: NAi010, 2014).
[14] Urban Fabric, Steenhuis, *De Lijnbaan*, 22.

car mobility. This meant that the old central shopping street of Rotterdam, the Hoogstraat, would not be restored to its former glory. It was a crucial decision and created yet another breach with the historical pattern of Rotterdam. Yet, the decision was made without regrets, since the narrow Hoogstraat (about nine metres wide) with its bustle of traffic and shoppers was regarded as a notoriously bad example by modern city planners. Like the Kalverstraat shopping street in Amsterdam, it was considered hazardous and overcrowded.[15] In fact, before the war, the Rotterdam elite of entrepreneurs had already been highly dismissive of the quality of its own city. Projects like the construction of the new town hall at the Coolsingel went hand in hand with ruthless slum clearance. Discussing the fast modernization process of pre-war Rotterdam, architectural historian Michelle Provoost speaks of the lack of nostalgia for the historic city, even 'self-hatred'.[16] Decades before the devastations of the war, the minds were already set for a new beginning. So, when in May 1940 the opportunity for a new start presented itself, the old, urban forms were soon forgotten as new kinds of urban spaces were envisaged to rebuild the city.

In true modern spirit, Rotterdam's novel urban spaces were to be generous, bright and clean. Accordingly, a world of spacious elegance and carefree comfort appears in the many beautiful

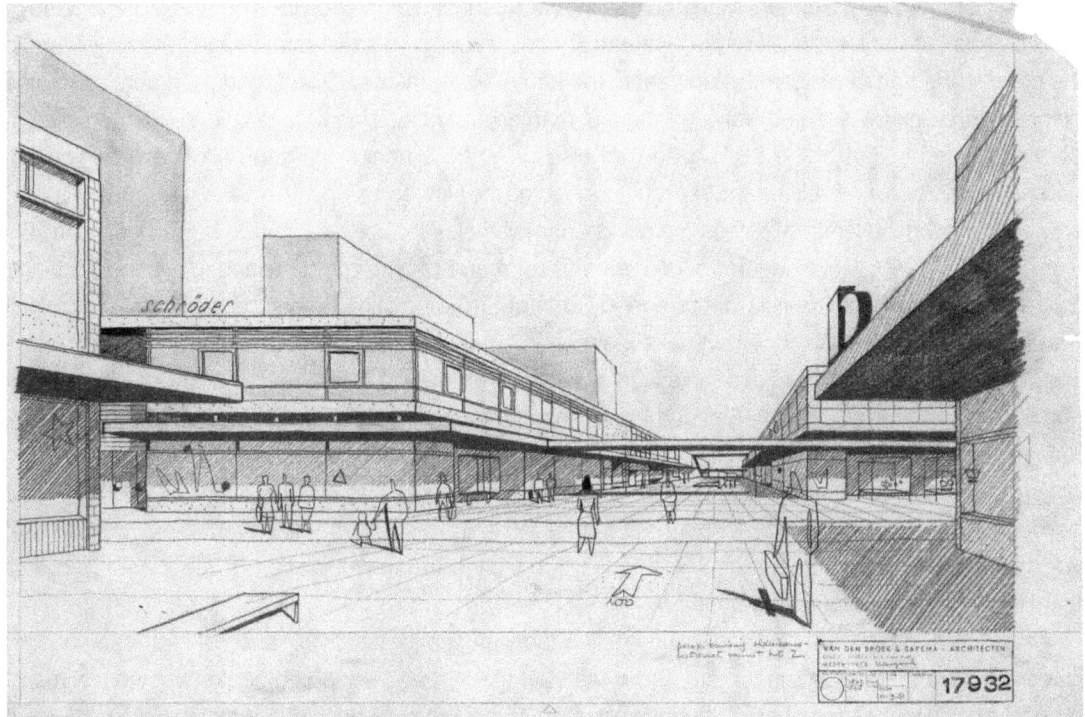

Figure 4.2 Early perspective drawing of the Lijnbaan shopping street by project architect Frans van Gool.
Source: Collection Het Nieuwe Instituut/BROX-g07t5-1.

---

[15]Ibid.
[16]Michelle Provoost, 'Massa en Weerstand: De Wederopbouw van het Centrum in het Interbellum', in *50 Jaar Wederopbouw*, ed. Martin Aarts (Rotterdam: 010Publishers, 1995), 65–96.

perspective drawings of the Lijnbaan that were made by Frans van Gool, the project architect of the van den Broek and Bakema office. These drawings betray the modern, middle-class lifestyle that the architects aspired to, including a hint of American glamour and optimism. The Lijnbaan was planned to be eighteen metres wide with two zones of five metres on each side to accommodate a smooth flow of shoppers, and a zone of eight metres wide with terraces, flower beds, kiosks and free-standing display boxes in the middle. The shops lining this pedestrian street were (and still are) all housed in two-storey high volumes; their architecture characterized by a continuous timber canopy that runs along the shop fronts and crosses the streets at regular intervals to protect customers from the rain. Overhead the shop facades consist of a regular and repetitive screen of vertical, prefab concrete elements that frame either windows or panels. A 1.10 metre module was maintained throughout the project, including in the design of the public space. Together with the continuous canopy, this module endows the Lijnbaan with urban and architectural coherence. On street level the shop owners were allowed to have individually designed shop windows, and even deviate from the perimeter block to create transitional spaces between the shop and the street, as long as the basic module was maintained and the shop windows were fully glazed.

On 9 October 1953, Herman Witte, the minister of Reconstruction and Housing and a civil engineer, officially opened the first phase of the Lijnbaan. The new shopping street ran between the Kruiskade in the north to the Van Oldenbarneveldtstraat in the south. Here, the new Bijenkorf department store was planned, strategically situated between the Lijnbaan and the Coolsingel, and built following a design by Marcel Breuer. Part of the first phase was also de Korte Lijnbaan (or 'short Lijnbaan'), which ran perpendicular to the main Lijnbaan street and connected the Lijnbaan proper to the new Schouwburgplein square in the west. Here, the temporary city theatre was situated, along with the new concert hall De Doelen (1955–1966), which the brothers Evert and Herman Kraaijvanger designed in a fittingly angular modern language characteristic of the period. East of the Korte Lijnbaan the, equally new, Town Hall Square was projected, that today still links the monumental town hall on the Coolsingel to the Lijnbaan. The second phase of the Lijnbaan involved a southern extension to the Binnenwegplein Square. Its realization was delayed until 1966 after the remains of the Coolsingel hospital were demolished. In the meantime, the office of van den Broek and Bakema had designed two large department stores on either corner of the extended Lijnbaan and the Binnenwegplein square: Ter Meulen, Wassen and Van Vorst between 1948 and 1951, followed by the furniture store De Klerk (1952–1954). These two sculptural volumes served as monumental corner stones connecting the new Lijnbaan to the Binnenweg and thereby to the old nineteenth-century city.

Finally and crucially, in 1954 the low-rise Lijnbaan was completed by a series of high-rise housing slabs just west of the shopping street. From the start the Lijnbaan shopping centre was conceived of as part of a mixed-use, high-density development. The apartment buildings were designed by local architects Hugh Maaskant, Arie Krijgsman and Herman Bakker.[17] Similar to the tight control that was applied to the architecture of the Lijnbaan shops, also here a strict ordering of the buildings around courtyards along with a precise spacing of the slabs resulted in a coherent urban ensemble, which

---

[17] To guarantee a collective outlook of the ensemble Maaskant acted as architectural supervisor to Krijgsman and Bakker.

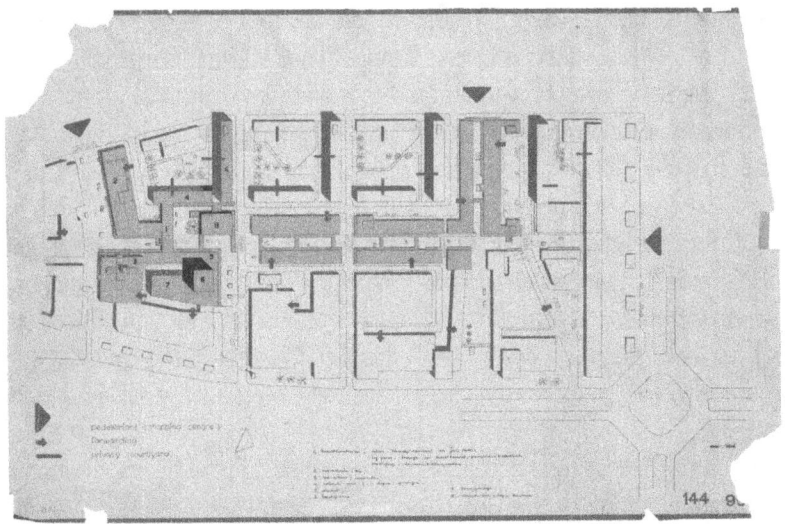

Figure 4.3 Urban lay-out of the whole Lijnbaan ensemble, including the series of high-rise slabs.
Source: Collection Het Nieuwe Instituut/BROX-g07ti-6.

was recently labelled an 'urban megastructure' by the Rotterdam collective Crimson Architectural Historians.[18] Although ahistorical – the Japanese architect Fuhimiko Maki only conceptualized the megastructure idea in 1964 – this speculative statement does provoke a re-evaluation of the whole project as an urban artefact.[19] Clearly, the Lijnbaan ensemble was the outcome of collective effort and involved teamwork. As such, it challenges conventional historiography in terms of easily identifiable architect-authors and unambiguous ideological intention. The persistent notion of individual authorship in modern architecture which depicts the architect as a heroic individual similar to the avant-garde artist has to make way for the concept of multiple authorship, while the presumption of a clear-cut ideological-artistic project underpinning the architecture has to be replaced by an understanding of the Lijnbaan ensemble as the outcome of a myriad of societal forces that represent the contemporary complexity and that are often contradictory. In the Lijnbaan case, the notion of multiple authorship comes to the fore not only in the development of its urban layout, but also at the level of the architecture produced in the office of the van den Broek and Bakema.

Transforming the urban block, blurring authorship in architecture

Examining the gradual development of the Lijnbaan block typology and the specific configuration of the shopping centre as a low-rise pedestrian street, a few observations can be made. As built, the Lijnbaan ensemble is the ultimate outcome of a step-by-step negotiation process during which the

---

[18]Crimson, *De Lijnbaan*, 42.
[19]Fumihiko Maki, *Investigations in Collective Form* (St. Louis: Washington University, School of Architecture, 1964). In Bakema's library there is a copy with a dedication by Maki.

originally proposed urban blocks were transformed into a larger pattern of interwoven open spaces and slabs. This process of negotiations involved the city department of planning, the elite of Rotterdam entrepreneurs, the shop owners who needed to replace their original premises and the various architects. Authorship inevitably becomes blurred in this process. In his memoirs Jaap Bakema, for instance, included an illuminating anecdote about the dynamics at play between the city department and his own office. Bakema became a partner of Jo van den Broek around the time the Lijnbaan job landed in the office, and it marked the beginning of their incredibly successful partnership in the postwar decades.[20] He suggests that Rein Fledderus, one of the designers working at the city department, had advised them to present their ideas in such a way that the director Van Traa could appropriate it as his own initiative. He furthermore claimed that this tactic turned out to be most successful as the proposition by van den Broek and Bakema was eventually integrated in an amended version of the original Basisplan.[21]

However, the shop owners' wishes had a bigger impact still on the transformation of the originally proposed urban block typology of the Basisplan. This collective of sixty-six individuals, who were hit by the bombardment, had held shops in temporary structures throughout the war years and its aftermath.[22] As Dutch law required that shops and the flats above them were owned by the same party, this collective demanded that no flats would be stacked onto their new property, because they lacked the resources to invest in housing. It was therefore decided that the new Lijnbaan would have low-rise shops only and housing would be recessed from the shopping street in a detached block configuration. To accommodate this changed set-up, the original Basisplan block typology was amended in 1947.[23] When the office of van den Broek and Bakema was eventually given the commission for the design of the shops in 1948, a second phase of consultancy followed. The architects had to meet all the demands of the individual shop owners for the specific layout of their shops. Bakema remembered that presentations were staged in the Hotel Atlanta at the Coolsingel, including a system of consulting hours for the retailers and their family to explain their wishes to the architects.[24] This eventually led to a modular system of standard shop types to accommodate the different wishes.

Also within the office of van den Broek and Bakema, authorship of the Lijnbaan ensemble remains blurred and has become a point of discussion. Architectural historian Wouter Vanstiphout suggests that the two partners followed different yet complementary agendas: van den Broek a more pragmatic, almost technocratic designer of urban systems, and Bakema a propagandist who expressed the

---

[20]For a history of the van den Broek and Bakema partnership: Hans Ibelings (ed.), *Van den Broek en Bakema. Architectuur en stedenbouw 1948–1988* (Rotterdam: NAi Uitgevers, 2000); Jean-Paul Baeten, *Een Telefooncel op de Lijnbaan. De Traditie van een Architectenbureau M. Brinkman, Brinkman en Van der Vlugt, van den Broek en Bakema* (Rotterdam: NAi Uitgevers, 1995).

[21]Jaap Bakema, unpublished memoirs in four volumes, written between 1975 and 1981 (private collection); the Lijnbaan comments in the second brown volume are dated 30 May 1980, 43–49.

[22]Numbers vary, sometimes 64, or 65 are mentioned. Urban Fabric, Steenhuis mentions 66, on pp. 22 and 25.

[23]Urban Fabric, Steenhuis gives a good overview of the various steps of the process on pages 34–37 and 60–61. Here too, Bakema suggests a collective dynamic between the shop owners, the Rotterdam elite (i.c. K.P. van der Mandele, director of the Chamber of Commerce and F.C. Bouman, director of the Holland-Amerika Lijn) and in this case Jo van den Broek, in Bakema, unpublished memoirs.

[24]Bakema, unpublished memoirs.

humanist ideology of the office.[25] Historian Bernard Colenbrander further complicates the issue of authorship by turning to the project architect, Frans van Gool. Due to the sheer amount of work, the office pioneered new organizational models based on the figure of the project architect, who was also credited in publications.[26] Nonetheless, this public recognition did not resolve tensions regarding authorship, quite on the contrary. Recalling his work on the Lijnbaan, van Gool claims full authorship of the project. He, however, simultaneously mentions a few conflicts between him and both his superiors regarding the detailing of the facade composition.[27]

Figure 4.4 Lijnbaan streetscape after completion.
Source: Photo by Jan Vrijhof, collection Het Nieuwe Instituut/BROX-fg07-2.

[25]Wouter Vanstiphout, Maak een stad. Rotterdam en de Architectuur van J.H. van den Broek (Rotterdam: Uitgeverij 010, 2005), 176; the architect Carel Weeber, former collaborator of Bakema and student of van den Broek, points to a more competitive and critical relationship between the two partners in an interview with the author, 2014, to be published in a forthcoming book on Bakema and his idea for an open society (Amsterdam: Archis, 2016).

[26]For instance in the monograph Architektur und Städtebau. Das Werk van den Broek und Bakema (Stuttgart: Karl Krämer Verlag, 1963). The listed project architects of the two department stores at the south corners of the Lijnbaan were (respectively) H.B.J. Lops and J.M. Stokla, and Lops and Van Gool.

[27]Bernard Colenbrander, Frans van Gool. Leven en Werk (Rotterdam: NAi Uitgevers, 2005), 13–15; Bakema acknowledges van Gool's role as co-author in his memoirs, pp. 44 and 49.

The idea of the pedestrian street also did not stem from the Lijnbaan project. It was already accepted as a starting point due to the negative perception of the old shopping streets with their mix of car traffic and shopping public. Still, van den Broek's role was substantial. As a member of two advising bodies, the so-called ASRO and OPRO, he prepared several studies.[28] He also authored two important preparatory reports for rebuilding the inner city, one was *Winkelstraten* (Shopping Streets) of 1944 and the other *Bouwvormen in de Binnenstad* (Building Forms in the Inner City) of 1946. Both contained typological studies of shopping streets in relation to the transformation of the conventional urban block.[29] Van den Broek was no stranger to such innovative typological work; he built his reputation on the meticulous studies he did throughout the 1930s.[30]

After van den Broek and Bakema were commissioned to design the Lijnbaan shops, the office remained involved in the development of the whole ensemble, including the urban layout of the high-rise housing blocks. Various options were discussed with the city department and ultimately the van den Broek and Bakema office drew the final version in 1950.[31] The original urban block typology of Van Traa's Basisplan, which was characterized by a hybrid programme and proposed a clear difference between street and court spaces, was now deconstructed into a composition of interrelated volumes and open spaces. Van den Broek already envisaged such new architectural freedoms when he published his 1946 report on new building forms for the inner city:

> The cityscape will be defined by plastic building volumes instead of two-dimensional street facades. Hence, architectural creativity will have a more valuable starting point than the treatment of front facades. Architects will have more freedom in terms of architectural concepts than in the design of facades lined up, in which case the necessity of lining up is limiting.[32]

Although van den Broek was not explicit regarding the kind of architectural concept he preferred, his affinities were clearly attuned to those circles of modern architects of which he himself was a prominent member. He favoured a mixture of the elementary language of Dutch Functionalism, the spatial concepts of De Stijl and references to Russian Constructivism. Van den Broek's speculation thus anticipated the radical transformation of the urban block as realized in the Lijnbaan. Throughout his career Bakema was much more upfront about his avant-gardist alliances than van den Broek. When defining

---

[28] The history is quite complicated due to the political situation during the war years. ASRO is the official body of the city and stands for *Adviesburo Stadsplan Rotterdam* or 'Advising Office City Plan Rotterdam'. OPRO was a parallel, independent think tank of architects, initiated by Rotterdam entrepreneurs, esp. Cees van der Leeuw, to provide critical input to the official process. OPRO stands for *Architectenwerkgroep Opbouw Rotterdam* or 'Architects' Working Group Reconstruction Rotterdam'; see also Wagenaar, *Welvaartsstad in Wording* and Vanstiphout, *Maak een Stad*.

[29] Both unpublished reports are in the collection of Het Nieuwe Instituut in Rotterdam; see also Urban Fabric, Steenhuis, 28.

[30] For an early study of van den Broek's contribution, see Rudy Stroink (ed.), *Ir. J.H. van den Broek. Projekten uit de Periode 1928-1948* (Delft: Delftse Universitaire Pers, 1981); Max Risselada documents the housing projects in the larger context of the development of Functionalism: Max Risselada (ed.), *Functionalisme 1927-1961. Hans Scharoun versus de Opbouw* (Delft: Publicatiebureau Bouwkunde, 1997); Wouter Vanstiphout provides a critical reading in relation to the building industry and local policies in Rotterdam in his dissertation *Maak een stad*.

[31] Urban Fabric, Steenhuis, 60; 73.

[32] Original quote: 'In plaats van door vlakke straatwanden zal het stadsbeeld bepaald worden door plastische bouwmassa's. Daardoor zal het architectonische scheppen een waardevoller uitgangspunt krijgen dan de behandeling van voorgevels. In de architectuuropvatting zullen de architecten vrijer kunnen zijn dan bij de vormgeving van aansluitende gevels, waarbij juist die noodzaak van "aansluiting" belemmerend werkt.' Source: van den Broek, 1946.

the Lijnbaan, he called the ensemble an example of 'plastic functionalism', a 'cluster' in line with the urban 'grouping concepts' that were developed within the Rotterdam CIAM group 'Opbouw' and later in 'CIAM – Team X'.[33] These references reveal how the Lijnbaan embodied Bakema's ideas for an open, egalitarian society, including his understanding of the idea of 'core'.

The Lijnbaan as an emblem of the open society

Parallel to the development of the Lijnbaan ensemble Bakema became involved in the post-war debates in CIAM. He attended the various post-war conferences starting with the reunion congress at Bridgwater in 1947 and quickly became one of the leading voices of a new generation of modern architects, who demanded that architecture and planning pay greater attention to sociocultural factors. Bakema spoke about how architecture and planning should further the 'spiritual growth' of man and should help to make people aware of the larger environment in which they live: modern architecture and planning was thus to move beyond the provision of basic material necessities such as housing. Bakema also promoted a relational understanding of the built environment. At the CIAM 8 conference in Hoddesdon in 1951, which focused on the theme of 'the heart of the city' or the idea of the 'core', he famously explained the idea as follows:

> There are moments in our life in which the isolation of man from things becomes destroyed: in that moment we discover the wonder of relationship between man and things. That is the moment of CORE: the moment we become aware of the fullness of life by cooperative action.[34]

Usually, this relational idea of architecture is placed next to Bakema's diagram of interrelations between people and buildings, the so-called 'friendship model', which he used to explain on Dutch national television in the early 1960s.[35] The friendship model illustrates Bakema's idea of an 'open society'. It represents both his interpretation and critique of the welfare state system of the post-war era.[36] The diagram shows a section of a city, which closely resembles the section of the Lijnbaan ensemble; an inverted pyramid with smaller elements and low-rise buildings in the middle and bigger buildings and high-rise projects shifted to the periphery. This diagram is a recurring motif in many of Bakema's urban schemes: the inner core reserved for pedestrians and a more intimate, human scale, and the outer edges for the large scale of the open landscape, car movement and high-rise development (see Figure 4.5).

Human scale and intimacy, pedestrianization, a modern articulation of monumental and civic space, all these elements are present in the 1952 report of CIAM 8 *The Heart of the City*, in particular in the

---

[33] Bakema, unpublished memoirs.
[34] Tyrwhitt, Sert, Rogers, *The Heart of the City*, 67. For a history of CIAM including Bakema's role: Eric Mumford, *The CIAM Discourse on Urbanism, 1928–1960* (Cambridge MA: MIT Press, 2000).
[35] Published as J.B. Bakema, *Van Stoel tot Stad. Een Verhaal over Mensen en Ruimte* (Zeist: Uitgeversmaatschappij W. de Haan, 1964) with the diagram on the cover.
[36] Dirk van den Heuvel, 'Towards an Open Society. The Unfinished Work of Jaap Bakema', in *Open: A Bakema Celebration*, ed. Dirk van den Heuvel, supplement for the Journal *Volume* 41 (2014) at the occasion of the Venice Biennale 2014, and the Dutch entry to the 14th international architecture exhibition.

Figure 4.5 Jaap Bakema, Diagram of friendship model, including note for 'transitional elements'.
Source: Collection Het Nieuwe Instituut/BAKE-42.

last chapter with the summary of conclusions of the conference.[37] Lewis Mumford's praise for the Lijnbaan must be set against the background of this international debate.[38] Unintentionally perhaps, the Lijnbaan with its transitional elements and the pedestrianized urban space can be considered a most eloquent demonstration of the principles laid out in *The Heart of the City*, including the way the Lijnbaan is carefully embedded and connected with the larger fabric of the modern city of Rotterdam and its monuments such as the town hall and the squares of Schouwburgplein and Binnenwegplein. Together with the careful attention paid to the transitional elements between indoor and outdoor spaces, what Bakema called the 'doorstep philosophy', the Lijnbaan also marks the shift from the CIAM discourse to the thinking of its successor Team 10.[39]

However, as mentioned, that the redefinition of a shopping street culminated in a civic space is still a refreshing surprise. Within CIAM circles in general or within the Rotterdam group Opbouw in particular, shopping was never regarded as belonging to the realm of the social. Bakema never presented the Lijnbaan at the post-war CIAM conferences, but preferred to discuss the more comprehensive planning schemes for the Rotterdam districts of Pendrecht and Alexanderpolder as developed by the Rotterdam CIAM group 'Opbouw'. One can only speculate about the exact reasons. Apart from the issue of blurred authorship, one might suspect a preference for all-encompassing urban schemes, from the house to the city, the valuation of high culture over everyday commerce, or even a relation with

---

[37] Tyrwhitt, Sert, Rogers, *The Heart of the City*.

[38] Lewis Mumford was expected to speak at CIAM 8, but eventually didn't participate, see Mumford, *The CIAM Discourse on Urbanism, 1928–1960*, 204–205.

[39] For a history of Team 10 and Bakema's role, see Max Risselada and Dirk van den Heuvel (eds.), *Team 10. In Search of a Utopia of the Present 1953–1981* (Rotterdam: NAi Publishers, 2005); Bakema re-appropriated this notion, which is usually attributed to his Team 10 fellows Aldo van Eyck and Alison and Peter Smithson in a response to the special issue of *l'Architecture d'Aujourd'hui* devoted to Team 10 in 1975, see J.B. Bakema, *Woning en Woonomgeving* (Delft, 1977), 197.

gender roles – shopping belonging to the realm of the feminine. The Austrian-American Victor Gruen was probably the first planner, who saw the social potential of shopping centres as a meeting space and a space for social interaction.[40] But a direct connection between the development of the Lijnbaan and his ideas seems non-existent, even when there are a couple of obvious American influences immediately traceable within the architecture of the Lijnbaan and the department stores designed by van den Broek and Bakema. Van den Broek noted in the journal *Bouw* his lessons from his trip to the United States and the new trends in shopping architecture; these included fully glazed windows and display techniques, light and air-conditioning technology, interior organization and logistics, escalators and the closed volumes of department stores which offer possibilities for billboard advertising and a new kind of architectural treatment of the facade as if foreshadowing Venturi and Scott-Brown's *Learning from Las Vegas*.[41]

Conclusion: How to protect a sound urban form?

Today, when visiting the Lijnbaan, the idea of an 'inverted' hierarchy is still visible with the low-rise shops in the middle and the many newly added high-rise buildings as an ever changing skyline encircling the pedestrianized heart of the area. Much of the subtle transitions between the small scale and the big scale have gone missing though. There are a few exceptions such as the new store by Kees Kaan, which houses a jeweller and a fashion shop, and which reads as an intensification of the quality of the architecture of van den Broek and Bakema's original building. Robert Winkel of Mei architecten works on the restoration of the Lijnbaan shops; a recent pilot project of his hand convincingly demonstrates that a radical approach can bring out the former clarity of the original architecture, rendering it actually rather contemporary.

Still, the overall process and the post-history of the Lijnbaan after its inauguration in 1953 show that the architecture of an open society and its specific urban spaces are not a given, but rather sites of contestations. Even though a crucial part of the Lijnbaan is now listed, these contestations continue. Although the listing of the first phase of the Lijnbaan and its concomitant juridical apparatus might protect the 'sound urban form' from disruption by developers, where this listing is not in place – as is the case in the second phase of the Lijnbaan – developers have much more freedom to propose new large-scale changes, which are harmful to the original design.[42] Hence, the conclusion seems only apt that the Lijnbaan remains a site for contestation of the spaces of the open society. It is in that sense that the 'sound urban form' still provides the framework for social interaction, whether the results will be as dignifying as the post-war decades of the welfare state remains to be seen.

---

[40]Victor Gruen and Larry Smith, *Shopping Towns USA. The Planning of Shopping Centers* (New York: Reinhold Publishing Corporation, 1960); Victor Gruen, *The Heart of Our Cities. The Urban Crisis: Diagnosis and Cure* (New York: Simon and Schuster, 1964).

[41]J.H. Van den Broek, 'Nieuwe Winkels en Warenhuizen in Amerika', *Bouw* (1948), 259–260.

[42]Currently, a debate is unfolding on the qualities of a redevelopment scheme for the southern extension of the Lijnbaan by the developer Multi Vastgoed with OMA and Wessel de Jonge as architects. See Ferrie Weeda, 'Forum Sloopt Architectuur Lijnbaan', *Vers Beton*, 27 November 2015, www.versbeton.nl/2015/11/forum-sloopt-architectuur-lijnbaan, accessed 15 July 2016.

Chapter 5

Displays of modernity: The urban restructuring of post-1963 Skopje
Jasna Mariotti

Introduction

On 26 July 1963, a destructive earthquake struck the city of Skopje, claiming more than 1,000 lives and causing tremendous damage to the city's urban fabric, ravaging about 85 per cent of its buildings.[1] Shortly after the earthquake, which was one of the most devastating earthquakes in the history of twentieth-century Europe, national and international parties offered aid, making the recovery of Skopje an unprecedented action of international solidarity and cooperation.[2] The radical urban transformations that the city experienced after the earthquake were informed by Yugoslavia's particular position in the post-war era. In 1948, the Tito–Stalin Split (or Yugoslav–Soviet Split) resulted in the country's expulsion from the Communist Information Bureau, which effectively banished Yugoslavia from the international association of socialist states and offered the country the opportunity to trace its own path of socialism.[3] In 1961 Yugoslavia became one of the six founding members of the Non-Aligned Movement. This Movement advocated for a middle course between the Western and the Eastern blocs, effectively placing Yugoslavia in a unique position 'in-between' that enabled the country to attract support from both sides.[4] As a result, after the earthquake, help for Skopje came from different corners of the globe. Not only Egypt and India, allies of Yugoslavia in the Non-Aligned Movement, but also Czechoslovakia, Romania and Poland from the East and France, Italy and UK from the West were among the eighty-two countries that contributed to the reconstruction of the city in need. Thanks to this extensive international aid, Skopje recovered quickly. Between 1963 and 1965 eighteen new neighbourhoods with 14,000 prefabricated units cropped up in the city[5] and, as houses were built, the traffic network was expanded and the water supply system improved. Prefabrication processes expedited the reconstruction process

---

[1] 'The Skopje Earthquake of 26 July 1963' [Le Tremblement de Terre de Skopje du 26 Julliet 1963], Report of the Unesco Technical Assistance Mission (Paris: UNESCO, 1968).
[2] Vladimir Ladinski, 'Post 1963 Skopje Earthquake Reconstruction: Long Term Effects', in *Reconstruction after Disaster: Issues and Practices*, ed. Adenrele Awotona (Aldershot: Ashgate, 1997), 73–107.
[3] Peter Siani-Davies, 'Introduction: International Intervention (and Non-Intervention) in the Balkans', in *International Intervention in the Balkans since 1995*, ed. Peter Siani-Davies (London: Routledge, 2003), 1–31.
[4] Ibid., 14.
[5] *Skopje – Grad na Solidarnosta* [Skopje – City of Solidarity] (Skopje: The City Assembly of Skopje, 1975), 168.

to such an extent that in October 1963 Edvard Kardelj, President of the Federal Parliament, pondered if 'this type of temporary and rapidly constructed unit should become a standard element of housing policy'.[6] This miraculous recovery also facilitated Skopje's growth; between 1961 and 1971 the city's population almost doubled, from 166,870 citizens in 1961 to 314,552 a decade later,[7] and also in the following years, this record growth continued, transforming Skopje from a rather small town into Yugoslavia's third-largest city, after Belgrade and Zagreb.[8]

The disciplines of urban planning and architecture took centre stage in the redevelopment of Skopje, and in its concomitant transformation from small town into large city. The clean slate that was created on Yugoslavia's 'non-aligned' territory invited designers from both East and West to project their urban visions, along with the sociopolitical models that they embodied, on the devastated Balkan city. This chapter looks at the urban restructuring of Skopje following the earthquake in 1963, focusing particularly on the development of the City Trade Centre and the materialization of visionary and novel ideas in the formation of the modern city.

The 1965 competition for the reconstruction of the city centre of Skopje

On 14 August 1963, less than one month after the earthquake, the existing master plan for the city of Skopje was declared void, signalling the need for the formulation of alternative models for the future development of the city.[9] The new master plan that was formalized in 1965 sparked intense public debate as it projected a rapid expansion of the city over the next twenty years, transforming Skopje into a regional capital of 700,000 citizens. Under the auspices of the United Nations, the Institute of Town Planning and Architecture of Skopje (ITPA) led the drafting process of the new master plan with the help of foreign experts, Doxiadis Associates from Athens and Polservice from Warsaw. Adolf Ciborowski, who was previously Chief Architect in Warsaw and coordinated city's post-war reconstruction, was appointed as Project Manager of Skopje's new master plan.[10]

The city centre, which the earthquake had almost completely destroyed, required immediate action. In 1964 the International Board of Consultants,[11] which was chaired by Ernest Weissmann

---

[6]Jack Fisher, 'The Reconstruction of Skopje', *Journal of the American Institute of Planners* 30, no. 1 (1964): 48.
[7]Demographic Research Centre, The Population of Yugoslavia, 1974 (Belgrade, 1974).
[8]Jasna Stefanovska and Janez Koželj, 'Urban Planning and Transitional Development Issues: The Case of Skopje, Macedonia', *Urbani izziv* 23, no. 1 (2012): 91–100.
[9]*Skopje – Grad na Solidarnosta*.
[10]United Nations Development Programme, *Skopje Resurgent: The Story of a United Nations Special Fund Town Planning Project* (New York: United Nations, 1970).
[11]The International Board of Consultants was formed by the United Nations and the Yugoslav Government shortly after the earthquake and was composed of international and Yugoslav experts in seismology and town planning. The president of the Board throughout the time of its activity was Ernest Weissmann. The work of this Board was financed from funds earmarked for the Master plan of Skopje and the meetings of the Board were organized by the General Directorate for Renewal and Reconstruction of Skopje and the Institute of Town Planning and Architecture of Skopje. The first meeting of the International Board of Consultants was held in March 1964 and the last one in May 1966. Source: Kole Jordanovski, *Skopje: Catastrophe, Reconstruction, Experience* (Skopje: Matica Makedonska, 1993), 141.

of the United Nations and comprised national and international experts in seismology and town planning, recommended the organization of an international competition for its reconstruction, possibly with help from the United Nations.[12] Acknowledging that the city centre should be 'radically replanned to the highest possible standard', the Board urged the most talented urban planners and architects to participate.[13] This competition marked a new beginning for the planning of Skopje. It earmarked the city as a testing ground for modern urban planning concepts and ideas and also as a site for collaboration and exchange between experts from different countries. Eight teams were invited to submit a proposal for the competition and in February 1965 two representatives from each team were invited to visit Skopje.[14] Amongst the invitees were four foreign teams – Luigi Piccinato (with Studio Scimemi) from Rome, Maurice Rotival from New York, Kenzo Tange from Tokyo and van den Broek and Bakema from Rotterdam – and four Yugoslav teams: Radovan Miscevic and Fedor Wenzler from the Croatian Institute of Town Planning in Zagreb, Eduard Ravnikar and associates from Ljubljana, Aleksandar Djordjevic and his colleagues from the Belgrade Institute of Town Planning from Belgrade and Slavko Brezovski and his associates from Makedonija-proekt from Skopje. According to the 1970 United Nations Development Programme report on the redevelopment of Skopje:

> It was made clear in the competitors' brief that the purpose of the competition was not to pick the firm to be entrusted with the preparation of a detailed city-centre plan: that remained the responsibility of the Skopje ITPA. The intention of the organizers, it was explained, was to obtain an ideal town planning scheme by enabling the ITPA to draw upon a fund of ideas contributed by a variety of highly skilled firms with a wide range of experience.[15]

Ernest Weissmann, a Yugoslav architect who had worked for Le Corbusier before joining the United Nations as an Assistant Director of the Bureau of Social Affairs and Director of the Centre for Housing, Building and Planning at the Department of Economic and Social Affairs, represented the United Nations and chaired the Jury.[16] Another eight jury members represented the United Nations, the International Union of Architects, the Yugoslav Town Planning Federation, the Yugoslav Architects Association and the local authorities. One rapporteur represented the local authorities and there were also six consultants, responsible for the protection of historical monuments, traffic and transportation,

---

[12]The United Nations were already present in Skopje after the earthquake through their role in the preparation of the master plan for the whole territory of the city. However, this was the first time that the United Nations were involved in sponsoring a competition, thanks to legal documents that were made official a few years earlier and that allowed the United Nations to organize and to finance an international competition open to a limited number of entrants. The competition for the reconstruction of the city centre of Skopje was accordingly organized by the United Nations Special Fund and the Yugoslav Government, in cooperation with the International Union of Architects, the Association of Yugoslav Town Planners and the Association of Yugoslav Architects. Source: United Nations Development Programme, *Skopje Resurgent,* 297–298.
[13]Ibid., 297.
[14]Ibid., 298.
[15]Ibid.
[16]Eric Mumford, *The CIAM Discourse on Urbanism, 1928–1960* (Cambridge, MA: MIT Press, 2001).

co-ordination with the Master Plan, the economic aspects of implementation, town development policy and earthquake engineering.[17]

On 20 July 1965, the Jury awarded the first prize to two teams. Three fifths or $12,000 was given to the team of Kenzo Tange from Japan, and the other two fifths, or $8,000 to the team of Miscevic and Wenzler from Zagreb. The jury decided on this rather unconventional distribution because '… there was no one entry which should be the single basis for implementing the reconstruction of the centre of the city of Skopje. Each of the entries contained a variety of promising ideas and proposals'.[18] In its report, the jury noted that Kenzo Tange's entry '… has dealt with many aspects of the plan in a serious, original and inspired way', pointing particularly to '[t]he architectural interpretation of larger structures and planning and design of the urban ensembles' as being 'of high quality'.[19] The entry of Miscevic and Wenzler in turn was praised for '… the opportunity it provides for realization in stages and thus for flexibility'.[20]

Shortly after the winners were announced, the international team with members from Japan, Zagreb and Skopje began collaborating on a new master plan for the city centre of Skopje which aimed to 'contain all the positive aspects of all the competition entries' and would – according to Adolf Ciborowski – '… be a base for a beautiful city for happy citizens'.[21] The 'Ninth Project', as the master plan that the team of Kenzo Tange, Miscevic and Wenzler, Polservice traffic engineer S. Furman and Skopje's ITPA drafted was called, was approved in 1966.[22]

When the master plan was drafted, Kenzo Tange was already an internationally renowned figure in the world of architecture and although the 'Ninth Project' was the result of international teamwork, it clearly took its cue from the ideas that Tange and his team had elaborated in their competition entry for Skopje. Nonetheless, working on Skopje's master plan also opened new frontiers for Tange, enabling him to introduce the ideas of the metabolist movement in Europe. Regarding his presence in the city, Tange noted that '[i]t has been most fortunate that I was able to have the opportunity of cooperating with Yugoslavian architects, concerning the Skopje Project'.[23]

---

[17] The members of the jury for the International Competition for the reconstruction of the city centre of Skopje were: Mr. J. Canaux – representing the International Federation for Housing and Planning; Mr. A. Ciborowski – representing the United Nations; Mr. T. Kirijas – representing the local authorities; Mr. A. Ling – representing the International Union of Architects; Mr. U. Martinovic – representing the Yugoslav Architects Association; Mr. M. Meyerson – representing the United Nations; Mr. V. Midic – representing the Yugoslav Town Planning Federation; and Mr. S. Sedlar – representing the local authorities. Rapporteur was Mr. L. Pota. Consultants of the Jury were: Mr. B. Cipan – protection of historical monuments; Mr. S. Furman – traffic and transportation; Mr. R. Galic – co-ordination with the master plan; Mr. K. Jordanovski – economic aspect of implementation; Mr. B. Popov – town development policy; Mr. P. Serafimov – earthquake engineering. Source: United Nations Development Programme, *Skopje Resurgent*, 364.

[18] Ibid., 370.

[19] Ibid., 373.

[20] Ibid.

[21] V. Boskovski, 'Skopje so 63,000 Novi Stanovi: Devettiot Proekt ke gi Sodrzi Site Dobri Resenija na Dosega Predlozenite Proekti' [Skopje with 63,000 New Apartments: The Ninth Project Will Contain all the Good Solutions of the so far Proposed Projects] *Nova Makedonija*, 30 July 1965, A6.

[22] United Nations Development Programme, *Skopje Resurgent*, 122.

[23] Kenzo Tange and Udo Kultermann, *Kenzo Tange, 1946–1969: Architecture and Urban Design* (New York: Praeger publishers, 1970), 7.

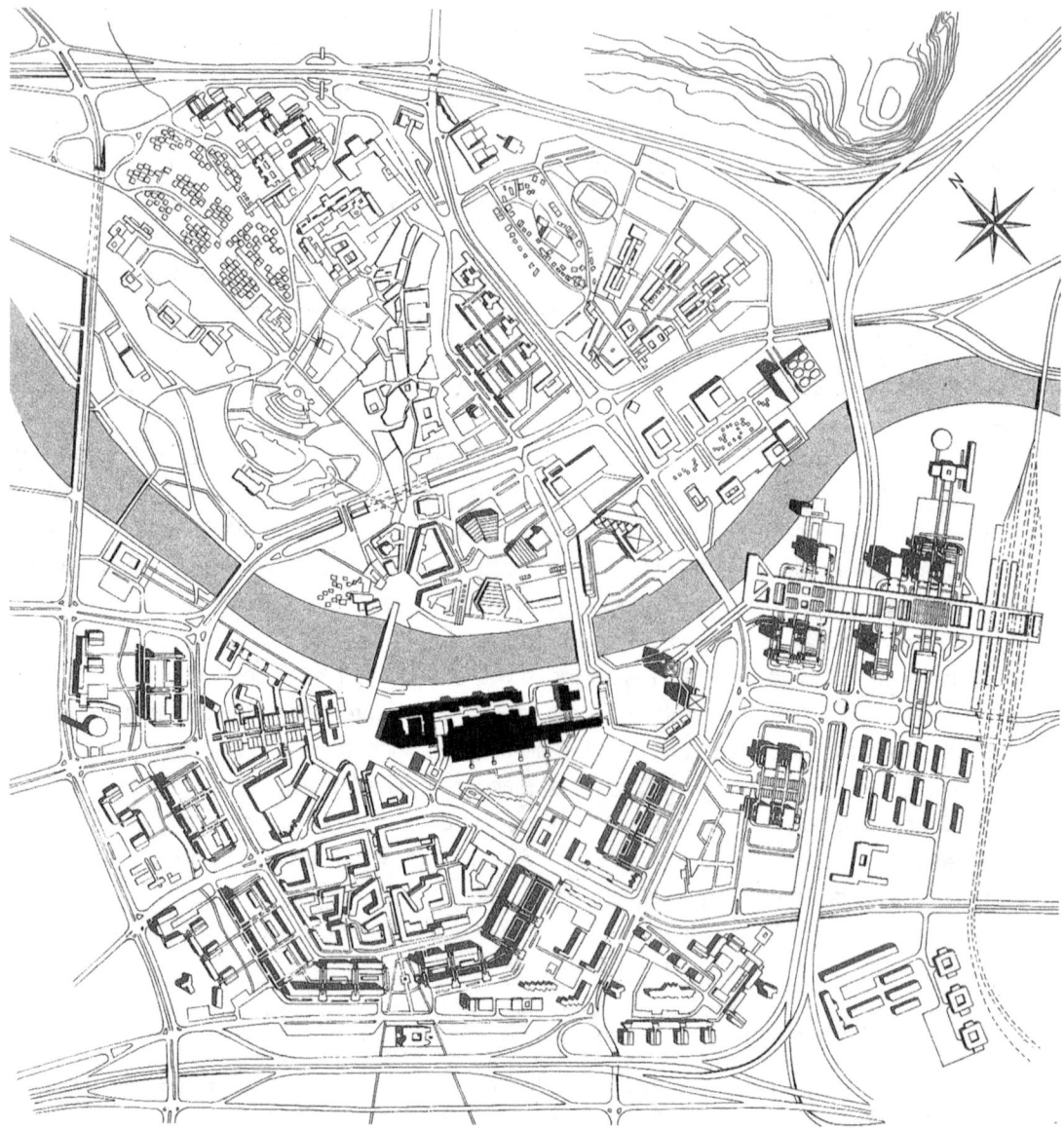

Figure 5.1 The 'Ninth Project' for the reconstruction of the central city area of Skopje, 1966.
Source: United Nations Development Programme, *Skopje Resurgent: The Story of a United Nations Special Fund Town Planning Project* (New York: United Nations, 1970), 331.

The city trade centre in Skopje

In the period following the competition, Skopje witnessed an internationalization of its architectural culture, which was supported both by the presence of foreign architects working in the city and through the growing influence of a young generation of Macedonian architects that were trained abroad. Gjorgji Konstantinovski, for instance, designed the Student Dormitory 'Goce Delcev' (1971–1975) and Skopje's

City Archives (1966–1968) after studying under Paul Rudolph in Yale, and Janko Konstantinov, who worked for Alvar Aalto in Jyväskylä in 1957[24] and built Skopje's Telecommunications Centre (1974) and Post Office (1979).

Shortly after the earthquake, several large-scale competitions were organized for different sites in the city. Beyond reconstruction, these competitions aspired to project new urban visions on the destroyed city. One of these competitions was for the City Trade Centre (*Gradski Trgovski Centar*). According to Ciborowski, Project Manager of Skopje's master plan, this project along the Vardar river, which was to incorporate the existing housing towers, was one of the priority areas for intervention in the frame of Skopje's renewal.[25] As a result, the idea to build a larger complex with shopping, restaurants and craft shops in the core of the downtown, where the new master plan had envisaged the construction of new commercial space, was accepted in 1966.[26] This marked the starting point for the construction of the City Trade Centre.

The master plan stipulated that the Trade Centre had to be located in the centre of the city, along the Vardar river, the central city square and the inner city park, in an area where pedestrian and vehicular traffic intersect, and was to incorporate areas for trade, catering and services.[27] While these programmatic prerequisites were included in the competition brief, the boundaries of the building site, or the materials to be used were not.[28] Held early in 1967, the competition for the City Trade Centre not only offered a testing ground for new concepts in architecture, but also tested the spatial possibilities of the site. Twenty-three competition entries from across Yugoslavia were submitted, several of which by prominent Yugoslav architects. After this first call, the jury invited five teams to submit their proposals for an internal competition,[29] and subsequently awarded the second prize – no first prize was awarded – to Živko Popovski and his team.[30]

At the time of the competition Popovski was a young Macedonian architect who had recently returned from the Netherlands, where he had worked in the architectural office of van den Broek

---

[24] Georgi Konstantinovski, *Graditelite vo Makedonija XVIII-XX Vek* [Architects in Macedonia XVIII–XX Century] (Skopje: Tabernakul, 2001).

[25] R. Damjanovski, 'Dobar od na Izgradbata i Obnovata na Skopje' [Good Track Record of the Reconstruction and Renewal of Skopje], *Nova Makedonija*, 9 February 1967, A6.

[26] Original quote: 'Izgradbata na Trgovskiot centar stana prioritetna zadaca vo oformuvanjeto na centralnoto gradsko podracje. Poradi ova, uste vo 1966 godina, vo akcijata za izgradba na nov deloven prostor, se prifati idejata, pokraj drugoto, vo jadroto na centarot na gradot, kade sto i so noviot urbanisticki plan bese predvidena izgradba na nov deloven prostor, da se izgradi eden pogolem kompleks od trgovski, ugostitelski i zanaetciski dukani.' In Tihomir Arsovski, Gavril Gavrilski and Trajko Stojkov, *Gradski Trgovski Centar* [City Trade Centre] (Skopje: Osnovna edinica za deloven prostor, 1981).

[27] Tihomir Arsovski, *Gradski Trgovski Centar Skopje* [City Trade Centre Skopje] (Skopje: Zavod za stanbeno i komunalno stopanisuvanje, 1969).

[28] Ibid.

[29] In the first round of the competition, the second prize was given to the team of Živko Popovski and to the team of Grujo Golijanin, Edvin Smit and Milan Sosteric. The third prize was given to the team of Janko Konstantinov, the fourth prize to the team of Radisav Popovic, Gordana Popovic, Andrej Smid and the rights were bought from the competition entry of Fedja Kosir. See Arsovski, *Gradski Trgovski Centar*.

[30] Živko Popovski, 'Opstojuvanjata na Gradskiot Trgovski Centar' [The Persistence of the City Shopping Mall], Interview by Ž. Mitevska, *Makedonsko Sonce*, 1999, http://www.makedonskosonce.com/broevi/1999/sonce287/Tekst15.htm, accessed 17 January 2015.

and Bakema in Rotterdam.³¹ While there, he worked – amongst other things – on the competition entry for the reconstruction of Skopje. When interviewed in 1999, Popovski noted that winning the competition for Skopje's City Trade Centre was '… probably … a result of my one-year stay at an expert's team in Holland'.³² Living and working in Rotterdam, and employed by van den Broek and Bakema, it is safe to assume that Popovski was familiar with the Lijnbaan, which was designed by van den Broek and Bakema in 1953.³³ Lined with shops, this linear pedestrian street had restored the inner heart of the city, which was damaged severely during the Second World War. It thus presented a suitable case study for the post-war reconstruction of inner cities and following its success, many more shopping centres followed 'from the Netherlands to deep in Russia and from South Africa up to Scandinavia'.³⁴

Popovski's competition entry for the trade centre reinforced the East–West axis of the city and melded the surrounding area, including the housing towers that were built along the river before the earthquake in 1959, into a coherent and cohesive whole. His horizontal linear structure stitched the fragmented urban tissue of the central part of Skopje together through an internal network of streets that cut through the volume and connected adjacent public spaces. The horizontality of the complex was interrupted only by the verticality of the existing housing towers; thus achieving a well-measured balance that was praised in the competition report: '[t]he proposed architectural ensemble represents an acceptable architectural and urban composition with a good layout of the shaping elements and volumetric proportions'.³⁵

Shortly after the competition for the City Trade Centre was finished, the drafting processes started. Due to the size and complexity of the complex, the Institute for Urbanism and Architecture of Skopje along with two of Macedonia's biggest architecture offices, the Institute of Studies and Design 'Beton' and the design organization 'Makedonija-proekt', were involved. Following the ideas set out in the competition entry, Tihomir Arsovski, Gelevski Živko and Markova Lidija worked together with Popovski to prepare the project's working drawings. Construction started on 11 October 1969 under the auspices of the Institute for Housing and Communal Works, and finished on 29 November 1972. The City Trade Centre was officially opened on 27 April 1973, little more than three years after construction began.³⁶ The opening ceremony was attended by state and city officials and featured prominently on the cover of daily newspapers, such as *Nova Makedonija*, which enthusiastically labelled the City Trade Centre 'a jewel for the city, a building for the future'.³⁷

---

³¹Georgi Konstantinovski, *Graditelite vo Makedonija XVIII–XX vek* (Kniga II) [Architects in Macedonia XVIII–XX century (Vol. 2)] (Skopje: Tabernakul, 2004).
³²Ibid.
³³Divna Pencic et al., *Skopje – An Architectural Guide* (Skopje: Coalition for Sustainable Development – CSD, 2010).
³⁴Michelle Provoost and Wouter Vanstiphout, 'Wijlen de Lijnbaan', last modified 1 September 2007, https://www.archined.nl/2007/01/wijlen-de-lijnbaan/, accessed 20 January 2015.
³⁵Original quote: 'Predlozeniot arhitektonski ansambl pretstavuva prifatluva arhitektonsko-urbanisticka kompozicija so dobar raspored na oblikovnite elementi i volumenskite odnosi.' In: Arsovski, *Gradski Trgovski Centar Skopje*.
³⁶Arsovski, Gavrilski and Stojkov, *Gradski Trgovski Centar*.
³⁷F. Josifovski, 'Otvoren Trgovskiot Centar' [The Trade Centre Is Opened], *Nova Makedonija*, 28 April 1973, A9.

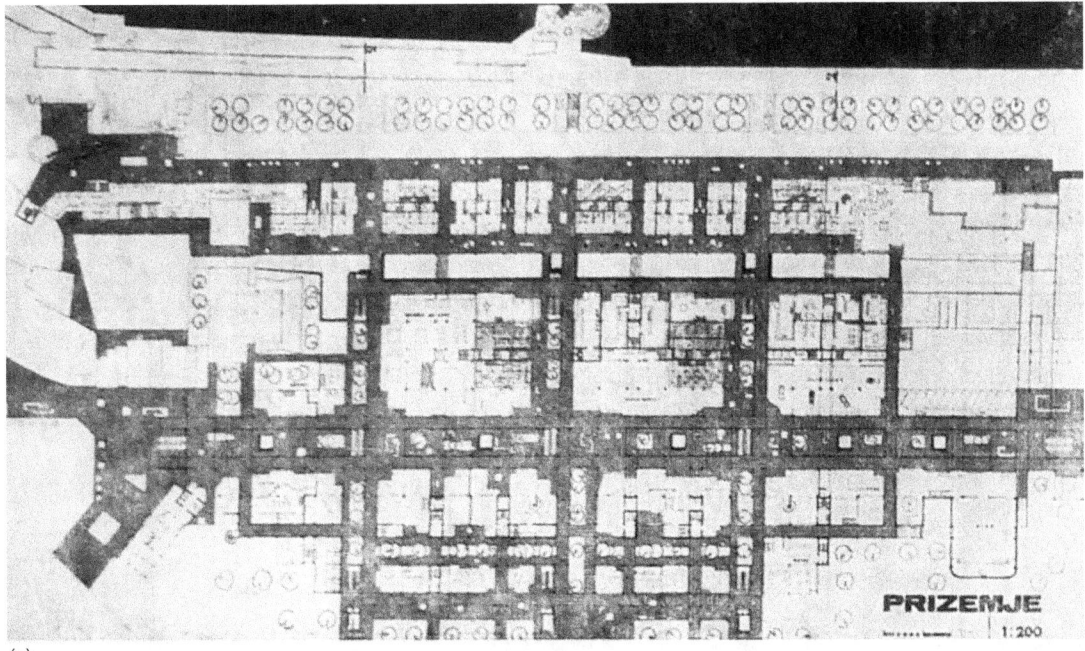

Figure 5.2 Živko Popovski's competition entry for the City Trade Centre: (a) ground floor plan, (b) model.
Source: Tihomir Arsovski, *Gradski Trgovski Centar Skopje* (Skopje: Zavod za stanbeno i komunalo stopanisuvanje, 1969).

100,000 square metres of shopping in the city centre

The City Trade Centre in Skopje housed an extraordinary diverse programme within its 100,000 square metres, including areas for trade, a hotel, catering, crafts, a cinema, banks, a post office and offices. These functions were carefully distributed over the different levels of the complex, depending on their size and the anticipated frequency of visits. Of the City Trade Centre's five floors, two were below ground, one was level with the ground and two floors were raised. The lowest floor provided parking and storage facilities, while the first floor below ground housed supermarkets and service areas. The ground floor along with the two upper levels were designated for commerce, trade and catering. The building's organizational scheme ensured that different activities within the complex were optimally connected, and the technology used to construct the complex was state of the art for its time. Popovski proudly claimed that 'there was no competition in the area between Athens and Vienna'.[38]

Figure 5.3 City Trade Centre in Skopje.
Source: Photo by Rumen Kamilov in Tihomir Arsovski, Gavril Gavrilski and Trajko Stojkov, *Gradski Trgovski Centar* (Skopje: Osnovna edinica za deloven prostor, 1981).

---

[38]Popovski, 'Opstojuvanjata na Gradskiot Trgovski Centar', Interview by Ž. Mitevska.

One of the most distinctive features of the building were the elevated streets that cut through the central part of the ground floor and the two upper levels, thus contributing to a dense, multi-level system of pedestrian streets and public spaces which were connected through spiral staircases and ramps. These interior shopping streets and promenades were 'freed' from the perils of vehicular traffic, which was restricted to the complex's perimeter. A myriad of entrances connected the internal pedestrian network of the City Trade Centre to the river quay, the park and the central city square, thus increasing the connectivity within the city while firmly embedding the building in its pedestrian network. Approximately two thirds of the complex' surface area or 62,257 square metres was 'built up' and one third or 35,103 square metres was public, open space.[39] This resulted in a pleasant variation between open and enclosed spaces, which is still one of the distinguishing features of the building today. A rigid structural grid in combination with a modular spatial organization ensured that in spite of its rich programmatic and spatial variety the complex did exude unity. This appearance of coherence was reinforced by a clever alternation between horizontal slabs and transparent commercial façades, which emphasized the building's linearity.

The City Trade Centre in Skopje has a dominant presence in the urban fabric, thanks to its location – at the very heart of the city – and its size; the building has one of the biggest footprints in the inner centre of Skopje. Nonetheless, the complex is highly permeable and in spite of its size functions as a single entity. It created a spine within the urban fabric that strongly contributed to the newly proposed East–West axis of the city. As such, it not only perfectly fulfilled its role as one of the key components of the 1966 master plan, but also proposed a new concept of urban centrality by positioning a shopping mall at the very heart of the city. Contrary to the American suburban shopping centre, which is disconnected from its surroundings – turned 'inside out', the 'public character' of the building can only be experienced from within – the City Trade Centre of Skopje was firmly anchored into its surrounding and strongly embedded in Skopje's urban fabric. With no front and no back, the complex is an impressive spatial construct that effectively stitched the devastated city centre back together.

Displays of modernity

Urban planning and architecture took centre stage in political and societal debates in Skopje after the 1963 earthquake as the city's built environment became a testing ground for novel urban planning models, reflecting the country's ambiguous position 'in-between'. Supervised by the United Nations, the city's reconstruction was propelled onto the international stage, and it became a national priority to rebuild it to the highest possible standards.[40] In the international limelight, Skopje's reconstruction held the potential to showcase Yugoslavia's 'modernity' to the outside world. While planning for Skopje was ongoing, socialist Yugoslavia played a significant role in the Non-Aligned Movement and its position at the intersection between the East and the West presented an opportunity to illustrate the speed of the

---

[39] Arsovski, *Gradski Trgovski Centar Skopje*.
[40] United Nations Development Programme, *Skopje Resurgent*.

(a)

recovery and the strength of its sociopolitical system to both power blocks: 'There are few examples in the world', said Ciborowski, 'where work undergoes as continuous and synchronized. But, this is the main requirement that we, as representatives of the UN, wanted to provide for your city. This is a wonderful methodology that should be applied by other organizations, not only in your country but in other countries around the world as well.'[41]

In post-earthquake Skopje the collaboration between experts from around the world made urban planning and architecture a global practice, as the city became a site where these 'global' modern ideas were materialized. After 1963, Skopje became a world city, aided by knowledge and technology from

---

[41]Original quote: 'Malku se primerite vo svetot – rece Ciborovski – kade sto se raboti vaka kontinuirano i sinhronizirano. No, toa e glavniot uslov sto sakavme i nie, kako pretstavnici na OON, da go obezbedime vo vasiot grad. Toa e prekrasna metodologija koja treba da ja primenuvaat i drugi organizacii ne samo vo vasata zemja tuku i vo drugi zemji vo svetot.' In: R. Damjanovski, 'Adolf Ciborovski Zadovolen od Tekot na Obnovata i Izgradbata na Skopje' [Adolf Ciborowski Satisfied with the Renewal and Construction of Skopje], *Nova Makedonija*, 13 October 1967, A9.

Displays of modernity: Post-1963 Skopje

(b)

Figure 5.4 Movement in the City Trade Centre in Skopje: (a) vehicular traffic is restricted to City Trade Centre's perimeter; (b) areas for pedestrian movement in the City Trade Centre.
Source: Photos by Rumen Kamilov in Tihomir Arsovski, Gavril Gavrilski and Trajko Stojkov, *Gradski Trgovski Centar* (Skopje: Osnovna edinica za deloven prostor, 1981).

both sides of the Iron Curtain, which was certainly facilitated through Yugoslavia's unique unaligned position. Popovski confirmed:

> After the devastating earthquake, the West and the East competed in Skopje with money and ideas, it was an interesting international game. Western civilization wanted to compete with the East on a different level, on the level of solidarity, with money and teams. The projects for the reconstruction

Figure 5.5 President Tito looks at the model of the executive design for the City Trade Centre.
Source: Tihomir Arsovski, Gavril Gavrilski and Trajko Stojkov, *Gradski Trgovski Centar* (Skopje: Osnovna edinica za deloven prostor, 1981).

were not solely on a level of architecture and design. The experts thought both sociologically and philosophically, and made a concept for a city that was supposed to be representing what Western civilization was considering to be a democratic and libertarian culture. Skopje needed to be prepared for the 21st century.[42]

The reconstruction projects for Skopje came into being in a system that was receptive to new ideas and are thus representative of the modernization programmes implemented in the country after the Second World War. The transformation of the city of Skopje was in itself a modern project. Skopje's

---

[42]Original quote: 'Po katastrofalniot zemjotres vo 1963 godina, Zapadot i Istokot vo Skopje se natprevaruvaa so pari i so idei, se vodese interesna megunarodna igra. Zapadnata civilizacija, sakase da se natprevaruva so istocnata na poinakvo nivo – na nivo na solidarnost, so pari i so timovi. Proektite za izgradbata ne se odnesuvaa samo na arhitektura i na dizajn. Ekspertite mislea i sociološki i filozofski, napravija koncept na grad sto trebase da bide reprezent na ona sto zapadnata civilizacija go smetase za demokratska i slobodarska kultura. Skopje trebase da se podgotvi za 21 vek.' In: Živko Popovski, 'Mozevme, no ne Napravivme Svetski Grad' [We Could Have, but We Didn't Do a World City], *Dnevnik*, 27 July 2004, http://okno.mk/node/35128, accessed 17 January 2015.

post-war display of modernity through its architecture and planning nonetheless illustrates Yugoslavia's distinctiveness from its counterparts on either side of the Iron Curtain. The City Trade Centre is a perfect example. Even though this building introduced the concept of a 'shopping centre' – an American import *par excellence* – into Yugoslavia's non-aligned territory, it did so in a radically different and explicitly 'non-capitalist' manner. The project envisioned a free flow of citizens and its significance is manifested through its public spaces, which take the shape of streets that cut through its core and are freely accessible to all – wealthy or poor, customer of *flâneur*. The City Trade Centre in Skopje presents a novel typology that introduces urbanity and reinforces connectivity in the very centre of the city, integrating commerce and the existing housing towers into a cohesive whole. The building is thus not only a complex display of modernity in Skopje after the earthquake, but also a display of the emergence of a society that incorporates knowledge and ambitious visions for contemporary tendencies, cultural freedom and modernization through its built environment. It is a manifestation of the vision for a modern Skopje that emerged from the rubble of the devastated city, expressing civic values, technological advancement and Yugoslavia's openness to incorporating tendencies from both East and West, both in its symbolic representation and in its material expression.

Part 2

Constructing consumer-citizens: Shopping centres shaping commercial collectivity

Chapter 6

Miracles and ruins, citizens and shoppers: Frankfurt 1963
Inderbir Singh Riar

The human penchant for romantic traditionalism was strengthened to some extent in the face of the ruins which surrounded us on all sides.

Bruno E. Werner, *Modern Architecture in Germany* (1956)

If anything, the Paris-based office of Georges Candilis, Alexis Josic and Shadrach Woods believed, with technocratic zeal and utopian faith, in building the architecture of the welfare state. Formed in 1955, the partnership – between Candilis, an Azerbaijan-born Greek who as a young man attended the 1933 meeting of the Congrès International d'Architecture Moderne (CIAM) that announced its consequential edicts on functionalist town planning, Josic, a Serbian refugee from Tito's dictatorship and Woods, an American with pre-war studies in engineering and later literature and philosophy – quickly began a successful career in mass housing, and soon entire *villes nouvelles*, suited to a society suddenly witnessing unprecedented economic growth. Their efforts would carry the first hopes of *Les Trentes Glorieuses* – a period felt, by the early 1960s, throughout Western Europe as one of unremitting prosperity, persistent modernization and presumably durable peace.

The call to reshape the norms and forms of post-war Europe accompanied an incipient challenge to modernist doctrine. Candilis–Josic–Woods were grounded in the architecture of Le Corbusier and the ideology of *urbanisme* – the city, rationally ordered by circulation and hygiene, was prophetically imagined always arising *ex nihilo* (hence assuaging anxieties of reconstruction in the aftermath of world war). Candilis and Woods also spearheaded Team 10, a group emerging from CIAM but rejecting its 'four functions' – the strict division of cities by habitation, work, leisure and circulation – in favour of more primal expressions of 'community'.[1] Attempting to satisfy Team 10 notions on spaces of 'change and growth', Woods would advance his influential models of 'stem' and 'web'. The ideograms were replete with bio-mechanical overtones of *flexibility* increasingly prevalent in architectural discussions. In both, tree- or tartan-like patterns were to engender 'open' or spontaneous experiences of urban life.

---

[1] Candilis and Woods supervised the construction of Le Corbusier's Unité d'Habitation in Marseilles in 1951. They followed it with housing projects in Morocco under the auspices of ATBAT-Afrique (a wing of Atelier des Bâtisseurs, the multidisciplinary team developing technical expertise for undertakings like the Unité). Josic joined ATBAT in Paris.

The desire to redeem functionalism, to liberate Western thought from determinist excess whether architectural or political, appeared forcefully in Candilis–Josic–Woods' noted but short-lived 1963 plan for rebuilding the war-damaged core of Frankfurt. Inside the mediaeval Römerberg district, a 'web' of cultural facilities and shopping concourses was to meet the demands of a new consumer society stepping from the shadows of a dark past. The effects of organized welfare state capitalism – here, shopping, entertainment and education – could, it was thought, be distributed by architecture as a way to remove the stain of Nazism. Like so many other schemes, particularly the 1957 Berlin International Building Exhibition, Frankfurt-Römerberg stood to emblematize, in the eyes of planners, politicians and the public alike, the *Bundesrepublik* as a beacon of democracy – an idea predicated on the triumphal return of modern architecture to the West German city.

Miracles

'No experiments!' Konrad Adenauer, the first and long-serving Chancellor of West Germany, thus exhorted his nation towards post-war economic success and political redemption. The rallying cry, heard throughout the 1957 federal election, captured Adenauer's Christian Democrat belief in the steadying hand of government on an unfettered economy bound by some ethical communitarian ideal; but it also implied a nagging fear of deep-seated cultural insecurities – over wartime loss or 'collective guilt' for fascism – surrendering to communist or revanchist sympathy. Seeking to restore faith in politics, Adenauer's Christian Democratic Union (CDU) promoted its *Soziale Marktwirtschaft* (social market economy) under the aegis of a conservative-corporatist welfare state. The CDU, which would rule from 1948 until 1969, had swiftly disavowed earlier enthusiasm for socialism and nationalizing industry in favour of managed capitalism.[2] Drawing on the Marshall Plan and a sudden industrial boon with the Korean War (a distant but palpable spectre of communist aggression), the German economy again began manufacturing chemicals, construction equipment, electrical goods, machine tools, optics and steel – all in lieu of armaments forbidden until NATO membership in 1955, another facet of rehabilitation under Western eyes. By 1954, the economy grew 8.8 per cent annually; next year, the country ran trade surpluses.[3] The ensuing *Wirtschaftswunder*, the 'economic miracle' masterminded by Adenauer's capable Economics Minister Ludwig Erhard, encouraged free markets tempered by a social safety net.[4] While new networks of roadways, mail, telephone, water, electricity, gas and sewage brought revelatory perceptions of communication and mass mobility to all citizens, the reintroduction of the *Betriebsrät*, the works councils outlawed by Nazism, gave greater senses of ownership in the economy at large.[5]

---

[2]Pól O'Dochartaigh, *Germany since 1945* (Houndsmills, UK: Palgrave MacMillan, 2004), 19, 23.
[3]Dennis L. Bark and David R. Gress, *A History of West Germany: From Shadow to Substance, 1945–1963* (Oxford, UK: Blackwell, 1993), 392–393.
[4]The paradigm of New Deal capitalism, lent by American bureaucrats assisting the drafting of the 1948 constitution, was to strengthen the economic, political and spiritual unity of West Germany as bulwark to communism.
[5]Arnold Symottel, 'From Starvation to Excess? Trends in the Consumer Society from the 1940s to the 1970s', in *The Miracle Years: A Cultural History of West Germany 1949–1968*, ed. Hanna Schissler (Princeton, NJ: Princeton University Press, 2001), 347.

Weimar era reformism and Bismarkian traditions of regulation were recovered in the promise to bind individuals to bourgeois democracy.

As much as it was predicated on a pacific equilibrium between state and capital, the 'miracle' owed to popular perceptions of measurable wealth. Subsequent booms in consumption – *Fresswelle* (the food wave), *Kleidungswelle* (the clothing wave), *Urblaubswelle* (the travel wave) – expanded taste cultures and material comfort.[6] The demand for things and the freedom to buy stabilized the budding republic in a collective consciousness able to recall pre-war hyperinflation, the Great Depression, wartime rationing and post-war hoarding followed by black marketeering (and now watching scenes of scarcity in East Germany). *Prosperity for All*, the title of Erhard's compiled writings published in 1957, caught the idea at the zenith of Adenauer's *Wiederaufbau* or 'reconstruction' politics. Individual encounters with modernization – televisions, refrigerators, washing machines, and automobiles at home; electric typewriters and punch cards at the office – were extended in sentiments of transnational cooperation when joining, first, the European Coal and Steel Community (its six signing foreign ministers were Christian Democrats) and, at the turn of the decade, the European Economic Community.[7] Affluence was to underwrite the social compact.

In this lay a reckoning with history. The embrace of managed *laissez-faireism* was a kind of 'denazification'. Erhard's wartime work at the Gesellschaft für Konsumforschung (Society of Consumer Research, which he cofounded in Berlin) undergirded his long-standing conviction that individual consumers – a force inimical to totalitarianism (*ex post facto* anti-fascism or burgeoning anti-communism) – could be the foundation of democracy.[8] The *Soziale Marktwirtschaft* was to chart a third way between capitalism and a planned economy by eschewing Anglo-American competition in favour of Catholic political thought emphasizing natural communities protected against excessive state intrusion and marketplace ravage.[9] At the same time, Adenauer's programme rested on bureaucratic continuity – his Secretary of State, Hans Globke, had penned Nazi commentaries informing the 1935 Nuremberg Race Laws – thereby exposing the limits of 'reconstruction'.[10] With the same officials once overseeing a fascist command economy now running an economically liberal republic, many wondered whether the wholesale shift to consumerism was inherently corrupted. Not dissimilar commentary from left and right warned of consumerism imperiling democratic self-realization based on shared understandings of a redemptive German humanist tradition – liberal, socialist or theological – and moral teachings. *Kultur* – what Norbert Elias had, immediately before the war, defined as the uniquely Germanic concept of intellectual, artistic and religious facts as opposed to political, economic or social ones (in other words,

---

[6] Michael Wildt, 'Consumption as Social Practice in West Germany', in *Getting and Spending: European and American Consumer Societies in the Twentieth Century*, eds. Susan Strasser et al. (Cambridge, UK: Cambridge University Press, 1998), 306ff.

[7] Arnold Sywottek, '"From Starvation to Excess?" Trends in the Consumer Society from the 1940s to the 1970s', in *The Miracle Years: A Cultural History of West Germany 1949–1968*, ed. Hanna Schissler (Princeton: Princeton University Press, 2001), 347.

[8] Alfred C. Mierzejewski, *Ludwig Erhard: A Biography* (Chapel Hill: The University of North Carolina Press, 2004), 13–26.

[9] Wolfram Kaiser, *Christian Democracy and the Origins of European Union* (Cambridge, UK: Cambridge University Press, 2007), 170; James C. Van Hook, *Rebuilding Germany: The Creation of the Social Market Economy, 1945–1957* (Cambridge, UK: Cambridge University Press, 2004), 139–188.

[10] West Germany safeguarded its seemingly fragile republic by outlawing neo-Nazi groups and the Communist Party.

works of art or philosophy 'in which the individuality of a people is expressed') – offered an antidote to the process-oriented or superficial effects of *Zivilisation* (and attendant threats of massification associated with the Third Reich).[11] The thesis carried Theodor Adorno and Max Horkheimer's *Dialectic of Enlightenment*, conspicuously republished for German audiences in 1947. Challenging the emancipatory project of Enlightenment reason, the Frankfurt School émigrés, poised to return to West Germany, apprehensively described a 'culture industry' when dismissing the standardized artistic fare of capitalism. Their critique underlay growing unease with the 'miracle'. Comfort was apparently too readily accompanied by smugness and self-satisfaction vitiating any viable sense of communality.[12] Fearing unceasing commodification of everyday life, with people seen as lost in a miasma of shopping and entertainment, thinkers such as Adorno and Horkheimer's student Jürgen Habermas reasoned that consumerism had robbed *Kultur* of its apposite adversarial role: to engage in political debate. A nascent 'public sphere' – Habermas' influential idea appeared at the very moment of Candilis–Josic–Woods's Frankfurt plan – risked being reduced to isolated spaces of private or familial intimacy instead of becoming a 'training ground for critical public reflection'.[13] Lessons in civics were still needed.

As such, and in the terms of Habermas's argument, modernism, as an equally educative and therapeutic institution, required reinstatement as the proper patrimony of German *Kultur*. One mid-1950s book, notably written in English, put it succinctly:

> Meanwhile it was quickly revealed, if at first only on paper, that, particularly in the field of architecture, ties with the creative thought of the period before 1933 had not been completely disrupted ... [and] it became clear that the students of Poelzig, Gropius, and Mies van der Rohe had not allowed the period of dictatorship to distort their architectural views.[14]

Works like Hans Schwippert's Bonn parliament begun in 1949, Egon Eiermann's West German pavilion at the 1958 Brussels world's fair or Mies' Neue Nationalgalerie commissioned in 1962 were promoted as maintaining an uninterrupted link between a pre-war 'international style' and the aesthetic-ethical values of the *Bundesrepublik*. Contemporaneity was paramount. As the newsmagazine *Magnum* recognized in a 1960 issue titled 'Haben die Deutschen sich verändert?' ('Have the Germans Changed?'), with a cover polemically contrasting photographs of a Nazi march, bombed-out buildings, and a cornucopia of foodstuffs, especially sausages:

> The Germans long to be part of the 'family of nations'. They are sick of standing apart, being alone, whether in a brilliant or in a miserable state. The yearning to be assimilated to the international standard of taste, desires and needs has engulfed their architecture as well as their menus. (No architect would dare to build an office block in any but the same style as his colleagues in Louisville, Nagasaki or Lyon. No urban restaurant would forgo serving 'Steak à la Hawaii' or Nasi Goreng.) The Germans

---

[11] Norbert Elias, *The Civilizing Process* (1939; Oxford, UK: Basil Blackwell, 1994), 4–5; Jan-Werner Müller, *Another Country: German Intellectuals, Unification and National Identity* (New Haven: Yale University Press, 2000), 23, 34.

[12] Paul Betts, *The Authority of Everyday Objects: A Cultural History of West German Industrial Design* (Berkeley: University of California Press, 2004), 129.

[13] Jürgen Habermas, *The Structural Transformation of the Public Sphere: An Inquiry into a Category of Bourgeois Society* (1962; Cambridge, MA: MIT Press, 1989), 29, 34; Betts, *The Authority of Everyday Objects*, 129, 239.

[14] Bruno E. Werner, *Modern Architecture in Germany* (Munich: F. Bruckmann, 1956), 12.

desperately want to strike lucky, and the world wants finally to have better luck with the Germans. So we are resolved to be happy and mediocre.[15]

Feelings of dispossession, alienation or political isolation were to be overcome in the outwardly modern forms of commodities, including buildings.

Receding impressions of deprivation led to another worry, almost an existential crisis. By 1960, unemployment dropped to 1.3 per cent, the housing shortage officially ended and West Germans saw themselves irrevocably enjoying ever-rising living standards.[16] Yet related nostalgia for Weimar modernism, upheld as untainted by Nazi *Volkskultur* (or Soviet socialist realism), contributed to a national act of suppressing memory: the affirmative heritage of modernist architecture, deliberately recast as stylistically inconspicuous ('happy and mediocre'), assisted in making the Third Reich invisible and imperceptible.[17] The wish for anonymity complemented Adenauer's paternalistic 'Chancellor Democracy' and its diminishing of traditions of oppositional liberalism – a situation that a pioneering American historian of German intellectual life traced to the post-nationalist language of the 1948 constitution or Basic Law:

> If the Junkers have disappeared and the military influence is in at least temporary eclipse, bureaucracy and industrialism have completely recuperated their wonted forms. Observers are in general agreement that democracy in Germany is still not so much a matter of active faith as a system of formal law and that its current liberal interpretation is the effect of Allied power, economic prosperity and anti-totalitarian resentment operating in a political vacuum.[18]

To many, the caesura encompassed an incapacity for confronting difficult histories. The mandarins of the 'miracle', tirelessly shaping a 'leisure society', were hardly preoccupied by *Vergangenheitsbewältigung*, a thorough reckoning of the past, but vigorously creating circumstances to forget it.[19] The resulting restorative vision of modern culture, including architecture tailored to *Wiederaufbau* needs, seemed incapable of fashioning an urban realm where society could regain some semblance of spiritual renewal.

Ruins

Along this long arc of tension, between economic miracle and social democracy, mechanized life and the rootedness of tradition, lay the conditions in which Candilis–Josic–Woods' Frankfurt-Römerberg

---

[15] Klaus Harpprecht, 'Die Lust an der Normalität', *Magnum* (April 1960), quoted in Wildt, 'Consumption as Social Practice in West Germany', 312.

[16] Bark and Gress, *A History of West Germany*, 395.

[17] Betts, *The Authority of Everyday Objects*, 187–188.

[18] Leonard Krieger, *The German Idea of Freedom: History of a Political Tradition* (Boston, MA: Beacon Press, 1957), 468.

[19] Theodor W. Adorno, 'The Meaning of Working through the Past' (1960), in *Guilt and Defense: On the Legacies of National Socialism in Postwar Germany*, eds. Jeffrey K. Olick and Andrew J. Pellerin (Cambridge, MA: Harvard University Press, 2010), 213–227. Adorno's critique – '"working through the past" does not mean seriously working upon the past, that is, through a lucid consciousness breaking its power to fascinate. On the contrary, its intention is to close the books on the past and, if possible, even remove it from memory' – rallied a 1960s generation dismayed by the perceived political compromises of the *Bundesrepublik*.

Figure 6.1 'Peace in our daily bread', CDU election poster, September 1953.
Source: Wiki Commons. This image was provided to Wikimedia Commons by the Konrad-Adenauer-Stiftung, a German political foundation, as part of a cooperation project.

proposal took hold. The programme followed that of countless cities: the removal of wartime rubble and reconstruction. Just as Germans in the 1930s had sought to re-establish a pre-war normality – respite from political conflict instability and financial catastrophe – West Germans of the 1950s craved recovery in the ambit of an advanced industrial nation ensuring material and cultural security.[20] The upheaval accompanying economic and urban growth was the accepted price of moving from *Zusammenbruchsgesellschaft*, the collapsed society of 1945–1949, to *Wirtschaftswunder*.

The Frankfurt-Römerberg architecture competition called for rebuilding a historic centre. On 22 March 1944, Allied night bombing levelled the city's medieval heart. 'I can still imagine Munich but no longer Frankfurt', wrote the Swiss architect and novelist Max Frisch; five centuries of urban tradition were replaced by simple footpaths winding through the destruction.[21] Now, the Hessian metropolis, briefly envisioned as the capital of the *Bundesrepublik* (Walter Gropius, the Bauhaus founder, had recommended as much during a quick return to his country in 1948), readied a *tabula rasa* for post-war ambitions. Candilis–Josic–Woods' winning project – set squarely between the *Dom* (cathedral), *Römer* (town hall) and Old St Nicholas Church, which had all survived bombardment – showed three terraced decks containing offices, markets, restaurants, workshops, art studios, galleries, auditoria, libraries, a

---

[20]Rudy Koshar, *Germany's Transient Pasts: Preservation and National Memory in the Twentieth Century* (Chapel Hill: The University of North Carolina Press, 1998), 245–246.

[21]Max Frisch quoted in Rudy Koshar, *From Monuments to Traces: Artifacts of German Memory, 1870–1990* (Berkeley: University of California Press, 2000), 155; K. Michael Prince, *War and German Memory: Excavating the Significance of the Second World War in German Cultural Consciousness* (Lanham, MD: Lexington Books, 2009), 77.

Figure 6.2 'Have the Germans changed?' 1960.
Source: *Magnum* Journal.

youth centre and music school, a cinema, a cabaret, an extension to the Historischen Museum and dwellings; below, two underground levels of parking and delivery roads allowed the complex to run autonomously. Approximating the dense fabric of European towns, the layout – multiple pedestrian routes leading to interior courtyards, roof terraces or the city beyond – could, the architects claimed, 're-establish the human scale and the relationship with the monuments'.[22] The metabolic intimacy of walking was to be restored by escalator and travellator, tools of *speed* and *consumption* nevertheless affording greater communion with others by reawakening quotidian experiences of the city. Desperate to supplant CIAM functionalism, but prey to its diagrammatic generalizations, Candilis–Josic–Woods drew on a Team 10 wish for a 'basic structure' supporting 'all the *prolongements du logis*: commercial, cultural, educational and leisure activities, as well as roads, footpaths and services'.[23] The corresponding 'web' accordingly used modular components, undoubtedly prefabricated and interchangeable, arranged on a divisible long-spanning structural grid. Here, deep in Frankfurt-Römerberg, was, Woods insisted,

---

[22] Georges Candilis, Alexis Josic and Shadrach Woods, 'Proposal for the Reconstruction of the Center of Frankfurt', *Le Carré Bleu* 3 (1963): n.p.
[23] Shadrach Woods, 'Urban Environment: The Search for System', in *World Architecture Today*, ed. John Donat (London: Studio Vista, 1964), 153.

nothing less than a 'framework' for a 'universal society' emerging from the 'breakdown' of preceding 'perceivable human groupings (villages and towns, classes, castes and sects)'.[24] Tinged by cybernetics discourse and systems theory, thus suggesting a totalizing model of history, Woods's schema was perfectly attuned to the operations of the welfare state – namely, the long-term management of 'wholes', whether people or cities.

The proposition neglected, though, the often desperate struggle between *Gemeinschaft* and *Gesellschaft*, between bureaucracy and kinship, as organizing principles of post-war life. Unlike before,

Figure 6.3 Frankfurt Altstadt, 1945.
Source: Wiki Commons. This image is the work of a US Air Force employee, made as part of that person's official duties. As a work of the US federal government, the image is in the public domain.

---

[24]Shadrach Woods, 'Web', *Le Carré Bleu* 3 (1962): n.p.

Kultur became adapted to *Amerikanismus* (the money economy) and bourgeois values.[25] Woods acknowledged the totalizing reality:

> Given the discipline of a continuous system frame, functions may be articulated without the chaotic results which we obtain when we pursue only the articulation of function without first establishing a total order. Indeed it is only within such a frame that function can be articulated. The parts of system take their identity from the system. If there is no order, there is no identity but only chaos of disparate elements in pointless competition.[26]

The 'search' for 'processes' revealed an architectural truth: 'we must dispense with the use of symbols and monuments, for the century has cast aside these crutches of authority. Indeed if authority can be said to exist it can only be through consent' – ballot-box democracy – 'and has no need of formalism or of allegories to impose itself'.[27] Woods' worldview – on architecture, on West Germany – betrayed an ingrained belief in an emancipatory modernism resisting ossified signs of power. Yet his deeply technocratic language disquietingly although unconsciously echoed a different rhetoric of 'order' (or 'discipline') previously imposed over politics (or 'chaos'). In 1933 or 1963, the modernizing impulse, left-wing or reactionary, held that society could be remade *in toto*. Stripping away the remnants of the past, the *deus ex machina* of the 'web' assured deliverance from former stylistic decadence by offering the barest means of place-making: strictly speaking, panels, ducts, columns.[28] Inside, a remarkable social world would grow: 'The problem of Frankfurt is not to make a museum of it, but to discover a system which the citizens can use to create their own environment.'[29] Granting the ability to remake the Römerberg complex – 'non-centric initially, poly-centric through use' – as a space of popular edification and commercialization was to guard against any authoritarian compulsion. Prefabrication as ethos, as purposefully appreciating the merits of obsolescence, would find users endlessly transforming spaces around them, thereby refusing to consecrate any outward style or political value.

This was the utopian dream. In their drive to make Frankfurters conform to principles of welfare state prosperity, Candilis–Josic–Woods, already expert in the *équipement* (including shopping) of the French *villes nouvelles*, saw the city centre as an architecture 'degree zero' unencumbered by style or convention. The considered a-formalism – a building drawn without façades – reflected the architects' vision of architecture and society unimpeded by *a priori* cultural codes.[30] The view on modernization was really an instance of late capitalism, or the penetration of industrialization into all aspects of life.[31] This too was part of the 'miracle': the obsession with economic advance at almost any expense abetted lifting the burden of 'memory' that went up in flames, along with centuries-

---

[25] Alan Colquhoun, 'Criticism and Self-criticism in German Modernism', in *Collected Essays in Architectural Criticism* (London: Black Dog, 2009), 302–312.
[26] Woods, 'Web', n.p.
[27] Ibid.
[28] Shadrach Woods, 'Frankfurt: The Problems of a City in the Twentieth Century', in *World Architecture Today*, ed. John Donat (London: Studio Vista, 1964), 156.
[29] Candilis et al., 'Proposal for the Reconstruction of the Center of Frankfurt', n.p.
[30] Alan Colquhoun, *Modern Architecture* (Oxford: Oxford University Press, 2000), 221.
[31] Fredric Jameson, 'Periodizing the 60s', in *The Ideologies of Theory: Essays 1971–1986* (Minneapolis: University of Minnesota Press, 1988), 205ff.

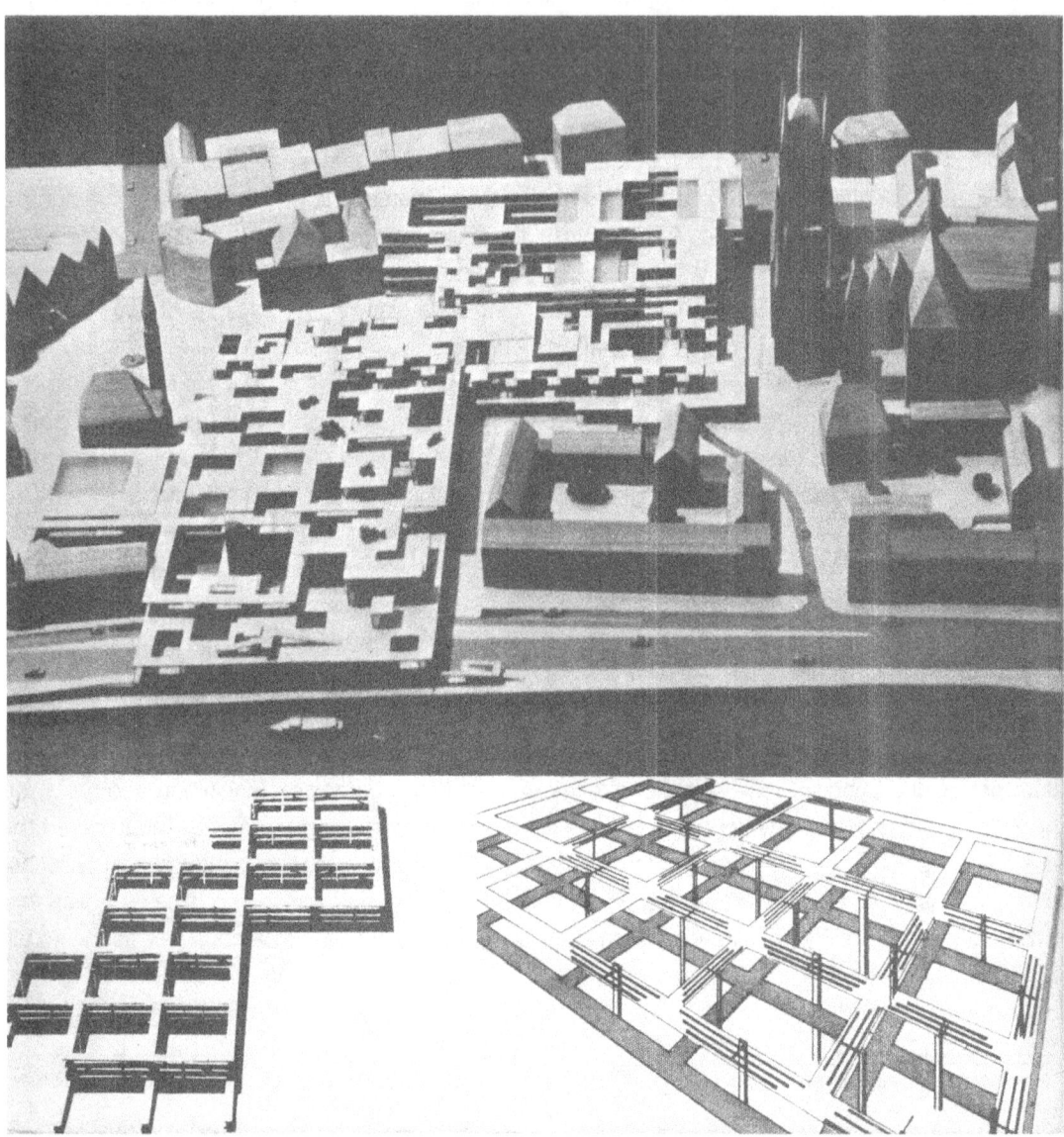

Figure 6.4 Candilis–Josic–Woods's Frankfurt-Römerberg 'web': a 'system' within medieval fabric.
Source: Le Carré Bleu 3 (1963): n.p.

old structures, between 1942 and 1945.³² Out of these ruins and their eventual disappearance, the architecture of reconstruction, whether the controversial reproduction of Goethe's destroyed house (symbol of German cosmopolitanism) in Frankfurt or Woods' 'system', eliminated ways of confronting the past.³³ Even as it promised a hopeful future of individual self-realization in an ever-changing commercial maze, Candilis–Josic–Woods' plan unwittingly added to effects behind what the psychoanalysts Alexander and Margarete Mitscherlich would describe in a best-selling book as 'the inability to mourn', their diagnosis of a population denying the horrors of the Third Reich by 'de-realizing' the Nazi period (and concomitant feelings of guilt). The obfuscation of history intertwined the present-day 'problem of political apathy' resulting from the deliberate redirection of social energy to consumerist distraction: West Germans, the Mitscherlichs observed, concentrated 'on the restoration of what had been destroyed' – building and cities – 'and on the extension and modernization of their industrial potential – down to, and including, their kitchen utensils'.³⁴ Making things and buying them had, it seemed, replaced the possibility of ever achieving shared senses of remembrance, thus identity.

As avatar of the 'miracle', Candilis–Josic–Woods' Frankfurt-Römerberg plan was finally to bring West Germany into European modernity. Despite the architects' insistence on cultural works, it was the commercial programme that fitted their plan to the *Bundesrepublik*. Elsewhere, increasing numbers of self-service stores – 'supermarkets' – guaranteed the plethora of choice while regimenting taste.³⁵ Shopping granted tranquillity unknown to several generations. Impressions of permanent affluence strengthened loyalty to the young republic and permitted greater emphasis on personal development.³⁶ As West Germans adopted industrialized forms of leisure – cars, televisions and holidays abroad – they began undoing the ties of neighbourhood-centred recreation and rest. It was a crucial sociological shift: whereas Nazi leisure was designed to unite and to bind, post-fascist leisure inclined towards dispersing and separating people from one another.³⁷ If individual efficiency and privatization of life were upheld as countering totalitarian massification, then the same phenomena also weakened expressions of collective space and time. The difficulty extended especially to Woods, who regarded 'society' as 'an unhierarchical association of autonomous individuals, with change providing the only constant element'.³⁸ Candilis–Josic–Woods' idealized 'open' future rested on the paradox that tradition had actually been destroyed by Nazism. The architects' plan became caught in this philosophical conundrum, one made even more nettlesome given West Germans' nagging suspicion of having turned

---

[32] W.G. Sebald, *On the Natural History of Destruction* (New York: Random House, 2003), 12–13.

[33] Walter Dirks, a leading Christian Socialist opposing the CDU reorientation towards free-market principles, would, as editor of the left-leaning monthly *Frankfurter Hefte*, denounce acts of architectural restoration for obliterating historical judgement in the late 1940s: 'There are connections between the spirit of Goethe House and the fate of its destruction'; Germans consequently needed the courage to accept both the 'bitter logic' that had reduced the Goethehaus to rubble and 'the verdict of history' as 'definitive'. See Koshar, *Germany's Transient Pasts*, 229–231.

[34] Alexander and Margarete Mitscherlich, *The Inability to Mourn: Principles of Collective Behavior* (1967; New York: Grove Press Inc., 1975), 8–9, 31ff.

[35] Sywottek, 'From Starvation to Excess?', 350.

[36] Wildt, 'Consumption as Social Practice in West Germany', 313–315.

[37] Betts, *The Authority of Everyday Objects*, 245.

[38] Woods, 'Urban Environment', 153.

the defect of industriousness, of immorally obeying orders, into a national virtue.[39] The organizational model to be imposed on Frankfurt may have corresponded to the Mitscherlichs' view that a welcome 'concept of "urbanity"' – 'cosmopolitanism' – was slowly reappearing; but the transformation anticipated in Römerberg – 'consumerism' as praxis – was simply another instance of escapist modernization that Alexander Mitscherlich condemned for contributing to the 'unlivability' of German cities by the mid-1960s.[40] 'Community' had, the argument went, been deformed by the interests of economic planning (including urbanism). Faced with designing big buildings for mass society, Candilis–Josic–Woods scarcely recognized, and possibly never accepted, that the very action of inhabiting their plan – to buy goods and ideas – was itself ideological, a process securing not the liberation of daily existence but its rationalization.

Ultimately, Candilis–Josic–Woods' unrealized plan only called into question whether traditional social-urban *Kultur*, which lay ruined, could be recreated with the tools of consumer-industrial *Zivilisation*. By chipping away at the 'Adolf Hitler Mountains', the dwindling but still looming piles of rubble, and by preserving individual buildings in an aesthetic context utterly dissimilar from the original neighbourhood setting, Frankfurt-Römerberg was spontaneously to generate a myth of origins in which West Germans saw themselves as happy modern consumers.[41] Ironically, Nazi Party officials and architects had once cultivated Frankfurt as a historical fantasy world, carefully conserving its picturesque *Altstadt* or old town to suit a kitsch consumer paradise.[42] Now, in 1963, its debris conferred conflicting notions on Germanness. For some on the left, 'ruins' demanded being left intact for the foreseeable future, thus becoming monuments to a shameful era and totems around which a more tolerant nation could arise.[43] For others, the mania to rebuild held little place for such bleak symbols. Ruins took on different powers: at first, by their removal, giving pride in reconstruction and a return to normality; but later, almost in their absence, enabling, the Mitscherlichs worried, a perverse logic of suffering, a 'one-sided memory' honouring those who died in the air raids but never 'the victims of the concentration camps, for the Dutch, Polish, or Russian victims of the Gestapo and the Special Squads'.[44] Perhaps acts of preservation could have assisted historical consciousness (or what the Mitscherlichs perceived as the German lack of empathy for the anguish of others); but the programme of urbanism in which Candilis–Josic–Woods participated was fundamentally arrayed against the pull of custom and national identity. Governed entirely by an inner functionality, the Frankfurt-Römerberg 'web' could never admit

---

[39]Alexander and Mitscherlich, *The Inability to Mourn*, 15.

[40]Alexander Mitscherlich, *Die Unwirtlichkeit unserer Städt: Anstiftung zum Unfrieden* (1965) quoted in Koshar, *Germany's Transient Pasts*, 277.

[41]Koshar, *Germany's Transient Pasts*, 246, 275.

[42]Ibid., 177–178.

[43]The Nazis had, well before the end of the war, celebrated their bombarded cityscapes as the ultimate sublime, the destruction giving sensations of human suffering as the sacrifice for a new Reich. Now, in the post-war decades, the preservation of historic buildings was to aid people in recognizing a natural connection between past and present without abusing history and style in the ways fascism had. A curious effect was the immediate creation in the late 1940s of large and realistic models of destroyed cities, including one of Frankfurt, with almost every tumbled brick rendered with exacting precision. See Helmut Puff, 'Ruins as Models: Displaying Destruction in Postwar Germany', in *Ruins of Modernity*, eds. Julia Hell and Andreas Schönle (Durham, NC: Duke University Press, 2009), 253–269.

[44]Alexander and Mitscherlich, *The Inability to Mourn*, 30.

any pretense to *völkisch*-ness, no matter how reassuring.[45] This was what it offered to the 'miracle'. The activities inside – grids upon grids of culture and consumerism – would acclimatize people to the good fortune of the present (while distancing them from any past difficulty). Candilis–Josic–Woods understood such intentions, having just designed an enormous commercial centre, truly a shopping mall, for Toulouse-Le Mirail, where another 'web' defined the new world of a French *banlieue* by the pressing logic of automotive mobility and mass retail.[46] Modernists to the last, the architects rarely considered these forces in opposition. Their Frankfurt labyrinth, leaving the mediaeval fabric behind, reached over to enclose a multilane fast road running along the Main river. To unite two cityscapes, to blur distinctions between old and new, was, as Woods insisted, to embrace 'our continuous society' (and never bygone 'compartmented societies').[47] The 'web' apparently could effortlessly negotiate *Altstadt* and *Autobahn*.

* * *

As the *Trümmer* or rubble scapes slowly vanished under architectures of the 'miracle', the psychology of metropolitan life changed forever. Out of places once pulverized beyond recognition and turned to dust emerged a world of cleanliness and order. In the desperate search for salubrity and stability, it was hard to know whether Candilis–Josic–Woods' plan befitted or lay at odds with a civic terrain riddled by histories of violence. Disinterring ruins could only uncover *necropoli*, a haunting archaeology of a horrible politics that many wished left buried and forgotten. Above, streets still experiencing the contradictions of denazification – anything overtly National Socialist, specifically neoclassical gigantism, had been ridiculed and razed; but fascist works in traditionalist and modernist veins continued to escape demolition – caused feelings of mediocrity and modesty in all efforts at rebuilding.[48] The insecurity left, in the eyes of the American architectural historian (and cold warrior) John Ely Burchard, who came looking for the West German 'phoenix', cities crowded with middling modernisms: 'curtains against which more brilliant individual achievements can be displayed'.[49] Reconstruction followed suit. In Frankfurt, an inconsistent strategy of preservation produced an inconclusive mediaeval–modern pastiche. The anodyne tableau of shopping district kitsch was, Burchard wrote, a 'failure': 'If this is what Ernesto Rogers meant when he called the Frankfurt restoration "a phenomenon of a merely culturalistic nature" … then he was no doubt completely right.'[50] Rogers, whose advocacy of architecture resolutely modern in technique but sensitive to historical context was denounced by Team 10 (and whose office partner Gianluigi Banfi was murdered at the Mauthausen-Gusen concentration camp), had dismissed the Römerberg results when describing recent European architecture in the American journal *Daedalus*: 'For the truth of an old environment cannot be repeated and the new requirements have not been

---

[45] Narratives of a triumphant modernism were also intended to counter the East German 'rediscovery' of classicism.
[46] Tom Avermaete, *Another Modern: The Post-war Architecture and Urbanism of Candilis-Josic-Woods* (Rotterdam: NAi Publishers, 2005), 303.
[47] Woods, 'Urban Environment', 152.
[48] Jeffry M. Diefendorf, *In the Wake of War: The Reconstruction of German Cities after World War II* (New York: Oxford University Press, 1993), 54–66.
[49] John Burchard, *The Voice of the Phoenix: Postwar Architecture in Germany* (Cambridge, MA: MIT Press, 1966), 2.
[50] Ibid., 26.

Figure 6.5 West German shopping district kitsch with the 'Römer Area' at upper left, shown in John E. Burchard, *The Voice of the Phoenix: Postwar Architecture in Germany* (Cambridge, MA: MIT Press, 1966), spread of page 25.
Source: Massachusetts Institute of Technology, by permission of MIT Press.

expressed.'[51] Perhaps the interregnum of old and new needed a greater view on the present than architecture could ever provide. On 20 December 1963, the Auschwitz trials began in Frankfurt. Over the next twenty-one months, as the city's resurrection continued, its residents met the legacies of a far different and vicious erasure of history.

Vergangenheitsbewältigung remained, however, elusive. The trials became hailed for using West German judges and law; but the verdicts proved inconclusive: in the end just a few 'monsters', the sadists behind the most heinous crimes, were ever isolated from many lesser 'fellow travellers', the supposedly ordinary or unwilling participants receiving lighter sentences or acquittal. With troubling circumlocution, West Germans could presume being free of culpability, free from a genocidal past – they were only neighbours living peacefully beside the perpetrators – and assiduously return to the tasks of the *Wirtschaftswunder*.[52] CDU demands of 'integration' – Adenauer's pursuit of democratization always

---

[51]Ernesto N. Rogers, 'The Phenomenology of European Architecture', *Daedalus* (Winter 1964): 370. On Rogers's confrontation with Team 10, see: Oscar Newman, *CIAM '59 in Otterlo* (Stuttgart: Karl Krämer Verlag, 1961).
[52]Rebecca Wittman, *Beyond Justice: The Auschwitz Trial* (Cambridge, MA: Harvard University Press, 2005), 6, 247; Norbert Frei, *Adenauer's Germany and the Nazi Past* (New York: Columbia University Press, 2002), 27–40.

involved assimilating compromised officials – trounced left-liberal pleas for 'justice'.[53] Under these conditions, Candilis–Josic–Woods' plan would have inevitably partaken in processes of exoneration: with its seemingly infinite programmes, their 'web' was to facilitate re-education to democracy via pedagogic means. Grids upon grids would lie atop ruins, a pacification of disturbing memories in architecture for the final conversion of former 'fellow travellers' to citizens and consumers.

That Candilis–Josic–Woods' Frankfurt-Römerberg plan coincided with Adenauer's last year as Chancellor was likely fitting. Whatever else, Christian Democrats had promised upheaval in all habits of consumption, whether of commodities or education or entertainment. Thus, also in 1963, Candilis–Josic–Woods won a competition to extend the Freie Universität Berlin (aptly named in 1948 at the dawn of the Cold War). Criticizing the atomization of knowledge, the architects again advanced a 'groundscraper' giving 'the minimum organization necessary to an association of disciplines'.[54] While the building would attain something of the social and political charge envisioned by Woods, far more radical ideas were in the offing. Mounting youth unrest, fully erupting in 1968, found a generation weaned on the *Soziale Marktwirtschaft* rejecting its institutions, including effects like Woods' 'web', for ostensive 'coca-colonization'.[55] On 2 June 1967, police killed a student, Benno Ohnesorg, during a demonstration against the visiting Shah of Iran in West Berlin. Towards the decade's end, Woods had, with increasing *nouvelle gauche* sentiment, sought architectures capable of resituating the 'man in the street'.[56] Now, shrill cries for direct action challenged the quest for a genuine public sphere once imagined in works like Frankfurt-Römerberg. A regime of home-grown West German terrorism would, in the early 1970s, coincide with severe global economic shocks upending the assumed ascendancy of an affluent society and regulated future of a European Community. All of it could only throw into crisis the compensatory project of welfare state urbanism as the ultimate vehicle of non-revolutionary reform.

---

[53] Jeffrey Herf, *Divided Memory: The Nazi Past in the Two Germanys* (Cambridge MA: Harvard University Press, 1997), 267, 291.

[54] Shadrach Woods, *Candilis-Josic-Woods: A Decade of Architecture and Urban Design* (Stuttgart: Karl Krämer Verlag, 1968), 208.

[55] A hilarious statement on 'coca-colonization' appears in the émigré director Billy Wilder's 1961 film *One, Two, Three*, in which James Cagney's harried Coca-Cola executive desperately tries to establish American-style consumerism in West Berlin. The student revolt aimed at delegitimizing a previous 'skeptical generation' (who, like Jürgen Habermas, were otherwise viewed as untainted by Nazism) for its fixation on democratizing German politics instead of the crypto-fascist features of the *Bundesrepublik* (not least given the CDU's selection of Kurt Georg Kiesinger, a former Nazi, as Chancellor in 1966). Yet by equating anti-fascism to anti-capitalism and anti-Americanism – an effect of a rebellion by those having only experienced widespread prosperity – the students paradoxically exculpated their parents (the 'Auschwitz generation'). See Müller, *Another Country*, 45–53.

[56] Shadrach Woods, *The Man in the Street: A Polemic on Urbanism* (Hardmondsworth, UK: Penguin Books, 1975).

Chapter 7

Collectivity in the prison of plenty: The French commercial centres by Claude Parent, 1967–1971
Tom Avermaete

They lived in a strange and shimmering world, the bedazzling universe of a market culture, in prisons of plenty, in the bewitching traps of comfort and happiness. Where were the dangers? Where were the threats? In the past men fought in their millions, and millions still do fight, for their crust of bread. Jérôme and Sylvie did not quite believe you could go into a battle for a chesterfield settee.[1]

In his 1965 novel *Les Choses*, Georges Perec describes the impact of mass consumption on a young couple, who work as part-time market researchers and dream of what they will be able to buy, impatient to consume: 'In the world that was theirs it was almost a regulation always to wish for more than you could have.'[2] Perec narrates how Jérôme and Sylvie wander through the mass consumer paradise, lost in the crowd, their focus not on their fellow shoppers but on the commodities themselves. He depicts the defeat of society where lifestyle is prioritized above interaction and communities are replaced by loose networks of acquaintances that are essentially interchangeable.

Such a world, for young adults from working-class background, had in the 1960s only just arrived in France. *Les Choses* narrates the story of a generation thrown into the turmoil of French modernization which was extremely swift and intense. According to scholar of French culture Kristin Ross:

> The speed with which French society was transformed after the war from a rural, empire-oriented, Catholic country into a fully industrialized, decolonized and urban one meant that the things modernization needed – educated middle managers, for instance, or affordable automobiles and other 'mature' consumer durables, or a set of social sciences that followed scientific, functionalist models, or a work

---

[1] Georges Perec, *Things: A Story of the Sixties*, translated by David Bellos (Boston, MA: David R. Godine, 1990), 49.
[2] Ibid.

force of ex-colonial labourers – burst onto a society that still cherished pre-war outlooks with all the force, excitement, disruption, and horror of the genuinely new.[3]

This period of growth, prosperity and abrupt social change became known as *Les Trente Glorieuses* or 'the thirty glorious years' and ranged from the liberation of France in 1944 to the economic downturn triggered by the oil crisis of 1973.[4]

Les Trente Glorieuses was also the era of the arrival of mass consumption in France. While consumption had served to differentiate class until the interwar period, the emergence of mass consumer society introduced more inclusive consumer patterns. Goods were no longer perceived as class specific and advertisers marketed products as classless. Mass distribution, which had formerly been resisted by the class-conscious French bourgeoisie, became more widely accepted because of the patronage of wealthy families.[5] However, that mass consumption was conceived of as classless did not mean that goods were affordable for the entire population or even a large proportion of it. French society experienced great change during the 1950s, but much of the working population did not gain the necessary purchasing power for the acquisition of new consumer goods until the 1960s.

Figure 7.1 Claude Parent, Centre Commercial Sens, 1967–1970. The capacity of the oblique function is activated to accommodate a new collective.
Source: Collection Frac Centre-Val-de-Loire, France.

---

[3]Kristin Ross, *Fast Cars, Clean Bodies. Decolonization and the Reordering of French Culture* (Cambridge, MA: MIT Press, 1996), 4.

[4]See Jean Fourastié, *Les Trente Glorieuses: La Révolution Invisible de 1946 à 1975* (Paris: Fayard, 1980). This decade also represents the stumbling and final collapse of the French Empire. It was marked by the first major Algerian uprisings in 1954, the referendum on African independence in 1958, the granting of that independence in 1960 and the Evian Accords that officially announced the hard-won independence of Algeria in May 1962.

[5]See Victoria de Grazia, 'Changing Consumer Regimes in Europe, 1930–1970: Comparative Perspectives on the Distribution Problem', in *Getting and Spending: European and American Consumer Societies in the Twentieth Century*, eds. Susan Strasser, Charles McGovern and Matthias Judt (New York: Cambridge University Press, 1998), 59–83. De Grazia explains how in the 1950s and 1960s mass distribution thrived amongst wealthy families who were cognizant of how to make their lives better, knew where to save money, had cars to drive themselves to new shopping centres, and had refrigerators at home to store food. De Grazia sees a 'one class market' taking shape by the 1960s.

Missionaries of mass distribution

The rapidly growing consumer society also witnessed the arrival of new actors in the built environment. From the late 1950s on the great names of mass retail appeared on the French firmament: Goulet-Turpin (1958), Carrefour (1959), Auchan (1961), Promodès (1961) and Intermarché (1970).[6] For many of these protagonists in the realm of mass consumption the United States was an important, albeit contested, point of reference.[7] Through the French national employers' federation (Conseil National du Patronat Français, or CNPF) they were able to participate in study trips to the United States that were organized from the late 1940s on.[8] Under the auspices of the Marshall Plan, the directors of the new mass retail companies were sent on 'missions' to study and evaluate the secrets of American prosperity and its relation to mass retail outlets. The United States government, acting first through the Economic Cooperation Administration (ECA), the agency that administered the Marshall Plan, and later through its successor, the Mutual Security Agency (MSA), conceived of and helped fund such travels.[9] Five hundred French missions and 4,700 delegates would visit American factories, farms and offices, but also supermarkets and shopping malls. France alone supplied over one-quarter of all trainees sent to the United States from Marshall Plan countries.[10]

Upon their return, the delegates of the retail companies reported that they had little to learn from the American firms at the technical level, but much to apprehend about selling. French business lacked market studies, adequate advertising and above all new concepts of self-service retail outlets. The French were impressed by the way the Americans were able to create a society in which the desire for a better life was central and not the fulfilment of basic needs as in post-war France: 'Americans have had the merit of finding the way to make their entire population live comfortably.'[11] As a mission report of 1954 indicates, the American strategy was to make everybody a consumer: 'This message of "Live better", repeated by all advertisers trying to sell their products, constitutes the background noise for all of American life – a sound punctuated by the ring of cash registers throughout the country.'[12] The means by which to achieve this generalization of consumer life were market research, advertising, standard products and generous credit combined with mass retail outlets.

---

[6]For a wider discussion of the introduction of these companies, see Chatriot Alain and Chessel Marie-Emmanuelle, 'L'Histoire de la Distribution: Un Chantier Inachevé', *Histoire, Économie & Société* 1 (2006): 67–82.

[7]Richard Kuisel illustrates how debates over American culture in post-war France were passionate in part because they were often based on the assumption that America was the inevitable future. Richard Kuisel, *Seducing the French: The Dilemma of Americanization* (Berkeley: University of California Press, 1993).

[8]On these study trips, see V. Guigueno, 'L'écran de la Productivité. Jour de Fête et l'Américanisation de la Société Française', *Vingtième Siècle* no. 46 (Avril–Juin 1995): 117–124 and 'What They Saw, What They Wrote, What We Wear. The American Experience in the Reports of French Marshall Plan Missionnaries', in *Catching up with America,* ed. D. Barjot (Paris: Presses Universitaires de Paris-Sorbonne, 2002), 197–206. On the mission of 1947: C. Lhermie, *Carrefour ou l'Invention de l'Hypermarché* (Paris: Vuibert, 2001), 5–6.

[9]International Cooperation Administration, *European Productivity and Technical Assistance Programs, A Summing Up, 1948–58* (Paris, 1959), 139.

[10]Some of these missions led to publications of insights and reports such as R. Uhrich, *Super-marchés et Usines de Distribution. Hier aux États-Unis, Aujourd'hui en France* (Paris: Plon, 1962).

[11]Claude Foussé, *Traits Caractéristiques De La Prospérité Américaine* (Paris: Société auxiliaire pour la diffusion des éditions de la productivité, 1953), 88.

[12]AFAP, *Rapport de la Mission d'Étude du Marché et Publicité* (1954), 8.

The missionaries of mass distribution in France were enthusiastic about the American strategy towards the good life, largely because they saw a great role for their own mass retail companies within it. But the trouble with France, as one report suggested, was that half its population was still outside the circuit of the economy and that it lacked the shop infrastructure to adequately spark the logics of mass distribution and consumption.[13] Many of the French missionaries, including Marcel Fournier of Carrefour, Gérard Mulliez of Auchan and André Essel of Fnac, therefore went on special training courses that were offered by the National Cash Register Company (NCRC) in Dayton. The main proponent of these courses, the Colombian businessmen Bernardo Trujillo, spoke of new mass retail outlets as 'factories for selling'. He urged participants to develop new spaces for mass consumption, based on the principle of self-service and equipped with abundant parking, where elements of entertainment would complement shopping.[14]

Exploring the spatio-dynamics of shopping

It was in this context of cross-Atlantic exchanges on mass consumption and the future of shopping that the young architect Claude Parent was contacted in 1954 through his friend, the sculptor Nicolas Schöffer, to design his first supermarket in Châtenay-Malabry for the already existing store chain of Goulet-Turpin. Parent had little relevant experience to approach this commission. He had studied at the École des Beaux-Arts in Toulouse (1936–1945) and had worked with the architect Ionel Schein.[15] With Schöffer he had experimented with projects for a 'Spatiodynamic City', which took the utopian form of housing

Figure 7.2 Claude Parent, Nicholas Schöffer, Design for supermarket at in Châtenay-Malabry, 1954. The project is composed of a series of large steel frame portico structures in which the various components of the shopping ensemble were situated.
Source: Collection Frac Centre-Val-de-Loire, France.

---

[13]The peasantry and the industrial workers might contribute as producers, but they still did not qualify as true consumers, as eager buyers of consumer durables.

[14]On the role of Trujillo, see Lhermie, *Carrefour*, 22 -26; E. Thil, *Les Inventeurs du Commerce Moderne: Des Grands Magasins aux Bébés-Requins* (Paris: Jouwen, 2000), 125 -127; B. Trujillo, 'Postface', cited in Thil, *Les Inventeurs*, 285 –311; Philippe Roger, *Rêves et Cauchemars Américains: Les États-Unis au Miroir de l'Opinion Publique Française, 1945–1953* (Villeneuve-d'Ascq, Presses Universitaires du Septentrion, 1996), 101; Rosa K. Walker, '*Tout sous un même toit*': *Le Discours sur l'Avenement du Supermarché et du Libre-Service en France, 1958–1963* (New York: Columbia University, 2002), 22.

[15]On this collaboration, see Silvia Berselli, 'Claude Parent and Ionel Schein: Une collaboration symbiotique en équilibre instable', in *Claude Parent, L'œuvre Construite, L'œuvre Graphique*, eds. Claude Parent, et al. (Orléans: HYX, 2010), 56–61.

on pilotis, with helicopters buzzing around the buildings and cars circulating between the pilotis.[16] These experiences, however, offered little guidelines for Parent to engage with the modern challenges that Jean Goulet, the director of the retail chain of Goulet-Turpin, posed to him. Goulet intended to create large new supermarkets that were inspired by an American model of self-service retail and that would offer a place to the rapidly developing principles of mass consumption and marketing.

Schöffer and Parent did not propose a supermarket, but a large commercial ensemble that, besides the supermarket, included several other places of consumption such as other stores, boutiques and cafes.[17] Their project was composed of a series of large steel frame portico structures in which the various components of the shopping ensemble were situated and which were connected through a large steel frame canopy, which was thought to act as a new collective space. The choice for the steel frame construction method was no coincidence; according to Schöffer and Parent, it installed the architectonic condition for the spatio-dynamics that the programme of mass consumption demanded. They believed that the steel frame structures could function as a perennial counter-form that emphasized the fleeting logics of mass consumption, while also offering an open frame in which the dynamic flow of consumer products, the many layers of publicity and the multiple advertisement and signs could be located.

Though schematic in nature, the project of Schöffer and Parent also clearly suggested that the supermarket should not be considered as an isolated figure but rather as a part of a larger set of mass consumption developments and above all – because of its interior structure – as a component of a new urban reality that was located in the fringes of the city. Jean Goulet was very enthusiastic about the proposal and was keen to realize such a larger urban and commercial ensemble in Châtenay-Malabry. However, Eugène Beaudouin, the renowned designer who was chief architect at the French service des Bâtiments Civils et des Palais Nationaux (BCPN) and responsible for the planning of the site in Châtenay-Malabry, rejected the proposal because of its unconventional character. Beaudouin considered the proposed shopping environment too large and too openly defined to be considered a worthwhile element of the new urban development. Schöffer and Parent's attempt to offer a frame for the logics and rhythms of mass consumption was considered an act of architectural imprecision. As a result, the project of Châtenay-Malabry was cancelled and Parent was asked by the directors of Goulet-Turpin to design more conventional supermarkets.

Coining the commercial centre

In 1957, Claude Parent joined Jean Goulet on a CNPF study trip to the United States to investigate the development of supermarkets and the first shopping malls in Detroit and Edina. Upon his return, Parent was asked to develop a series of supermarkets – also called *grand surfaces* – for the firm Goulet-Turpin at Antony (1958), Nanterre (1958), La Celle-Saint-Cloud (1958–1960) and Athis-Mons

---

[16]Nicolas Schöffer, Guy Habasque and André Giraud-Bours, *Nicolas Schöffer: [Space, Light, Time]* (Neuchâtel, Switzerland: Éditions du Griffon, 1963).
[17]Nadine Labedade, 'Nicolas Schöffer', *Frac Centre,* http://www.frac-centre.fr/index-des-auteurs/rub/rubprojets-64.html?authID=253&ensembleID=575&oeuvreID=7783, accessed 1 December 2015.

(1959). In all of these projects Parent continued his experiments with large spans in steel and concrete that would offer a lot of flexibility to house the dynamic programme of mass consumption.

It would, however, take until the end of the 1960s before Parent received his first commission for a series of full-fledged 'commercial centers' (*centres commerciaux*) from Goulet-Turpin. At the edge of existing cities or in the proximity of new towns (*villes nouvelles*) he designed four new commercial centres for Tinqueux (1967–1969), Sens (1967–1970), Ris-Orangis (1967–1970) and Epernay-Pierry (1968–1970) in a time span of two years. Parent's point of departure for all of these commissions was that the new reality of mass distribution and consumption had to be paired with a new fangled architectural approach. His commissioner, Jean Goulet, who was hailed in the national newspaper *Le Figaro* for his sharp critique of 'the triumph of the hangar style' in new shopping centres, shared Parent's point of view.[18] Parent was critical, even dismissive, of the way that the new programme of the commercial centre was approached in architectural terms in the United States. He repeatedly condemned the architecture of the American shopping centre as 'architectural pollution'[19] and a 'simulacrum': 'An architecture that is ignorant of its specific means, covers its misery by selling itself to the industry, by identifying to the object and by adoring the golden calf of the automobile. It flees the responsibility of imagining its future by becoming more mobile.'[20]

Parent was particularly dismissive of the conservative architectural approach of the American shopping centres, which was based on very conventional spatial conceptions and in its collective zones merely mimicked the urbanity of the American main street or even of an idealized version of the European city. As an alternative Parent proposed a whole new spatial conception, which would be more in tune with the new reality of mass consumption and mass production: the oblique function.

Figure 7.3 Claude Parent, Model of Centre Commercial Ris-Orangis, 1967–1970.
Source: Collection Frac Centre-Val-de-Loire, France.

---

[18] J.C.M., 'GEM…Le Contemporain', *Le Figaro*, 20 April 1971.
[19] Claude Parent, 'Simulacre', *Architecture Principe* no. 5 (1966): 3.
[20] Ibid., 1.

He had been experimenting with his theories of the oblique function since the mid-1950s in the context of commissions for churches, claiming that these out-of-the-ordinary functions offered the appropriate setting to test a new relation between body and space, as well as a new way of moving through buildings.

The main architectural strategy to achieve this novel relation between body and space, Parent believed, was to discard the idea that architecture was composed of horizontal and vertical planes and to introduce the inclined surface. Such an architecture of inclined surfaces, an 'oblique architecture' in Parent's words, would not only create a new relation between different architectural elements such as

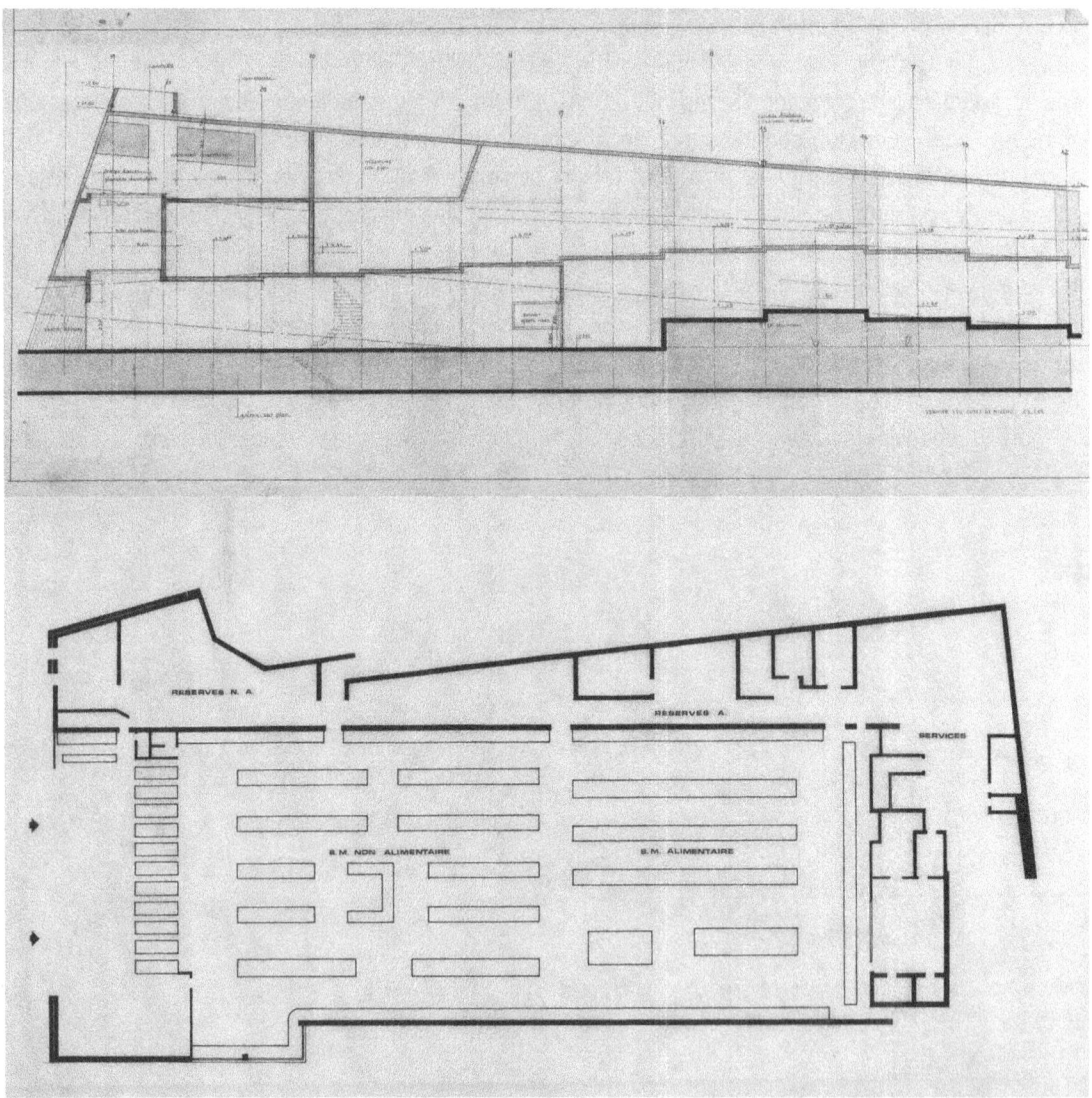

Figure 7.4 Claude Parent, section and plan of Centre Commercial Ris-Orangis, 1967–1970. The oblique function made transition spaces obsolete and combined the diverse spaces of the commercial centre in a continuous landscape.
Source: Collection Frac Centre-Val-de-Loire, France.

floors, walls and ceilings, but would also introduce a new fangled experience of space. By rearticulating the conventional geometry of space, the habitus of spatial experience would be dislocated and the possibility for a new perception would emerge. As early as 1957, when he designed his own house in Paris, Parent developed the spatial syntax of such an architecture of disequilibrium, which took the form of a dwelling space that 'seemed to rise up, fracture and then tumble back down to the ground'.[21]

A new realm of people, goods and information

The typology of the commercial centre offered Parent a new opportunity to elaborate his conceptions of an oblique architecture. It was especially the capacity of the oblique function to accommodate a new collective that interested him in his designs for the commercial centres. Parent believed that the non-conventional character of oblique architecture, its very dislocation of the traditional spatial definitions of the horizontal and the vertical, provoked the possibility for a new articulation of the social realm.

However, Parent did not define the social realm in terms of the relation between the public and the private, between the collective and the individual. He also distanced himself from the understanding of the social realm in terms of age groups as the French government applied in new housing estates, differentiating between children, adolescents, grown-ups and the elderly.[22] For Parent, all of these categories seemed obsolete within the world of the commercial centre. He was convinced that the very practice of mass consumption was modernizing and cut across these different categories. More specifically, he held that the practice of mass consumption had the emancipatory power to redefine the very character and composition of the social realm. Such a new social realm would no longer be composed of simple gatherings of individuals, but rather of new and complex formations of people, goods and information. The commercial centre with its dense flows of consumers, its endless stream of commodities and thick clouds of advertisements was considered as one of the ideal places where such a new formation could emerge. Parent imagined that the people, products and information could develop new affinities and enter into new relations. Just as many of his contemporaries, he strongly believed in the agency of the consumer-citizen that would be able to fashion these new relationships between people, products and information and by doing so create an entirely new collectivity.

This new collectivity between people, products and information was however not something that would grow naturally according to Parent. Many of the commercial centres in the United States were predefining these relationships and thereby turned the consumer-citizen into a 'dupe' – a mere plaything of commercial strategies. Parent envisaged a more heroic role for the consumer-citizen, one that implied an active and critical position *vis-à-vis* fellow consumers, products and publicity. The consumer would become the main and independent agent of the new collective realm: 'The oblique function forces

---

[21]Frederic Migayrou, 'The Definition of a Critical Architecture', in *The Function of the Oblique: The Architecture of Claude Parent and Paul Virilio 1963-1969*, ed. and trans. Pamela Johnston (London: Architectural Association, 1996), 60.
[22]See my discussion of this in Tom Avermaete, 'A Thousand Youth Clubs: Architecture, Mass Leisure and the Rejuvenation of Post-War France', *The Journal of Architecture* 18, no. 5 (2013): 632–646.

man to be consciously participative and offers a specific "POTENTIAL CHARGE" to each individual, stimulating his autonomy.'[23]

Architecture could play an important role in the constitution of a new individual consumer but also of a new commercial collective realm. The oblique concrete architectural landscape that Parent designed was the sturdy support for this fleeting new formation. Parent thought of his shopping centres as large concrete landscapes; continuous topographies that had to be explored by the citizen-consumer. This continuous character was a propinquity of the oblique form of the landscape that erased many of the traditional thresholds such as stairs, steps and entrance doors that could be found in more traditional shopping centres.

The oblique function made transition spaces obsolete and combined the diverse spaces of the commercial centre in a continuous landscape. The continuity of the concrete landscape did, however, not only rely on the oblique function. It also depended on an inclusive attitude *vis-à-vis* the various components of the mass consumption programme. In his concrete landscape, Parent included a set of spaces that were normally treated as separate from the very building of the commercial centre. Infrastructural spaces such as loading quays and parking spaces were incorporated in Parent's concrete logic and became full-fledged parts of the collective landscape of mass consumption: 'Concrete used in a roughly casted fashion ... emerges as a zoomorphic element from the floor of the parking and upward.'[24]

Parent's commercial centres were designed to bring a whole new experience of shopping to France. In the commercial centre of Sens, citizen-consumers park their cars on a futuristic-looking concrete landscape from which a large mountainous concrete formation arises. After entering one of the cavern-like entrances in this formation, visitors find themselves on a sturdy interior landscape of oblique paths and surfaces. Closed off from the outside world and disoriented by the oblique function, they climb the landscape and gradually discover a modern universe of mass consumption. Along their path towards the main hypermarket they are confronted with three levels of niches with commercial functions such as newspaper shops and fashion boutiques but also exhibition spaces in which installations on modern furniture, decoration and design prepare the mind of the consumer for the world consumer goods to come.

Following the example of the Galleries Lafayette in the city centre of Paris, Goulet-Turpin paid ample attention to these exhibitions about contemporary design, interior decoration and furniture. Jean Goulet maintained in several interviews that 'the education of the public is nowadays achieved in the big shops'.[25] Even though the Goulet-Turpin chain could not invite grand international curators like the Italian designer Gio Ponti that Lafayette showcased, they did collaborate with national initiatives on furniture and design such as the Centre de Création du Meuble (CREAC) to bring the objects and atmospheres of modern life to the visitor.

---

[23]Claude Parent, 'Structure', *Architecture Principe* no. 3 (1966): 7.
[24]Notes accompanying the design of the commercial centre in Sens, see also Audrey Jeanroy, 'Claude Parent', *Frac Centre*, http://www.frac-centre.fr/index-des-auteurs/rub/rubprojets-64.html?authID=143&ensembleID=370&oeuvreID=7661, accessed 20 December 2015. 'Le béton dans son emploi en brut de décoffrage souligne le mouvement implicite de l'architecture. Celle-ci se définit comme une flèche géante vers l'entrée, comme une émergence zoomorphe depuis le sol du parking'.
[25]Interview with Jean Goulet, *Le Figaro*, 20 April 1971.

Collectivity in the prison of the plenty

Educating the new consumer-citizen was part of the ambition of the new French commercial centres of Goulet-Turpin and the exceptional architectural experience that Parent created within his concrete shopping topographies contributed to these educational ambitions. The redefinition of walls and floors into an oblique formation was symbolically paired with the re-articulation of goods into commodities. Together the oblique architecture and the commodities installed the atmosphere of a new material *bien-être* (well-being) that was for sale in the *centre commercial* – echoing the strategy of creating a desire to 'Live Better' that the missionaries of mass retail had encountered some years earlier in the United States. As the critic Gerald Tassiot noted in the journal *Art et Architecture*, Jean Goulet understood all too well that the architectural design of Claude Parent played a paramount role in articulating the atmosphere of modern life that could be purchased in his shops. Tassiot, however, questioned the role that designers should play in providing such 'an architecture that sells'.[26]

One of the most prominent characteristics of the commercial centres by Parent is without a doubt their telluric concrete quality. The centres are vast concrete landscapes that seem to create a novel topography while being firmly bound to the territory that they are situated in. This particular choice for the large-scale use of concrete might be looked upon as part of a wider research that Parent had also pursued in other oblique projects such as the well-known church of Sainte-Bernadette-du-Banlay in

Figure 7.5 Claude Parent, Centre Commercial Ris-Orangis, 1967–1970. Infrastructural spaces such as loading quays and parking spaces were incorporated in Parent's concrete logic.
Source: Collection Frac Centre-Val-de-Loire, France.

---

[26]Gérald Gassiot-Talabot, 'Une Architecture qui Fait Vendre', *Art et Architecture* no. 10 (1969): 17.

Nevers of 1962. However, Parent maintained that his material preference corresponded to an ambition to support the 'light' logics of mass consumption by a more grounded and perennial architecture. The unconventional formal composition of the commercial centres provokes associations with the contemporaneous experiments to articulate future spatial systems in science-fiction movies, but their concrete material presence also grounds them strongly in the here and now. The vast concrete commercial centre was for Parent simultaneously a distinct universe of mass consumption and another ordinary element in the suburban territory of Sens. In his view, the concrete topography of the commercial centre complemented the already existing landscape of old villages and new suburban developments in the southern territory of Paris in a self-evident way.

In the photography that Parent commissioned for Sens, this dual role and the resulting ambiguous characteristics of the commercial centre were intentionally staged: the landscape of mass consumption is pictured as the receptacle of the newest shopping carts that enable the practices of mass consumption, and of a wooden push car which reminds viewers of an older form of trade – though this last one appears as uprooted. The message is clear: both the long-standing inhabitant of the village and the new suburban dweller participate in the modernity of the commercial centre, they are part and parcel of it. The oblique architecture enables this simultaneity; by deconstructing and redefining the spatial articulations it not only dissolves the borders between inside and outside but also between building and territory and as such opens the field for a new collectivity that is composed of *habitués* (regulars) and newcomers, of consumers, traffic and information.

Retroactive collectivity

On 3 September 1969, the first Goulin-Turpin commercial centre opened in Ris-Orangis in the South of Paris along the national road N7. It had taken one year and 10,895 tons of concrete and steel to complete the building. The commercial centre was welcomed by the professional press as 'the equivalent of the commercial street in the traditional city'[27] and in popular newspapers like *L'Express,* it was positively presented as 'a cathedral of consumption'.[28] For generations of shoppers the commercial centre of Ris-Orangis would become the site where they discovered the burdens and pleasures of mass consumption with advertisements, standard products and self-service counters at their disposal. An inhabitant of Ris, who was a child at the time, remembers the appearances of sport champions like the skiers Jean-Claude Killy and Marielle Goitschel, the soccer player Raymond Kopa and the cyclist Raymond Poulidor. 'It was the biggest commercial centre in the area, the trendy place of Paris, a sporting goods company had moved, the stars came to sign autographs and promote the brands', he recalls.[29] The same promotional strategies were applied in the other commercial centres at Sens, Tinqueux and Epernay-Pierry.

---

[27]Ibid.
[28]*L'Express*, 19 October 1970.
[29]Matt Olson, Ro Studio Blog, http://www.letemps.ch/lifestyle/2015/05/29/un-supermarche-bientot-inscrit-aux-monuments-historiques, accessed 1 December 2015.

In spite of all the architectural efforts and commercial strategies that were deployed to turn the commercial centres of Claude Parent into true centres of social life, they did not live up to the expectations of their designer. The new collectivity engendered by the oblique architecture was not as spectacular as expected and did not substantially differ from the collective formations in other shopping centres in France. Throughout the years the commercial centres changed owners, were heavily transformed and painted and gradually became generic and unremarkable occurrences in the vast suburban landscapes in which they were constructed.

Or so it seemed. A few years ago the retail firm Carrefour announced its plans to demolish the commercial centre of Sens because it no longer complied with the state-of-the-art logics of mass consumption at the beginning of the twenty-first century. Surprisingly, this quite ordinary news generated an extraordinary and broad public movement almost instantly. Letters were published in newspapers, blogs were started and web pages published – often by people that were not professionally involved with architecture and urban planning.[30] These citizens argued that they recalled the visit to the oblique architecture of the commercial centre as a meaningful and unforgettable life experience that should be protected and preserved as trace of a meaningful past. In 2011, their plea to protect and safeguard the centre was heard and Parent's commercial centre in Sens became the first protected commercial monument of the second half of the twentieth century in France.[31] Many years after its conception the collective of Parent's commercial centre stood up, forcefully fought and victoriously won its 'prison of plenty'.

Figure 7.6 Claude Parent, Centre Commercial Sens, 1967–1970. The landscape of mass consumption as the receptacle of mass consumption, and of older forms of trade.
Source: Collection Frac Centre-Val-de-Loire, France.

---

[30]Matt Olson, Ro Studio Blog, http://www.rolublog.com/2009/11/afin-de-poursuivre-notre-action-de-protection-du-centre-commercial-de-sens-dessine-par-monsieur-claude-parent-jai-fait-editer-une-carte-postale-de-soutien-qui-doit-agir-comme-une-petition-amusante-e/, accessed 1 December 2015.
[31]'Un centre commercial de Claude Parent devient monument historique', *Le Moniteur*, 21 June 2011, http://www.lemoniteur.fr/article/un-centre-commercial-de-claude-parent-devient-monument-historique-14822565, accessed 1 December 2015.

Chapter 8

Hello, consumer! Skärholmen Centre from the Million Programme to the mall
Jennifer Mack

In every person's heart, there are, of course, two souls: a socialist who wants to share with others, not just keep everything for himself, and a capitalist who wants to keep what he has for himself. That is expressed in the tensions and conflicts between all the demands on society on the one hand, and citizens' willingness to pay taxes on the other.

Albert Aronson, Executive Director, Svenska Bostäder,
developer of Skärholmen, 1968[1]

On 8 September 1968, in front of 150,000 people, Prince Bertil of Sweden inaugurated Skärholmen Centre, the nucleus of a new town that featured outdoor squares, shopping and community services on the outskirts of Stockholm.[2] This *centrum* – 'Scandinavia's largest suburban town centre'[3] – emerged in the heyday of the so-called Million Programme, as welfare state politicians and architects constructed over one million dwelling units between 1965 and 1974, often in suburbs developed at high speed, on previously unbuilt land, and along new transit lines.[4] In Stockholm, they followed not only the guidelines that the national Housing Board developed in publications like *God Bostad* (Good Housing) but also

---

All translations from the Swedish are by the author. I would like to thank the editors and Helena Mattsson for their thoughtful comments on earlier drafts of this chapter.

[1] Barbro Salaj, 'Hej konsument. Demokratin bakom Skärholmen', *Sveriges Television*, 23 October 1968.

[2] '150 000 invigde nya Skärholmen. Ström av premiärpublik kom med fyllda T-tåg', *Svenska Dagbladet*, 9 September 1968, 1; Ulf Hård af Segerstad, 'Skärholmens budskap: "Du skall konsumera!"', *Svenska Dagbladet*, 9 September 1968, 5; Whim, 'Fyrverkeri och prinstal invigde nya Skärholmen', *Svenska Dagbladet*, 9 September 1968, 10; 'Nu börjar kriget om kunderna. Skärholmens centrum invigt med fyrverkeri och barngråt', *Dagens Nyheter*, 9 September 1968, 7; 'Lennart kom bort i Skärholmen', *Dagens Nyheter*, 9 September 1968, 13.

[3] '150 000 invigde nya Skärholmen'.

[4] The Million Programme *centrum* model was used across Sweden: from Rinkeby in Stockholm to Angered in Gothenburg to Ronna in Södertälje. All of these new centres were designed to include social, cultural and commercial facilities from the outset.

the strict prescriptions included in the municipality of Stockholm's *Planstandard 1965*, forming rings around major Swedish cities.[5]

This chapter examines Skärholmen Centrum from its opening through the 1980s to unravel the complicated threads linking Swedish 'community' and 'consumerism' and how they played out in this high-profile, planned environment. Skärholmen shifted from what Prince Bertil proudly described as the 'mecca of urban planners'[6] to an object of public disgust just days after its inauguration. American observer Marquis W. Childs famously labelled the Swedish 'Middle Way' in 1936 as a marriage between socialism and capitalism; this chapter argues that the *centrum* synthesized both the synergies and dissonances of this pairing in urban and architectural design.[7] When the new complex appeared in a Swedish public television programme called 'Hello, Consumer!' (*Hej konsument!*), images depicted conveyor belts of identical new goods traveling into the retail space and shopping carts of the new everyday resident. While the new city nucleus became a paradigm of the civic infrastructure that Social Democratic politicians aspired to spread over the newly modern and freshly urbanized country, it was met with accusations of being merely a shopping centre in semantic disguise.

Figure 8.1 Inauguration ceremony of Skarholmen Center, September 1968, photograph by Gino Forsell. *Source:* Håkan Forsell.

---

[5]*Planstandard 1965: Förslag till stadsplanestandard för nya flerfamiljshusområden i Stockholm* (Stockholm: Stockholms stadsbyggnadskontor, 1965). In this publication, the authors write: 'With the tight timeframe that is now the rule, one can speak of a single, continuous planning design and production process in which the phases overlap. The more comprehensive planning and local development planning are interwoven, the greater the need to identify the general principles that must guide the urban planning work early on' (3).

[6]'Nu börjar kriget'.

[7]Marquis W. Childs, *Sweden: The Middle Way* (New Haven: Yale University Press, 1936).

Using representations of Skärholmen in the media, including architectural trade journals, television and radio programmes, and newspaper articles from its inauguration to the 1990s, this chapter traces the tensions between Skärholmen's conflicting roles, represented alternately as a consumer paradise and civic purgatory. If civil society and the market are typically presented as architectural and social antagonists in histories of burgeoning European welfare states from the 1930s to the 1960s, recent scholarship has argued that they were actually intertwined in an osmotic relationship from the outset: an interconnection that becomes emblematic in Skärholmen.[8] This chapter investigates how the civic and the commercial were, in fact, continuously complementary from the 1930s to the 1960s, and how new forms of civic engagement found ways to seep into this paragon of commerce by the early 1970s.

The social *Centrum*

Strategically locating cultural and social programme features like community centres and the Workers' Educational Association near to stores – which would naturally draw customers – served as a legitimate basis for political involvement to develop *centra* like Skärholmen across Sweden: they furthered the cause of Social Democratic community building.[9] Government reports known as the State's Public Investigations (SOU) highlighted these new urban landscapes as spaces of interchange, where modern Swedish citizens were to meet in state-sanctioned ways. Stringent state regulations on commerce (such as limited opening hours) met new standardized products requiring ever-larger 'self-service' shops and refrigeration.

The Ministry of the Interior's seven-part *Boendeservice* reports highlighted these social aims. Sociologists Mats Franzén and Eva Sandstedt argue that the definition of 'service' shifted from part one (published in 1968, when Skärholmen was inaugurated), offering a vague definition that left the content implicit, to part two (published in 1970), emphasizing the possible iterations for social and ideological programme pieces.[10] While the *centrum* took an ostensibly civic role from its inception, the focus on service in the later reports emphasized facilities to encourage social interactions between citizens as a critical planning problem.

Here, for example, an avian enthusiast might join a birdwatching 'study circle' or a new mother might learn about infant sleep patterns from a housewives' group. The carefully researched 'service' (including everything from day cares to kiosks to laundry rooms) on offer would contribute to the development of a society in which social and cultural functions reinforced the Social Democratic ideologies of the time.[11] Shopping – seen as complementary to these services – should be streamlined and modernized.

---

[8]On Skärholmen, see Helena Mattsson, 'Where the Motorways Meet: Architecture and Corporatism in Sweden', in *Architecture of the Welfare State*, eds. Mark Swenarton, Tom Avermaete, Dirk van den Heuvel (London: Routledge, 2014), 154–175. See also Kenny Cupers, *The Social Project: Housing Postwar France* (Minneapolis: University of Minnesota Press, 2014); Dirk van den Heuvel and Tahl Kaminer, 'Defying the Avant-Garde Logic: Architecture, Populism, and Mass Culture', *Footprint Journal* 8 (2011): 1–5.

[9]Mats Franzén and Eva Sandstedt, *Välfärdsstat och byggande: Om efterkrigstidens nya stadsmönster i Sverige* (Uppsala: Arkiv förlag, 1981).

[10]Ibid., 34–35.

[11]Johan Rådberg, *Doktrin och täthet i svenskt stadsbyggande 1875–1975* (Stockholm: Statens råd för byggnadsforskning, 1988), 376.

According to the tenets of both *Jantelagen* (literally the 'Jante Law', the unwritten but pervasive rule that no Swede should regard him- or herself as better than any other) and 'Middle Way' Swedish governance, however, it should also be discreet. Commerce provided an opportunity to display Swedish modernity and ingenuity but was to remain primarily a necessity component of the design.

While the SOU reports emphasized social and cultural 'residential service' (*boendeservice*) in new town centres like Skärholmen, the reality was that the innovative complex primarily dedicated its floor space to commercial functions.[12] Skärholmen Centrum opened with 73,771 square metres of retail area (shops and restaurants), compared with only 10,308 square metres devoted to social purposes and 9,064 square metres dedicated to educational, leisure, cultural and gathering spaces.[13] Social Democratic 'resident service' reports aside, Skärholmen developed overtly and proudly as both a *centrum* and a shopping centre.

As architectural historian Helena Mattsson has recently argued, in fact, the story of the Million Programme has typically been 'oversimplified' to omit what was actually a strong 'Swedish corporatist policy'.[14] From the political point of view, a new kind of citizen would be produced through consumption and catered to in these spaces; personal development for the advantage of the Swedish state was paramount, but the way to achieve this was nonetheless through a 'corporatist democracy'.[15] In the space of the town centre, the reality was that the development of Skärholmen depended on a deep and abiding alliance between commerce and civic functions where, for example, a shop window in the new complex advertised a 'new happy city' where 'new beautiful clothing habits, inside and out' would be on offer.[16]

Such representations appeared as a unifying theme of descriptions of Skärholmen's appearance, where commentators contended that shopping comprised the primary component of the neighbourhood's architectural image. Ulf Hård af Segerstad, writing for the national newspaper *Svenska Dagbladet*, described this as follows:

> When the visitor stands with his back against the subway station, which itself is one long bazaar building, he sees literally nothing other than this castle for merchandise. This consumer organization's

---

[12]The seven-part Boendeservice series, which the Ministry of the Interior (Inrikesdepartementet) undertook, appeared from 1968 to 1973. Specifically, these are SOU 1968:38, *Boendeservice 1* (Stockholm: Inrikesdepartementet, 1968); SOU 1970:68, *Boendeservice 2. Mål, finansiering av lokaler, utvecklingsprojekt* (Stockholm: Inrikesdepartementet, 1970); SOU 1971:25, *Boendeservice 3. Kommunstudien* (Stockholm: Inrikesdepartementet, 1971); SOU 1971:26, *Boendeservice 4. Projektstudien - en redovisning av aktuella serviceanläggningar* (Stockholm: Inrikesdepartementet, 1971); SOU 1971:27, *Boendeservice 5. Totalkostnadstudien - en diskussion av ekonomiska konsekvenser av några former av boendeservice* (Stockholm: Inrikesdepartementet, 1971); SOU 1971:28, *Boendeservice 6. Strukturstudien - tio uppsatser om samhällsförändringar som påverkar boendeservice* (Stockholm: Inrikesdepartementet, 1971); and SOU 1973:24, *Boendeservice 7. Verksamheter. Planering och organisation. Ekonomiska frågor. Exempel* (Stockholm: Inrikesdepartementet, 1973).

[13]These included standardized, up-to-the minute amenities like libraries, hobby spaces, sobriety clubs, churches, post offices, youth centres and stores offering industrialized goods. For more on standardization and the interface between modernist architecture and consumption, see Helena Mattsson and Sven-Olov Wallenstein (eds.), *Swedish Modernism: Architecture, Consumption and the Welfare State* (London: Black Dog, 2010).

[14]Mattsson, 'Where the Motorways Meet', 154–175.

[15]Ibid., 157–158.

[16]Image in montage included in Salaj, 'Hej konsument'.

Domus Palace has dressed in an architectural masquerade costume of nearly Egyptian type, with powerful, rounded wall columns and other vertical and horizontal articulations whose only purpose, with the massive brown-red building mass, is to express power.[17]

If the power of Skärholmen was the power of shopping, such opportunities to purchase new modern products in this late modernist urban environment should be available to the region at large, including some areas that had yet to be built.

A regional centre

Skärholmen Centrum closely adhered to the models that government officials had envisioned for all of urban Sweden, operating as a premier example of the *centrum* type and the largest to date. Formally, as in other *centra* across Sweden, the designs for Skärholmen drew on American planner Clarence Perry's notion of 'neighbourhood unit', which provided scientific principles to determine walking distances between shopping areas and housing, and for children between home and school, focusing on six critical elements: size, borders, open spaces, institutions, shops and an internal traffic system.[18] They also incorporated design ideas from CIAM's Functional City, typically providing a strict separation between vehicular and pedestrian traffic.

In Stockholm, Million Programme areas comprised transit-oriented developments, as it was in Skärholmen; storefronts and the subway entrance lined the *centrum*'s rectangular, open square. Even so, planners envisioned Skärholmen as a 'regional' rather than merely a neighbourhood centre, with a catchment area serving 300,000 people across newly expanded municipal boundaries. Unlike earlier *centra*, its users were not limited to those in the immediate surroundings, and many of these would live in the projected, nearby new municipality of Botkyrka, for which ground on Million Programme urban planning and architectural interventions had not broken upon Skärholmen Centre's inauguration. Arriving from beyond traditional neighbourhood borders by car, these shoppers would speed from the new surrounding highway into a spot in a modern parking garage. As a major node in an emerging regional network, Skärholmen's plan relied on new understandings of both transit and distance.

The City of Stockholm's public housing company, Svenska Bostäder (literally 'Swedish Housing', SB), emphasized this regional character in its overview of the project: a booklet entitled *Skärholmen* and published in 1968.[19] Outlining the area's features and proudly describing the intentions behind its designs, SB argued that Skärholmen would surpass the expectations of a mere neighbourhood unit. Instead, as Executive Director Albert Aronson declared, 'Skärholmen Centrum will become the

---

[17] Hård af Segerstad, 'Skärholmens budskap'.

[18] See Clarence Perry, *The Neighborhood Unit: A Scheme of Arrangement for the Family-Life Community*, 'Regional Plan of N.Y. Regional Survey of N.Y. and Its Environs', *Monograph* 1, vol. 7 (1929).

[19] Many architects were involved in the project. Principally, the firm of Boijsen & Efvergren took responsibility for the *centrum*'s design, although Mattsson points out that they came to the commission late in the process and were relegated a role 'to elaborate a plan already settled'. Mattsson, 'Where the Motorways Meet', 172. Others involved were Hans Borgström & Bengt Lindroos, C.E. Sandberg, S. Ancker, B. Gate, S. Lindegren and Svenska Bostäder's own architectural office.

Figure 8.2 Aerial photograph of Skårholmen Centre from the E4 highway.
Source: Photograph by Cogg Bildbyrå in *Arkitektur* 11 (1968): 32.

commercial, social, and cultural node for the Southwestern part of Greater Stockholm.'[20] A product of the newly drawn boundaries for the city, Skårholmen will be, he added, 'a symbol for Greater Stockholm'.

Established in 1944, SB itself is a municipally owned and operated company, yet Aronson's text emphasized principally the *centrum*'s commercial functions. Swedish consumers were here to be treated to a display of every modern influence on shopping available, from mass-produced goods to refrigerated perishables to superstores offering an unprecedented scale and speed of new 'self-service' consumption. Care was also taken to ensure that – with many construction companies involved – the distribution of stores would be meticulously planned 'to avoid incorrect siting and double establishment'.[21] Like SB, the new commercial tenants believed in the future of the suburbs and the

---

[20]Svenska Bostäder, *Skårholmen* (Stockholm: AB Svea, 1968).
[21]Ibid., 5.

Figure 8.3 Terraced building and subway entrance in Skärholmen Centre.
Source: Photograph by Sune Sundahl in *Arkitektur* 11 (1968): 37; and ArkDes.

new consumer on wheels who would visit them. As in town centres elsewhere, new tenants were not difficult to find.

Two months after Skärholmen Centrum's inauguration, the cover of the November 1968 issue of the Swedish journal *Arkitektur* featured milk cartons; this new industrial packaging signified the issue's concern with commercial urban design and the heated debates it provoked in a Middle Way welfare state democracy.[22] The key point of contention concerned whether or not new centres should function principally as places for shopping and expand to offer larger goods and faster service. In one article, 'Service and Centres as Planning Problems', Bertel Granfelt wrote:

> Although the public sector – above all the municipalities – had a great influence on the planning of the 1930s and 1940s, the American vision has come to dominate the Swedish centre planning at times. Social centres (*samhällscentra*) have in this case become synonymous with commercial centres (*kommersiella centra*), with the primary role going to the private sector, especially retail, as the chief mediator of an ever-increasing flow of goods to the consumers.[23]

This 'ever-increasing flow of goods', in other words, meant that the *centrum*'s commercial functions often eclipsed its social and cultural ones.

---

[22]*Arkitektur* 11 (November 1968).

[23]Bertel Granfelt, 'Service and centra som planeringsproblem', *Arkitektur* 68, no. 11 (1968): 4. Other articles addressing Skärholmen and the problem of the *centrum* included one by its designers: Wilhelm and Dag Efvergren, 'Skärholmens centrum', *Arkitektur* 68, no. 11 (1968): 32–39. For more on the arguments about the character of the *centrum* more generally, see the debate article, 'Handeln och konsumenten', *Arkitektur* 68, no. 11 (1968): 14–25.

Figure 8.4 South-facing outdoor staircase in Skårholmen Centre.
Source: Photograph by Sune Sundahl in *Arkitektur* 11 (1968): 36; and ArkDes.

Similarly, a 1968 broadcast on Swedish public television, entitled 'Hello, Consumer. The Democracy behind Skårholmen',[24] discussed the interplay between a *centrum* designed to accommodate both shopping and the socialist tendencies of the Social Democratic government. The programme featured images of Skårholmen shoppers, as well as close-ups of identical products available for purchase traveling down conveyor belts and in shopping carts. 'Hello, Consumer!' presented the space as a collision between the idealized social agendas of the national government's *Boendeservice* and the new possibilities for shopping that mass-produced goods, self-service stores and the industrialization and unprecedented scale of consumption offered.

---

[24]Salaj, 'Hej konsument'.

Figure 8.5 Cover of the November 1968 issue of *Arkitektur*.
Source: Photograph by Arne Barthelson in *Arkitektur* 11 (1968): front cover.

In the programme, Docent Lars Persson, responsible for conducting research on retail spaces for the trade commission, argued that Skärholmen's development outlined the precariousness of this dual agenda. He said: 'One builds as it were fancier and fancier centres, while retail itself has as a goal to reduce costs in order to maintain competitive prices, to reduce prices.'[25] If the design of Skärholmen Centrum reflected new ideas of luxury and Swedish social solidarity at the same time, the triumph of one over the other seemed inevitable from this perspective. He continued in this vein, noting that retailers subsidized the costs of the *centrum*'s social and commercial components: 'Here, one can of course

---

[25]Ibid. It is not entirely clear that it is Persson who made these remarks, as the person who says them is not introduced. Salaj's voiceover mentions Persson immediately afterward, and an interview with Persson conducted is then heard.

speculate about the questions: What kind of suburban centres would we get if we let the commercial part, so to speak, take care of itself on its own terms? Would we even get any cultural, social centres in the suburbs? Is it the case that we pay for the culture with the cost of food?'[26]

In Skärholmen, in other words, public 'service' research had advanced an agenda for social and cultural programmes in theory that not even the premier Stockholm municipal housing company could privilege in reality. Social Democrats hoped that urban Sweden would be a place where commerce would be secondary and the training of citizens would be paramount, yet the limited influence of Svenska Bostäder's commissioned architects, Boijsen & Efvergren, and their late arrival on the scene meant that these designers could develop the *centrum* less as a civic centre and more as an unbounded mall.[27] The heavily dichotomous reception of Skärholmen after its construction (wherein its developers attempted to defend the centre as journalists led the charge against it) reflects this conundrum, and its architectural design increasingly took the blame for dissonances between vision and reality, stated in terms of producing residents who were passive rather than active.

Demolish Skärholmen!

Just two days after Prince Bertil's speech, Lars-Olof Franzén's article, 'Demolish Skärholmen!' (*Riv Skärholmen!*) appeared in the national newspaper *Dagens Nyheter*, beginning what became known as the 'Skärholmen Debate'.[28] Mats Franzén and Eva Sandstedt write that the central concerns of what actually grew into a 'suburbs debate' were two pairings: the active and the passive resident and community versus isolation.[29] Skärholmen's passive resident was linked in particular to concerns about extreme consumerism: shopping would leave the citizen with no other purpose in life. As Hård af Segerstad had written the day before Franzén's polemic appeared: 'Inside the zone of the Temple of Things and the Palace of Gadgets, in the centre of the Centre, there is no place for those who have no money in their purses or those who demand more from their environment than basic material gratification.'[30]

Following this ominous logic, Lars-Olof Franzén pilloried 'a suburban centre that is one of the most misanthropic that has been constructed to this point, an import, too late, of American city planning from the end of the 1940s that was already outdated then'.[31] He specifically sharpened his sword on condemning automobile traffic in the service of commercial enterprises, decrying the area's lack of attention to the needs of the everyday resident, particularly the pedestrian:

> It is namely not the idea that you should walk there even if you live relatively close by. You should drive your car, and you should drive it into a parking structure for four thousand cars, and then you

---

[26]Ibid.

[27]Mattsson notes that architects were conspicuously absent from most discussions and representations of the designs: Mattsson, 'Where the Motorways Meet', 164.

[28]Lars-Olof Franzén, 'Riv Skärholmen!' *Dagens Nyheter*, 10 September 1968, 5.

[29]Franzén and Sandstedt, *Välfärdsstat och byggande*, 21 and 29.

[30]Hård af Segerstad, 'Skärholmens budskap'.

[31]Franzén, 'Riv Skärholmen!'

will drive a car away from it. The function motorist – the function consumer, but no place for the entire person.[32]

Rather than a new centre of community life for new model citizens that the welfare state purported to support, he lambasted what he rather regarded as an overt and seemingly myopic emphasis on commercial functions: easy access from the highway to the 4,000-car parking garage taking precedence over meaningful civic and collective space. Franzén wondered if Skärholmen's planners had 'consciously neglected our right to an environment where people want to be and to meet each other, even when they are not on their way to buy a furniture set or a beer'.[33] Naked consumerism, it seemed, had sullied opportunities for the kind of personal development that Swedish politicians and designers claimed to envision.

In the aftermath of Franzén's modest proposal to demolish the newly built Skärholmen, a flood of similar articles washed across the country's newspapers during the autumn of 1968. With titles like 'Hold onto your wallet! New town centres will strip us of a half billion', 'Skärholmen's message: 'You shall consume!'', 'The point of Skärholmen? Offer community service or sell opulence' and 'Demolish Skärholmen or fire the urban planners?', they assaulted the focus on shopping, the neglect paid to spaces for community service, and the planners and architects themselves.[34] In one piece, Albert Aronson angrily defended a series of accusations previously made by the critic Olle Bengtzon, who in turn answered:

> Nothing of all that should give life and substance and make the centre into something more than a commodity market was finished when Skärholmen was inaugurated with a Prince speech and half a billion in advertising. On the other hand, department stores and shops were developed from the beginning for customers from Botkyrka City, which was not even begun.

Others noted that the buildings meant to house commercial functions had been built much earlier and more completely than the community infrastructure that the plans for Skärholmen had promised. 'We really regret that it turned out like that', said Director of Planning Göran Sidenbladh, on national television. He continued: 'We believe that the people who live in these neighbourhoods here are more dependent on the non-commercial part of the centrum than the commercial part to acclimate themselves.'[35]

This debate stoked the fires of ongoing concerns over the conflicts between Social Democratic agendas – and the very values said to be at the heart of their political platform – and the economic variables that shaped Swedish town centres. In Skärholmen, stores opened with fanfare, princely

---

[32]Ibid.
[33]Ibid.
[34]Olle Bengtzon, 'Håll hårt om planboken! De nya centra ska plocka oss på en halv miljard', *Expressen*, 4 September 1968; Hård af Segerstad, 'Skärholmens budskap'; Albert Aronson and Olle Bengtzon, 'Målet med Skärholmen? Bjuda samhällsservice eller sälja överflöd', *Expressen*, 10 October 1968. This article is formulated as a debate between Svenska Bostäder's Albert Aronson and Expressen's critic Olle Bengtzon; Lars Gyllensten, 'Riv Skärholmen eller avskeda stadsplanerarna?', *Dagens Nyheter*, 12 September 1968. For more, see the November 1968 issue of *Arkitektur*.
[35]Salaj, 'Hej Konsument'.

speeches and glittering curtain walls of glass, but a gaping hole remained on the site where a community sports hall should have been. Had Skärholmen's planners forgotten its citizens and replaced them with apathetic consumers?

Mrs Norman's milk and meat

'Skärholmen a threat against HOUSEWIVES. Woman attack: They drink secretly.'
> Headline in newspaper, shown in montage of 'Hej konsument', 1968.

Skärholmen's urban planning and incomplete civic architecture posed, it was claimed, particular challenges for housewives. Media reports in 1968 claimed that their passive lives in the neighbourhood led them to alcoholism. In a debate about Skärholmen held on 24 September 1968 at the City Museum in Stockholm, Aronson answered why he as a Social Democrat did not lead the project towards social functions and away from the 'consumer society'. Later, one unidentified participant wryly described the assumptions he had met about his everyday life in Skärholmen:

> Now, I am apparently a bore who takes the subway to and from work and am so tired when I come home that I just eat and then watch TV and go to bed because I have nothing else to do. Besides that, my wife is on the road to alcoholism, and my child, who is three months old, is going to become a gangster. I don't know if I am going to agree with that.[36]

He did agree with critics who lamented that adequate civic functions like day cares, youth centres and sports facilities remained unfinished. The consumer had apparently trumped the citizen at Skärholmen's opening, but was this vision of public life as bleak as the reality?

As the consumer faced the state, in fact, Skärholmen Centrum became a locus of action, not just for the apparently alternating visions of utopian community-building activities or dystopian, mindless consumption of industrialized goods. In the nexus of this apparent power struggle and battle over discourse and the detritus of unrealized planning projects, Skärholmen became the site of one of the most high-profile consumer advocacy actions in Swedish history, using the space of the centrum for unplanned activism in critique of state actions: specifically empowering the consumer. And it was housewives who led the charge. In spite of itself, Skärholmen paradoxically succeeded in building community: even if this community assembled around the protest of the very principles of the centre itself.

The rising cost of food – especially dairy products and meat – led to the formation in 1972 of a grassroots group of seven residents calling themselves the Skärholmen Committee, who sought lower food prices and the elimination of food taxes. Comprising entirely women and led by a twenty-three-year-old mother of two, Ann-Marie Norman, the group became popularly known as the 'Skärholmen Wives'. In protesting the exorbitant grocery prices of the times, the group called attention to the everyday

---

[36] Ibid.

economic plight that middle- and working-class Swedes experienced during the economic downturn of the early 1970s.[37]

In contrast to the depictions of the Skärholmen as an unsalvageable, overly commercialized space where 'passive' shoppers were to be enticed to buy more than they needed just to keep the stores alive,[38] the Skärholmen Committee used the commercial and civic spaces of Skärholmen Centrum both as the focus of their discontent and as the locus of their protests. The Wives' active community engagement directly reclaimed and reprogrammed the supposedly over-commercialized spaces upon which so many detractors had founded their disapproving assessments of Skärholmen. Picketing outside local stores during their 'strike week' from 21 to 28 February 1972, the group refused to buy milk or meat during that time, saying on the first day of the boycott that they would stop buying milk for seven days and would continue to refuse the purchase of meat 'until further notice'.[39] In their charge to engender effects beyond the confines of the suburb itself, the Skärholmen Committee called on others to join them in boycotting these products in a 'milk action'. They sought not just to raise awareness of how pricing affected their families and their food choices, but to provoke action: the government should control the market.

That Saturday, on 26 February 1972, a group of 6,000 gathered in central Stockholm to demand that the government 'LOWER FOOD PRICES!'[40] They had invited Prime Minister Olof Palme, who did not make an appearance. Despite his absence, Norman spoke passionately about the stakes of this action to the group at Sergel's Square, saying:

> Recipes for 'poor man's dishes' have suddenly become popular in newspapers. We'll most likely be told how to make bread out of bark soon... We can only coldly state that it's not working now.[41]

They delivered their list of demands to his office the following Monday instead. With the high-profile debate and unusual group of consumer-protestors, the Skärholmen Wives were invited to join a televised debate later that month, featuring the Minister of Trade, Kjell-Olof Feldt. While the results were not immediate, the mobilized outcry of the Skärholmen Committee put pressure on Prime Minister Palme to take action. Eventually, using the power of state control over pricing, Palme intervened and restricted the cost of dairy products in December 1972. This measure remained in place until 1 January 1975.

In this sense, Skärholmen – criticized above all for producing 'passive consumers' – became the nucleus of an *active* movement with *active* consumers. From the 'regional' marketplace of Skärholmen Centrum, where everyday practices of Swedish citizenship were to be reinforced, the Wives not only disrupted the status quo but also motivated the state to contain the commercial forces that Lars Franzén and others had argued were out of control. If early critics read Skärholmen Centrum as a planned

---

[37] See 'Mjölk-strejk mot höga matpriser', *Aftonbladet*, 18 February 1972; 'Hon startade köpstrejken – nu ringer hela landet', *Expressen*, 19 February 1972.

[38] Aronson and Bengtzon, 'Målet med Skärholmen?'

[39] Robert Hartman, 'Stopp för mjölken i Skärholmen!' *Aftonbladet*, 21 February 1972.

[40] 'Dags för barkbröd?' *Svenska Dagbladet*, 27 February 1972, 1. The newspaper also contended that one protestor had yelled: 'Filet Mignon for the People!'

[41] Lena Högardh, 'Pengarna har man i kassen och maten ryms i portmonnän', *Svenska Dagbladet*, 27 February 1972.

capitalist free-for-all, it became, by the 1970s, a civic space of activism that specifically challenged both commercial domination *and* the 'planned' civic life of the community spaces described in *Boendeservice*. Here, the social functions of the town centre were realized as designed, but, rather than finding their expression in new forms of civic responsibility and recreation, focused on establishing the rights of the new consumer, remaking Mrs Norman and other housewives from alcoholic and apathetic to politically powerful.

Under glass

God is dead and sick in Skärholmen
a slum that doesn't even know what it's missing
that believes that it has to be like this
and pulls down its blind Venetian blinds

From Ylla Eggehorn's poem, '70-talets slum' ('The Slum of the 1970s'), 1970[42]

With press like 'Demolish Skärholmen!' and other negative assessments of their monolithic architecture and unfinished outdoor areas, Million Programme areas were increasingly stigmatized by the 1970s, and those who could move away did so.[43] As architects searched for ways to revamp the common urban environments that the space of the centrum itself represented, they increasingly permitted shopping an even more prominent position in the foreground of renovation planning. Many efforts seemed to contradict each other, as some argued that the 'rationalized' service the Million Programme produced had dissatisfied citizens, so they made spaces for consumers instead. Others emphasized new ways to bring 'democracy' into these much-maligned suburban spaces where, it was argued, top-down planning had forgotten the people for whom the designs were created.

During the 1980s, new design principles – again imported from the United States and beyond – led to the redesign of a large portion of Skärholmen Centrum's space in accordance with the new typology of the indoor shopping mall. The same month that Skärholmen opened, one newspaper critic, Ulf Hård av Segerstad asked: 'Why, one asks oneself, hasn't this compact town centre been expanded to a satisfactory galleria complex?'[44] This provocation took decades to become material reality but occurred, most dramatically, when major sections of Skärholmen's pedestrian shopping streets were

---

[42]Ylva Eggehorn, *Ska vi dela* (1970).
[43]For more on how the Million Programme became an ontological crisis not only for Swedish urban planning and architecture but also Social Democratic politics, see Karl-Olov Arnstberg, *Miljonprogrammet* (Stockholm: Carlssons, 2000); Thomas Hall, 'Urban Planning in Sweden', in *Planning and Urban Growth in the Nordic Countries*, ed. Thomas Hall (New York: E. & F.N. Spon, 1991), 167–246; Thomas Hall and Sonja Vidén, 'The Million Homes Programme: A Review of the Great Swedish Planning Project', *Planning Perspectives* 20 (July 2005): 301–328, among others.
[44]Hård av Segerstad, 'Skärholmens budskap'.

covered in glass in 1984. This defined them as a formal contrast to the social and cultural *centrum* functions housed around the open square of the late 1960s.

Some social services, such as public psychologists and health clinics, remained housed on upper stories of the complex; they were, in effect, hidden from view, as impressive atria and multi-level consumer spaces shifted the *centrum* more fully to the use of shoppers. With atria and entertainment facilities claiming increasing space, the *centrum* of the 1980s moved further and further away from the social engineering imagined in the *Boendeservice* reports and closer to the typologies of a neoliberal, international postmodernist architecture.

Along with these physical changes, ownership of Skärholmen Centrum shifted increasingly away from the public. Following the trend of other *centra* across urban Sweden such as Vällingby, Skärholmen's keys have been increasingly handed over to private actors. Underlying Aronson's attitudes and SB's development in the 1960s, despite its early 'consumerist' critiques, were the notions that Social Democratic politics expected a wide swath of Swedish society to use Skärholmen and that it would be open to all citizens. Increasing control of private interests have partitioned its spaces and remade its profile.

As renovation trumped demolition, the *centrum*'s supposed architectural failures ultimately required a radical physical change that seemed, in a sense, to reify the terms of critiques that articles such as 'Demolish Skärholmen!' and its peers had vilified: the outdoor public passages became an indoor mall. As Aronson, Sidenbladh and others behind the original plans acknowledged, Skärholmen's 'consumerism' originally served as the economic force driving its supposedly more virtuous functions: one not quite operating in the shadows. If this focus on commerce quickly became an epithet for the centre's critique after Skärholmen opened, it had evolved into an openly stated and desired design feature less than two decades later. Where did this leave the citizen?

From the Million Programme to the mall

In the ideal view, the Million Programme *centrum* offered a well-researched civic and commercial environment in which everyday post-war Swedes would find their bearings in the new modern society. As a pedagogical space, it was an important component of Social Democratic modernization and community building. Even so, as media reports and SB's promotional literature of the 1960s indicates, the reality was that Skärholmen Centrum – one of the most widely discussed and debated in urban Sweden – devoted 66 per cent of its total area to shops and restaurants, and only 9 per cent and 8 per cent to social and cultural activities, respectively. If this *centrum* supposedly housed more passive consumption than active community, the education in collective living that Swedish citizens were meant to gain there perhaps emerged most meaningfully in the actions of Skärholmen Wives. Consumers gained a social consciousness, and became active participants in public life in this new town centre, although not in the ways that developers, planners and architects had envisaged.[45]

---

[45] For more on attitudes and innovations during renovations of Million Programme areas, see Birgitta Johansson (ed.), *Miljonprogram – utveckla eller avveckla?* (Stockholm: Forskningsrådet Formas, 2012) and Ola Broms Wessel, Jennifer Mack and Tim Anstey (eds.), *Future People's Palace* (Stockholm: Arvinius, forthcoming).

But are the Wives merely an inspiring footnote in what is otherwise a doomsday scenario for welfare state planning? Did consumption trump the social and cultural roots of the state project? At first glance, it may appear that Skärholmen Centrum's renovation under glass has not created notably more space for civic functions, especially during its more recent rebranding under the nickname and accompanying logo 'SKHLM – The Capital of Shopping', a play on the abbreviation for Stockholm, STHLM. Rather than serving as the pinnacle of a suburban Sweden in which Skärholmen would be a regional focal point, this *centrum* now entices users from the entire capital to this geographic periphery. On the other hand, Skärholmen Centrum as constructed comprised not only the shops along what were previously outdoor streets, but also its public squares: Skärholmstorget and Måsholmstorget. From some views, they appear to be the shadow spaces of the mall, housing another kind of (unplanned) commercial and civic space already evident in the 1980s. From another, an open marketplace became representative of the alternative forms of shopping that many residents of the area also esteem.

In 'The Orient in Skärholmen', broadcast on the Swedish Radio channel P1 in 1988, Alvar Janson interviewed various purveyors of fruits and vegetables – mostly immigrants. He began his report with a hawker selling bananas and continued:

> Yes, that how it sounded when it got cold, autumnally cold, outside the revolving doors into Scandinavia's largest shopping centre, which is glazed, rather impersonal, but heated and above all sells intensively. For there outside is Skärholmen's other face. That's where the un-Swedish square with all the immigrants that provides life and colour and contrast is located. Almost like in the Orient.[46]

This Skärholmen comprises a fluid environment where Skärholmen Centrum's chain stores – such as the Swedish clothing retailers H&M and Lindex – and local salespeople running the market on the square share many of the same clientele.

Skärholmen cannot be naively viewed through the utopian lenses of industrialized urban planning of the mid-1960s. At the same time, calls to 'Demolish Skärholmen!' as a commercialized perdition – when the paint had barely dried on its town centre – appear equally naïve in their pessimism. From the active political actions of the Skärholmen Wives to open-air markets of the 1980s to the mixture of commercial and community centre today, Skärholmen is more than *either* a failed civic centre with nothing but commerce and drive-by urbanism on the edge of the capital *or* the triumph of capitalist consumerism. Whether users interact with it as a mall, a civic space, a locus of personal development or all of the above, they find themselves in search of a Sweden in search of itself.

---

[46] Alvar Janson, 'Orienten i Skärholmen', Sveriges Radio, 19 November 1988.

Chapter 9

Milton Keynes' Centre: The apotheosis of the British post-war consensus or, the apostle of neo-liberalism?
Janina Gosseye

Introduction

In preparation for the official opening of Milton Keynes' shopping centre by newly elected Prime Minister Margaret Thatcher, the Milton Keynes Development Corporation (MKDC) drafted an 'Imaginary dialogue between the Chairman [of the MKDC] and the Prime Minister'.[1] Expecting Mrs Thatcher to question 'why... the exchequer [should] continue to invest taxpayers funds in the future development of Milton Keynes'[2] and propose that '... it should be possible for the exchequer to reduce dramatically the levels of public investment in Milton Keynes',[3] the MKDC was clearly troubled by the impending visit and felt that Lord (Jock) Campbell of Eskan, its Chairman, needed to be well prepared for this encounter and the harsh line of questioning that (they imagined) would inevitably ensue. But was this fear justified? Admittedly, Milton Keynes was a grand outcome of the UK's post-war consensus and stood for everything that Thatcher opposed. But surely the symbolism of the opening of (then) Europe's largest indoor shopping centre – the architectural embodiment of a liberal economy and a harbinger of global capitalism – at the heart of this new town on the cusp of her election would not have gone unnoticed? Oddly enough, this symbolism *did* seem to elude the architects, planners and politicians involved in the development of Milton Keynes's shopping centre. For them, the Centre was not a 'shopping centre' but a piece of civic infrastructure that would benefit the community at large.

Questioning if Milton Keynes' Centre was the apotheosis of the post-war consensus or an apostle of neo-liberalism, this chapter demonstrates the complex ways in which public and private interests were interwoven in British post-war urban development. Already prior to the assumed 'neo-liberal turn'

A longer version of this chapter has been published in Janina Gosseye, 'Milton Keynes' Centre: The Apotheosis of the British Post-war Consensus or, the Apostle of Neo-Liberalism?', *History of Retailing and Consumption* 1, no. 3 (2015): 209–229.

[1] 'Opening of Central Milton Keynes by the Prime Minister – Tuesday, 25 September 1979', MKDC Consignment 8298, Box 4, File 3, 40–43, Centre for Buckinghamshire Studies (Aylesbury).
[2] Ibid., 40.
[3] Ibid., 41.

of the late 1970s, local governments worked in close collaboration with the private sector, leading to different public–private partnership constellations, the importance of which, British historian Peter Shapely has argued, was highlighted by the construction of countless shopping centres.[4] As a result, contrasting and (at times) conflicting goals and aspirations were projected onto (and incorporated in) shopping centre designs. Milton Keynes' Centre offers an excellent example in this respect. Combining writing by the MKDC with contemporary architectural critique of the Centre and popular discourse, the chapter iterates how Milton Keynes' architects and planners endeavoured to reconcile these different interests in their design. It also exposes their struggle to relate the architecture of the Centre to new social ideals that emerged in post-war years and define a novel formal language able to respond to the ongoing political and economical transformations that gradually dismantled the welfare state and paved the way for the 'triumph' of neo-liberalism.

Milton Keynes: The birth of Britain's biggest and best new town

In 1942 – in the throes of the Second World War – Churchill's coalition government issued a report entitled *Report of the Inter-Departmental Committee on Social Insurance and Allied Services*. Drafted by Sir William Beveridge, a highly regarded economist, this document rapidly became the blueprint for the modern welfare state. It detailed five giant social evils that beset the British people – illness, ignorance, disease, squalor and want – and also set forth the remedies: national health care for all, full employment, universal secondary education, state insurance against sickness, unemployment and old age and, last but not least, subsidized housing.[5] When the war ended, Beveridge's words were translated into deeds. One of the first points of action for the incoming Labour government was to devise creative solutions to alleviate the pressing housing deficit. Advice emanating from both the state and town planners as early as 1944 advocated for the adoption of the neighbourhood unit as a model for housing design in Britain.[6] Two years later, in the 1946, the British parliament passed the 'New Towns Act'. This act enabled the government to designate areas of land for the formation of new towns and regulated the establishment of development corporations, each of which was responsible for the building and management of one of the projected new towns.[7] Over the following decades, three development 'waves' led to the creation of about two dozen new towns in England and Wales; twelve between 1946 and 1950, five between 1961 and 1964 and six between 1968 and 1971.[8] The neighbourhood unit became an important component of these new towns.[9] British advocates of this planning model were

---

[4]Peter Shapely, 'Governance in the Post-war City: Historical Reflections on Public-Private Partnerships in the UK', *International Journal of Urban and Regional Research* 37, no. 4 (July 2013): 1289.

[5]Victoria De Grazia, *Irresistible Empire: America's Advance through 20th Century Europe* (Cambridge, MA: The Belknap Press of Harvard University Press, 2005), 339–340.

[6]Ministry of Health, *Design of Dwellings* (London, 1944); Ministry of Health/Ministry of Works, *Housing Manual 1944* (London, 1944), cited in: James Greenhalgh, 'Consuming Communities: The Neighbourhood Unit and the Role of Retail Spaces on British Housing Estates, 1944–1958', *Urban History* 43, no. 1 (November 2015): 158.

[7]Peter Hall and Mark Tewdwr-Jones, *Urban and Regional Planning* (London: Routledge, 2010), 68–71.

[8]Brian Harrison, *Seeking a Role: The United Kingdom 1951–1970* (New York: Oxford University Press, 2009), 154–155.

[9]Anthony Goss, 'Neighbourhood Units in British New Towns', *The Town Planning Review* 32, no. 1 (1961): 66–82.

convinced that the neighbourhoods they produced would present the sort of physical environment which promoted 'neighbourliness' and suggested that a causal, deterministic relationship existed between spatial arrangement and the production of 'community spirit'.[10] The careful positioning of retail facilities in particular was attributed a key role in the production of community formation and in 1944 the Retail Advisory Committee on Town Planning was formed at the behest of the Ministry of Town and Country Planning.[11]

Over the following two decades, growing economic prosperity and social stability led to the emergence of a mass consumption society in Britain, which was supported by revolutionary changes in the structure of the retail sector, including the implementation of self-service,[12] the establishment of supermarkets, the expansion of shopping areas in pedestrian zones of city centres and – last but not least – the development of shopping centres. Well aware of the growing importance of what was then described as the new 'Retailing Revolution', the government became instrumental in supporting the growth of new shopping centres.[13] In the early 1960s, the Ministry of Housing and Local Government,[14] which was – amongst other things – responsible for the designation of new towns, created a working party to assess the distribution, size and growth of shopping centres. It aimed to advise local authorities on shopping provision and trends in towns in the same region. However, although the state promoted the growth of shopping centres, it also recognized that building them required capital, expertise and political will; thus necessitating the public and private sectors to work together.[15]

While several shopping centres were built at the heart of existing city centres in an attempt to revitalize inner city areas, some of the earliest shopping centres were located at the heart of new towns. This was perhaps not entirely coincidental given the strong involvement of the Ministry of Housing and Local Government in the development of shopping centres. In 1955, the 'Town Centre' of the new town of Cumbernauld, which is widely accepted as the UK's first 'shopping centre', was inaugurated and several others soon followed suit. So, when Richard Crossmann, the Minister of Housing and Local Government, designated the construction of Milton Keynes new town in 1967, not only was the retailing (and consumer) landscape in Britain undergoing intensive and comprehensive transformations, but the synergy between the development of a shopping centre and (or 'at the heart of') a new town was also well established.[16]

---

[10]Clarence Perry, who in 1929 had originally presented the concept of the neighbourhood Unit, had remained relatively silent on its ability to develop social relations. See Greenhalgh, 'Consuming Communities', 6.

[11]Greenhalgh, 'Consuming Communities', 13–14.

[12]See Gareth Shaw, Adrian Bailey, Andrew Alexander, Dawn Nell and Jane Hamlett, 'The Coming of the Supermarket: The Processes and Consequences of Transplanting American Know-How into Britain', in *Transformations of Retailing in Europe after 1945*, eds. Ralph Jessen and Lydia Langer (London: Ashgate, 2012), 39.

[13]Shapely, 'Governance in the Post-war City', 1293.

[14]The Ministry of Housing and Local Government was the successor of the Ministry of Town and Country Planning. It was originally formed as the Ministry of Local Government and Planning in January 1951, when functions of the Ministry of Health were merged with the Ministry of Town and Country Planning, which had been created in 1943. Its name was changed to the Ministry of Housing and Local Government by the Conservatives after the October 1951 general election.

[15]Shapely, 'Governance in the Post-war City', 1293.

[16]Michael Edwards, 'City Design: What Went Wrong at Milton Keynes?' *Journal of Urban Design* 6, no. 1 (2001): 87.

Of all the new towns that had been constructed up until then, Milton Keynes was to be the largest as well as the most ambitious and most modern. Located in North Buckinghamshire, it was to provide for overspill from the towns in the south of the County and also destined to contribute towards housing London's surplus. In May 1967, the MKDC was established and preparations to develop a 'strategic plan' began in December that same year.[17] In early 1970, Lord Campbell, Chair of the MKDC and a representative of the Labour Party in the House of Lords, presented the Plan for Milton Keynes to the Minister. The macrostructure of this plan was based on a grid of roads, spaced at about one kilometre intervals, with land uses coarsely distributed across the entire designated area.[18] At a local level the plan relied on an even distribution of so-called 'activity centres'. These grouped together different services inside the grid and ensured that wherever you were in the city, you were never more than a six-minute (or 500 metre) walk away from the nearest public facility. Complementing these local nuclei was a large centre located at the heart of the new town which was to offer '... most of those services and facilities which serve the whole population of the city' and following the MKDC's advice needed to include a substantial shopping centre.[19]

In September 1979, after a rather halting development process, the Centre was festively opened.[20] Just like the architects and planners of the mid-1940s had deemed retail facilities within the neighbourhood unit capable of promoting 'neighbourliness' and 'community spirit', so too did the designers of Milton Keynes' Centre believe that this new shopping centre would support community formation and civic education within the new town through its spatial arrangement. However, the Centre was not only to operate on a local level, but it also needed to put Milton Keynes firmly on the regional map and, to satisfy its investors, was to function as a major commercial hub between London and Birmingham.[21]

Not a shopping centre but a city centre

It was not unusual for new towns to have a shopping centre at (or *as*) their core. Cumbernauld and Irvine in Scotland and Runcorn in England, for instance, all had such a commercial facility embedded in their centre. But the shopping centre in Milton Keynes was different. In May 1979, a few months before the building's opening, the Royal Institute of British Architects (RIBA) published a lengthy piece in its monthly journal, entitled 'The Shopping Centre', which plainly stated: 'It [the shopping centre at Milton Keynes] owes no allegiance to its new town brothers at Cumbernauld, Irvine and Runcorn.'[22] This text was authored by Derek Walker, Chief Architect and Planner of Milton Keynes, who contended that the building was '... a strange animal in conventional shopping terms' and '... a far cry from the dumbell

---

[17]Milton Keynes Development Corporation, *The Plan for Milton Keynes*, volume 1 (March 1970), 3.
[18]Edwards, 'City Design', 88.
[19]Milton Keynes Development Corporation, *The Plan for Milton Keynes*, volume 1, 30–31.
[20]Terence Bendixson and John Platt, *Milton Keynes: Image and Reality* (Cambridge: Granta Editions, 1992), 145.
[21]Brian Burrows, 'Milton Keynes: A Model for Regenerating Our Cities?' *Long Range Planning* 20, no. 1 (1987): 72.
[22]Derek Walker, 'Central Milton Keynes: The Shopping Centre', *RIBA: Central Milton Keynes Annual Report* 5 (1979): 213.

[sic.] concept of earlier American centres or the prison-camp exterior/ seedy nightclub interior mode of many recent commercial ventures in France and England'.[23]

In the early 1970s Walker commissioned architects Stuart Mosscrop and Christopher Woodward to design the shopping building. Taking their cue from Walker, Mosscrop explained that: 'We were determined we would not design a "shopping centre",' and continued:

> This building type of ours was the biggest in Europe when it first opened. But all other modern shopping places were modelled on Victor Gruen, the American architect who in the '50s came up with the "blobs" – tarmac machines for spending money, entirely enclosed … No, we thought … [t]his is going to be the first place that we actually make for *all the people* in Milton Keynes.[24]

Taking inspiration from the European arcades or *passagen*,[25] Mosscrop and Woodward structured the Centre around two large pedestrian arcades, twelve metres wide, fourteen metres high and 800 metres long that ran east–west along the length of the building and were connected by secondary pedestrian routes at ninety-metre intervals. These secondary interior walkways almost seamlessly connected the Centre to the exterior (outdoor) city grid, while the extensively glazed primary arcades effectively subdivided the building into three commercial strips. The outer two strips were designed to contain smaller 'unit shops' and the wider middle band was designated to house the large-space-use department and variety stores. This middle band also comprised two large public squares: an outdoor garden court, called 'Queen's Court', and a spacious indoor hall: 'Middleton Hall', which – in reference to the great public facilities in Italy – was paved with travertine. Located at the heart of the new town, firmly anchored in the city grid, and housing an array of different spaces – large indoor- and outdoor squares, as well as high and light, and low and narrow arcades – the spatial design of the Centre, its architects believed,

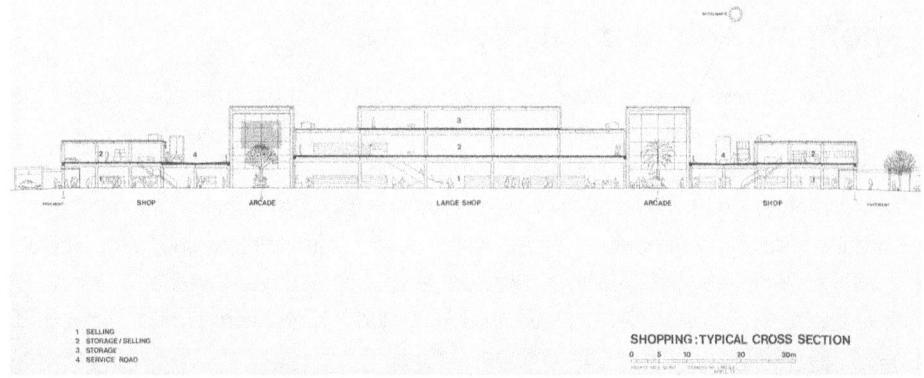

Figure 9.1 Schematic cross section of Milton Keynes shopping centre.
Source: MKDC Collection, Centre for Buckinghamshire Studies (Aylesbury), archive location: Lib/ 15 and 16.

---

[23]Ibid.

[24]Stuart Mosscrop, Interviewed by Roger Kitchen, in *The Story of the Original CMK*, ed. Marion Hill (Milton Keynes: Living Archive, 2007), 27.

[25]Christopher Woodward, Interviewed by Roger Kitchen, in *The Story of the Original CMK*, Hill, 25.

Milton Keynes' Centre 143

Figure 9.2 Aerial view of Milton Keynes shopping centre, seen from the south-west.
Source: MKDC Collection, Centre for Buckinghamshire Studies (Aylesbury), archive location: MK/ Photo/ 3/ 33.

would construct community spirit in Milton Keynes: it was a hub for face-to-face interaction, both a locale of everyday sociability and a venue for major events.

Walker, Mosscrop and Woodward basically thought of the shopping centre as an extension of the city grid: a network of (covered) streets and squares, which was accessible 24/7.[26] To that end, the Centre had air curtains instead of doors, which made it permanently accessible and able to attract people at all hours; a true city centre.[27] To visualize the Centre's aspired urban atmosphere, the architects commissioned renowned architectural renderer Helmut Jacoby to make a set of illustrations of the design.[28] In one of his drawings showing the Garden Court, Jacoby prominently included a group of chortling children playing with a ball, accompanied by a dog in the foreground; another drawing depicting Middleton Hall, foregrounded an amorous young couple while placing an elderly person in a wheelchair almost at the centre of the tableau. Jacoby clearly wanted to emphasize the accessibility of

---

[26]Hill, *The Story of the Original CMK*, 63–65.

[27]Mosscrop, Interviewed by Roger Kitchen, in *The Story of the Original CMK*, Hill, 63. Due to complaints of shop tenants regarding 'freezing winds' howling through the building, doors were however installed shortly after its opening, much to the dismay of the architects and planners involved in its design. See Derek Walker, Interviewed by Roger Kitchen, in *The Story of the Original CMK*, Hill, 63.

[28]Walker, Interviewed by Roger Kitchen, in *The Story of the Original CMK*, Hill, 65.

Figure 9.3 Architectural drawing of Middleton Hall by Helmut Jacoby, 1974.
Source: MKDC Collection, Centre for Buckinghamshire Studies (Aylesbury), archive location: Box of Photographs marked 'Misc Photos Identifiable Not Catalogued'.

the shopping centre, both literally and figuratively speaking, as he consistently included people of all shapes and sizes, young and old, male and female in his illustrations. Most remarkable about Jacoby's drawings of Milton Keynes' Centre, however, is that even though he consistently showed its arcades and squares crowded with people, very few (in fact almost none) were actually carrying shopping bags. Jacoby had thus clearly well understood the architects' desire to create a 'city centre' before a 'shopping centre'.

Not a shopping centre but a civic centre

In his 1979 RIBA article Walker expressed the hope that once opened, Milton Keynes' shopping centre '… will symbolically become a centrepiece for community activity [which] will hopefully inculcate the right kind of civic pride …'.[29] Like many of his contemporaries who highly valued civic pride as an aspiration for urban development and as a symbolic form of power,[30] Walker, together with Mosscrop and Woodward, consciously wrought to translate these aspirations into the design of Milton Keynes' shopping centre. One of the Centre's key design features destined to contribute to the inculcation of civic pride was its ambitious interior landscaping scheme. Supported by the extensive glazing of the main arterial walkways, which allowed natural light to penetrate deep into the building, Mosscrop and Woodward integrated approximately forty plant beds, each approximately 25 m² in surface, in these two urban corridors.[31] Designed by Tony Southard of the MKDC landscape department in collaboration with the architects, the landscaping scheme sought to give each of the Centre's two 'streets' a unique

---

[29] Walker, 'Central Milton Keynes: The Shopping Centre', 213.
[30] Peter Shapely, 'Civic Pride and Redevelopment in the Post-war British City', *Urban History* 39, no. 2 (May 2012): 310–328.
[31] Tony Southard, Interviewed by Roger Kitchen, in *The Story of the Original CMK*, Hill, 117.

Figure 9.4 Interior view of one of the Centre's two large pedestrian arcades, with a view through to the Queen's Court (outside).
Source: MKDC Collection, Centre for Buckinghamshire Studies (Aylesbury), archive location: MK/Photo/ 4/ 2.

character. The more shaded north arcade was given typical temperate forest and tropical plants with dark, dense foliage, while the south arcade was landscaped with plants from hot, dry climates, the foliage of which is generally paler, smaller and less dense.

Walker, Mosscrop and Woodward made the decision to include lush vegetation in the shopping centre against the advice of commercial surveyors, who informed them that it would impede consumption.[32] Commercial success was however not a top priority for the designers and certainly ranked lower than the Centre's ability not only to 'inculcate' but also to express 'the right kind of civic pride'. They aimed to create a civic centre more than a shopping centre. Nonetheless, it is safe to assume that the architects also believed that the unique atmosphere bestowed upon the Centre by the landscaping scheme would become one of its key 'selling points' and would thus inevitably support its commercial aims. The local press indeed soon picked up on the Centre's distinctive design. An article published in the *Milton Keynes Express* of 21 September 1979 pointed out that 'unlike [in] some of the earlier covered shopping centres in Britain, the plants are not an afterthought but an integral part of the original design' and reported that one writer had already described visiting central Milton Keynes as 'like shopping at Kew Gardens'.[33] This likening must have pleased the architects as Kew Gardens not only contained the largest collection of living plants in the word, but was also a prime location for the cultivation of civic pride in the UK.[34]

Once built, the MKDC cleverly used the Centre's distinct vegetation to lay claim to Milton Keynes' urban superiority to attract prospective shoppers to the new town. Ahead of the shopping centre's

---

[32] Frank Henshaw, Interviewed by Roger Kitchen, in *The Story of the Original CMK*, Hill, 117.
[33] 'Shop in Kew at New City', *Milton Keynes Express* (supplement), 21 September 1979, 27.
[34] In Britain, the relationship between landscape architecture and civic pride was by then already well established. Professor of landscape architecture Ian Thompson has, for instance, posited that in Britain '19th century legislation opened the way ... for local authorities to make provision for municipals parks and very soon these became matters of civic pride'. Source: Ian Thompson, *Landscape Architecture: A Very Short Introduction* (Oxford: Oxford University Press, 2014), 8.

Figure 9.5 View of Liliane Lijn's kinetic sculpture, entitled 'Circle of Light', which was hung from the Midsummer Arcade shortly after the Centre's opening.
Source: MKDC Collection, Centre for Buckinghamshire Studies (Aylesbury), archive location: MK/Photo/3/11.

opening, it issued a beautifully illustrated brochure, with a colourfully drawn composition of the flowers, shrubs and trees that could be found inside the shopping centre on the front, and a perspective drawing of the building from above indicating precisely which vegetation could be found where on the back.[35] In the margin next to this drawing, a short caption suggested that '[w]ith such distinctive quality of the interior landscape, shopping in Central Milton Keynes is a uniquely pleasant and stimulating experience'.[36] This statement beautifully illustrates how the MKDC inextricably linked the need to market the shopping centre (and by extension the new town of Milton Keynes) to the inculcation of civic pride. It also corroborates Peter Shapely's suggestion that the inculcation of civic pride was part and parcel of urban development projects in post-war Britain and was – as it had been in early modern England – structured around architecture and the use of 'public' space. Now, however, it was no longer mirrored in the choice of Gothic or classical styles of design, but through a modern architecture of steel, concrete and glass; through new public spaces and, last but not least, through public art.[37]

Soon after its opening, the Roland Collection of art was on display in the shopping centre. *The Milton Keynes Express* reported: 'Pablo Picasso and Henry Moore are not names you generally associate with doing the shopping, but thousands of city shoppers have been popping in to see the works of these and other artists in a temporary gallery in Central Milton Keynes. What's more, there are hopes that the gallery will one day become a permanent feature.'[38] While Lord Campbell, Chairman of the MKDC,

---

[35] Promotional brochure for Milton Keynes Shopping Centre, issued in 1978, found in MKDC lib 19/20-21, folder containing two advertising leaflets for Central Milton Keynes shopping, Centre for Buckinghamshire Studies (Aylesbury).
[36] Ibid.
[37] Shapely, 'Civic Pride and Redevelopment in the Post-war British City', 310–328.
[38] 'Shoppers meet Picassos', *Milton Keynes Express*, 28 September 1979, 38.

credited the architects for changing '… the space of a shopping area into a perfect exhibition area',[39] Kenneth Robinson, chairman of the Arts Council, underlined that '[i]t is vital that this kind of exhibition should be available to people going about their business shopping, and able to drop in [as] this is the way you make converts to the enjoyment and appreciation of the arts'.[40] The Development Corporation also commissioned various artworks to be installed inside the shopping centre. In February 1980, a £18,000 'kinetic sculpture' by American sculptress Liliane Lijn was, for instance, suspended from the ceiling above Midsummer Arcade. The installation of this sculpture was accompanied by an exhibition of drawings that showed how the sculpture was made.[41] The MKDC thus not only sought to inculcate civic pride through the design of the shopping centre, but also encouraged the civic education of Milton Keynes' residents through the integration of art in the building and the programming of various public events and exhibitions.[42]

More than a shopping centre, the building was to become a civic centre, which through its design would craft better citizens. Instead of having an underground delivery system, or even one at the rear, the Centre's delivery routes were placed on top of the building. This decision was quite controversial, but had strong practical and economic motives. Mosscrop pointed out that underground servicing was very expensive, and suggested that '[u]p there, you only have to take them 3 m high and they get ventilation and light free of charge'.[43] In a recent interview, Woodward however intimated that pragmatism and cost-effectiveness were not the sole motives informing this decision. He contended that by placing the delivery routes on top of the Centre in direct view of the shoppers – these service roads were located on the low, outer bands of shops and thus clearly visible from the two main fourteen metre high arcades – the design team aspired to create a continuous reminder of the labour involved in the functioning of the Centre.[44] Beyond cultivating the individual shopper and inculcating civic pride, the building's design thus also aimed to heighten the social (or 'class') consciousness of its shoppers.

The commodification of urban life

Ahead of the Centre's opening, the Central Milton Keynes Advertising Agency was given the delicate task of launching an advertising campaign. This campaign was to instil confidence in private investors, while maintaining the depiction of the Centre as a city/civic centre servicing the local community. Countering (or perhaps rather 'complementing'?) descriptions by the local press – which was commonly keen to support claims to greatness – of Milton Keynes' Centre as the 'Biggest Buy in All Europe'[45] and

---

[39]Ibid.
[40]Ibid.
[41]'Let There be Light with Sculpture – Cost of £18,000', *Milton Keynes Mirror*, 27 February 1980, 22. See also: 'The Circle of Light', *Milton Keynes Express*, 28 September 1979, 59.
[42]Hill, *The Story of the Original CMK*, 109.
[43]Mosscrop, Interviewed by Roger Kitchen, in *The Story of the Original CMK*, Hill, 113.
[44]Christopher Woodward, Interviewed by Janina Gosseye, 13 January 2014.
[45]'Biggest Buy in All Europe', *Milton Keynes Express* (supplement), 23 March 1979, 24–25.

a 'Palace of Varieties',[46] the Advertising Agency advised that the campaign was to depict the Centre as 'friendly and human and warm and inviting',[47] giving clear instructions to avoid any reference to 'bigness', 'inhumanity' and 'coldness'.[48] This inviting and humane, campaign rhetoric not only neatly coincided with the democratically inspired unconditional access to the shopping centre that MKDC's architects, planners and politicians aspired to, but also advanced the Centre's commercial aims. A similar egalitarian rhetoric was used by Thatcher to promote the sell-off of council estates. This policy was rolled out at the opening of Milton Keynes' shopping centre and was cleverly (as it emphasized the supposed 'democratic' and 'egalitarian' foundations of the initiative) coined the 'right to buy'.[49] But the 'right to buy' was not a right available to all residents of Milton Keynes as Roger Kitchen, a social worker of the MKDC, pointed out in an article in the *Milton Keynes Express*: 'There are many people', he wrote, 'the less well off – the people for whom Milton Keynes was intended to provide housing – who will never be in a position to afford the glossy life style the development corporation continues to portray in its undampened enthusiasm'.[50] Kitchen thus suggested that by subsuming Milton Keynes' 'city centre' in a shopping centre, not only the quality of urban life became a commodity, but also the city itself.

Rather than a city or a civic centre, some suggested that the new shopping centre introduced the neoliberal ethic of intense possessive individualism as a template for human socialization in Milton Keynes. Sue Aplin, a researcher from Brunel University, for instance wrote:

> I think the centre fulfils some deeper need in these pilgrims who travel from as far as Nottingham and Peterborough. It is a communal meeting place to which they can go and be contained as part of a group with a shared destination and purpose…there is something very alluring about the centre, standing on the highest point for miles around and incorporating mystical elements in its design. The building's interior has some of the symbolic content of a cathedral with aisles and naves on axes, and high central spaces which reduce human form. There are seven altars where you can pay respect to favourite saints in the form of Boots, Marks & Spencers and British Home Stores. The order of identity of a particular time is normally represented by a structure be it a mound, a stone, a pyramid, a temple, a castle, cathedral or palace. Today the new shopping centres, like Milton Keynes, … have become potent symbols of our time to today's communities.[51]

This somewhat incongruous conflation of the Centre with the country's great medieval cathedrals, which suggested that in Milton Keynes consumerism had become a religion, was however not plucked out of thin air. In September 1979, a few months after Bill Jowett, manager of the Milton Keynes

---

[46] 'Palace of Varieties', *Milton Keynes Express* (supplement), 21 September 1979, 16–17.

[47] 'Central Milton Keynes: Shopping as It Should Be – The Launch Plan: Advertising and Promotion', found in: MKDC lib 22/2, Brochure on the launch plan, advertising and promotion for Central Milton Keynes entitled 'Shopping as It Should Be', Centre for Buckinghamshire Studies, Centre for Buckinghamshire Studies (Aylesbury).

[48] Ibid.

[49] After the opening of the shopping centre Thatcher and her entourage visited the Galley Hill home of Peter and Patricia King, who had (by then) lived in Milton Keynes for more than six years. During this visit, she presented them with the deeds of their house, making Mr and Mrs King the first couple to make use of the substantial discounts offered by Thatcher's new government to tenants who wanted to buy their (council) homes. See 'She's Nice, Say Labour Voters', *Milton Keynes Express*, 28 September 1979, 3.

[50] Roger Kitchen, 'Glossy Life Style', *Milton Keynes Express*, 23 March 1979, 31.

[51] Sue Aplin, 'A Potent Symbol', *The Architects' Journal: Reflections on Milton Keynes Shopping Centre*, 22 October 1980, 801.

Shopping Management Company, suggested that '[o]ne of the most exciting ideas is for Middleton Hall to become the "cathedral" of Milton Keynes',[52] reverend Robin Baker, rector of the newly created city centre parish, soon joined in his enthusiasm, and – agreeing that 'Middleton Hall has almost a cathedral feel about it' – opted to host that year's harvest festival in the shopping centre.[53] As Milton Keynes had no church at that time, reverend Baker's enthusiasm was not entirely surprising. Although it had the world's largest shopping centre, Milton Keynes lacked not only a church, but also quite a few facilities that one would expect to have been constructed prior to such a large commercial structure, including a hospital[54] and a train station.[55] By building the 'biggest and best' indoor shopping centre in Europe at the heart of Milton Keynes before some of these basic civic facilities, the MKDC gave citizens the instruction that shopping was the civic value of Milton Keynes.

The official opening of the Centre[56] was largely overshadowed by demonstrations held in 'honour' of the visit of Prime Minister Thatcher. 'Prime Minister gets Rowdy Reception', the *Milton Keynes Express* headlined on 28 September 1979, continuing that during the official opening of the shopping centre Thatcher was met by a 'mob' of protesters, who 'booed and heckled throughout her 10 minute speech in Middleton Hall'.[57] This protest was however not directed against the 'multi-million tribute to the consumer society', as the *Milton Keynes Mirror* called the shopping centre,[58] and the neo-liberal ring of this development. Instead, protestors who 'noisily shouted', as an 'unmoved'[59] Thatcher walked through the shopping centre, railed against government spending cuts to Milton Keynes that had (supposedly) made the development of Milton Keynes' Centre possible. Many regarded the development of the Centre as a form of 'government' expenditure that was necessary to attract private investment and guarantee the survival of Milton Keynes.[60] In the late 1960s and 1970s, as many old industrial cities

---

[52]'Biggest Buy in All Europe'.

[53]'Planning Harvest Festival in Shop Centre "Cathedral"', *Milton Keynes Express* (supplement), 21 September 1979, 12.

[54]G. Farmer, 'The Cash Should Be Going towards a Hospital', *Milton Keynes Mirror*, 5 March 1980, 9. See also Bendixson and Platt, *Milton Keynes: Image and Reality*, 146.

[55]'Green Light for New £7.8m Station Plan', *Milton Keynes Mirror*, 20 February 1980.

[56]Although Margaret Thatcher 'officially' opened Milton Keynes' shopping centre on 25 September 1979, the shopping centre had already opened to the public more than one month earlier, on 9 August 1979. See 'Prime Minister to Open City Centre', *Milton Keynes Express*, 6 July 1979, 1; 'Prime Minister to Open City Centre', *Milton Keynes Mirror*, 11 July 1979, 1; 'Mrs Thatcher Puts off Visit', *Milton Keynes Express*, 3 August 1979, 1; 'Super City Centre Has Lift-Off!', *Milton Keynes Mirror*, 15 August 1979, 1; 'Crystal Palace Opens', *Milton Keynes Express* (supplement), 21 September 1979, 2; 'As Thatcher Opens the City Centre … Hundreds in Protest over Cuts', *Milton Keynes Mirror*, 26 September 1979, 1; 'Prime Minister Gets Rowdy Reception', *Milton Keynes Express*, 28 September 1979, 1.

[57]'Maggie Is in a Fighting Mood: Noisy Hecklers at City Centre Demo', *Milton Keynes Express*, 28 September 1979, 3.

[58]'Supershop … We're Number One in Europe!', *Milton Keynes Mirror*, 8 August 1978, 1–2.

[59]Ibid., 9.

[60]The Milton Keynes Development Corporation was faced with severe cuts in their budget. 'City in Danger if Tories Win' *Milton Keynes Express* announced on 6 April 1979, claiming that 'the new city and its long-awaited hospital would be on the danger-list if the Conservatives win the election'. Attracting private investment was thus seen as a necessity to guarantee the survival of the city, which was confirmed in a June 1979 article, stating: 'The government has cut Milton Keynes Development Corporation's budget this year by £3m but this week an MKDC spokesman claimed it would have little effect on the development of the new city. For there has been "increasing support" from private investors, rising from £40m last year to £60m this….' See 'Government Cuts MKDC budget', *Milton Keynes Express*, 29 June 1979, 15. This was not unusual, as Peter Shapely has pointed out: 'From the late 1950s through to the late 1970s, local government in Britain worked (often closely) with the private sector to secure investment and redevelopment.' Source: Shapely, 'Governance in the Post-war City', 1288.

like Manchester, Liverpool and Birmingham plunged into economic decline, local authorities (not in the least development corporations) needed to 'sell' their cities, both literally and figuratively speaking, in order to attract investment. Failure to do so, Shapely claims, would have meant missing out on major investment opportunities, leading inevitably to accusations of incompetence.[61] Many (if not most) Milton Keynes' residents thus silently condoned the MKDC's rather pragmatic and business-minded approach. They did not rail against the shopping centre for commodifying public space in Milton Keynes, but (quite on the contrary) joyfully proclaimed: 'I feel that the shopping centre has given a heart to the city … it is a joy to shop at Central Milton Keynes, it is just what Milton Keynes needed and in my opinion shopping as it should be'[62] and: 'On my first shopping expedition in the city centre my biggest reaction was a sense of community, at last here is a place where the people of Milton Keynes could come and feel at home.'[63]

Enveloping the public and the private in a (post-) modern jacket

While the local popular press and many Milton Keynes residents marvelled at their new shopping centre, some national commentators were more critical about this development. In a television programme called 'Shop', executive producer of arts and features for Anglia TV John Swinfield for instance blandly labelled the complex 'Shopping out of a test-tube – its countenance is smooth anonymity'.[64] Not entirely public nor completely private; not a real shopping centre, but not a wholesome civic or city centre either; constructed at a turning point from modernism to post-modernism; and seemingly entrenched between welfare state ideals and neo-liberal politics, the Centre's ambiguous position in-between in particular became a point of contention.

Architectural critics were maddened and baffled by Milton Keynes' shopping centre. In *The Architects' Journal* of October 1980 some questioned the dubious way in which the Centre promoted 'consumer society values' while others deprecated the shopping centre for its 'failure to follow orthodox marketing practices in the lack of inviting signs and "razzamatazz"'.[65] Terry Farrell, for instance, expressed his 'unease' about 'the way the designers knowingly or unknowingly contributed to the overall institutional effect with an obsessive use of grids and anonymous mirror glass',[66] and continued: 'The '60s argument that anonymous buildings and frameworks allow people freedom to do what they like is clearly mistaken; creative, personal prompts are needed to prevent pubs looking like railway buffets and public

---

[61] Shapely, 'Governance in the Post-war City', 1292; Shapely, 'Civic Pride and Redevelopment in the Post-war British City', 314.
[62] 'City's New Heart', *Milton Keynes Mirror*, 30 January 1980, 22.
[63] D. Parker, 'A Sense of Community', *Milton Keynes Mirror*, 6 February 1980, 15.
[64] 'Shopping Out of a Test-Tube?', *Milton Keynes Express*, 25 January 1980, 6.
[65] David Embling, 'Editor's Comment', *The Architects' Journal: Reflections on Milton Keynes Shopping Centre*, 22 October 1980, 806.
[66] Terry Farrell, 'Endless Arcades', *The Architects' Journal: Reflections on Milton Keynes Shopping Centre*, 22 October 1980, 798.

squares like exercise yards.'[67] Thus unmistakably categorizing the Centre as an utterance of a bygone architectural era – modernism – Farrell expressed a desire for the architects to 'breathe more fun into the whole mixture'.[68] The tone of Peter Smith's contribution was even less forgiving. After railing against the Centre's 'inexorable gridsquare', 'blank walls' and the 'perverse' handling of parking and first floor servicing, he concluded: 'No, Milton Keynes, I can't rate you very highly in my shopping centre stakes. Most of the tasteless developers' schemes up and down the country have more go, more sense of place about them. I don't even think that one can blame (or credit) Mies or the Modern Movement with this phenomenon, or rather mania.'[69]

The architects and planners of the Centre had of course been given a very daunting task. At a time when architecture was increasingly turning away from the blandness and failed utopianism of the modern movement, allowing for 'complexity and contradiction' to enter the profession, and the precedents of shopping centres that had 'architecture' were few and far between, they had to manage the expectations of private companies who needed to be seduced to open a shop in the building while attempting to imbue the shopping centre with a sense of civic 'dignity' befitting a city centre. It is then no surprise that they relied on the modern methods they were familiar with, leading to what Nikolaus Pevsner has labelled 'a sleek Miesian steel-framed and glass-clad style'.[70] The only discernible post-modern element of Milton Keynes' Centre was its mirror glazing, which some scholars have qualified as one of the most complete signifiers of postmodernity: it not only signifies the postmodern agencies that absorb and project all contexts as surface effects or simulacra but also denotes the very technology of reproduction, which centrally defines the post-modern moment.[71]

More than with form and design idiom, the local community was concerned with the financing of this glass and steel leviathan. In 1979, for instance, when the MKDC announced that it had set aside half a million pounds for the advertising campaign for the shopping centre,[72] Borough Councillor David Taylor questioned why public funds should be invested in the marketing campaign of a shopping centre. 'Who Pays City Publicity Bill?', he openly asked in a letter to the *Milton Keynes Express*, questioning if it is '[m]orally right to spend public money advertising a selection of private companies?'. [73] The most pertinent debate regarding the shopping centre's finances was however raised in a short note sent to the *Milton Keynes Express* by resident Gwen Howick, suggesting that the shopping centre had been

---

[67] Ibid.

[68] Ibid., 799.

[69] Peter Smith, 'Shopping Inside the Gridiron', *The Architects' Journal: Reflections on Milton Keynes Shopping Centre*, 22 October 1980, 805.

[70] Nikolaus Pevsner, Elizabeth Williamson and Geoffrey K. Brandwood, *The Buildings of England: Buckinghamshire*, second edition (London: Penguin Books, 1994), 489.

[71] John D. Dorst, *The Written Suburb: An American Site, an Etnographic Dilemma* (Philadelphia: University of Pennsylvania Press, 1989), 107; Neil Leach (ed.), *Rethinking Architecture: A Reader in Cultural Theory* (London and New York: Routledge, 1997), 224–255. Frederic Jameson through the analysis of the Bonaventure Hotel in Los Angeles similarly links mirror glazing to postmodernism and capitalism: Frederic Jameson, *Postmodernism, or the Cultural Logic of Late Capitalism* (Durham: Duke University Press, 1991).

[72] '£500.000 Promotion', *Milton Keynes Express*, 26 October 1979, 7.

[73] David Taylor, 'Who Pays City Publicity Bill?', *Milton Keynes Express*, 2 November 1979, 8.

Figure 9.6 Exterior view of Milton Keynes' shopping centre, showing its mirror glazing.
Source: MKDC Collection, Centre for Buckinghamshire Studies (Aylesbury), archive location: 000953 DGM Press and info Photos 1.

made too ornate at the expense of housing estates.[74] Her suggestion received an impassioned reply in the following edition of the newspaper by an anonymous 'shopper', who pointed out that

> the shopping building was funded by the Post Office Pension Fund. They invested their money in the future of Milton Keynes. They would not have spent that money on housing. In a capitalist society that is their choice. They, after all, have to think of their members' future needs and they need a good return for their investment.[75]

The fact that the Post Office Pension Fund put up £24 million[76] for the development of Milton Keynes' Centre indeed placed the MKDC in a very advantageous position. It not only freed the corporation from entering into a partnership with a private developer, which might have compromised the design, but it also provided a welcome rebuttal against claims that the MKDC was squandering taxpayers' money.

---

[74] Gwen Howick, *Milton Keynes Express*, 8 February 1980.
[75] 'Hurrah for Shops Centre', *Milton Keynes Express*, 15 February 1980, 8.
[76] 'Opening of Central Milton Keynes by the Prime Minister – Tuesday, 25 September 1979', Centre for Buckinghamshire Studies.

Although the 'Royal Mail' was part of the public sector, its pension scheme was not run in a similar way to other pension schemes for public sector workers. Contrary to most public sector pension funds, which were paid for directly out of general taxation, the Post Office Pension Fund relied on contributions from workers and the growth of the scheme's assets to pay for worker's pensions, while the company was liable to pay for any shortfall out of its own revenue. In theory, the anonymous 'shopper' whose letter was published in the *Milton Keynes Express* was thus right: the money invested into the shopping centre did not come from taxpayers' purse, but from a private fund. However, as the decades rolled past and the expenses of the Post Office Pension scheme steadily increased, also the deficit between the fund's assets and liabilities grew. By the early 2000s, when talks started about the privatization of the Royal Mail, this deficit was estimated at £37,5 billion. So, when in March 2012 the Royal Mail was privatized in one of the largest government sell-offs in generations and the service was sold for £28 billion, the company's future obligations, which were tied up in the Post Office Pension Fund and which amounted to approximately £10 billion, were nationalized. This deal thus relieved the (now private) Royal Mail of its immense pensions deficit by effectively passing this financial burden on to the UK's taxpayers.[77]

This entanglement between the public and the private (both in economical and spatial terms), which started in the post-war decades and was strongly supported (and elaborated) by Thatcher's regime, has made it increasingly difficult to qualify precisely what the country's 'public' assets are and what are its private ones. In Milton Keynes' (shopping) Centre, the public sphere – or 'civic realm' – was intimately enmeshed with private interests. Here, citizens became consumers who, MKDC's politicians, planners and designers hoped, would through the spatial design of the shopping centre and through encounters with exotic foreign plants and modern artworks become 'elevated' citizens with a keen community spirit and heightened social consciousness.

Conclusion

Untangling the construction history of Milton Keynes' Centre, this chapter set out to demonstrate the complex ways in which public and private interests became increasingly entangled in Britain's post-war urban development and to uncover how architects and planners responded to the ongoing political and economical transformations that gradually dismantled the welfare state and paved the way for the 'triumph' of neo-liberalism. In Milton Keynes, Derek Walker, Stuart Mosscrop and Christopher Woodward sought to create a city centre that was able to inculcate civic pride, educate the public and engender social consciousness, while responding to the economic aims of its private investors. The resulting design was a function of the synergies and dissonances between these

---

[77]Mitch Feierstein, 'Royal Mail Pension Nationalisation: Far from Providing a Windfall, It Turns MPs into Hypocrites and the Rest of Us into Debtors', *Daily Mail*, 20 March 2012, http://www.dailymail.co.uk/debate/article-2117106/Royal-Mail-pension-nationalisation-Far-providing-windfall-turns-MPs-hypocrites-rest-debtors.html, accessed 1 November 2015; David Kingman, 'The Privatisation of Royal Mail: What about the Pension Scheme?' *Intergenerational Foundation: Fairness for Future Generations*, 25 September 2013, http://www.if.org.uk/archives/4280/the-privatisation-of-royal-mail-what-about-the-pension-scheme, accessed 1 November 2015.

different aspirations. Although the Centre commodified urban life in Milton Keynes and introduced the neoliberal ethic of intense possessive individualism as a template for human socialization, it did create a modern heart for the new town. This chapter thus evidences that Milton Keynes' Centre was neither the apotheosis of the post-war consensus nor an apostle of neo-liberalism, but both simultaneously, as the building expresses the confluence of these antagonistic socioeconomic ideologies in its material form.

Chapter 10

Shopping as a part of a political agenda: The emergence and development of the shopping centre in socialist Croatia, 1960–1980

Sanja Matijević Barčot and Ana Grgić

Introduction

In (former) socialist countries the theme of consumerism has for a long time been neglected in sociological and anthropological research. A possible explanation for this dearth, which has also manifested itself in the field of architectural history, could be found in the widespread assumption that consumerism only played a significant role in capitalist contexts. Socialist realms are, by contrast, believed to rely upon the ideological basis of social egalitarianism, which implies an essentialist perception of human needs. In such contexts, a distinction is made between those needs that are 'true', human and deeply authentic and those that are 'false', imposed and, as such, cannot lead to true happiness.[1] This compliance with the 'codes' imposed by egalitarianism has legitimized the portrayal of socialist economies as morally superior to capitalist ones. However, in socialist countries, it is the State that controls production and, consequently, all major sectors of the economy. The State thus determines what the 'true' needs are and dictates the ways in which and the extent to which these needs will be satisfied. Feher, Heller and Marcus, all affiliates of the Budapest School of thought, have described this political system as a 'dictatorship over needs'.[2] In such a system the wish to possess things merely because they are new, exciting or modern is deemed morally and politically incorrect, while destitution and self-denial in the name of a 'nobler' cause is highly valued and has assumed the effect of a 'social glue'.[3] The general assumption is therefore that consumerist culture, whereby values are determined by purchasing power and material ownership, is incompatible with the ideological premise of socialism.

---

[1] Breda Luthar, 'Remembering Socialism: On Desire, Consumption and Surveillance', *Journal of Consumer Culture* 6 (2006): 233.
[2] Ferenc Feher, Agnes Heller and Gyorgy Markus, *Dictatorship over Needs* (New York: St. Martin's Press, 1983).
[3] David Crowley and Susan Emily Reid, 'Introduction: Pleasures in Socialism?', in *Pleasures in Socialism: Leisure and Luxury in the Eastern Bloc*, eds. David Crowley and Susan Emily Reid (Evanston: Northwestern University Press, 2010), 10.

Yugoslavia, of which Croatia was an integral part until 1991, represents a unique case due to the peculiar political position that the country assumed after the conflict of the Yugoslav President Tito with Stalin in 1948.[4] As a result of this conflict Yugoslavia was expelled from the Inform-bureau (the East European association of Communist parties) and withdrew from the Eastern Bloc. Yugoslav society subsequently increasingly rejected the so-called 'Soviet' model that had, up to then, permeated all aspects of life: from politics to economy to culture. But the dispute with Stalin did not prompt Tito to abandon socialism; it motivated him to seek another path, a sociopolitical ideology that would prove to be superior to Soviet socialism. This new path was found in 'self-management' socialism[5] and was, according to American historian Patrick Hyder Patterson, 'a decidedly *socialist* conception that claimed to be more faithful to the original vision laid out by Marx'.[6] Starting from 1950, in an attempt to distinguish Yugoslavia's socialist path from the Soviets', the government increasingly dismissed certain methods of rigid state control that had been the basis of economic policy during the previous five years. That year political leader Boris Kidrič stated: 'To think that the uncontrolled torrent may be eliminated…is a folly, idealism…the one to be able to do it would be – God!…Today we have to allow the onset of somewhat chaotic economic laws, as well a number of other laws….'[7] Kidrič's statement was symptomatic of Yugoslavia's increasing rejection of Soviet-style socialism and signalled the advent (and acceptance) of new economic models, which were much more in-tune with liberal economy market mechanisms. Although the State still provided a regulatory framework by delineating a macroeconomic plan, the imposed constraints were much less restrictive and gave Yugoslav businesses greater economic independence.[8]

---

[4]The reasons for the so-called Tito-Stalin split were numerous and complex and are still the subject of research and interpretation. A commonly accepted thesis suggests that the dispute arose because of Tito's unwillingness to submit to Moscow's policies and forfeit his influence in the Balkan. See, for example, Wayne S. Vucinich (ed.), *At the Brink of War and Peace: The Tito Stalin Split in a Historic Perspective* (New York: Columbia University Press, 1982); Jeronim Perović, 'The Tito-Stalin Split: A Reassessment in Light of New Evidence', *Journal of Cold War Studies* 2 (2007): 32–63.

[5]The political concept of 'self-management socialism' was first publicly presented by Tito's chief theoretician Edvard Kardelj, in his speech at the National Assembly in 1949. Central to Kardelj's speech was the idea that the future development of socialism must be based on citizens' participation in governance and decision-making processes. In June 1950, the first law establishing workers' self-management, the Basic Law of Management of State Economic Enterprises by Working Collectives, also known as the Law on Handing over Factories to the Workers, came into action. Although the subsequent development of self-management included many formal mechanisms of workers' participation in decision-making processes, in reality these merely legitimized decisions that had been taken previously, rather than implemented a true form of workers' self-management, as social processes and important economic decisions still remained in the hands of political power. Duško Bilandžić, *Hrvatska moderna povijest* (Zagreb: Golden marketing, 1999), 314–339.

[6]Patrick Hyder Patterson, *Bought and Sold: Living and Losing the Good Life in Socialist Yugoslavia* (Ithaca: Cornell University Press, 2011), 27.

[7]'Misliti da se stihija može ukloniti…je glupost, idealizam…onaj tko bi likvidirao stihiju bio bi – Bog!…Mi danas moramo dozvoliti početak stihijnog [sic.] djelovanja ekonomskih zakona i niza drugih zakona ….' Boris Kidrič, lecture given at the Institute of Social Sciences in Belgrade on 21 June 1950, quoted in Bilandžić, *Hrvatska moderna povijest*, 321; translated by the authors.

[8]The Yugoslav economy is often labelled a form of 'market socialism'. Attempting to reconcile the socialist premise of egalitarianism with (ruthless) market dynamics that aspire to increase profit by eliminating the competition, this system applied a 'correction' by claiming or 'confiscating' the majority of companies' profit, leaving only a certain amount at the company's own disposal. As such, the state was able to guarantee the wage of every employee regardless of the company's profitability. Ibid., 327–328, 410.

In parallel with these internal reforms, Yugoslavia's international position also changed. Following its separation from the Eastern Bloc, Yugoslav politics gradually opened up to the West, which granted the country abundant financial aid, thanks to its important geostrategic position. After Stalin's death in 1953, however, diplomatic relations with the USSR were re-established and Tito assumed a leading role in the formation of the Non-Aligned Movement in early 1960s.[9] Yugoslavia's foreign policy and international position thus increasingly became a careful balancing act between East and West, as Tito manoeuvred the country into an exceptionally opportune political position 'in-between'. According to an issue of *Time* magazine published in 1965, Yugoslavia's position necessitated permanent oscillation between 'communist iron control' and 'flirting with capitalism', and proved to be extremely precarious in economic terms.[10] Nonetheless, Tito's cunning manipulation of Yugoslavia's in-betweenness resulted in economic prosperity and effectuated a sort of economic miracle in the following decades. In fact, its position 'in-between' meant that Yugoslavia enjoyed the best of both worlds: socialist ethics and capitalist models. This position of course brought about some unease and contradictions, most notably with regard to the country's stance on consumerism.

The emergence of consumerist culture

At the height of Yugoslavia's economic growth, which had increased employment and heightened purchasing power, the State's highest political body, the Central Committee of the League of Communists of Yugoslavia, decreed that a higher living standard was to become a key goal of the country's economic policy. To that end two economic development guidelines were introduced: one aimed to increase public investments in welfare, including housing, education, healthcare and culture, and the other encouraged personal consumption.[11] Furthermore, in 1958, this same political body drew up a programme that envisaged *udobniji život*, or a 'more comfortable life' for Yugoslav citizens, including the ownership of 'various objects of consumption' - *različitih predmeta potrošnje*. This programme was to ensure *bolje usluživanje potrošača robom*, a 'better catering to the consumer's needs', a concern for *svakodnevne potrebe i opskrbu*, 'everyday needs and supply' and also *odmor i zabavu*; 'rest and

---

[9]The Non-Aligned Movement was created to give those countries that had not formally aligned with either of the two power blocs political clout. Most partisans of the Non-Aligned Movement were Asian and African countries that had recently gained independence after the demise of the colonial system. Tito was among the first to recognize their political potential and, although they often adhered to resolutely different ideologies and political beliefs, the new relations that subsequently grew between Yugoslavia and these countries resulted in cultural cooperation and provided significant business opportunities. For Yugoslavian architects the country's participation in the Non-Aligned Movement meant that they could get involved in a range of planning and design projects in fellow Non-Aligned states. Ibid., 373–383.

[10]'Yugoslavia: Half Karl & Half Groucho', *Time*, 7 May 1965, http://www.time.com/time/magazine/article/0,9171,898778-2,00.html, accessed 14 April 2015.

[11]The budget of socialist Yugoslavia was basically distributed over two kinds of investments: 'capital investments' (in industry and infrastructure) on the one hand and 'social standard investments' on the other. While the first five-year plan, drafted in 1947, prescribed almost exclusively 'capital' investments to assist the country's intensive industrialization, the focus of the new state investments, following the political changes in the 1950s, was geared towards projects that would directly improve people's everyday lives. Bilandžić, *Hrvatska moderna povijest*, 387.

recreation'.[12] While it confirmed that personal improvement should not trump common interests, the programme did posit that personal happiness could not be subordinated to so-called 'higher causes'. It thus marked a loosening of the 'dictatorship over needs'.

During the Cold War, consumption became a weapon in the superpowers' fight for citizens' 'hearts and souls' and an essential component of America's cultural imperialism.[13] When in 1957 America placed a supermarket at the heart of its exhibit at the Zagreb Fair, this display was well received by Yugoslav citizens.[14] It also impressed those in power, to such an extent that the Yugoslav government decreed that sixty similar supermarkets were to be opened across the country as soon as possible.[15] Particularly fascinating about this novel symbol of American modernity was that it enabled customers to – through 'self-service' – choose the item that they wished to purchase themselves. So, by exporting the supermarket, America exported the sense of freedom, the freedom of choice.[16] This experience was of special significance to the citizens of a country in which no freedom of choice existed. Over the following decade, which was rife with political and ideological introspection, the belief that 'quality of life' was a basic human right increasingly took root. And so, by the early 1960s some goods that countries behind the Iron Curtain could only dream of had become available in Yugoslavia.[17] Although this emerging consumerism in Yugoslavia did not attain Western standards in terms of choice and abundance, from the perspective of the Eastern Bloc it was nonetheless enviable.[18] Yugoslav statistics from the 1960s and the 1970s show a steady growth of private consumption, which in some years even exceeded 10 per cent.[19] These 'successes' soon quashed the critique of committed Marxists,

---

[12] Igor Duda, 'Svakodnevni život i potrošačka kultura u Hrvatskoj 1970-ih i 1980-ih' (PhD diss., Sveučilište u Zagrebu, 2009), 15, citing *Program Saveza komunista Jugoslavije. Prihvaćen na Sedmom kongresu Saveza komunista Jugoslavije 22.–26. travnja 1958. u Ljubljani* (Zagreb: Stvarnost, 1965); translated by the authors.

[13] See, for example, Victoria de Grazia, *Irresistible Empire: America's Advance through 20th Century Europe* (Cambridge, MA: Belknap Press of Harvard University Press, 2005).

[14] Before the Zagreb Fair, the United States displayed the supermarket at the exhibitions in Paris, Vienna and Rome. However, the supermarket exhibition at the Zagreb Fair turned out to be the most spectacular one, as it surpassed the until then most visited Roman exhibition which was attended by more than 400,000 people. Radina Vučetić, 'Potrošačko društvo po američkom modelu (jedan pogled na jugoslavensku svakodnevicu šezdesetih)', *časopis za suvremenu povijest* 2 (2012): 291, citing Robert H. Haddow, *Pavilions of Plenty: Exhibiting America Abroad in the 1950s* (Washington, DC: Smithsonian Institution Press, 1997).

[15] Ibid., 292.

[16] Ibid., 289–297.

[17] A variety of well-known European and American products were produced under license in Yugoslavia, so Yugoslavians could enjoy products of Western brands. Vučetić, 'Potrošačko društvo po američkom modelu (jedan pogled na jugoslavensku svakodnevicu šezdesetih)', 281.

[18] At the time, a renowned American tourist guide explained that the living standard in Yugoslavia was growing steadily, but had not yet reached the level of comfort achieved in Western countries. The guide did note that the basic necessities and consumer goods were available in almost every household and that food was plentiful and cheap. Fodor, *Fodor's Modern Guides: Yugoslavia* (New York: McKay, 1968), 46–47, cited in Igor Duda, *U potrazi za blagostanjem: O povijesti dokolice i potrošačkog društva u Hrvatskoj 1950-ih i 1960-ih* (Zagreb: Srednja Europa, 2014), 57–58.

[19] Bilandžić, *Hrvatska moderna povijest*, 388. The extreme growth of personal consumption has been associated with the exceptionally low cost of housing and healthcare. Patterson writes: '… in 1966 a worker earning the average personal income would have had to work 16 hours to pay the monthly rent on an average apartment of fifty square metres. Simply to buy a pair of men's leather shoes, however, she would have had to work longer – almost 18 hours'. Patterson, *Bought and Sold*, 42.

Figure 10.1 President Tito and his wife visiting the supermarket prototype at the Zagreb Fair, 1957.
Source: Photograph by Ladislav Benko, Hrvatski državni arhiv, Croatian State Archives, Zagreb, Croatia.

who questioned the possibility of attaining consumer satisfaction without succumbing to consumerist values and ethics.[20] And so, as the marketing and advertising industry grew on a par with consumption, shopping increasingly came to be seen as a legitimate way of spending one's free time, complementing the programmed socialist leisure that up until then had consisted solely of cultural and political education and 'uplifting' physical and social activities. From the 1960s on, the State began to invest in

---

[20]Patterson, *Bought and Sold*, 149.

new facilities that would enable and stimulate consumption, just like it had previously invested in the development of so-called 'homes of culture'.

Shopping and city development

In the early 1960s a retail network of specialized shops, supermarkets and department stores was set up following a State decree, which was financed with contributions by socially owned trading companies and public funds.[21] Two distinct – in terms of urban planning – retail typologies emerged in the following decades. The first was the so-called 'centre'. Designed as a quasi-autonomous spatial complex, the 'centre' was generally constructed at the heart of new state-financed housing developments which started to appear in the outskirts of cities and which were invariably designed in accordance with CIAM concepts of urban planning. They contributed to the urban expansion and decentralization of the city centre in terms of trading and services and ranged from small nuclei offering just a few basic necessities, such as food shops, basic services, and spaces for social and political activities, to large cores containing a wide programmatic array, including self-managed community offices, community halls, reading rooms, supermarkets, textile shops, newsagents, tobacconists, stationery shops, restaurants, confectionery and pastry stores, hairdressers, tailors and sometimes even a cinema. The built form of the 'centre' was a function of its programmatic complexity, and generally took the shape of an urban

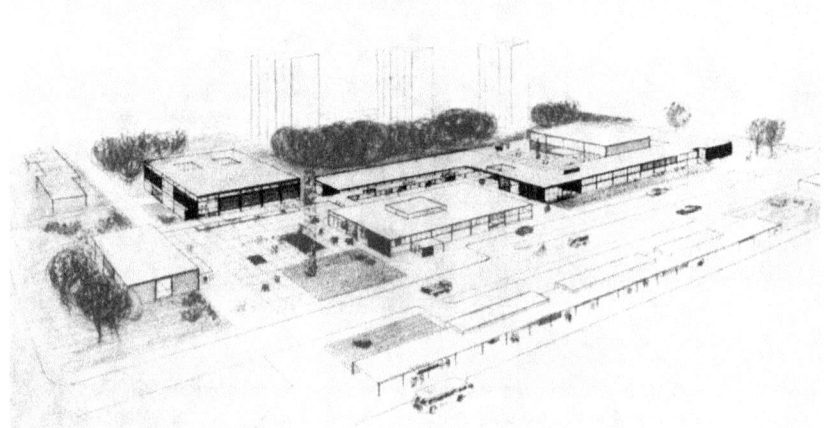

Figure 10.2 Centre of the Trnsko housing estate, Zagreb, 1963. Architects: Aleksandar Dragomanović, Radovan Nikšić, Edo Šmidihen.
Source: Croatian Museum of Architecture, Zagreb, Croatia.

---

[21]The shopping facilities within the new housing estates were considered a part of the local community services. Their construction was therefore financed mainly by public funds. These funds were raised through a taxation scheme, stipulating that investors who built housing units had to contribute 20 per cent of the price of the each built apartment to the municipality. Monies obtained through this scheme were also used for the construction of other communal facilities, such as schools and kindergardens. Sanja Matijević Barčot, 'Utjecaj društveno organiziranih modela stambene izgradnje na arhitekturu Splita 1945–1968', PhD dissertation, Sveučilište u Zagrebu, 2014, 159.

cluster built up of different functional pavilions. These pavilions were often located along an open-air pedestrian walkways or public squares. The 'centre' not only provided basic services, but also accommodated the social life of the local community, offering venues for informal socializing, political activities and cultural events. The role that these Yugoslav 'centres' were envisaged to play was not unlike what Victor Gruen had originally imagined for the American shopping centre, which was to offer a spatial framework supporting the social cohesion of new city areas by offering an array of social, civic and commercial services.[22]

If the 'centre' was to create an urban atmosphere *ab ovo*, the other retail typology that popularized in 1960s Yugoslavia added another layer to existing urban fabrics. The downtown department store emerged in tandem with new regulations for city centres and was commonly commissioned by city administrations to direct post-war reconstruction and boost inner-city development. In early post-war years, most good-sized cities had commissioned regulation plans or/and – at least – architectural studies projecting the future development of the city centre. During the 1960s, as a result of the sociopolitical and economic changes that had occurred in the country, these regulation plans were often severely altered, most commonly to increase commercial capacity, sometimes even by replacing the cultural facilities. One such example is the 'Regulation Project of City Centre Extension' in Split. This proposal by Berislav Kalogjera used a broad range of modern elements, including overlapping volumes, designed passages, shaded porches, semi-covered and open pedestrian squares, to interfere with the irregular structure of the existing urban tissue and imitate the medieval city core. Kalogjera arranged business and trading facilities along irregular pedestrian paths and dispersed shopping over the entire volume, creating a higher concentration in its southern part. The project also featured a new architectural typology, never before seen in Split: the department store, which was built on the very edge of the historical city core. During the project's realization department stores were incorporated in several other locations in the area. After Prima, the first department store, another three were built: Maja, Salon namještaja Prima (Prima furniture store) and Dalma. These all embraced a bold, modern formal language and significantly contributed to the complexity of the city's public space.

Like elsewhere in war-torn Europe, the 'downtown' department store became an integral part of the process of re-urbanization. Informed by CIAM's concept of the 'core' and Bakema's theories about the humanization of the centre, the department store became a tool for urban reconstruction and revitalization. It was used either as an 'urban patch' – the department stores Maja and Prima in Split and Korzo in Rijeka are good examples – or an 'urban magnet', as can be seen in the department stores Prehrana in Osijek, Dalma in Split and Ri in Rijeka. These department stores were carefully integrated in new pedestrian zones through a thoughtful articulation of their open spaces. By 1970 thirteen department stores had opened in Croatia, a number that by 1980 had increased to sixty.[23] These department stores were organized in chains, which distributed their shops over the country's territory and regions. The acronyms of the locations in which these retail facilities opened were commonly

---

[22]Many of these planned 'centres' were however never fully realized. Often public funds would run out after the housing construction had been completed, and trading companies, although socially owned, seldom dared to risk the investment. Zdenko Kolacio, 'Opskrbni Centri', *Arhitektura* 3–4 (1961): 3–4; Petar Mudnić et al., 'Stanovanje', *Urbs* 6 (1966): 77–110.
[23]Duda, 'Svakodnevni život i potrošačka kultura u Hrvatskoj 1970-ih i 1980-ih', 38.

Figure 10.3 Prima department store in Split, 1966. Architect: Antun Šatara.
Source: State Archives in Split, Split, Croatia.

absorbed in their nomenclature: PRI-MA for Primorski magazin, DAL-MA for Dalmatinski magazin, NA-MA for Narodni magazin and so on. These department stores targeted all the demographic groups regardless of their economic capacity and therefore represented new common spaces, open to all.

Typological development: From department store to shopping centre

During the 1960s department stores gradually added a recognizable, new, 'modern' layer to Croatia's existing urban fabrics. A noteworthy example is the Maja department store in Split. Here, the department store's contemporary commercial design was directly confronted with the city's built heritage. Built into the Baroque city bastion of Priuli, it was connected to the old wall by its position and architectural articulation and engaged in a dialogue with the external space by virtue of its recessed ground floor along Marmont Street and its prominent, horizontal upper storey that opened up onto a large terrace overshadowing the ground floor. These architectural elements facilitated and enhanced the urban atmosphere, as they created a pleasant and lively meeting point along Marmont Street. The complex was furthermore to be connected to the remains of the bastion by a diaphanous volume, which would bridge the void that had recently (and quite brutally) been created to accommodate new traffic regulations, and embed the wall in the city's pedestrian network.²⁴ Although this part was never realized, citizens' response to the architectural ensemble was remarkable and the complex soon became the focal point of Split's social life.²⁵

The Prima department store, which was located in the immediate vicinity of the Maja department store and which – according to Kalogjera's urban plan – needed to accentuate the entrance to the new, modern extension of the city centre was built in 1966 on the site of the previously planned concert hall. There it played an ambitious and prominent role in the city's urban life; a role that had originally been assigned to the concert hall. The complex, which also housed a cinema, was designed by Antun Šatara, who in 1966 was awarded the prestigious Republic prize of 'Borba' for its powerful and well-proportioned architectural design. Bernardo Bernardi, another distinguished Croatian architect who had previously worked on several projects of national significance, designed the department store's interior.²⁶

Given their commercial character, it is rather peculiar that department stores in Yugoslavia were often built on exceptionally valuable urban sites, designed by architects of repute and, that they were often the subject of major architectural competitions. However, since the concept of the department store in socialist Croatia generally exceeded its commercial features, and was commonly attributed a broader social and political role (albeit indirectly), this should not come as a surprise. That said, architects who were involved in the design of these new commercial centres were often confronted with a lack of information on the programmatic and functional features of this novel typology. Not only did they lack access to professional international literature, but they also regularly had to deal with investors who were insufficiently prepared for the task, leaving them largely to their own resources.²⁷ In spite of these difficulties, or perhaps precisely because of them, they achieved admirable results, qualitative in both architectural and urban articulation:

> With regard to the commercial function a freer and more richly articulated layout and composition of business parts of buildings were aimed at enabling their better utilisation in terms of displaying and presenting the merchandise. Frequent perforations of these parts and a free pedestrian communication between them were to contribute towards the attractiveness of space, and thereby a better marketing of the merchandise.²⁸

---

²⁴The demolition was conducted in two phases between 1947 and 1951. Slavko Muljačić, 'Kronološki pregled izgradnje Splita u XIX. i XX. stoljeću (1806–1958)', in *Zbornik Društva inženjera i tehničara u Splitu*, DIT, Split (1958): 90; Berislav Kalogjera, 'Split – studija regulacije gradskog centra', *Urbs* 3 (1959–1960): 29–30.

²⁵For the citizens of Split, the large open terrace on the top floor of the Maja department store was especially attractive. It was used as the summer extension of the self-service restaurant 'Bastion' situated on that floor. Slavko Muljačić, 'Kronološki pregled izgradnje Splita 1944–1969', *Urbs* 8–9 (1969): 80–81. The popular dancing venues that were organized on that terrace in the 1960s still exist in the collective memory of that generation.

²⁶The most significant project by Bernardi was the interior design of 'Moše Pijade' Workers' University in Zagreb (1961). Other notable projects include: the interior design of the Zagreb airport (1966), hotel 'Marko Polo' in Korčula (1961–1971) and the interior design of hotel 'Maestral' in Brela (1965).

²⁷'Natječaj za idejnu skicu robne kuće i kina u Zagrebu', *Arhitektura* 3–4 (1961): 15–18.

²⁸'S obzirom na trgovačku funkciju nastojalo se slobodnijom i razgranijom tlocrtnom dispozicijom i kompozicijom poslovnih dijelova zgrada omogućiti što bolju njihovu upotrebu u smislu izlaganja i prezentacije robe. Česte perforacije tih dijelova i slobodne pješačke komunikacije među njima treba da pridonesu atraktivnosti prostora, a time i plasmanu artikala.' Berislav Kalogjera, 'Split – studija regulacije gradskog centra', *Urbs* 3 (1959–1960): 29; translated by the authors.

Unencumbered with the dictate of profitability, which affected the design of commercial facilities elsewhere, the discourse on the development of department stores in post-war Croatia emphasized the typology's social significance. City administrations treated it as an important project for the city, spending as much attention on it as on other important public projects. This gave architects great freedom and also justified high construction costs.[29] Many department store designs secured their authors prestigious awards; for example Prima in Split, Prehrana in Osijek, Nama Trnsko in Zagreb.[30]

During the 1970s the architectural design of department stores became more complex. Apart from the actual store, they increasingly hosted an array of ancillary facilities, including clubs, conference venues, cinemas, banks, offices, hotels, auction halls and parking spaces. The 'commercial centre' in Split by Vuko Bombardelli is, for instance, a good example. Its design ostensibly follows Kalogjera's urban scheme, as its various functions are located in a dispersed conglomerate of interconnected volumes, with entrances at several levels. Featuring porches, passages and roof terraces the complex demonstrates a successful blend of modernist spirit and Mediterranean influences. Nonetheless, of the planned complex only the Dalma department store was realized, with a square whose urban role fades in comparison with the one that Bombardelli had originally envisaged. A similar story unfolded in Rijeka, where an exceptionally ambitious project for the Ri department store was realized following the winning competition entry of Ninoslav Kučan, Boris Babić and Vjera Kučan.[31] Here, the department store was used as an urban planning tool to connect the old city, Rijeka's main street Korzo, to the harbour. The project occupied two housing blocks, as it spanned the street and crossed the main thoroughfare between Korzo and Riva. The original proposal envisaged a pedestrian bridge and stairs descending down to the very end of the shore, which were unfortunately never realized. Even so, the commercial attraction of the department store did contribute to the creation of an informal pedestrian link between the harbour and the city. Following contemporary developments in architectural practice, the Ri department store was entirely pre-fabricated. Plated in a lacework of aluminium trusses, which were designed to display large advertising boards, the façade had an industrial aesthetic, which became the target of intense public debate. Nonetheless, the store's opening in 1974 elicited a highly emotional response from Rijeka's citizens. Approximately 30,000 people attended this event and local newspapers expressed their admiration for the complex's technical composition, making the department store a symbol of the city's progress and prosperity.[32]

---

[29]According to the prominent Croatian art historian Duško Kečkemet, the department store took a representative character and became the ultimate meeting place for the whole citizenry, and, as such, took on a social role that was originally intended for public buildings such as community halls, theatres and auditoriums for social meetings. Kečkemet was quite critical towards this phenomenon, especially as he once, while attending a meeting at the city administration, witnessed a statement in which the construction of department store was equalled to the historical cultural outreach of constructing a temple or church. Therefore, Kečkemet was particularly affected by the fact that the city government not only made no effort to build 'more valuable' public facilities, but also proudly pointed to the construction of a department store as a symbol of the city's progress and success. Duško Kečkemet, 'Robne kuće – hramovi suvremene civilizacije?', *Vjesnik*, 5 December 1978, 11.

[30]Darko Venturini, 'Robna kuća "Prehrana" u Osijeku', *Arhitektura* 97–98 (1968): 27–33; 'Robna kuća "Prima" u Splitu', *čovjek i prostor* 173 (1967): 1, 11.

[31]'Izvještaj ocjenjivačkog suda natječaja za izradu idejnog rješenja robne kuće u Rijeci', *čovjek i prostor* 215 (1971): 14–16.

[32]Ervin Dubrović, *Ninoslav Kučan* (Rijeka: Muzej grada Rijeke, 2006), 39–49.

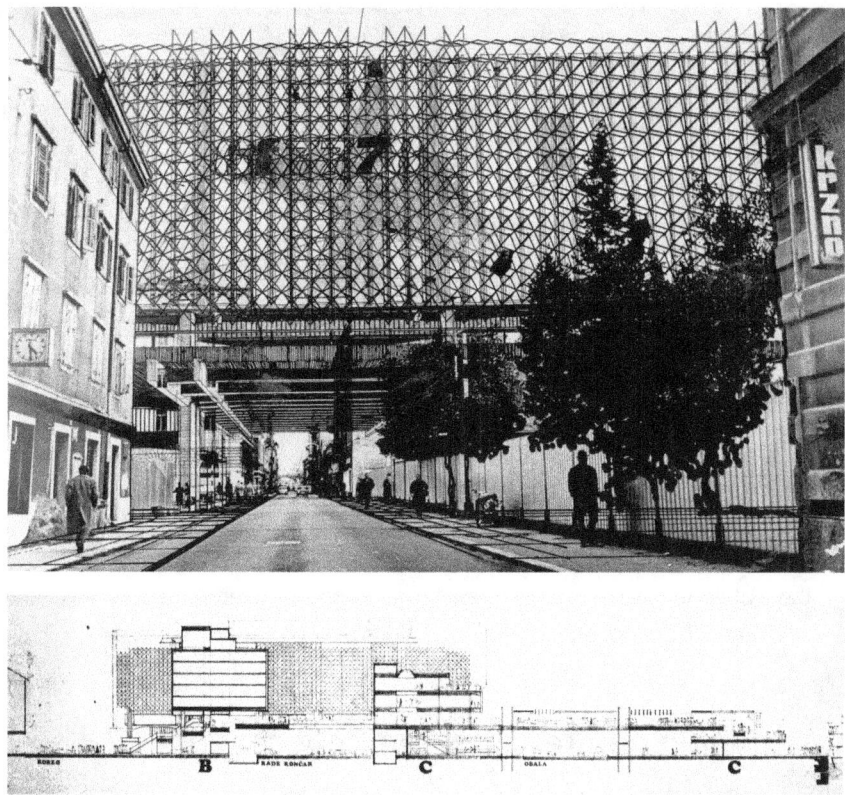

Figure 10.4 Ri department store in Split, 1966. Architects: Ninoslav Kučan, Boris Babić, Vjera Kučan.
Source: Private collection of Vjera Kučan, Rijeka © Kučan family.

The most elaborate example of commercial architecture in post-war Croatia was the Koteks shopping centre in Split, designed by local architect Slaven Rožić in 1978. When it was inaugurated it was widely considered – largely because of its size, its lavish retail offer and its multi-level underground parking, which made it a regional magnet – the first 'true' shopping centre in Yugoslavia.[33] Located on a terrace of the former quarry, it covered, together with the Gripe sports centre that Rožić designed in collaboration with Živorad Janković, an area equivalent to an entire housing estate of 1960s Split. Greatly exceeding the scale of existing department stores, retailing in Koteks was set in a complex spatial dialogue with the shopping centre's external public spaces. Its shopping facilities were articulated through highly pronounced tectonics, as the elements of the Mediterranean urban inventory – shaded terraces, pergolas, squares and flights of stairs – were blown up to a hypertrophic scale, creating a true public urban space. However, as the complex was exclusively dedicated to shopping, the dynamics of its use were reduced to the shops' opening hours, and its urban dimension was never fully achieved.

---

[33]Darovan Tušek (ed.), *Split Arhitektura 20. stoljeća* (Split: Sveučilište u Splitu Građevinsko-arhitektonski fakultet, 2011), 121.

Figure 10.5 Koteks shopping centre in Split, 1981. Architect: Slaven Rožić.
Source: State Archives in Split, Croatia.

Nevertheless, the Koteks shopping centre remains an excellent example of a local interpretation of architecture for modern leisure consumption.

Socialist shopping centres after the political shift

The heyday of Yugoslav consumerism ended in the late 1970s when the economic crisis revealed all the weaknesses of the country's inconsistent and contradictory economic system. Rising unemployment, pay cuts, deprivation, extreme inflation, shortage of consumer goods, queues in front of stores…made the 1980s a period of disillusionment. The break-up of Yugoslavia and the political shift of the 1990s led to a drastic change of sociopolitical paradigm. In Croatia this change was accompanied by a collapse of spatial and urban planning policies, as well as a change in consumerist culture. Privatization brought chaos, which, among other things, resulted in department stores falling victim to either second-rate architectural conversions commissioned by their new owners or closure and long-term vacancy due to dubious ownership issues. In Split the Maja department store was adapted, retaining only little of its original urban qualities, while the Prima department store changed its interior design to cater to individual tenants. The conversion also included a roof-top extension. Here an oval café was built, which is commendable insomuch as it seems to have *recognized*, if not solved, a problem that many downtown department stores are confronted with today; poor circulation on the upper floors. The interior of the Dalma department store has sunk into obscurity, after having lost the features of its open selling space completely. Meanwhile, the Koteks department store is visibly decaying, while the social dynamics and urban quality of the surrounding town continue to decrease. The Ri department store in Rijeka has been transformed into a number of small shops, which have difficulty surviving. The department stores in Zagreb and Osijek suffer the same fate. At the same time, the construction of large ex-urban shopping malls following the introvert American shopping typology seems to be gaining momentum.

Conclusion

Consumerist culture transformed post-war Croatia into a highly peculiar socialist society, which Jean-Luc Godard quite succinctly described as 'the children of Marx and Coca-Cola'.[34] Disagreement exists among historians regarding the impetus for this transformation; some argue that this consumerist shift revealed common people's wishes and desires, while others claim it was the result of a deliberate 'top-down' undertaking. The latter group contends that the government encouraged consumerism so citizens, indulging in the joys of shopping, would feel content and would care less about political issues. For Tito, consumerism thus became a means of obtaining loyalty. It gave citizens a sense of freedom, which the government – in a true Machiavellian fashion – turned into a means of control.[35] Regardless of which hypothesis is correct, fact remains that in the period between 1960 and 1980, Yugoslavia became a consumerist society that to a certain extent resembled the West. There are nonetheless differences, one of which can be found in its commercial architectural design.

While the design of shopping centres in Western capitalist societies often lacked architectural ambition, as 'self-respecting' architects shunned the commission, fearing that their design freedom would be constrained by commercial demands, shopping in socialist Yugoslavia received an entirely different reception by architects and authorities alike.[36] Here, shopping became the subject of architectural competitions, and its design was commonly awarded to the most prominent national architects. Socialist shopping facilities were also attributed social and urban significance; they defined and created public space and were to express the success of Yugoslavia's modern society. The architecture of socialist shopping, as the selected examples demonstrate, was thus often of high quality. Today these buildings not only constitute valuable architectural heritage, but also cultural heritage. They are part of the collective memory and identity of a particular post-war generation of Yugoslavs, and as such deserve much greater recognition than they have thus far received.

---

[34]*Masculin Féminin*, directed by Jean-Luc Godard (Paris, Stockholm: Anouchka Films et al., 1966).
[35]Patterson, *Bought and Sold*, 290–291.
[36]References are to Daniel Herman, 'High architecture', in *Harvard Design School Guide to Shopping*, eds. Rem Koolhaas et al. (Köln, London: Taschen, 2002), 392.

Chapter 11

Unico Prezzo Italiano: Corporate consumption and retail architecture in post-war Italy
Daniele Vadala'

Recent scholarship has argued that in post-war Western Europe shopping centres were regularly funded by governmental authorities and often formed integral components of urban reconstruction and urban development projects. In this context, it is suggested, the shopping centre's role exceeded that of commercial entity as it was perceived as a potential building block of the welfare state, able to assist in the construction of a more egalitarian society.[1] Such scholarship claims that in post-war Europe the shopping centre, which often included an array of 'social' functions, thus adopted social significance and fostered a sense of collectivity.

This hypothesis is to some extent confirmed in the case of post-war Italy. Even though the downtown department store model, which first emerged during the fascist regime, persisted in the country until the mid-1970s,[2] changes did occur as it accommodated a new culture of consumption that expressed the ideals of a diverse group of actors, including entrepreneurs, designers and local municipal bodies. Their interests converged in a 'democratic' consumption space that reflected the values of the emerging middle class, who became a key protagonist in this democratic phase in Italy's

---

I would like to thank Matteo Iannello (Architect and curator of the Calandra Archive, Palermo) and Arianna Cona (Fondazione Per Salvare Palermo) who kindly helped to provide the photos of the Upim building in Messina; Alessandro Cavallaro (Architect, Catania) for the photo of La Rinascente building in Catania, and last but not least, I would like to thank Sergio Pitrone (M.Sc. student Business and Service Management, Università Cattolica del Sacro Cuore, Milan) for his invaluable support in the archival research.

[1] Janina Gosseye, 'Collectivity and the Post-war European Shopping Centre', *Lusofona Journal of Architecture and Education* no. 8–9 (2013): 245–264.

[2] The enduring success of the department store model offers the most direct explanation for the late introduction of shopping centres in Italy. These gained popularity only around the end of 1980s, when they manifested themselves as private enterprises with mono-functional commercial areas. One of the first and most interesting examples is the Centrotorri, which was built in 1988 in a commercial area in the outskirts of Parma and comprised a project by Aldo Rossi. That same year the Centro Commerciale Bonola in the Gallaratese district near Milan was inaugurated. The work of Michele Sernini is a reference point on the advent of shopping centres in Italy in the late 1980s, following new national bylaws in the retail sector. See Michele Sernini, 'I Centri Commerciali Dieci Anni Dopo', *Commercio, Rivista del Centro di Studi sul Commercio dell' Università Bocconi* no. 63 (1998): 33–59; Michele Sernini, 'I Centri Commerciali Integrati in Italia: Quando il Developer Diventa Urbanista', *Archivio di Studi Urbani e Regionali* no. 33 (1988): 3–28.

history.³ Starting from the late 1950s, as consumer experience increasingly assumed a central role in Italy, retailers adopted new labour practices and opted for new architectural languages that could reflect emerging lifestyles, and convey ideals of freedom and modernity. Around this time, a new generation of young architects entered the profession. They contributed to a new phase of modern architecture that was in tune with the premises of post-war Neorealism. Their work was characterized by a sense of freedom and a fruitful hybridization between the urban and rural, and included the popularization of traditional motifs.⁴ Some critics have interpreted their work as an 'Italian retreat from modern architecture', thus sparking an intense debate on the history and theory of modern architecture.⁵ This controversy over the role of technology and tradition in modern architecture – and the search for a third option in-between – had a strong effect on the department stores planned by La Rinascente-Upim after the Second World War.

This chapter traces the post-war history of La Rinascente-Upim through the analysis of a select number of case-study department stores⁶ to demonstrate how the company – through its corporate image, employment policies, product pricing and, most importantly, through the architectural design of its stores – attempted to contribute to the formation of a novel, democratic Italy, while walking a fine line between tradition and modernity.

Mass retailing and labour in Italy before the Second World War

The pervasive spread of retail chains in post-war Italy cannot be understood without taking the primary role that mass retailing had under Fascism into account. One of the key players was

---

³This 'involvement' of the middle class, included both the department store's employees and customers. The department store took on the role of 'cultural mediator'. It introduced the public to an entirely new range of products that were displayed in a modern retail environment, with special attention paid to the window dressing. In this regard, the department store played an important role in enhancing social mobility in Italy. The young Giorgio Armani, for instance, began his career in the fashion industry in the 1960s as window dresser at La Rinascente in Milan: 'Armani remained there for seven years, learning the nuts and bolts of merchandising and discovering that he had a flair for retailing that enabled him to work his way up to the position of menswear buyer and later fashion coordinator.' See S. Dow, *Business Leader Profiles for Students*, Volume 1 (Detroit: Gale Group, 1998), 39.

⁴Michelangelo Sabatino often dwells on the concept of the 'hybrid' in his ground-breaking study on post-war Italian architecture: 'By reinventing tradition, Italian architects, during and after fascism, constructed a hybrid modernity that was at odds with avant-garde radicalism and its insistence on the *eclipse of history*.' See Michelangelo Sabatino, *Pride in Modesty: Modernist Architecture and the Vernacular Tradition in Italy* (Toronto: University of Toronto Press, 2010), 7.

⁵Reyner Banham, 'Neoliberty: The Italian Retreat from Modern Architecture', *Architectural Review* 125 (April 1959): 230–235. For a recent interpretation of the debate between Reynher Banham and Ernesto Rogers, see M.L. Segura, 'Neoliberty & Co.: The *Architectural Review* against 1950s Italian Historicism', *Cuadernos de Proyectos Arquitectonicos* no. 4 (September 2013): 98–107; A. Vidler, 'Troubles in Theory Part III: The Great Divide: Technology vs Tradition', *Architectural Review*, 24 July 2012, http://www.architectural-review.com/essays/troubles-in-theory-part-iii-the-great-divide-technology-vs-tradition/8633393.article, accessed 20 August 2015.

⁶These case studies have not been selected because they are representative of all La Rinascente-Upim department stores built in post-war Italy, but because they are examples *par excellence* of the company's ability to develop a precisely defined corporate model, able to convey both modernity and social progress, while adhering to tradition. By 1965 La Rinascente-Upim 'was by far the leading group in the retail sector, controlling 55 per cent of the stores' sales surface and ranking among the top 35 European companies in that sector (the only Italian company to do so)'. See Emanuela Scarpellini, 'The Long Way to the Supermarket: Entrepreneurial Innovation and Adaptation in 1950s–1960s Italy', in *Transformations of Retailing in Europe after 1945,* eds. R. Jessen and L. Langer (London: Ashgate, 2012), 55–69.

La Rinascente-Upim, which was originally established in 1917 when Senatore Borletti,[7] who had close ties to the fascist regime since 1923, took over the UPIM department store created by the Bocconi brothers in Milan.[8] Thanks to this acquisition, the La Rinascente-Upim group experienced substantial growth over the following decades. In this period, several UPIM stores, which targeted consumers with small incomes by selling cheaper products than La Rinascente, opened across the country; thus helping the company to survive the crisis of the 1930s: 'Not only was the UPIM a success, but it also helped the Rinascente to get over the crisis years of the early 1930s, and as a result, 14 of the 19 Rinascente branches were transformed into UPIM stores.'[9] 'UPIM' stands for Unico Prezzo Italiano Milano (Italian One Price Milan), and was inspired by an American entrepreneurial model that distributed mass-produced goods through chain stores that were spread throughout city centres. Despite the brand name, UPIM department stores had around fifty different prices for its products; significantly more than Woolworths, which had five and which was considered the reference model for the one-price-store.[10] UPIM stores were successful and by the end of 1932, twenty-two *Grandi Magazzini* were operational,[11] not only in Milan, Rome and other major urban areas in Italy's industrial north, but also in mid-sized urban areas across the country.

The presence of a well-trained staff, able to mediate between customer and product, was a key aspect of the novel shopping experience in UPIM's *Grandi Magazzini*. To this end La Rinascente-Upim established a school for its sales personnel in Milan in 1933. Here, employees were instructed by teachers who were trained in countries where modern retail distribution was more mature, including Switzerland and France.[12] The two-year course was free for boys and girls between fifteen and seventeen years of age that held a grammar school diploma, and the curriculum paid ample attention to sales techniques and skills such as observation, affability, tact, countenance, smile, politeness, punctuality, responsibility,

---

[7] Senatore Borletti is the son of Rodolfo and brother of Aldo, founder of the Veglia Borletti, a company that grew up manufacturing all the on-board devices of Fiat cars: 'for years, millions of motorists continued to drive while keeping an eye on the name Veglia-Borletti on the dasboard'. See G. Garuzzo, *Fiat: The Secrets of an Epoch* (Cham/Heidelberg/New York/Dordrecht/London: Springer, 2014).

[8] The business created by Ferdinando and Luigi Bocconi in 1877 was initially called Aux Villes d'Italie and then Alle Citta d'Italia and was clearly inspired by the French Le Bon Marché.

[9] V. Zamagni, *The Economic History of Italy 1860–1990* (Oxford: Clarendon, 1993), 313. By the start of the Second World War, Upim-La Rinascente had become by far the most successful group in the retail sector. Thirty-five shops had opened by 1939 and fifty-five were operational by 1943. See also V. Zamagni, 'Alle Origini della Grande Distribuzione in Italia', *Commercio* no. 10 (1982): 74–87.

[10] Woolworths was founded in the 1880s and began its expansion into Europe in the early twentieth century, inaugurating its first shop in Liverpool in 1909. By 1930, 444 Woolworths shops were operational worldwide. Woolworths owed its success to a simple but effective formula; they offered a wide range of cheap, mostly household products in large stores where customers could browse without being pressured to buy. See G. Shaw et al., 'Structural and Spatial Trends in British Retailing: The Importance of Firm-Level Studies', in *The Emergence of Modern Retailing 1750–1950*, eds. N. Alexander and G. Akehurst (London: Frank Cass, 1999), 90; Y. Cassis, *Big Business: The European Experience in the Twentieth Century* (Oxford: Oxford University Press, 2004), 45.

[11] J. Morris, 'The Fascist Disciplining of the Italian Retail Sector', in *The Emergence of Modern Retailing, 1750–1950*, eds. Alexander and Akehurst, 150.

[12] M. Luporini, 'L'École des Vendeurs dans les Grands Magasins Rinascente-Upim', in *VI Congresso Internazionale dell'Insegnamento Tecnico*, Roma, 28–30 December 1936 (Milano: Tipografia Turati, 1937), 5. See also M. Morandi, *Formare alle Professioni: Commercianti e Contabili dalle Scuole d'Abaco ad Oggi* (Milano: Franco Angeli, 2013), 103.

sense of order and loyalty. In the second year of the course, the focus lay on the development of vending skills in relation to the reception and acquaintance of clients.[13] The school also provided after-work courses in tailoring, household economy and gymnastics, in compliance with the social programme of Fascism that highly valued physical training and feminine work. The education promoted a communitarian vision which likened the company to a large 'family' of managers and employees with shared interests. As of 1936, this stance was reflected in the title of the company magazine, *La Famiglia Rinascente-Upim* – 'the Rinascente-Upim family'.[14]

Rinascente-Upim: Creating a progressist business model

Its strong position in the Italian market offered the Rinascente-Upim group the capacity to immediately resume activity after the Second World War, starting with the reconstruction of its main seat

Figure 11.1 Rinascente building in Milan, c. 1955.
Source: Postcard, author unknown.

---

[13]Luporini, 'L'École des Vendeurs', 15. The popularity of the personnel employed in the Upim stores is vividly reflected in Eric Lamet's novel remembering his childhood in Milan: 'I became the little darling of some of the salesladies of the local Upim store located on via Meravigli.' See E. Lamet, *A Child al Confino: The True Story of a Jewish Boy and His Mother in Mussolini's Italy* (New York City: Adams Media, 2010), 37.

[14]The Italian term *famiglia* (family) has a double meaning in this case; it not only signifies a 'family nucleus', but also an 'entrepreneurial nucleus', with a certain paternalistic attitude. In 1947, the magazine was rebranded and was given the subtitle: *Cronache della Rinascente-Upim* with a section on *Rassegna di Vita e di Lavoro nei Grandi Magazzini* (review of life and work in the department stores).

next to the Piazza del Duomo in Milan. The sober rationalist building that was inaugurated in 1952 replaced the former magnificent art-deco structure that was bombed by the Allied Army in 1943. Milan continued to be the headquarters of the company, which in post-war years adopted the ambition to spread a sense of modern and sober elegance over the largely rural country that Italy still was. Just as the workers in the American Ford company became the principal buyers of the cars they were producing,[15] so too did the numerous employees of the Rinascente-Upim department stores become not only the company's best consumers, but also the strongest promoters of its modern outlook and progressive vision. The controversial *clausola di nubilato*, or the 'condition of being unmarried', which was included in most standard Italian employment contracts was, for instance, not implemented by Rinascente-Upim.[16] The company desire to 'modernize' Italy's post-war society thus also advanced the emancipation of women as in regions with a very high level of female unemployment, like Sicily, being employed by Upim became '... a goal to achieve and defend at any cost, even for many female high school graduates'.[17] Furthermore, the company did not see their support of 'working women' as a threat to a woman's femininity. On the contrary, female staff enjoyed the 'privilege' of wearing pleasant dresses and having a curled hairdo, offered by Rinascente-Upim's fitted uniform designs and coiffeur service.[18]

La Rinascente also expressed its modern, progressive attitude through different aspects of its organization, most notably through its product range and through the spatial design of its stores. The integration of escalators in the stores, for instance, introduced – besides a joyful game for generations of children – a truly modern practice to post-war Italy, while the well-assorted selection of mid-range and high-end products (offered by UPIM and La Rinascente respectively) made modern comforts available at fair prices to Italy's middle-class families. These same families became full-fledged participants in Italy's *miracolo economico* (economic miracle), as they were offered consumer environments that responded to their expectation of building a better future.

La Rinascente-Upim's comprehensive strategy to develop a corporate image was a key aspect that from the mid-1950s gained increasing importance. Designers such as Max Huber, Bruno Munari and Tomàs Maldonado were actively involved in defining all the different aspects that formed the corporate identity of the group: from the size and shape of the buckets and the famous corporate logo with a capital 'R' preceded by a minor 'l' to the design of a coordinated set of options for the arrangement of the shop windows, available to all the stores of the group.

---

[15] P. Scieur, *Sociology of Organisations: An Introduction and Analysis of Collective Organisations* (New Delhi: PHI Learning, 2012).

[16] M. Boneschi, *Milano, l'Avventura di una Città: Tre Secoli di Storie, Idee, Battaglie che hanno fatto l'Italia* (Milano: Mondadori, 2007).

[17] 'L'assunzione all'Upim o alla Standa, anche per molte diplomate disoccupate, è oggi considerata un traguardo da raggi-ungere e difendere in ogni modo.' See C. Ottaviano, 'Il Lavoro', in *Essere donne in Sicilia*, eds. Simona Mafai et al. (Roma: Editori Riuniti, 1976), 146.

[18] Boneschi, *Milano, l'Avventura di una Città*.

Figure 11.2 Cronache della Rinascente, 1954. Cover design by Max Huber.

Corporate but popular: Modern architecture according to *la* 'R'

In the late 1950s, the criticism on the course of modern architecture in Italy that Reyner Banham raised in the pages of the *Architectural Review* evolved into a wider debate on the exhaustion of modernism and the role of architectural traditions. In the pages of *Casabella* architects like Ernesto Nathan Rogers pointed out that architects' attention for the pre-existing codes of the European city was self-evident. Such arguments intended to prompt a return to the most progressive instances of the Modern Movement while connecting them to the formal languages of Western architectural history.[19] Also, in the policies of the Rinascente-Upim group this discussion on the relation between modern and historical traditions played an important role. Generally the group's expansion strategies were underpinned by a well-defined, modern corporate image. On an urban and architectural level, however, the company aimed for projects that were undoubtedly modern but simultaneously engaged with the different locales of the Italian architectural tradition – an approach that has been qualified as an 'architecture

---

[19] Ernesto Nathan Rogers, 'Continuità o Crisi?' *Casabella-Continiità* no. 215 (April/May 1957): 3–6. For a recent evaluation of Ernesto Nathan Roger's contribution to post-war architectural culture, see Anna Giannetti and Luca Molinari (eds.), *Continuità e Crisi: Ernesto Nathan Rogers e la Cultura Architettonica Italiana del Secondo Dopoguerra* (Firenze: Alinea, 2010).

of differences'.[20] This 'regionalist' tendency explains the architectural variety of the projects that were realized by the Rinascente-Upim group outside Milan, as the case studies in Rome and in the Sicilian towns of Messina and Catania will illustrate.

The Rinascente department store in Rome

Franco Albini had already designed some wicker chairs for la Rinascente, when the practice he held with Franca Helg was commissioned to design a new store at the edge of the so-called 'Quartiere Umbertino' in Rome in 1957. This store was located at the corner of Piazza Fiume and Via Salaria, facing the remnants of the Aurelian Walls, the outer ring of the imperial city. An early design proposal envisioned a parking lot on the roof and an escalator tube on the outside of the building. This adjoining element, which bears clear resemblance with the famous design that Renzo Piano, Richard Rogers and Gianfranco Franchini made a decade later for the Centre Pompidou in Paris, aimed to maximize the retail area while emphasizing the movement of people coming into the store from the street. Albini's second design was however much more conservative. It hid the ventilation ducts behind the façade panels and accentuated the floor levels with a kind of trabeation of steel beams that 'emphasizes its palazzo-like form'.[21] When the building was completed in 1961, Reyner Banham passed an ambivalent judgement on Albini's Rinascente: although he endorsed the first project as a well-composed expression of environmental control – later echoed by other critics of the Marxist school, such as Tafuri and Tentori – he also openly praised the quality of the final project. Banham regarded the corrugated-panelled façade that hid the ventilation ducts as a proper response to a worrisome technical issue in modern architecture, contrasting it with Louis Kahn's approach in the Richards Laboratories, which he derided as 'Ducthenge'.[22] Surprisingly Ernesto Rogers, who was considered a great opponent of Banham, adopted a similar stance regarding Albini's work in Rome. Although the editor of *Casabella* did not undividedly laud the final design, he was mainly positive about the result because it represented a modern architecture that while losing 'some of its objective rigor [and] some of its conceptual clarity, gains a greater wealth of vibrations'.[23]

Franca Helg explained the transition from the first 'machinist' solution to the final design as a basic balancing act of two main concerns: 'the respect for tradition on one hand and the necessity to express ourselves in a way congruent with our times on the other'.[24] Helg thus emphasized how tradition in architecture should be regarded as 'the collective awareness of the continuity of the past and the present, the continuous integration of customs, ethics and cultures of all times, a sort of collective recognition of permanent cultural values'.[25] With this in mind, it should come as no surprise that the management of La Rinascente gave Helg and Albini this commission, as they clearly shared the

---

[20] P. Zermani, *L'Architettura delle Differenze* (Roma: Kappa, 1988).
[21] T. Kirk, *The Architecture of Modern Italy: Vision of Utopia, 1900-Present* (New York: Princeton Architural Press, 2005), 181.
[22] Reyner Banham, 'Louis Kahn: The Buttery-hatch Aesthetic', *Architectural Review* no. 131 (1962): 204.
[24] Ibid., 181.
[23] Kirk, *The Architecture of Modern Italy*, 182.
[25] Ibid., 182.

Figure 11.3 Rinascente building in Rome, 1955.
Source: Fondazione Franco Albini, Milan Courtesy of Fondazione Franco Albini.

company's search for a more attentive attitude towards modernity and tradition. Furthermore, there was no risk that the firm would regress into the realm of *pastiche* – or into Banhamian 'Neoliberty'[26] – as Albini made it clear that he regarded tradition both as a method and a way to modernity: 'Tradition, as a discipline, is a safeguard against fantastical license, against the fleeting quality of fashion and the damaging errors of mediocrity.'[27] It was in this frame of mind that the striking vision of the reddish crushed stone panels, ideally hanging like gigantic rugs, from successive entablatures cast upon the skies of Rome could be forged; 'almost a memory of the architectural orders, seized in their primal arrangement'.[28]

---

[26]'Neoliberty' can only be fully understood in the context of Reyner Banham's primeval formulation (see note 5) as a polemic argument against the post-war developments of Italian architectural culture, seen by the British architecture critic as a retreat from the progressive instances of modern architecture. Gillo Dorfles criticized Banham for creating confusion by his use of the term 'neoliberty' arguing that 'neobaroque' would probably have been a more precise definition. See Gillo Dorfles, *Architetture Ambigue: Dal Neobarocco al Postmoderno* (Bari: Dedalo, 1984), 76.

[27]Ibid., 182.

[28]'quel comporre per trabeazioni sovrapposte. Quasi un ricordo degli ordini architettonici colti nella loro prima matrice' See A. Cortesi, 'Lo Studio Albini & Helg e la Questione della Tecnologia negli Anni '60', *Ottagono* no. 37 (1975): 54–63.

Going south: La Rinascente in Sicily

Similar attempts to articulate a balanced confrontation between modern consumption models and a sense of place, this time responsive to the urban fabric of the Mediterranean, can be recognized in the projects of La Rinascente-Upim in Messina and Catania. Given the comparable scale and the close cultural ties that existed between these two cities on the Ionian coast of Sicily, these developments followed parallel and sometimes converging trajectories – even though they did diverge in the end. In both cases the intervention involved the replacement of important buildings along the main street of the city; the bombed historical palace of the Spitaleri family along Via Etnea in Catania and the low-rise art deco Grand Hotel along Viale S. Martino in Messina, which was property of the great actor Angelo Musco. Another common feature was the idea – partially accomplished in Catania but more fully developed in Messina – of a mixed-use development, which combined the shopping centre with housing.

The UPIM building in Messina was situated on a large plot that was originally planned as a large residential redevelopment along Viale S. Martino, the main road of the late nineteenth-century

Figure 11.4 Upim building in Messina: exterior view, c.1963.
Source: Archivio Roberto Calandra, Palermo Courtesy of Archivio Roberto Calandra.

downtown.²⁹ The building was developed by Sismiconsult, a group of architects and engineers that Roberto Calandra had formed in 1962 (with Cutrufelli, D'Amore, De Cola). When it was completed in 1963, it was the first steel building ever built in Italy within a first category seismic zone. At an urban level, the intervention clearly applied the neighbourhood unit principle that Calandra had studied during his post-graduate term at Columbia University in New York and that he wrote a piece on for the journal *Metron* in 1946.³⁰

The architecture was characterized by an exposed steel structure with a rigid grid layout and a masonry infill, which could be perceived as a slightly eccentric gesture in a Mediterranean port town like Messina. Its architectural design was clearly informed by Albini's final project, which had been published shortly before the Sismiconsult team started developing their design. Both projects are characterized by an intricate dialectic between steel structure and masonry panels. La Rinascente in Rome was clad in prefabricated panels of granulated granite and red marble dust, while Calandra used a continuous clinker cladding, which was entrenched within the building's steel structure. In both projects, this dialectic choice of materials was intended to establish a material relationship with the surrounding (historic) urban fabric. Other important similarities between Albini's La Rinascente in Rome and Calandra's UPIM in Messina included the use of a recessed ground floor and the architects' careful attention to texture, colour and shadow; elements they thought could contribute to the building's relation with the urban scenery. The UPIM store in Messina was given a wide urban gallery that was 'carved' out of the block, and that was 'relaxed' or 'classical' in character. This covered public interior was animated by shop windows and functioned as an antechamber to the apartments and the offices above. It was clad with marble panels set in a steel structure, which varied from rough panels at the bottom to polished finishings at the top, thus creating subtle variations in the stone's white grey colour. This exaltation of the inherent preciousness of marble – enhanced by the juxtaposition with modern materials, such as steel – in public or collective places, such as covered plazas, made this project an exponent of this 'subtle line of active classicism' that remains at the very core of modern architecture.³¹

When Roberto Calandra designed the UPIM store in Messina, Carlo Scarpa was commissioned to design the new Rinascente in Catania. By that point, a strong connection existed between the two men. In 1953 a long-lasting friendship had started between Scarpa and Calandra, which ended with the death of Scarpa in 1978. Both architects favoured an original approach to modernity in which materiality was considered the key element able to establish a relationship with the past. Both Calandra and Scarpa were members of a select group of Italian architects, including (among others) Albini and Helg, Ignazio

---

²⁹This part of Messina underwent huge transformations after the great earthquake of 1908 and was from the 1950s on further redeveloped at a higher density than the too restrictive ratio that had governed the reconstruction of the city after 1908. For a comprehensive discussion on the role that the great earthquake had in stimulating a profound revision of the urban fabric of Messina, see G. Parrinello, *Fault Lines: Earthquakes and Urbanism in Modern Italy* (Oxford: Berghahn Books, 2015), 21–104. For an account on the architecture and urban design in post-earthquake Messina, see L. Di Leo and M. Lo Curzio, *Messina, una Città Ricostruita: Materiali per lo Studio di una Realtà Urbana* (Bari: Dedalo, 1985), and G. Campione, *Il Progetto Urbano di Messina dal Terremoto al 1948* (Roma, Reggio Calabria: Gangemi, 1993).

³⁰*Metron* was an architectural journal founded by Bruno Zevi in 1945. See R. Calandra, 'La Teoria Americana della Neighborhood Unit', *Metron* no. 6 (1946): 58–68; M. Iannello, 'Roberto Calandra: Architetto e Maieuta', in *Archivi di Architettura a Palermo Memorie della Citta'*, XVII–XX Secolo, eds. M. Pecoraro and P. Palazzotto (Palermo: 40due, 2012), 120–131.

³¹D. Vadala', 'The Silent Seed of Modernity: How Marble Made Rationalism', in *Radical Marble: Architectural Innovation from Antiquity to the Present*, eds. W. Tronzo and N. Napoli (London: Ashgate, forthcoming 2016).

Figure 11.5 Upim building in Messina: public gallery, c.1963.
Source: Archivio Roberto Calandra, Palermo, Courtesy Archivio Roberto Calandra.

Gardella, Giancarlo De Carlo and Lina Bo Bardi. In their work, this group strongly embraced traces of the past – both in terms of historical characteristics and also in terms of building cultures.[32] Unfortunately, Scarpa's Rinascente was never built.[33] Art critic Giovanni Carandente described the project as follows:

> He thought he could use for the façade the materials most fitting to the site, lava stone, white marble and steel, feeling how important it was to preserve the chromatic field of the original baroque that essentially defines the streetscape. But he intended to produce an utterly new design. He considered a compact block of lava stone, etched by vertical courses of white marble.[34]

Figure 11.6 Rinascente building in Catania, 1957.
Source: Photo Alessandro Cavallaro, 2015.

---

[34]'Pensava di usare per la facciata i materiali più consoni al luogo, pietra lavica, marmo bianco e ferro, sentendo quanto fosse importante serbare intatto il continuum cromatico del barocco etneo che praticamente definisce l'intera via. Ma intendeva progettare una forma del tutto nuova. Immaginava un blocco compatto di pietra lavica intercalato da ricorsi verticali in marmo bianco.' See Dal Co and Mazzariol, *Carlo Scarpa*, 204.

[32]G. Carandente, 'Vent'anni di lavoro', in *Carlo Scarpa, 1906–1978*, eds. Francesco Dal Co and G. Mazzariol (Milano: Electa, 1984), 204.

[33]The failure of Scarpa's project in Catania derived mainly from the growing discomfort of the client regarding the delay of the project's delivery. This is confirmed by Giovanni Carandente, who had the important role of facilitator in the initial talks between Scarpa and the Dukes of Misterbianco, who owned the area. Carandente wrote: 'Sicily could have been endowed with an entire edifice designed by Scarpa along one of her more notable streets, if unfavourable conditions and the slowness in designing wouldn't have impeded it.' Original quote: 'La Sicilia potrebbe inoltre fregiarsi di un intero edificio progettato da Scarpa su una delle sue vie più illustri, se condizioni sfavorevoli e la lentezza di progettazione da parte sua non lo avessero impedito.' See Carandente, 'Vent'anni di lavoro', 204. This delay was not unusual and was consistent with Scarpa's approach to architectural design, which Francesco Dal Co described as 'lavorando con prudenza e lentezza', or: 'working with prudence and slowness'. See Francesco Dal Co, 'Carlo Scarpa: il Mestiere dell'Architetto', in *Interpretazioni Veneziane: Studi di Storia dell'arte in Onore di Michelangelo Muraro*, eds. M. Muraro and D. Rosand (Venezia: Arsenale Editrice, 1984), 481. For a more recent study on the activity of Carlo Scarpa in Sicily, see the extensive work of Matteo Iannello, *Carlo Scarpa in Sicilia 1952–1978* (Tesi di dottorato, Università degli Studi di Palermo, 2012), 123–134.

Like the UPIM building in Messina, Scarpa's Rinascente was to consist of offices and apartments, with commercial functions on the ground and mezzanine floors. Contrary to the projects in Messina and Rome, however, Scarpa did not recess the ground floor, most likely because he wanted to align the new volume with the late baroque *rettifilo* of Via Etnea. Scarpa's project was completed by a local practice, and while it respected the overall original scheme, it only comprised thirty apartments along the main street, thus losing the textural complexity of Scarpa's vision.

Conclusion

In post-war Italy social differences were commonly connected to the country's strong urban–rural divide. Until the late 1980s – when the department store model began to be eclipsed by the shopping centre paradigm – going downtown and entering an UPIM store made this difference more impalpable. Retail buildings were then considered public places where people could take part in modernity, regardless of class or gender. The exceptional endurance of the department store model in Italy in the post-war decades can in this sense be considered both its cause and effect. While this model had its roots in pre-war, fascist times, in post-war years these 'retail palaces' resolved issues that in other Western European countries were largely addressed by urban planning and welfare policies.[35] In countries, such as Sweden, France and England, the shopping centre was inscribed into the social welfare state system, but in Italy the shopping experience remained an almost exclusively private enterprise. Nevertheless, these private groups succeeded – not in a small part thanks to their architecture – to shape modern, progressive and above all 'democratic' commercial places that created valuable 'public' spaces in the urban fabric.

Apart from La Rinascente-Upim's architectural developments, also its urban strategy – erecting modern department store not only in representative locations in major Italian city centres, but also in the downtown areas of smaller towns – was geared towards 'democratization', by making modern consumption models accessible to Italians of different age, gender and class and introducing modern products as well as sales techniques into (even) peripheral parts of the country. The strategic central location of the department store in the urban core of Italian cities thus gave them a 'civic value'.

Finally, the implementation of a new organization of labour also played a key role in La Rinascente-Upim modernization campaign. Cleverly training its personnel and carefully selecting its product range to suit the needs of a diverse audience, the company introduced modernity in Italy's retail environment. During the 1960s, organizing a range of events, such as the 'British Week', La Rinascente-Upim became a 'place to be'; a symbol of progress and democracy, which offered freedom of choice: from Milan to Catania and 'from the fridge to the miniskirt, it is la Rinascente that sells for the first time those items that will change the Italian way of life'.[36]

---

[35] Gosseye, 'Collectivity and the Post-war European Shopping Centre'.
[36] 'Baptised by an Artist', *La Rinascente*, https://www.rinascente.it/rinascente/en/aboutus/123/, accessed 16 June 2015.

Part 3

Shifting forms of shopping: Between dense and tall and the low-slung (suburban) shopping mall

Chapter 12

The creation of civic identity in post-war corporate architecture: Marcel Breuer's Bijenkorf in Rotterdam, 1953–1957

Evangelia Tsilika

When the 'Magazijn De Bijenkorf' in Rotterdam[1] celebrated its grand opening on 16 October 1930, nobody could anticipate the short lifespan that this strikingly modern glass palace would have. Partly destroyed ten years later by the German raids that demolished the historical centre of the city, Willem Dudok's creation was abandoned by the Bijenkorf's General Management, which acceded to the idea of demolition to comply with the new plans for the city's reconstruction. A few years later, in 1953, Marcel Breuer was commissioned to design the new Bijenkorf (meaning 'Beehive') on the Coolsingel Boulevard, not far from its old site. Breuer's complex, which consisted of a department store, an office annex, a movie theatre and a construction field office, was produced during – what can be qualified as – the most creative period of the architect and his office. During this time, he worked on many challenging commissions, including the UNESCO Headquarters in Paris (1952–1958), St. John's Abbey in Collegeville, Minnesota (1953–1961) and two other projects in the Netherlands: the Van Leer Office Building in Amstelveen (1957–1958) and the American Embassy in The Hague (1956–1959), which garnered international recognition. This chapter examines how Breuer, having studied in depth the nature of the project within the particularities of its time and place, created an extremely functional and expressive building with a civic character, that was able to fulfil its *raison d'être* – retail – in a simple and economical way, while assuming a pivotal role in the planned reconstruction of the city, as it became a landmark for post-war Rotterdam.

The way to the new Bijenkorf

The dynamics and decisions that shaped the idea of the new Bijenkorf were set in motion long before the company appointed Breuer as the architect. The principal decision made by the Bijenkorf management was twofold: on the one hand it involved the demolition of the surviving part of Dudok's building and on the other hand, the relocation of the store higher on the Coolsingel Boulevard, following

---

[1] The Bijenkorf in Rotterdam was the third branch of the Dutch department store to open after the company's flagship store in Amsterdam in 1909 and a store in The Hague, which opened in 1926.

suggestions made in the plan for the city's reconstruction.² This plan of 1946, known as the 'Basic Plan', presented a new urban concept that was to transform the image of Rotterdam. One of its proposals was to straighten and widen the old Boulevard and open it up to the river, where, as Cornelis van Traa suggested, 'the prosperity comes from'.³ Van Traa, the architect of the reconstruction plan, deemed the store's new location as crucial for the city as for the company.⁴ Its altered position indeed placed the Bijenkorf at the new epicentre of the administrative and commercial activity of the city, on a spacious corner plot in the middle of the Coolsingel's west bank, near City Hall and opposite the Chamber of Commerce. The new store would furthermore be within walking distance from another department store of Dutch origin, Vroom & Dreesmann, to the east of the Coolsingel⁵ and, most importantly, would be strategically located next to the new Lijnbaan shopping centre, a project informed by the city's desire to bring private shopkeepers back to the centre of Rotterdam.⁶ This planned 'commercial' vicinity could be considered a Dutch transplant of the American 'regional' shopping centre model which made the department store an anchor of the shopping centre.⁷

The company realized that regardless of how successful and progressive the old Bijenkorf had been in its time, it was now outstripped.⁸ Designed according to the prevailing type for the department store in pre-war Europe,⁹ Dudok's multi-storey building had amply fenestrated facades and a glazed light atrium, which rose through the floors and inundated the sales areas with natural light. When the decision to reconstruct or raze the building presented itself, this layout however no longer corresponded with the expectations of contemporary retail design. Already in the early 1930s, department stores in the United States, concerned about their commercial viability, had introduced the concept of the

---

²A letter of agreement between the city and the company dated 14 January 1949 stipulated that the Bijenkorf's old building would be relinquished and the store would relocate to a new plot (marked on the map as block RO-AF-31AM-8). This initial agreement was followed by negotiations concerning the financial terms of the exchange. Source: 'Stukken betreffende de voorbereiding voor en kostenramingen van de nieuwbouw', Archief van de Koninklijke Bijenkorf Beheer N.V., Stadsarchief Amsterdam.

³C. van Traa, 'Nieuwe Bijenkorf te Rotterdam', *Bouwkundig Weekblad* 75a, no. 38 (1957): 2.

⁴'The Beehive moved to another location and that movement deserves a statement, because, in my eyes, this was a particularly good solution, both for the Beehive and for the city of Rotterdam.' See ibid. Additionally, in C. van Traa, 'Rotterdam's Nieuwe Bim', *Bouw* (July 1948), 204, van Traa stated that the City Council was not entirely satisfied with his plans for the Coolsingel and requested modifications be made to the design for the west bank, as it lacked important buildings and character when compared to the east bank. Van Traa tried to solve this problem with the aid of commercial establishments.

⁵Vroom & Dreesmann rebuilt its store on the Hoogstraat in 1950, when the centre of the city was still deserted. See T. Lanterman, 'Planung, Wiederaufbau, Neubau', in *Rotterdam: Den Neubau einer Stadt*, ed. C. van Traa (Rotterdam: Verlag Ad. Donker, 1957), 66.

⁶Van Traa, 'Rotterdam's Nieuwe Bim', 204. Van Traa believed that the proximity of these two commercial complexes was crucial for their establishment and success. He believed that the Lijnbaan might have not been realized if the construction of the Bijenkorf on the west bank of the Coolsingel had not been expected and that vice versa the Bijenkorf might have not been built if a shopping centre had not existed in its immediate vicinity. See Van Traa, 'Nieuwe Bijenkorf te Rotterdam', 2.

⁷For a detailed analysis, see Richard Longstreth, *The American Department Store Transformed, 1920–1960* (New Haven: Yale University Press, 2010), 1, 172–180, 221.

⁸Discussions on the programme and character of the new building had started within the executive board as early as 1946 and intensified after 1949 with the plot-exchange agreement. See 'Stukken betreffende de voorbereiding voor en kostenramingen van de nieuwbouw', Archief van de Koninklijke Bijenkorf Beheer N.V., Stadsarchief Amsterdam.

⁹According to Meredith L. Clausen, this type was established by the Parisian 'Magasin au Bon Marché', in 1876: Meredith L. Clausen, 'The Department Store: Development of the Type', *Journal of Architectural Education* 39, no. 1 (1985): 20–29.

fully air-conditioned store, which was more enclosed and which was equipped with an elaborate lighting system designed to eliminate shadows and glare, while emulating 'natural' daylight. The new 'windowless' store was to protect the merchandise from direct exposure to sunlight and thus avoid discolouring.[10] Following deteriorating economic conditions in the United States after the Wall Street Crash of 1929, commercial design had furthermore turned to more simple and moderate architectural solutions that banned some of the 'indulgences' of the old type, such as glazed atria surrounded by open galleries, grand staircases, monumental entrances, domed corner rotundas, luxurious materials and ornamentation.[11] This American evolution of the department store's building type was music to the ears of post-war investors in Europe who, despite the recent (hard-gained) economic prosperity and social stability, preferred to economize on both time and means.

Disenchanted with Dudok's design and informed by a 1949 report on 'The future of the department store' drafted by Martin Lederman, the firm's consultant,[12] the Bijenkorf's management decided to modernize the store and turned towards the American models of consumption for inspiration. Lederman's report furthermore motivated the company's executives to hire an architect from across the Atlantic for their Rotterdam project. To find a suitable candidate, they undertook several trips to the United States, and after a 1953 visit to a branch of the Abraham & Strauss suburban department store, a big warehouse in Hempstead, Long Island, built in 1951–1952, commissioned Marcel Breuer to design the new Bijenkorf.[13] Breuer had been the consulting architect for the exterior design of the Abraham & Strauss store, which he kept windowless above the ground level and clad in white-painted brick. Abraham Elzas, the Amsterdam-based architect of the firm, was asked to support Breuer's work locally and the two entered into a partnership.[14] Finally, the New York-based retail architect Daniel Schwartzman, who had collaborated with Breuer on the Abraham & Strauss project, was also hired by the Dutch company to consult on interior design.[15]

Nonetheless, notwithstanding the significant influence that the city and the company's management had on the design of the new Bijenkorf, and in spite of the intensive interaction between all the architects engaged in the project, it would be incorrect to think of the new Bijenkorf as anything other than the work of Breuer's unique mind. Breuer alone is to be attributed for the building's careful mediation between

---

[10]Richard Longstreth, 'Sears, Roebuck and the Remaking of the Department Store, 1924–42', *Journal of the Society of Architectural Historians* 65, no. 2 (2006): 238–279, and Longstreth, *The American Department Store Transformed*, 1, 38, 47–49.

[11]Clausen, 'The Department Store'.

[12]Martin Lederman, 'The Future of the Department Store', 1949, Archief van de Koninklijke Bijenkorf Beheer N.V., Stadsarchief Amsterdam.

[13]Archief van de Koninklijke Bijenkorf Beheer N.V., Stadsarchief Amsterdam.

[14]It was agreed that Breuer would have the last word in design matters and that he was free to choose the consultants for the technical matters. See 'Bespreking Betreffende de Nieuwe Bijenkorf te Rotterdam ten Kantore van de Heer A. Goudsmit op 28 July 1953', Archief van de Koninklijke Bijenkorf Beheer N.V., Stadsarchief Amsterdam. Elzas had participated in the discussion that succeeded the 1949 agreement, which set the guiding lines and prerequisites prior to the design of the new building.

[15]Daniel Schwartzman was responsible for 'the layout and size of the different departments and their relation to each other', and was also engaged to advise on '... the detailed merchandising requirements of these departments, including fixtures, accessories, etc.'. See 'Contract of collaboration between Marcel Breuer–A. Elzas and Daniel Schwartzman on 1 March 1954', Marcel Breuer Papers, 1920–1986, Archives of American Art, Smithsonian Institution.

formal expression and function as he succeeded in attaining a balance between opposing forces commanded by the design brief. On the one hand, the building had to be 'practical' in its use, allow for the implementation of rationalized retail processes, comply with technical requirements and offer economical solutions in line with contemporary consumer practices while adhering to demands imposed by the free market economy; on the other hand it needed to offer a certain aesthetic pleasure and symbolism, representative of the optimism driving the reconstruction of the war-torn town, while offering Rotterdam residents a new locale of collectivity able to express the values of the unfurling welfare state.

A form for the function

After having obtained the commission, Breuer did not simply transplant the American department store model in Europe, but carefully adapted his design to the particularities of both the city and the postwar European reality. First of all, he treated the building as a purpose-built entity. To respond to the programme of functions defined by the company and in search of an economical solution, he developed his own definition of the department store: 'Essentially', he said, 'a department store is a big, empty box built around a central circulation core, with the walls closed to provide ample storage.'[16] And so, befitting the new economic circumstances, a compact 'box'-like architecture – a 26.5 metres high parallel-piped with a total floor area of about 36,000 square metres, of which 15,000 square metres were sales area – arose, which was able to accommodate large numbers of customers, display and store an abundance of goods, offer flexibility in the interior layout and operate under conditions of artificial lighting and ventilation to support and protect the merchandise.

The circulation of the original 1957 new, five-level department store also conformed to Breuer's definition of the typology, as a set of escalators placed in a prominent central position connected the large sales halls with uniform layouts.[17] Ancillary staircases were situated around the three sides of the sales halls, while lifts and restrooms were located at the rear, along with the circulation of goods and personnel, which took place unobtrusively, behind the scenes. With this new approach, a straightforward relation between the pragmatic character of a retail establishment and its formal expression was achieved.

Breuer's arrangement not only provided adequate space for retail, the core activity of the department store, but also for a range of customer services, intended to optimize the sales.[18] These included an espresso bar in the basement; a snack buffet on the ground floor; a hair salon, a post office and a travelling agency on the first floor; a restaurant with a capacity of 500 on the second floor; and a bakery on the third floor. The offices and employees' facilities on the fourth floor opened onto roof gardens. On the north side of the 'box', Breuer annexed a three-level volume containing offices, workshops, storage, packaging and pricing areas, as well as spaces for the building's technical installations.

---

[16] 'Bijenkorf Project', *Time Magazine*, 3 June 1957, 74.

[17] The use of escalators was a rather recent innovation of the mid-1940s. See Longstreth, *The American Department Store Transformed*, 52.

[18] Historically, the provision of non-commercial activities and services was a technique used to engage customers and keep them satisfied within the commercial environment to increase spending. See Clausen, 'The Department Store', 21.

Figure 12.1 Bijenkorf, ground floor plan, 1954.
Source: Stadsarchief Amsterdam.

Figure 12.2 Bijenkorf interior, 1957.
Source: Robert Doisneau/Rapho.

This volume also included a cinema theatre, the 'Cineac', on the first floor able to accommodate 600 moviegoers.[19] The 'Cineac' was directly connected to the restaurant and also had a separate entrance from the Coolsingel to ensure accessibility when the store was closed.

Figure 12.3 The 'Cineac' on the Coolsingel Avenue, 1957.
Source: Robert Doisneau/Rapho.

---

[19]From morning until midnight, the 'Cineac' would project the latest news on the big screen. See 'Het Bijenvolk', Archief van de Koninklijke Bijenkorf Beheer N.V., Stadsarchief Amsterdam.

Figure 12.4 Night view of the 'Bijkorama' display pavilion, 1957.
Source: Robert Doisneau/Rapho.

On the western side, adapted to the scale of the neighbouring Lijnbaan shopping centre, 'Bijkorama', a delicate crystalline pavilion that served as both exhibition space and advertising area,[20] was attached to the building.

Border adjustments of modern approaches

In the elemental form of the 'box', the functional requirements of the department store found their ideal expression. Breuer nevertheless had to defend this clear-cut volume – along with the modernist 'form follows function' axiom – to the city planning committee that, in an effort to widen the Coolsingel and give prominence to the few surviving buildings, such as the adjacent Hotel Atlanta, had imposed a

---

[20]In reality this area was used less for art exhibitions and more for merchandising promotions (i.e. as an automobile showroom) and special events, thus exploring the ambiguity of the term 'exhibition'.

double building line on the avenue's west bank.[21] After negotiations Breuer succeeded in replacing the protruding volume proposed by the city with a large independent monumental sculpture at the corner of the boulevard: Naum Gabo's twenty-five metres high constructivist work.[22]

When it came to the window-treatment, Breuer was also clear about his modern approach. Aware of the importance of qualitative lighting for a department store, and well-informed about the American developments in the field of artificial lighting, he dismissed the extensive use of exterior windows.[23] Uninterrupted by load-bearing elements, Breuer thus obtained the freedom to sheath the three-bay skin of his 'box' in striated Roman travertine slabs without revealing the interior floor division in the building's façade. Only a few large horizontal windows betrayed the presence of interior spaces in need of natural light: the restaurant on the second floor and the offices and employees' facilities on the top floor. On the ground floor Breuer used continuous plate glass windows to create display areas and establish a visual connection between the building and the street. The supremacy of solid over void did not change even when he added vertical slit windows to the pattern created by the travertine slabs. This element, whose only utilitarian purpose seems to be catering to the customers' desire to view some articles in daylight,[24] was the outcome of a careful calculation of the balance between solid and void. It ensured that also at night, in the dark, the store would be compelling. Thanks to its dramatic artificial lighting, the 'box' appears perforated as its interior is disclosed and its enclosed character begins to decompose. Standing in stark contrast with the solidity of the travertine walls was the office annex on the north side. It had an aluminium skeleton and a refined, highly elaborated curtain wall with references to De Stijl. The alternated use of transparent, translucent and opaque glass on this curtain wall responded to the daylight requirements for the different functions housed inside the annex, ranging from offices to the technical installations.

Breuer however avoided stereotypes and kept an experimental character in his design by subtly twisting modern elements and giving them an ambiguous character, thus revealing the ongoing struggle of opposites. Belonging to a less rigid generation of modern architects,[25] he was quite comfortable with features of classicism and – in the spirit of balancing contrasts – employed some of its basic aesthetic features, such as symmetry,[26] ratio, harmonious proportions and rhythm in the building's elevations,

---

[21]This protruding corner structure was to rest on columns, so that the full pavement width would remain available for the pedestrians. See Van Traa, 'Rotterdam's nieuwe bim', 204.

[22]Breuer was responsible for the final approval of Gabo's work. Their cooperation was 'on the same organizational lines as with Schwartzman'. See 'Meeting of Architects and Dr. van der Wal in Paris on Tuesday 27th and Wednesday 28th of May 1954, Archief van de Koninklijke Bijenkorf Beheer N.V., Stadsarchief Amsterdam.

[23]According to a contemporary publication, the new Bijenkorf would be the first department store in Holland to have 'closed upper floors': 'Four Stores', *Architectural Record* (May 1955): 206.

[24]This consideration was made by the company. See 'Stukken betreffende de voorbereiding voor en kostenramingen van de nieuwbouw', Archief van de Koninklijke Bijenkorf Beheer N.V., Stadsarchief Amsterdam.

[25]Breuer placed himself and his post-war projects in a period that he calls the 'second epoch of the architecture we call modern'. Following the revolutionary, early avant-garde modernism, a period of 'interlocking philosophy and realization' arose, which witnessed the emergence of a softer form of modernism, less iconic and more realistic. See Marcel Breuer, Typescript of lecture 'History of Modern Architecture' [undated], Marcel Breuer Papers, 1920–1986, Archives of American Art, Smithsonian Institution.

[26]Breuer believed that '[s]ymmetry is just as much a part of our means as asymmetry'. Source: Ibid.

mixed with more 'modern', asymmetrical elements.[27] Examining the relationship of the whole to the parts, he achieved an asymmetrical balance by, for example, placing the large horizontal windows near the edges of the volume, or by inverting weight distribution, lifting the 'heavy' elements up high above the ground. In doing so, Breuer gave motion to the rigorous and largely opaque prism, converting static balance into dynamism.

Balancing corporate and civic identity

Covering all three sides of the store with travertine stone, Breuer avoided the one, distinct and representational *façade*. Still, despite the homogeneity of the material, the treatment of the building's skin was not uniform. Variation was introduced through the alternation of cladding patterns on the different

Figure 12.5 Corner detail of the east and south façades of the Bijenkorf, 1957.
Source: Robert Doisneau/Rapho.

---

[27]Walter Gropius, 'The Theory and Organization of the Bauhaus', in *Bauhaus 1919–1929*, eds. Herbert Bayer, Walter Gropius and Ise Gropius (New York: The Museum of Modern Art, 1938), 30.

elevations: the cladding on the Coolsingel and Lijnbaan elevations was made of hexagonal plates, while the cladding on the in-between Van Oldenbarneveltstraat elevation was made of rectangular plates with the same height as the hexagonal ones. The crucial moment occurred where the two patterns met. There, at the edges of the 'box', a modern thinness was revealed; Breuer deliberately exposed the artificiality of the cladding and, hence, the nature of his construction. He also managed to transform a traditional material with a strong texture like stone into a clear-cut slab, by using it with great accuracy and formalism. The question why Breuer chose to use stone, a material with such an optical and historical weight, instead of aluminium, steel, glass or concrete, which were the prevailing and highly advocated building materials of modernism, however remains.[28] Perhaps the answer resides in this material's capacity to endow the building with a monumental character, as well as a sense of permanence and stability.

Questions on a new monumentality, along with speculations on the role of public buildings within the realm of modern architecture, already arose during the war and were extensively covered by the CIAM discourse on urbanism, in 1949 and 1952. Was modern architecture appropriate for the design of civic buildings and their social dimension?[29] Was a return to the *façade*, the nineteenth-century element of representation,[30] necessary? In its essence, a building's facade separates the private space of the interior from the public space of the city, protecting and, at the same time, projecting the enclosed functions. It is the public image of the building that transmits information and meaning about its character and its relationship to the urban environment, also contributing to the shaping of the latter. In this sense, architecture always has a role to perform within society, being an exponent of collective memory and shared values. And still, was there a distinction between the architectural expression of 'public buildings' and 'utilitarian buildings'?[31] And more importantly, could a commercial establishment be considered a public building? Noted architectural critic and former president of CIAM Sigfied Giedion considered the department store a utilitarian building and focused predominantly on its technological innovations that rendered it a symbol of modernity for nineteenth-century architecture.[32]

---

[28] According to Longstreth, these materials were '... heralded as embodying the latest in architectural treatments [of department stores]'. See Longstreth, *The American Department Store Transformed*, 56.

[29] 'The reconquest of the monumental expression' for Giedion would be the most difficult challenge of modern architecture. See Sigfied Giedion, 'The Need for Monumentality', in *New Architecture and City Planning: A Symposium*, ed. Paul Zucker (New York: Philosophical Library, 1944), 552. On the civic element of the urban environment and the role of the monument, see José Luis Sert, *Can Our Cities Survive? An ABC on Urban Problems, Their Analysis, Their Solutions* (Cambridge, MA: The Harvard University Press, 1947), 232–233.

[30] This approach was strongly advocated by Gottfried Semper, a prominent architectural theorist of the mid-nineteenth century. He believed that the *façade* should create its own rhetoric – mainly through cladding – being a project of representation and bearer of important attributes of the building, including its monumental character. See Gottfried Semper, 'Style in the Technical and Tectonic Arts or Practical Aesthetics: A Handbook for Technicians, Artists, and Patrons of Art', in *The Four Elements of Architecture and Other Writings*, trans. Henry Mallgrave and Wolfgang Herrmann (Cambridge: Cambridge University Press, 1989), 255; Wolfgang Herrmann, *Gottfried Semper: In Search of Architecture* (Cambridge, MA: The MIT Press, 1984), 178.

[31] José Luis Sert, 'Centres of Community Life', in *The Heart of the City*, eds. J. Tyrwitt, J.L. Sert and E.N. Rogers (London: Lund Humphries, 1952), 13.

[32] For Giedion the department store constituted 'a new building problem ["product of the industrial age"], apparently governed solely by practical considerations'. See Sigfied Giedion, *Space, Time and Architecture: The Growth of a New Tradition* (Cambridge, MA: Harvard University Press, 1941), 234, 242.

However, as historians Geoffrey Crossick and Serge Jaumain point out: 'The freedom of entry, the great architectural presence, the anonymity of the participants, and the theatrical style all placed the department stores in the public sphere.'[33] Moreover, in the mid-nineteenth century, 'as consumption itself became a social activity associated with leisure and entertainment, ... consumer institutions [increasingly] centred on those parts of the city close to theatres and bourgeois street life'.[34] Crossick and Jaumain furthermore argue that 'as buildings of height and grandeur rose in the city skies where churches spires and towers had once stood unchallenged', department stores became part of 'a new urban monumentalism'.[35]

With the creation of a 'timeless' architecture, Breuer once more revealed his determination to balance opposing forces; this time by reconciling the impermanence of fashion – the driving force of a department store – and the ephemeral character of the selling techniques with the desire to exude stability and reliability – characteristics befitting a public institution. Commissioned to design a new building on a corner block in the heart of the new centre of Rotterdam, which was going to be largely defined by new buildings, Breuer cleverly used materiality and classical composition techniques to give the building civic gravity. He was well aware of the visual significance of the Bijenkorf's enveloping surfaces and their capacity to simultaneously communicate civic and corporate identity, and clearly state the building's function within the urban structure.

In an effort to express the building's corporate identity in clear and memorable manner, Breuer imaginatively[36] used a clever marketing strategy, basing his design on the beehive, a theme that derived from the brand name of the store – the 'Bijenkorf'. With a geometric reduction of this concept, the hexagon[37] – the Coolsingel and the Lijnbaan elevations were clad with hexagonal panels – he created a strong public image and 'narrative' for the building that allowed Rotterdam's citizens to connect with it.[38] The motif that these panels created, which was both ahistorical and atemporal, conveyed a sense of eternity and gave the building monumental quality. It also resembled a tattooed surface; a constructed social skin charged with an urban and social function of reflecting a distinctive and recognizable identity of the bearer,[39] an element that, although it is part of the building, belongs to both the building and

---

[33]Geoffrey Crossick and Serge Jaumain (eds.), *Cathedrals of Consumption: The European Department Store, 1850–1939* (Brookfield: Ashgate Publishing Company, 1999), 32.

[34]Ibid., 23.

[35]Ibid., 21. For the monumental character of nineteenth-century department stores, see also Clausen, 'The Department Store'.

[36]Historically, Clausen points out, the identity of a department store was advertised only through the signs affixed to its facades – 'like the gigantic billboard overhead bearing the store's name'. See Clausen, 'The Department Store', 23.

[37]The use of a visual symbol to express the building's identity by integrating it into the building's design was an innovative element of Breuer's architecture. In his 1960 landmark publication *Shopping Town USA*, Victor Gruen also emphasized the value of the – 'simple and original' – symbol. See Victor Gruen and Larry Smith, *Shopping Town USA: The Planning of Shopping Centers* (New York: Reinhold Publishing Corporation, 1960), 165.

[38]Loyal to the Bauhaus logic of total design and believing in the expressive capacity of the details to reveal meaning, Breuer also used the geometry of the hexagon for the creation of a logotype for the department store – its 'trademark' – to be used in labels and advertisements, and for the design of the door handles, certain furniture and the construction site kiosk (a network of three elevated hexagonal cells) that was erected on the plot, serving as full-scale publicity during the construction.

[39]Claude Lévi-Straus, referring to the example of face-painting decoration used by an Indian tribe in central Brazil, concluded that 'one should be painted to become a man; he who remained in his natural state was not distinguished from animals'. See Claude Lévi-Straus, *Tristes Tropiques* (Paris: Librairie Plon, 1955), 160–165.

the city. The beehive concept also influenced the design of the building on a more symbolic level; it operated as a metaphor for the great concentration of people and activities in this building that attempted to restore an urban density that had been lost during the war.

Building a new collectivity

The old centre of Rotterdam needed upgrading already before the war erupted. Large parts of the population were living in dismal conditions and the city's infrastructure was unable to meet the demands of its port, which by the 1930s had become the largest in Europe.[40] After the Germans bombed the city, necessitating the clearance of rubble, the 'impatience to build from scratch – from emptiness – an entirely new, better city' soon became obvious.[41] Rotterdam's city architects, W.G. Witteveen and C. van Traa, his replacement, were eager to build a modern city, which could convey an image of affluence, consumerism and welfare and which would be able to accommodate the economic and logistic functions required by its large international port.[42] To this end, the 'Basic Plan' was reduced to a dynamic but rather neutral layout, intended to create opportunities for private building initiatives. The new plan designated the centre of the city for economic, commercial and recreational functions, while the residential function was moved to an urban zone around the centre. This exclusion of dwellings, however, risked resulting in a lack of vitality in the centre and attributed a pivotal role to commercial functions in the process of re-vitalizing the city core. Shopping became a key activity, which was to lure people to the newly constructed (partly empty) centre. The collective memory of the inhabitants, which was embedded in the streets and stones of the city and which was lost during the bombing, was thus replaced by a new form of collectivity: consumerism.[43]

In this framework, the role of the new department store could not be reduced to that of a temple of consumerism or a symbol of corporate power that would enforce the image of Rotterdam as an economically thriving place; it also had to tackle the revitalization of an empty city centre and become a symbol of urban regeneration.[44] Breuer's enclosed edifice had to offer compactness and intensity of public life with the integration of manifold human activities in the controlled and orchestrated shopping experience. As such, its role in Rotterdam's new centre resembled that of the typical American

---

[40]Han Meyer, 'Rotterdam, the Promise of a New Modern Society in a New, Modern City – 1940 to the Present', in *Out of Ground Zero. Case Studies in Urban Reinvention*, ed. Joan Ockman (Munich: Prestel Verlag, 2002), 89.

[41]Kees Schuyt and Ed Taverne, *Dutch Culture in a European Perspective (4) 1950: Prosperity and Welfare* (Hampshire: Palgrave Macmillan, 2005), 161.

[42]This image of Rotterdam, as described by van Traa's 'Basic Plan', incorporated – under the auspice of the Chamber of Commerce – ideas that influential 'modern-minded business people' had expressed during the war. See ibid., 161–162.

[43]When describing the cultural history of consumption Crossick and Jaumain explain the term 'consumer culture', as '... one in which groups constituted by class and gender could find social definition through the acts of buying as much as of consuming'. See Crossick and Jaumain, *Cathedrals of Consumption*, 2.

[44]According to Longstreth the department store had '[t]raditionally ... fostered urban growth simply by virtue of its existence', a fact that was known and widely used in the 1960s by shopping centre planners and developers in the United States and later in Europe. See Longstreth, *The American Department Store Transformed*, 221; M. Jeffrey Hardwick, *Mall Maker: Victor Gruen, Architect of an American Dream* (Philadelphia: University of Pennsylvania Press, 2004), 204, 221.

suburban shopping centre of the 1960s, which Victor Gruen deemed able 'to play the role not merely of a commercial centre, but of a social, cultural and recreational crystallization point'[45] and to offer 'emerging' communities a common ground.

The new Bijenkorf offered Rotterdam not merely another retail establishment, but a civic institution, a communal space built on private interests. By combining the commercial and business functions (the office annex) under one roof and offering leisure facilities (hair salon, espresso bar, snack buffet, restaurant), and cultural amenities (cinema, theatre, exhibition pavilion, works of art in permanent exhibition[46]) next to the regular customer services, a pleasing and ever-busy nucleus of activity was created, making the metaphor of the beehive a three-dimensional reality. This compactness and intensity of public life enhanced Rotterdam's urban activity and helped the Bijenkorf to become a focal point in a rather bland area. Breuer thus offered a new interpretation of the nineteenth-century concept of the department store adapted to inner-city, post-war Rotterdam.

---

[45] Victor Gruen, *The Heart of Our Cities. The Urban Crisis: Diagnosis and Cure* (New York: Simon and Schuster, 1964), 191; Gruen and Smith, *Shopping Town USA*, 11, 24.

[46] Apart from Naum Gabo's work, there was a sculpture of Henri Moore on the loggia of the restaurant and a 'glass-in-glass window' by Van Doesburg in the corridor leading from the ground floor to the 'Bijkorama'.

Chapter 13

The shopping centre comes to Germany: Frankfurt's Main-Taunus-Zentrum at the crossroads of mass-motorization and retail economics
Steffen de Rudder

Cars rolled along the streets in 'conspicuous caravans' to get to the new shopping centre, wrote the *Frankfurter Allgemeine Zeitung*, reporting a logjam of 70,000 cars in downtown Frankfurt.[1] Those who did not own a car, and in the mid-1960s that was still the majority of people in Germany, just walked the few kilometres in single file from Hoechst or Unterliederbach. The opening of the first rural German shopping centre on 2 May 1964 was a spectacle. In fact, this was not just a new type of retail business, but at that point, the largest shopping centre in Europe.[2] Photographs taken on the opening day show substantial crowds, with people marvelling at the modern complex, the sheer size of the site, the abundant variety of products and services and attractions such as a Kindergarten specifically for customers, or the thirty-two metre 'vending machine aisle'.

Here, a new culture of consumption became visible, a culture that imparted a bright, modern and friendly feel with unmistakable roots in America. The idea for Germany's first shopping mall, 'Main-Taunus-Zentrum' (MTZ) near Frankfurt, had been developed by the Canadian Bennet Group and the banker Frederik Burton from Toronto; the second site in Germany, the 'Ruhrpark' near Bochum which opened the same year, was an investment by Los Angeles building contractor Edward Roberts. American investors had been watching the interplay between increasing purchasing power, the mass motorization boom and a lack of space in built-up city centres and spotted an opportunity to transpose the successful American shopping mall model to Germany. This chapter examines to what extent the West German shopping centre resembled its American predecessor, how it was adapted to German society and why it became successful as a business model but not as public space.

---

[1] '50 Jahre Main-Taunus-Zentrum. Die Verkaufsmaschine', *Frankfurter Allgemeine Zeitung*, 1 May 2014, 24.
[2] Ibid.

Figure 13.1 The first shopping centre in Germany: 'Main-Taunus-Zentrum' near Frankfurt, 1964.
Source: ECE Projektmanagement G.m.b.H. & Co. KG, Hamburg, copyright holder unknown.

Figure 13.2 Geographical centre of a region with 1.7 million potential consumers: the fields of Sulzbach/Taunus.
Source: ECE Projektmanagement G.m.b.H. & Co. KG, Hamburg, copyright holder unknown.

Location

Whereas pre-war retail in Germany was about large urban department stores and local corner stores, the American style shopping centre moved the retail business from city to the countryside. It is therefore no coincidence that neither MTZ near Frankfurt nor the Ruhrpark near Bochum bear the names of these cities but make reference to landscape features of their sites. 'Main-Taunus' refers to a district in the middle of Hesse between the Taunus mountains in the North and the Main river in the South. Located in close proximity of large cities like Frankfurt, Wiesbaden and Mainz, this is one of Germany's most densely populated areas.

The overall concept of MTZ can be interpreted as the antithesis of the European city – no history, no density, no truly public space, no church and no town hall – but at the same time one that evokes it with the idea of the urban street: 'In the heart of the countryside [is] a street of shops 400 meters in length. ... Whatever you're looking for, you will find it at the MTZ. All the products and services you will find in a city. But without the traffic noise and without the traffic lights.'[3]

The Canadian investors' interest was not in the city, but in the region. In the latter phase of the *Wirtschaftswunder*,[4] the area between the Main and Rhine rivers was optimally situated; it was one of the strongest economic areas in the Federal Republic, densely populated and equipped with above-average purchasing power. This was about finding a location in the geographical centre, a place where all the lines crossed; a hub that would bring together 1.7 million potential consumers. That location

---

[3]Advertising brochure MTZ, 'Verkehrsverbindungen zum Main-Taunus-Zentrum', 1964.
[4]The term *'Wirtschaftswunder'* describes West Germany's unexpected fast economic recovery after the Second World War that went along with high industrial production, full employment, mass motorization and the implementation of German welfare state.

turned out to be thirty-three hectares of empty arable land, owned by the municipality of Sulzbach, at the intersection of an *autobahn* and a federal highway just outside Frankfurt. That was important because the city was afraid of losing its own retail business and would not have authorized a shopping mall within its borders. A key argument in the choice of location was the availability of vast amounts of space, which was used for thousands of parking spaces and which guaranteed the freedom to be able to expand *ad libitum*.

References

There were no direct models for the structure and architecture of the shopping centre in Germany, and architects were not yet familiar with this brief. The frequently cited Lijnbaan project by van den Broek and Bakema in Rotterdam (1953) must be viewed as a reference, although this was a shopping mall in an inner-city context and part of a larger urban development concept. The same goes for the widely acclaimed Vällingby project near Stockholm, which also comprises a shopping mall, but is located at the heart of a new residential area. There was great familiarity with American shopping centres as a direct example, and German architecture drew much of its inspiration from the American figureheads of German modernism, such as Walter Gropius and Mies van der Rohe, who had emigrated to the United States in the 1930s and once there, had been involved in the continued development of modernist architecture. This is also why looking to America was so important during the phase of new orientation in the post-Nazi era. Many architects of the German post-war modern age such as Helmut Hentrich and Hubert Petschnigg, and Friedrich Wilhelm Kraemer and Frei Otto toured the United States, visited the major practices and studied the manifold traits of modern architecture, which was at a more advanced stage in its development.

There was an awareness of the American shopping centre genre, which was the subject of excursions and discourse in the German trade press. For example, a delegation of the Association of German Retailers as well as the Economic and Construction Ministry travelled across the United States in 1963 and visited the latest examples of the American shopping mall from Boston to San Francisco. Titled 'The Retail Business in Urban Construction. Shopping centres in the US – European Consequences', a ninety-page travel report was released the following year, published by the Rationalization Board of Trustees of the German Economy.[5]

The delegation identified the 'fast and extensive' process of suburbanization as the dominating trend, characterizing it as a 'population movement'.[6] It is described as a 'unique phenomenon', which was to this extent only possible in the United States.[7] In a comprehensive analysis the authors compare the American and German situation, looking at geography, size of country, economic development, housing construction, way of living and even racial segregation.[8] They conclude that the countries

---

[5] Erwin Thomas, *Einzelhandel im Städtebau. Shopping Centers in den USA – Europäische Konsequenzen* (Frankfurt: Verlag für Wirtschaftspraxis, 1964).
[6] Ibid., 69.
[7] Ibid.
[8] Ibid., 78.

Figure 13.3 Berlin architects Schwebes and Schoszberger: design for the central street of shops.
Source: ECE Projektmanagement G.m.b.H. & Co. KG, Hamburg, copyright holder unknown.

are too different to simply transplant the American shopping centre to Germany and advise that these should only be built in the open countryside in particular cases, when establishing modern shopping facilities in a city centre is impossible or when traffic problems are too grave to be solved.[9]

Architecture

It cannot be ascertained whether the architects of MTZ, Paul Schwebes and Hans Schoszberger, had seen a typical American shopping mall with their own eyes; thus far a biography of the Berlin architects has not been published. We do know that Schwebes and Schoszberger had numerous contacts in the United States through their Berlin building projects. They served as contact architects for the construction of the Hilton Hotel in Budapester Straße, designed by the American Charles Luckmann and completed in 1957. Their biggest project, 'Zentrum am Zoo', a 200-metre long block of buildings flanked by two high-rise slabs, constructed between 1955 and 1957, emerged as a German–American cooperation. It was financed with the help of the European Recovery Program, the US government's reconstruction initiative for Western Europe better known as the Marshall Plan.

---

[9]Ibid., 82.

But it was not just through their experience dealing with American partners that Schwebes and Schoszberger emerged as suitable partners for the pending project. They had also built numerous department stores and business premises, mostly in West Berlin, and were therefore qualified to design a shopping mall.[10] They were representatives of an elegant-functional building style that is viewed as formative for Berlin post-war modernism. One of their best-known buildings is the 1956 Hardenberg House on the corner of Knesebeckstraße and Hardenbergstraße in Charlottenburg, once home of Berlin's largest bookstore. With its curved, neatly arranged glass façade and paper-thin, cantilevered roof, this is one of the most outstanding examples of 1950s Berlin architecture. Nonetheless, their 'Zentrum am Zoo' project was more famous still. The main body of the project, the 'Bikini-Haus', owes its name to an open-sided floor in the middle that separates the building into a lower section and an upper section. The lower section accommodates shops, while the upper floors were originally used for the production of women's apparel, later as office space.[11]

The visual vocabulary of MTZ includes only a few elements of this sophisticated, elegant 1950s architecture. At best, it is the light awnings of the shop buildings, the slender steel supports and the horizontally arranged facades of the central street that are reminiscent of the practice's showcase buildings. It can be assumed that in their approach to MTZ, Schwebes and Schoszberger were not pursuing high architectural aspirations. The project does not appear in the architecture museum's collection at Berlin's Technical University, a collection that includes the vast majority of Schwebes and Schozberger's work; any further traces of original design drafts have been lost. The centre left no traces in German architectural history; so far it has been mentioned only once. Under the heading 'temple to consumerism' – a title that for a centre that is modest at best in comparison with its American ancestors is somewhat misleading – there is a small chapter in an exhibition catalogue edited by Deutsches Architekturmuseum Frankfurt.[12] The text provides a formal description, but does not comment on the architecture or layout of the centre.

The fact that the architecture played a subordinate role befits the character of the construction brief and the intentions of the developers. A shopping centre out in the countryside did not need to be as showy as the metropolitan consumer temples of the 1920s. More important and crucial for the success of the business model was the seamless organization of the shopping excursion, which essentially had to fulfil three conditions: optimized vehicle accessibility with generous parking facilities, simple access from parking to shopping and maximized window display space for product presentation.

As a result, the rural shopping mall reverses the usual architectural treatment of the front and back of a building: The outside becomes the back, the inside the front. Outside, leading to the parking lots, are the back doors, where deliveries take place and empty packaging piles up. Inside, leading to the central

---

[10]Although in 1966, after Main-Taunus-Zentrum, Schwebes and Schoszberger built a similar shopping mall in Hamburg (Elbe-Einkaufs-Zentrum), most of their projects were planned for Berlin. Another well-known building is 'Telefunken-Hochhaus', a high rise standing at the dominant east–west axis at Ernst Reuter-Platz. Department stores, among others, were 'Karstadt-Kaufhaus' at Schloßstraße in Berlin-Steglitz and 'Warenhaus Neckermann' at Kantstraße and Wilmersdorfer Straße.

[11]The 'Zentrum am Zoo' (1957) is now a listed building. It reopened in 2014 after a full refurbishment.

[12]Romana Schneider, Winfried Nerdinger and Wilfried Wang (eds.), *Architektur im 20. Jahrhundert. Deutschland* (München: Prestel Verlag, 2000), 212.

street of shops, is the 'public' space, the side that is actually on show. But even in this inwardly turned exterior, the concept of an architecturally designed façade no longer plays much of a role: to ensure optimal pedestrian accessibility, the design is generally a single-story development, and to ensure maximum visibility for the product range, the entire façade is shop windows. The architecture, at least in this early phase of shopping design, takes a back seat behind the products themselves.

The organization of the entire complex is quite simple: At its heart is the central mall, which is perfectly straight, and has shops of varying widths opening out onto it on both sides. In accordance with what is known as the *Knochengrundriss* or 'bone floor layout', 'anchor outlets', which in MTZ were added five years later, are located at both ends of the mall. Visitors enter the mall either via entrances positioned along the sides, or via the two ends. Anyone walking up and down the mall once can be certain not to have missed anything. This arrangement results in a good internal density and diversity of the shops, while simultaneously guaranteeing great manageability.

Reception

MTZ rapidly proved to be an economic success and garnered huge public attraction. During the first year, retailers achieved a turnover of eighty-five million Deutschmarks; ten years later, this figure increased over tenfold. But although the reaction of the general public was positive, resonance in the trade press was negative. Two of Germany's leading architectural journals formulated hostile critiques – interestingly, from diametrically opposed perspectives.

In 1966 *Bauwelt*, for example, published a special issue titled 'Wandel im Handel' (Trade Transformation), which presented the new developments affecting the retail sector – self-service, supermarkets, shopping malls – mainly in a negative light. Journalists saw 'images of supply and

Figure 13.4 Rejected by critics, overrun by consumers: the shopping crowd in the central street of shops, 1964. *Source:* ECE Projektmanagement G.m.b.H. & Co. KG, Hamburg, copyright holder unknown.

wastefulness' and commented on examples of new retail architecture with quotes from retailers' associations that described the emergence of the shopping mall as a threat and a sign of cultural decline. For example, the Dortmund Declaration of Independent Small and Medium-Sized Businesses is quoted as saying that the 'exhaustion of all possibilities to prevent the building of rural shopping centres' will be needed to 'avert the decline of existing urban and town centres'.[13] MTZ is mentioned on two pages, but appears unworthy of further comment.

The journal *Baumeister* similarly comments on the mall in great detail and predominantly in a negative tone.[14] 'Upon closer examination', the publication states, the shopping mall is turning out to be 'a huge disappointment'. *Baumeister* is particularly critical of the organization of MTZ's parking lots, which are accessible from one of the roads running around the building. This road is however also used for deliveries and therefore represents a permanent barrier for customers between parking lot and shopping mall entrances. This may be one aspect reflecting the relative inexperience of the architects with the new building type. Schwebes and Schoszberger projects in downtown West Berlin had never included parking lots covering several thousand square metres. The publication also reserves sharp criticism for the architecture of the complex: 'The buildings are more or less basic functional boxes, ... all of which lack the definitive aura of a bazaar, Vällingby or every second American centre, they are bland and expressionless.' The summary is nothing short of damning: 'terribly petit-bourgeois and primitive, it will probably never establish itself as a model'.[15]

In contrast to the more conservative *Bauwelt*, *Baumeister* does however not appear to fundamentally question the shopping mall as an architectural genre. On the following pages, journalists compare the Frankfurt mall with Victor Gruen's Southdale Shopping Centre, built in Minnesota in 1956, where all the aspects 'missing in Frankfurt' have already been realized.[16] Southdale is portrayed as a new creation in urban construction that does not try to be a 'copy of the city', but an 'imaginative distillation' of those aspects that 'make the city so compelling'.[17]

Frankfurt's building director Erhard Weiß, who naturally viewed the countryside shopping mall as competition for the city's retailers, also commented on the 'first typically American German shopping mall' in a conference paper: It is, he wrote, 'the typical picture of a non-integrated shopping centre'.[18] 'The asphalt parking lots and the large expressways', Weiß continued, isolate 'the mall completely from the countryside'. He saw rural shopping malls as symptomatic of the lack of effort invested in the rejuvenation of the cities themselves and believed that a 'large-scale destruction of land' was taking place; a process driven not by the needs of consumers, but by real estate speculation.[19] Weiß also criticized the mass motorization and suburbanization trends, which was rather unusual for a German

---

[13]'Wandel im Handel', *Bauwelt* 47 (1966), 1362.
[14]'Main-Taunus-Zentrum', *Baumeister* (1964), 739.
[15]Ibid.
[16]Ibid., 741.
[17]Ibid.
[18]Erhard Weiß, 'Das Nordwest-Zentrum in Frankfurt am Main – Geplante Mitte eines neuen Stadtteils', in *Einkaufszentren in Form von integrierten oder selbständigen Siedlungsgebilden*, ed. Kurt Giesen (Essen: Vulkan-Verlag, 1966), 72.
[19]Ibid., 76.

urban planner in the 1960s. Without making direct reference to the American model, he summarized his views by saying it was 'horrifying to see how new trends are declared quickly and almost without contestation to irrefutable frameworks ... whether this be for cars or detached houses'.[20]

Weiß expressed his criticism in 1966, two years after the opening of MTZ and therefore at a time when the phenomenon was far from widespread. He was not the only one to have these misgivings. The discourse on suburbanization and city deterioration was already taking place in the trade press and the public arena before these developments had really taken hold. Already in 1962, the well-known architecture critic of the weekly newspaper *Die Zeit* criticized MTZ, citing the dangers of suburbanization, even though the centre was only in the planning stage at the time.[21] The first harsh critique of modern urban development came in the 1964 article 'The Murdered City' by Wolf Jobst Siedler and Elisabeth Niggemeyer;[22] in 1965 Alexander Mitscherlich published a similarly positioned polemic 'The Inhospitableness of Our Cities'.[23] Both publications reference Jane Jacobs, whose book *The Death and Life of Great American Cities* had already been published in Germany in 1963 and was broadly acknowledged.[24]

Jane Jacobs wrote her famous book at a time when the process of suburbanization and city deterioration was in full swing in the United States, and the consequences of mass motorization for city, countryside and way of living had already made themselves blatantly obvious. This close relationship with the United States, resulting in a view of America that was equally admiring and disparaging, was the reason why these phenomena were discussed in Germany before they had even become a reality.

Shopping

Shopping malls did indeed not develop in the same way as they had done in the United States. Up to and including the year 1971, there were only nineteen such malls in Germany.[25] This decelerated development was in line with the differing nature of the two countries' housing situation. Areas of owner-occupied and suburban housing in Germany never reached American dimensions, neither in surface area nor in population. Also the dominance of the car as sole means of transportation never assumed comparable proportions in Germany. Large sites outside cities such as MTZ with more than 45,000 square metres of retail space were only worthwhile for investors and operators in conurbations such as that between Frankfurt and Wiesbaden or in the Ruhr Valley region. This did not change until after German reunification, when a great number of large shopping centres opened in the former East Germany, over a short period of time and without prolonged planning regulation procedures. Today,

---

[20]Ibid., 77.
[21]Manfred Sack, 'Arznei für die kranke Stadt: Das Shopping Center im Grünen ersetzt die City nicht', *Die Zeit*, 1962, 44.
[22]Wolf Jobst Siedler and Elisabeth Niggemeyer, *Die gemordete Stadt: Abgesang auf Putte und Straße, Platz und Baum* (Berlin: Herbig, 1964).
[23]Alexander Mitscherlich, *Die Unwirtlichkeit unserer Städte. Anstiftung zum Unfrieden* (Frankfurt: Suhrkamp, 1965).
[24]Jane Jacobs, *Tod und Leben großer amerikanischer Städte* (Berlin: Bauwelt Fundamente, 1963).
[25]Bernd R. Falk (ed.), *Shopping Center Handbuch* (München: Welsermühl, 1973), 25.

there are an estimated 700 shopping malls in Germany,[26] including 450 with more than 15,000 square metres of sales areas (MTZ 1964: 38,000 m²).[27]

The retail sector in Germany also witnessed a parallel development. Two commercial architecture genres existing side by side as alongside the extensive shopping malls outside the cities, the big downtown department stores of retail concerns such as Karstadt, Horten or Hertie also re-emerged.[28] The department store culture of the 1910s and 1920s, which saw the establishment of stores such as Alfred Messel's magnificent Warenhaus Wertheim in Berlin, came to an end as a result of Aryanization, expropriation and wartime destruction. The typical multi-storey downtown department store building developed after the war from the late 1950s. This type of building, more modest and functional than its predecessor, commonly a voluminous box-like structure with a large grid façade, was for decades a defining feature of the West German inner-cityscape.

The first building of this kind was the Merkur department store in Duisburg, built in 1958 and designed by Helmut Rhode and Harald Loebermann. Better known was the Horten department store in Stuttgart built in 1960 and designed by Egon Eiermann, built in countless variations right through to the 1970s with the familiar honeycomb façade named after Eiermann himself. A building in this style was also later added to MTZ complex. In the city, department stores occupied half or an entire block, and this often meant that historically significant buildings were torn down – in the case of Stuttgart, even an icon of the modern age such as the Schocken-Kaufhaus by Erich Mendelsohn. This was how typical West German inner-city retail architecture contributed to the process of urban deterioration. Although this 'strategy' was quite dissimilar from that of the countryside shopping mall, which drew purchasing power and consumers out of the city centres, the result was no less effective. Nevertheless, department stores with their large-scale screen facades generated a stylistic impulse, and their architecture has left a stronger impression on the visual memory than the introverted shopping mall. But the shopping centre was certainly not less successful. In photos from the 1960s and 1970s, MTZ appears perpetually busy, sometimes even quite crowded. The range of products and services on offer included typical urban functions such as a bank, post office, doctors' surgeries and a total of six cafés and restaurants. However, all these had to close at 6 pm, in accordance with Germany's strict trading laws. Consequently, another (quite different) image of the mall emerged; one that was equally characteristic but never photographed: a picture of total emptiness – the aisle of shops with no shoppers, the deserted parking lots. On weekdays from 6 pm on and on Saturday afternoons, this was the reality of the rural shopping precinct.

This is probably the most crucial difference with the typical American shopping mall. MTZ never became a meeting point, a place to be, to meet or to stay longer than for running the errands. It never became a hangout for teenagers, because they simply could not get there and because there was nothing that attracted them. MTZ and its successors never produced the open and accessible public space that typical European city centres provided. In the United States on the other hand,

---

[26]Dieter Schmoll, 'Von Horten zur urbanen Mal', in *Retail Architecture S-XXL: Entwicklung, Gestaltung, Objekte*, ed. Jons Messedat (Stuttgart: av edition, 2015), 17.

[27]'50 Jahre Main-Taunus-Zentrum: Die Hausfrauen haben entschieden', *Frankfurter Allgemeine Zeitung*, 2 May 2014, http://www.faz.net/aktuell/wirtschaft/50-jahre-main-taunus-zentrum-die-hausfrauen-haben-entschieden-12916596.html, accessed 1 March 2015.

[28]Schmoll, 'Von Horten zur urbanen Mal', 17.

American teenagers would drive from their suburban homes to the nearest shopping mall, which was often the only place to go, and which was at times even open 24/7. This transformed the American shopping centre into a social hub that, although private property, offered a semi-public space within American society. As a result, the American shopping mall is bound up with so many stories, memories and biographies, and appears in numerous films as a place that defines an everyday culture that is specifically American.[29] When the number of malls in the United States began its decline in the year 2007, the issue of 'dead malls' took centre stage as a plethora of photographic essays, websites, blogs and even a Wikipedia entry dedicated to the declining US shopping mall document and (at times) lament its demise. These instances provide evidence of how deeply mall culture is embedded in American collective memory.[30]

Figure 13.5 Expressway intersection as *raison d'être* and the shopping centre as a function of mass motorization, MTZ brochure, 1964.
Source: ECE Projektmanagement G.m.b.H. & Co. KG, Hamburg, copyright holder unknown.

---

[29]See, for example, John Landis, *The Blues Brothers* (USA: Universal Pictures, 1980) ('The mall chase'); James Cameron, *Terminator 2: Judgment Day* (USA: Carolco Pictures, 1991); Quentin Tarrantino, *Jackie Brown* (USA: Miramax and A Band Apart, 1997).

[30]'Dead Mall', http://en.wikipedia.org/wiki/Dead_mall, accessed 1 March 2015; see also http://deadmalls.com/, accessed 1 March 2015.

Transport

The genesis of the shopping mall as an architectural typology in the context of urban construction is linked to two major development tendencies: rationalization in the retail sector and mass motorization. Both phenomena manifested themselves in the United States in the early 1940s and emerged in Germany twenty years later albeit in a modified form. In the case of MTZ, increasing levels of car ownership in the 1960s played a significant role. The automobile industry in particular took centre stage in achieving the German 'economic miracle'. The Volkswagen Beetle became one of the most prominent symbols of West Germany's post-war economy and society. When the millionth Beetle rolled off the production line in 1955, this was an event in which the entire nation participated.[31] The five million mark was passed just seven years later, in 1962. Car ownership levels in Germany had increased eightfold between 1950 and 1960 and continued to accelerate in the following years.[32] MTZ was built during a peak period in this development trajectory, which dramatically changed life in both the cities and the country. It was the availability of a car that made it possible to move out of the city and into the countryside, and it was only the mass availability of the car that made the shopping mall at the intersection of two highways conceivable as a business model.

The car first and foremost promised freedom, the opportunity to leave one's ancestral home at any time, and travel in any direction. It broadened employment possibilities and invited to overcome the boundaries of one's own mobility. Motorization created endless new possibilities, and also new obligations: the narrow streets of the old city centres could no longer cope with traffic volumes and were permanently and hopelessly clogged.

The history of housing and urban development clearly demonstrates the interdependence of trade and transport, and how new means of transport result in new commercial forms and new markets. Within this historic continuity also lies the typical shopping mall on the expressway intersection, which can be seen in this sense as a function of mass motorization. The relationship between choosing the concept and the location of MTZ and motor traffic circumstances was clearly explained in a 1961 edition of *Der Spiegel*:

> Densely populated residential areas are pushing themselves further and further away from the city centre. This means it takes consumers with purchasing power a while to reach downtown shopping areas, and their cars are then clogging up the narrow streets where there are insufficient parking lots. ... As an alternative to inner-city shopping precincts that are increasingly difficult to get to, the suburban resident is being offered a complex of department stores and specialist stores under one roof, which is more easily accessible to him.[33]

---

[31] The gold-coloured and velvet-lined jubilee car was produced on 5 August 1955. The day began with a thanksgiving service at the Volkswagen plant in Wolfsburg, followed by a draw of fifty Volkswagen beetles and ended with the presentation of the *Bundesverdienstkreuz* (Order of Merit of the Federal Republic) to managing director Heinrich Nordhoff. The three-day festivities were attended by 400 foreign and 600 German journalists. *Der Spiegel* covered the event with an eleven-page article and a photo of Nordhoff on the cover of the magazine. 'In König Nordhoffs Reich', *Der Spiegel* 33 (August 1955), 16–26.

[32] Heidrun Edelmann, *Vom Luxusgut zum Gebrauchsgegenstand: die Geschichte der Verbreitung von Personenkraftwagen in Deutschland* (Frankfurt: Schriftenreihe des Verbands der Automobilindustrie, 1989), 14.

[33] 'Einkaufzentrum: Mit Kindern und Kegeln', *Der Spiegel* 46 (November 1961), 42.

The article concluded that the shopping mall will 'match in diversity and quality the range of shops and services offered on the "Zeil", Frankfurt's famous high street'.[34] In this commentary, *Der Spiegel* issues a very early description of the self-fuelling system of advancing motorization: Motor traffic solves the problems caused by motor traffic, and it does so with yet more motor traffic. The city of Frankfurt exacerbated the problem by trying to solve it. Following a long discussion concerning a new transport system to make urgently needed improvements to the local public transport network, in 1961 the city assembly voted in favour of the most expensive and complex option: the construction of a new subway system. As a result, almost all main roads in downtown Frankfurt were building sites for many years. They brought motor traffic to a complete standstill and flushed frustrated motorists out onto the parking lots of MTZ.

In 1965, one year after the mall's inauguration, still only 50 per cent of customers did their shopping by car; 27 per cent came by bus and 23 per cent on foot.[35] With rising car ownership and the expansion of the federal highway and freeway network around Frankfurt, it was not long before no one was coming to the shopping mall on foot. A direct bicycle route from the nearby town of Sulzbach was established a few years ago, but these days about 90 per cent of visitors nonetheless come to the centre by car.

From an economic perspective, MTZ was the right concept in the right place at the right time. Today the region is even more densely populated, better connected to the road network and with even more purchasing power than fifty years ago. The complex has continually expanded over the years, adding further department stores, a movie theatre, parking blocks and a second aisle of shops. With 91,000 square metres of retail space, it is the third largest shopping centre in Germany today. The old buildings have been altered to such an extent that no identifiable features of the original MTZ remain. Its architecture was never important, and its disappearance has been neither acknowledged nor bemoaned by either customers or experts. The centre's prominent feature is not its form, but its economic logic. Its commercial fundament is a highly developed automobile culture that is deeply anchored in German history and society, and which offers a convenience thus far unequalled by other transportation systems. As long as this does not change, as long as store tenants pay the free parking and the roads are paid for by the public purse, the business model will not be called into question.

Adaption

In the German adaption of the American shopping mall in the 1960s, three factors led to a transformation of the original model. Firstly, in the post-war Federal Republic, the American 24/7 concept did not apply, but rather the iron principle of a 'social market economy'. The strict regulation of the labour market and in particular strict laws governing the hours of trading meant that shopping centres remained closed at times that were key to the consumer, in the evenings and for most of the weekend. They thus never evolved into surrogates of urban public life as they did in the United States. Secondly, while the German public welcomed the innovation from the United States, many urban planners and experts viewed the shopping mall and suburbia as negative examples of a typically American residential development. Even

---

[34] Ibid.
[35] Klaus Wolf, 'Das Shopping Center Main-Taunus – ein neues Element des rheinisch-mainischen Verstädterungsgebietes', in *Berichte zur deutschen Landeskunde* 37, Heft 1 (1966), 92.

Figure 13.6 Street – centre – landscape: Main-Taunus-Zentrum and Taunus mountain range, looking north-west, 1964.
Source: ECE Projektmanagement G.m.b.H. & Co. KG, Hamburg, copyright holder unknown.

before the first shopping centre opened, the debate began over how this development could be prevented. Finally, despite mass motorization and suburbanization, the downtown department store was able to establish itself firmly as a formative figure that put up strong competition to the countryside shopping mall. Victor Gruen, who was familiar with both worlds as a pioneer of the American shopping centre and Austrian Jewish émigré, had already predicted this development in 1966: 'The resistance of European cities to forces that might break up the city centre is considerably greater than in the United States', he wrote.[36] The old European city, which had already survived many phases of destruction, again turned out to be a resilient culture and in spite of all the obstacles, also emerged as a functioning economic model.

The examples of German or European shopping centres that were built after 1989 in completely altered circumstances in eastern Germany and Eastern Europe may turn out to represent an independent typology of the genre. Immediately after the German reunification, when the old system was gone but new laws, urban regulations, administrative procedures and routines were not yet fully established, and (former) East Germans yearned for the products of Western consumerism, large-scale shopping centres cropped up like mushrooms, establishing a new retail monoculture. It is likely that the biographies of these locales will feature the shopping mall as a social hub and part of everyday culture.

---

[36]Cited in Natalie Hochheim, *Entstehung der Shopping-Center in Hamburg* (Hamburg: Universität Hamburg, 2003), 7.

Chapter 14

Built for mass consumption: Shopping centres in West Germany's boom years
Olaf Gisbertz

In Germany today, it seems that no other building type from the late modern age has fallen into such disrepute as the *Einkaufszentrum* or 'shopping centre'. Once euphorically hailed by German city planners as the path to 'additional urbanity',[1] these building projects of yesteryear – mostly built in the 1960s and 1970s – have long since lost their lustre. Changes in consumer behaviour, new construction standards and a recent trend towards the revitalization of downtown areas have brought about a shift in thinking. Even though architectural concepts geared towards car-oriented shopping have remained popular, the early shopping centres of the boom years have lost public acceptance and are generally considered outdated. Yet, these large-scale structures still shape the built environment of numerous towns and cities today.

When the shopping centre concept as first conceived by Victor Gruen in the mid-1940s[2] arrived in West Germany in the early 1960s, it promised architects and town planners a tool to structure the sprawling suburbanization. At that time, many architectural and urban planning projects were realized in the country in the frame of the *Wiederaufbau* (reconstruction).[3] Although the construction of new buildings continued to grow well into the early 1970s, existing models were increasingly questioned and the critique of modernism reached its peak. After 1973, when the consequences of the oil and economic crisis were felt, the proliferation of large-scale projects quickly diminished and a smaller yardstick for buildings gained popularity.[4] Nonetheless, in this time of decline the first academic compendiums focusing on mass consumption and 'the planable city' appeared in West Germany. Based on empirical studies of existing shopping centres, these handbooks[5] attempted to legitimize

---

[1] Friedemann Wild, 'Foreword', in *Warenhaus und Einkaufszentren*, eds. Walter Pawlik and Ute Busche-Sievers (München: Callwey, 1972).

[2] Victor Gruen was a Viennese architect who migrated to the United States in 1938. There, together with his (then) wife Elsie Krummeck, he conceived of the concept of the shopping centre in the mid-1940s. See M. Jeffrey Hardwick, *Mall Maker: Victor Gruen, Architect of an American Dream* (Philadelphia: University of Pennsylvania Press, 2004).

[3] Jörg Eschenkamp, *Die Bundesrepublik Deutschland 1945/49–69* (Stuttgart: UTB GmbH, 2013).

[4] Uta Hassler and Catherine Dumont d´Ayot, *Bauten der Boomjahre: Paradoxien der Erhaltung* (Gollion: Infolio, 2009), 19.

[5] Klaus Wolf, *Geschäftszentren, Nutzung und Intensität als Maß städtischer Größenordnung: Ein empirisch-methodischer Vergleich von 15 Städten der Bundesrepublik Deutschland* (Frankfurt am Main: Waldemar Kramer, 1971); Bernd R. Falk (ed.), *Shopping Center Handbuch* (Munich: GWI, 1973).

'the planable' in the world of consumption. They suggested that when planning shopping centres, parameters such as the overall plot size, enclosed space, size of sales area and diversification of commercial enterprises according to strategies of sales marketing needed to be carefully considered in relation to questions of design and traffic. In the 1960s the Main Taunus Zentrum in Frankfurt (1964) and the Ruhrpark Shopping Centre in Bochum (1964), both exceeding 15,000 m² in surface, were among the largest facilities in West Germany. They offered a template for the planning of later (smaller) centres,[6] such as Braunschweig (1971) and Augsburg (1971). Here, design motifs for the centre's entry and exit recurred, as well at the layout of the multi-storey car parks, the interior design with multi-level shopping arcades interconnected by escalators, and the arrangement of different sales sectors in line with current consumer behaviour; albeit on a much smaller scale and in a radically different setting: near small- and medium-sized towns.

This chapter examines the design motifs of the shopping centre in post-war West Germany and investigates the role that this commercial typology assumed in city planning and urban development in the country. It investigates to what extent the West German shopping centre was formally and conceptually indebted to its American ancestor and questions the future viability of shopping centres in Germany from today's perspective.

Mass consumption for a mass society

Following the American example, the architecture of administration and commerce popularized in West Germany from the mid-1960s on. The first shopping malls were built in Frankfurt (1964), Bochum (1964) and Oberhausen (1971), on 'green-field' sites in the periphery. Soon thereafter, shopping centres cropped up all over West Germany, and by the 1970s moved from peripheral locations to the centre of large cities. For instance, in 1965 the Pepper-Zentrum (later called Europa-Center), designed by Helmut Hentrich and Hubert Petschnigg among others became a defining feature of downtown West Berlin. During the post-war reconstruction era, the city centre had already been given a modern look with the Bikini tower block, designed by Schwebes & Schoszberger in 1956–1957 and the Kaiser Wilhelm Memorial Church designed by Egon Eiermann in 1957–1961. The high-rise building of the Pepper-Zentrum added a new, widely visible silhouette in International Style. During the boom years, the West German consumer frenzy spread rapidly, aided by the rise of shopping centres and shopping arcades. Shopping was no longer seen as a means to an end (getting living supplies), but became an end itself, a leisurely pursuit.

Although 'shopping' interfered with essential parts of cities and their periphery from the late nineteenth century on, it was (somewhat surprisingly) only much later that the social sciences began to concern

---

[6] By the end of 1977 research conducted by the Ifo-Institut demonstrated that there were no less than 600 shopping centres in West Germany, which accounted for about 10 per cent of the country's retail sales. Around 10 per cent of these 600 shopping centres had a surface area of more than 25,000 m², 28 per cent had a surface area between 5,000 and 25,000 m² and the majority (amounting to 42 per cent of the more than 600 shopping centres) had a surface area of 1,000–5,000 m². Source: Helmut Vogel, *Das Einkaufszentrum als Ausdruck einer kulturlandschaftlichen Innovation dargestellt am Beispiel des Böblinger Regionalzentrums* (Trier: Zentralausschuss für deutsche Landeskunde, 1978), 25.

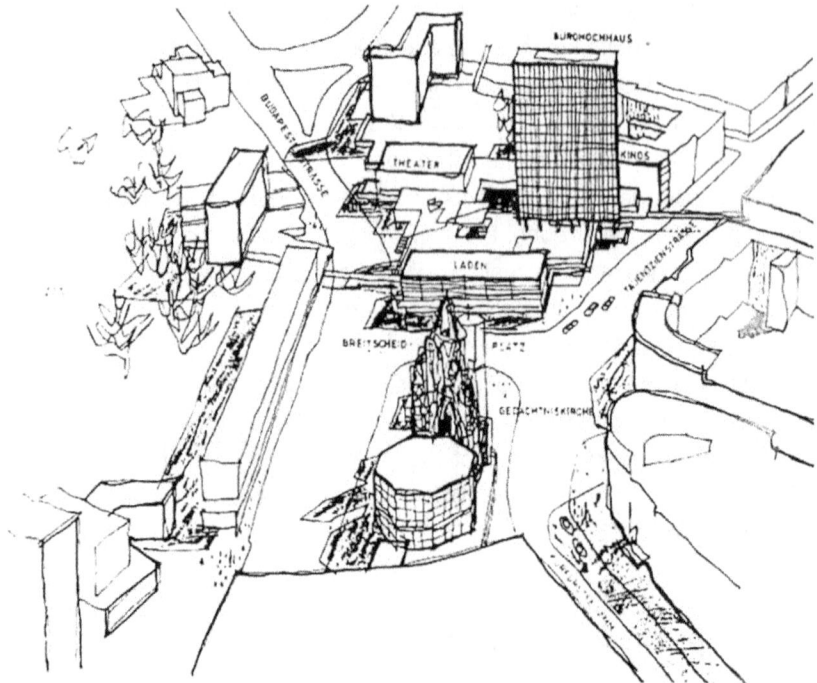

Figure 14.1 Pepper-Center (Europa-Center), Berlin, Helmut Hentrich & Hubert Petschnigg et al., artistic consultation Egon Eiermann, urban planning and consultation Werner Düttmann, Berlin 1963–1965, draft 1962.
Source: Die Bauwelt 35 (1963): 1002.

themselves with the phenomenon of the 'availability of things'.[7] In German language sociology, which became a key discipline of urban planning in West Germany simultaneously with the rise of shopping centres, architectural manifestations of consumption have only begun to be addressed in recent years.[8] This particular field assigned a key role in the 'democratization' of consumption to the department store, which was labelled an 'academy of modern life culture' by Edwin Redslob in the 1920s, as it supposedly – just like Alfred Messel's famous Wertheim building at the Leipziger Platz in Berlin (1903–1906) – opened itself up to the masses.[9]

In West Germany mass consumption however only developed in the decades following 1945. At this time – the time of the 'economic miracle' (*Wirtschaftswunder*) and the consolidation of post-war

---

[7] Dominik Schrage, *Die Verfügbarkeit der Dinge: Eine historische Soziologie des Konsums* (Frankfurt am Main/New York: Campus Verlag, 2009).

[8] Kai-Uwe Hellmann and Dominik Schrage (eds.), *Das Management der Kunden: Studien zur Soziologie* (Wiesbaden: VS Verlag für Sozialwissenschaften, 2005).

[9] Heike Delitz, 'Gebaute Begehrlichkeit: Zur Architektursoziologie der Konsumgesellschaft in Deutschland', in *Das Management der Kunden*, eds. Hellmann, Schrage, 45; Paul Göhre, *Das Warenhaus* (Frankfurt am Main: Rütten & Loening, 1907).

society[10] – it complemented existing department stores and small retailers. Simultaneously with the rise of the shopping centre, critical voices were raised in architectural journals publicly questioning this planned world of consumption.[11] Retail sector representatives and unions in particular deplored the preference of sites outside city centres for the development of shopping malls over more central locations. The shopping centre was, however, subject to early considerations by politicians and parties as well as business administrators, architects, lawyers and geographers. A scientific interest arose in the commercial typology's development, significance and planning. Initially, the focus rested on the shopping centre's location, planning, financing, administration and management,[12] while later studies from the field of empirical urban geography addressed questions of business structure, change of use, catchment areas, functional effects on the city and potential subsequent problems in terms of traffic density and spatial development.[13]

Mega structures – shopping for the masses

In West Germany shopping in architectural mega structures first began in a conurbation near Frankfurt: the Main Taunus Zentrum, which opened on 2 May 1964, was the first shopping centre in the Federal Republic.[14] Roughly six months later, on 13 November 1964, the Ruhrpark shopping mall in Bochum opened its doors. Similarly to the Main Taunus Zentrum, a location with a good transport connection was chosen for the Ruhrpark. Shopping was now only a short drive away in one's car, and parking was abundant. Located in the country's most densely populated agglomeration of North Rhine-Westphalia, the Ruhrpark quickly became widely accepted and intensively used. Also, with around 76,000 m² of commercial space, it remained the largest shopping mall in Germany for a long time. Modelled after its North American prototypes,[15] the Ruhrpark shopping centre was one-storey high and had arcades laid out at two staggered angles between the large anchor stores, Quelle, C&A and Karstadt.[16] An American firm had been involved in the planning, but the overall responsibility rested on Düsseldorf-based architect Hans Ulrich Freisleben.

Today little however remains of this early layout: All the stores and storefronts have been converted several times since 1964. In the five decades since its opening, the commercial space of the Rurhpark has quintupled, thus enabling the facility to retain its position as the largest shopping centre in Germany. Only two large neon signs with blue diamonds and white 'ruhr park' lettering at the entry of the car

---

[10]Hermann Glaser, *Die 60er Jahre: Deutschland zwischen 1960 und 1970* (Hamburg: Ellert & Richter, 2007), 82–85.
[11]*Bauwelt* 47 (1966): 1246.
[12]Heinz Heineberg and Alois Mayr, 'Shopping-Center im Zentrensystem des Ruhgebiets', *Erdkunde* 38 (1984): 98–114.
[13]Ibid.
[14]Klaus Wolf, 'Das Shopping-Center Main Taunus – ein neues Element des rhein-mainischen Verstädterungsgebietes', *Berichte zur deutschen Landeskunde* 37 (1966): 78–97.
[15]Thomas S. Gasser, *Das Shopping Center in Nordamerika: Einkaufszentren in Europa* (Bern: Paul Haupt, 1960).
[16]Heinz Heinberg, 'Der Ruhr-Park in Bochum – das größte Shopping-Center Deutschlands', *LWL: Geographische Kommission für Westfalen, Westfalen Regional*, http://www.lwl.org/LWL/Kultur/Westfalen_Regional/Wirtschaft/RuhrPark, accessed 11 December 2015; Markus Harzenetter, Walter Hauser, Udo Mainzer and Dirk Zache, *Fremde Impulse: Baudenkmale mi Ruhrgebiet* (Münster: Coppenrath, 2010), 267.

Figure 14.2 Ruhr-Park, Bochum, Hans Ulrich Friesleben et al., opening 13 April 1964, aerial photo.
Source: Photo by H. Lohoff, reproduced from Jürgen Dodt and Alois Mayr (eds.), *Bochum im Luftbild: Festschrift zum 20jährigen Bestehen der Gesellschaft für Geographie und Geologie Bochum* (Paderborn: Schöningh, 1976), 79.

parking – relics from a bygone period – remain from the original building. It was however only in the early 1970s that new shopping centres began to mushroom across West Germany. The typology then varied widely depending on its size, location and functional outfit with regard to retail stores and service provision.[17] Many smaller shopping centres were built across West Germany, which often became integral parts of downtown areas and districts. At that time, shopping centres and shopping arcades became much discussed in various German architectural journals, such as *Bauen und Wohnen*, *Bauwelt* and the *Deutsche Bauzeitschrift*.

Shopping as an urban experience

When the *Deutsche Bauzeitschrift* published by Bertelsmann devoted an entire issue to 'commercial buildings' in 1973, the large shopping centres of West Germany had already been built. By then it must

---

[17]Heineberg and Mayr, 'Shopping-Center im Zentrensystem des Ruhgebiets', 100.

have seemed paramount to comprehensively address the architecture of consumption. The original, American model of the 'green-field' shopping mall was however barely mentioned in the issue. This was – according to the editors – a conscious decision informed by the lack of American conditions in Germany:

> In Germany, most existing and prospective shopping centres with a commercial space exceeding 15,000 m² are located not directly in the city centre, but at intra-urban locations on the outskirts and suburban parts of towns and cities. Shopping centres in the United States, which were built in open countryside at a considerable distance from towns and cities due to the disastrous inner-city traffic and parking situation, can evidently not be put on a par with our familiar urban shopping areas, whose typical character is not least based on their close interrelation with the urban experience.[18]

Precisely how this urban shopping experience in close proximity to the town centre was thought of became clear through various examples of shopping centres shown in the issue, among which were the Mannheim-Vogelsang centre, the town centre of Leverkusen, shopping centres in Ulm-Böfingen, Wolfsburg-Detmerode and Hamburg-Langenhorn, which were all built in the late 1960s and early 1970s. A striking feature of these complexes is that they were not exclusively dedicated to shopping, but also included a residential component. Their aesthetic relied on the use of reinforced concrete panels or modular constructions composed of prefabricated construction elements. Typologically they were composed of a high-rise tower or slab that hovers over a shopping arcade on the ground floor. Whenever there were several levels – often including basement levels – these were typically accessed via escalators and bridges with parapets of washed concrete of varying grain size. Raw concrete, or *béton brut*, was often used, which visibly displayed the formwork.

These complexes – comprising both housing and shopping – were seen as microcosms, and the covered shopping areas were to invite people to come in and browse. They were thus not merely thought of as places of commerce, but as essential centres of communication in new town districts outside the actual city centres. The Forum Steglitz, for example, which was built in 1967–1970, was even intended as a 'centre of urban life'.[19] Erected on the former Born market in the middle of an existing district of the Wilhelmini Kaiser era in Berlin, this shopping centre was constructed with a precast concrete skeleton following the design of Berlin architect Georg Heinrichs in collaboration with Fin Bartels and Christoph Schmid-Ott. Two crossbar structures on pylons spanned the length of the glass cube, the eaves of which were interrupted on the sides by eight access shafts. Inside, the floors housing different department stores were arranged around two atriums and interconnected through a number of ramps and escalators. From the outside, with its illuminated advertisements, the Forum mainly addresses the urban audience on the busy Schlossstraße in south Berlin. Today, the building is still entirely bound to this paradigmatic view of a time when big-city traffic – according to the concept of the *Autogerechte Stadt*[20] – was considered the primordial factor in urban planning

---

[18]Cited from S. Nagel and S. Linke (eds.), *Bauten des Handels: Läden, Warenhäuser, Einkaufszentren* (Düsseldorf: Gütersloh, 1973), 25.
[19]Ibid., 30.
[20]Hans Bernd Reichow, *Die autogerechte Stadt: Der Weg aus dem Verkehrs-Chaos* (Ravenburg: Otto Maier Verlag, 1959).

Figure 14.3 Forum-Steglitz, Georg Heinrichs in collaboration with Fin Bartels and Christoph Schmid-Ott, 1967–1970.
Source: S. Nagel and S. Linke (eds.), *Bauten des Handels: Läden, Warenhäuser, Einkaufszentren* (Düsseldorf: Gütersloh, 1973), 31, 33.

and architectural design. Even though the Forum obtained its very own subway stop, and thus – contrary to its American ancestors – 'plugged into' the public transport network of Berlin, the complex predominantly addressed drivers speeding by its large façades. These façades however did not allow a 'sneak preview' of the atmosphere inside the centre. Already before the First World War German architect Peter Behrens described how motorized traffic would affect viewing habits and would call for an architecture of closed and quiet forms, an architecture which would 'avoid any impediments by aiming for compactness'.[21] A closer look at the Forum's construction images reveals that – rather typically for the architecture of the 1960s and 1970s – a 'second look'[22] is required to do justice to the twofold façade structure of the Forum Steglitz with its delicate lattice work between partly paned parapet elements in front of the paned aluminium primary structure against which it was set. Also inside the centre, the Forum Steglitz exhibits some pioneering elements of shopping centre architecture, including the glass parapet elements on the escalators and store levels as well as a (now no longer extant) pneumatic ceiling in the atriums.

For German planners and architects, shopping centres in the UK and Scandinavia played an exemplary role. An overview of shopping centres published in the *Deutsche Bauzeitung* in 1973 for instance included the Frölunda Torg shopping centre near Gothenburg by architects Hijalmar Klemming and Erik Thelaus as well as the Helsinki-Kannelmäki shopping centre by Erkki Karvinen. Scandinavia started building shopping centres early on.[23] These however did not follow the American model of stand-alone shopping malls outside of town centres at busy traffic intersections, but were seen as integral elements of suburban planning.[24] In Sweden, the 1947 urban planning law made such large-scale architectural projects viable through radical means, including expropriation. These designs attracted a great deal of attention from architects and urban planners and quickly became 'true places of pilgrimage for West German heads of state and district council delegations'.[25]

Also England became a point of reference for West Germany. A well-known example was the Old George Mall shopping centre, which was built in the late 1960s near the cathedral in the historic centre of Salisbury (England) following the design of architects Bernhard Engle & Partners. Erected in the middle of an existing apartment complex, it was an early example of a shopping centre inserted into inner-city neighbourhoods to revitalize urban areas. The planning even took into account historic landmarks by integrating small-scale construction forms and existing building materials such as brick and wood into the building's façade. The spatial arrangement of the interior of the shopping centre however corresponded with the typical layout of shopping centre architecture. It consisted of two shopping arcades positioned at an angle, which made the block accessible from two sides. These arcades opened onto a piazza with fountains, trees and benches.

---

[21] Peter Behrens, 'Einfluss von Zeit- und Raumnutzung auf die moderne Formentwicklung', in *Jahrbuch des Deutschen Werkbunds* (Jena: Eugen Diederichs, 1914), 7.
[22] Sonja Hnilica, Markus Jager and Wolfgang Sonne (eds.), *Auf den zweiten Blick: Architektur der Nachkriegszeit in Nordrhein-Westfalen* (Bielefeld: Transcript, 2010).
[23] Nagel and Linke, *Bauten des Handels*.
[24] Gasser, *Das Shopping Center in Nordamerika*, 4.
[25] Vogel, *Das Einkaufszentrum als Ausdruck einer kulturlandschaftlichen Innovation*, 62.

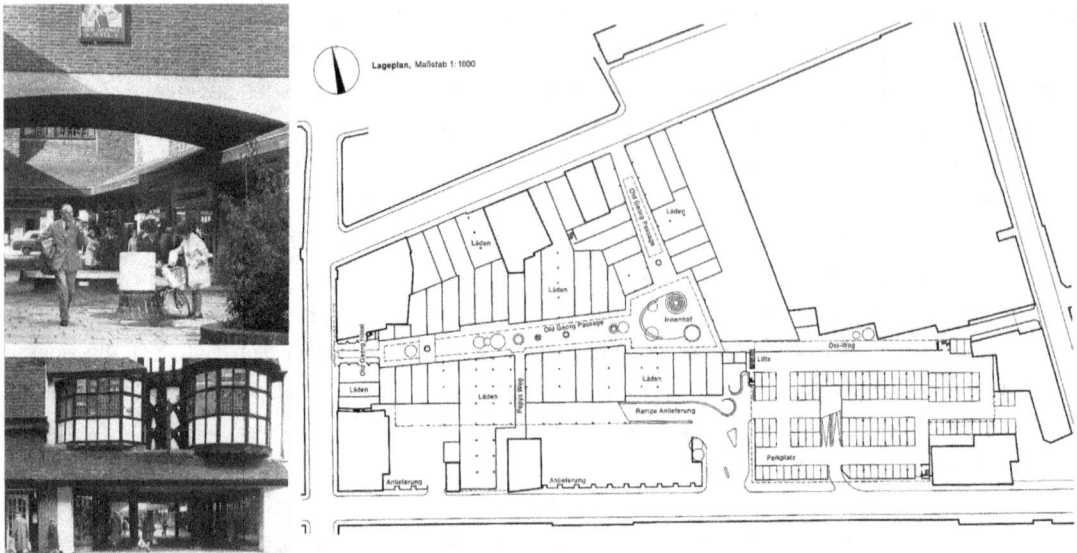

Figure 14.4 Old George Mall in Salisbury (UK), Bernard Engle & Partners, ground plan and views of existing buildings. *Source:* S. Nagel and S. Linke (eds.), *Bauten des Handels: Läden, Warenhäuser, Einkaufszentren* (Düsseldorf: Gütersloh, 1973), 80, 81.

Projects such as the one in Salisbury were frequently emulated in Germany in the late 1970s as urban planning concepts for downtown locations. This included the redesign of downtown areas in many small and medium-sized towns and villages. Such locations are still very popular today as everything is within walking distance and the projects' spatial design offers a highly multifunctional hybrid for shopping as an urban experience. Many 'regional' shopping centres on the other hand have undergone multiple modernizations, as their large volumes and (often) exposed raw concrete forms increasingly attracted criticism.

The ability of shopping centres to be transformed

Comparably to the United States, an important prerequisite for the rise of the shopping centre in West Germany was the increasing motorization and altered shopping behaviour of the population. Between 1960 and 1978, the number of cars per hundred inhabitants increased from eight to thirty-five and according to surveys carried out by the German Federal Statistical Office, sixty-two out of every hundred West German households owned a car in 1978.[26] Also consumer behaviour changed as a result of altered employment conditions. Empirical studies have shown that married women in particular increasingly preferred 'one-stop-shopping'; a large weekly shopping trip for all the necessary goods and services which required only one single parking effort.[27] These large shopping trips were made possible,

---

[26] Heinz Heineberg (ed.), *Einkaufszentren in Deutschland: Entwicklung, Forschungsstand und Probleme mit einer annotierten Auswahlbibliothek* (Paderborn: Schöningh, 1980).
[27] Ibid.

thanks to the increased storage capacity that the introduction of refrigerators and freezers had created. By 1978 these appliances had found their way into nearly all West German households.[28]

Apart from the few early large shopping centres that were built in green-field sites throughout 1960s, planners in West Germany preferred very different solutions to those that they observed in America.[29] Seemingly following Gruen's advice, who at the 1966 International Congress of Commerce and Urban Development recommended that Europe should not erect shopping centres in 'green-field sites' but should opt for locations closer to (existing) town centres,[30] they were built closer to (or in) existing city centres.

Many of these former mercantile building structures still exist in German cities today and often shape urban conglomerates through their large-scale building structures. In Augsburg the so-called Schwaben-Center, which was built in 1968–1971, and which drew the attention of several architectural

Figure 14.5 Schwaben-Center, architectural planning consortium (Brockel and Müller; Hans von Peschke and Rudolf Götz, Pröll and Müller and Hans Schrammel), in collaboration with Manfred Sabatke, 1969–1971.
Source: S. Nagel and S. Linke (eds.), Bauten des Handels: Läden, Warenhäuser, Einkaufszentren (Düsseldorf: Gütersloh, 1973), 54–55.

---

[28] Ibid., 22.
[29] Wild, Warenhaus und Einkaufzentrum.
[30] The 'Survival of Cities' remained a great concern for Gruen, even though his shopping centre concept was soon discredited for causing the precise opposite effect: Victor Gruen, Das Überleben der Städte: Wege aus der Umweltkriese. Zentren als urbane Brennpunkte (Wien: Molden, 1973).

journals,[31] for instance, represents such a prototypical new city district aimed at encouraging both shopping and living while offering enough parking spaces for the motorized consumption society. As an investment property it however quickly received as much bad press as its concrete-dominated shopping plaza, which formed the base of the high-rise apartment complex towering over it.[32] Today the Schwaben-Center still accommodates the same functions, although the department stores inside the complex have been refurbished several times. The same is true in Braunschweig, where between 1966 and 1972 an entire new district including a new train station and adjacent shopping arcade were built as a new gateway to the city. Like a pavilion, it spans between three points, formed by the apartment buildings, under a delicate roof. Its construction was accompanied by high expectations, but the first problems arose shortly after the shopping arcade was officially opened and finding tenants for the stores was difficult. Today most of it is used as commercial space, and the living units above the shopping centre are very popular. However, modifications required to meet contemporary Energy Saving Regulation standards were carried out with little consideration for the original architectural qualities of the complex. The unique graphic impression created by the concrete façade panels with projecting joints, which were intentionally left visible, is now, for instance, lost. Long before that, in 1999, the footbridge crossing the busy multiple lane streets in front of the complex had been demolished in resistance to the *Autogerechte Stadt*,[33] the long since obsolete manifest of urbanization in the German *Wiederaufbau* (reconstruction) after the Second World War.

Even if the increasing motorization had promoted the building of shopping centres with adjacent and integrated parking lots in Germany, the architectural planning and urban design of these complexes had little in common with typical American shopping malls. In West Germany, the shopping centre was usually planned as an integrated large-scale component of an urban development project while only a few of the early shopping centres, such as the Main Taunus, followed the American 'greenfield' approach. In Germany, the shopping centre was thought of as a building type which not only promised a return for investors, provided it was based on market- and location-driven planning, but was also considered by town planners as a means of re-vitalizing and urbanizing inner-city districts. Nonetheless, bad planning and false prognoses often recurred, as did design deficiencies, which were not always easy to remedy. For example, significant wind circulation around the outer façades and entrances of the Europa-Center had a negative effect on pedestrian flow outside the complex. Not even the later addition of display cases to the entrance passages could effectively remediate this situation.[34] Already in the 1970s substantial modifications were made inside the centre to 'protect the Europa-Center from weather effects, redesign the front and improve the interior acoustics for better communication, improve access, establish comprehensive security features in the context of meeting regulations of the time and make technical improvements'.[35]

---

[31] Nagel and Linke, *Bauten des Handels*, 54–55.
[32] Michael Hörmann, 'Das Schwabencenter in Ausgburg kampft ums Überlben', *Augsburger Allgemeine*, 9 May 2015.
[33] Reichow, *Die Autogerechte Stadt*.
[34] Bernard Butzin and Heinz Heineberg, 'Nutzungswandel und Entwicklungsprobleme integrierter Shopping-Center in West-Berlin', in *Einkaufszentren in Deutschland*, ed. Heineberg, 69.
[35] 'Europa-Center-Tage', Press release by the Europa-Center company, 25 October 1976, cited in: Ibid.

The 'shopping centre' as a type is nonetheless far from outmoded in Germany. This becomes clear when we look at new suburban housing developments as well as new districts near town centres in which mass consumption projects are integrated in an effort to cater to the current *zeitgeist*.[36] The era of the 'green-field' shopping centre in Germany only began in earnest after the German reunification in 1989, particularly around the outskirts of cities in former East Germany. After the turn of the millennium, many municipalities succumbed to the offers made by project developers for the building of shopping centres and malls in downtown areas. These developments have since given rise to controversial discussions; some consider the shopping centre a 'big seller',[37] while others see it as nothing more than an 'assault on the city centre'.[38]

---

[36] Kerstin Dörhöfer, *Shopping Malls und neue Einkaufszentren: Urbaner Wandel in Berlin* (Berlin: Reimer, 2008). For Example, the Alexa Shopping Centre in Berlin, which was built between 2004 and 2007.
[37] Ellen Bareis, *Verkaufsschlager: Urbane Shoppingmalls. Orte des Alltags zwischen Nutzung und Kontrolle* (Münster: Westfälisches Dampfboot, 2007).
[38] Walter Brune, Rolf Junger and Holger Pump-Uhlmann, *Angriff auf die City: Kritische Texte zur Konzeption, Planung und Wirkung von integrierten und nicht integrierten Shopping-Centern in zentralen Lagen* (Düsseldorf: Droste, 2006).

Chapter 15

The drive to modernize: Remodelling Birmingham city centre, 1945–1965
Jo Lintonbon

Introduction

Stimulated by growing consumer confidence, an expanding world of goods and the promise of a leisured society, a modern 'New Britain' was constructed, socially, politically and materially, in the late 1950s as the immediate post-war austerity years gave way to a new period of affluence. Across the country, bomb-damaged cities embraced comprehensive redevelopment and the motorcar in their reconstruction programmes. In Birmingham, this meant a radical transport modernization programme undertaken by the Corporation,[1] and the construction of a new retail complex by private developer Laing Development Co. Ltd. Described by Nikolaus Pevsner as one of the most exciting shopping centres yet built in the country, the Bull Ring Shopping Centre, epitomized the adventurousness and optimism of 'Britain's most transatlantic city'.[2] Its design was informed both by Gruen and Smith's *Shopping Towns USA* and by delegation visits to the United States.[3] Yet, while a direct lineage to its American counterpart was implied, there were distinct differences in the Bull Ring proposal, which, fairly quickly after opening, proved to be limiting to its commercial success and to the vitality of its surrounding context. A curious product of idealism and commercialism, the Bull Ring was both an object of civic ambition and a commercial experiment, determined architecturally by a challenging site context and an unfamiliar urban typology. As Professor of History, Arthur Marwick has suggested, the legacy of the desire to create concrete symbols of progress in post-war Britain was an ugly jungle of urban motorways and high-rise buildings,[4] and this in turn stimulated a critical interest in 'townscape'.[5] This chapter takes the major remodelling of Birmingham's city centre between 1945 and 1965 as its case study to assess contemporary cultural influences at play in the design and development of the Bull Ring Shopping Centre, and the errors made by a generation of pioneering designers, politicians and developers.

---

[1] The Corporation was the local administrative body of the Municipal Borough, incorporated in 1838 and governed by a Council. It became Birmingham City Council in 1986.
[2] Anthony Sutcliffe and Roger Smith, *The History of Birmingham Volume 3, 1939–1970* (London: Oxford University Press, 1974), 479.
[3] Victor Gruen and Larry Smith, *Shopping Towns USA: The Planning of Shopping Centers* (New York: Reinhold Publishing Corporation, 1960).
[4] Arthur Marwick, *British Society since 1945* (London: Allen Lane, 1982), 123.
[5] Gordon Cullen contributed to the campaign run by *Architectural Review*, publishing *Townscape* (London: Architectural Press) in 1961.

The post-war context

A climate of optimism in Britain, evidenced in the political and social experience of the British population in the period after the end of the Second World War, had a marked impetus on urban renewal and the remaking of Britain socially and architecturally. Austerity following the war's end, dominated by shortages of consumer goods and food, bomb-damaged housing and the economic loss of one quarter of the national wealth, was tempered by the promise of social reform and tangible improvements designed to improve the quality of life.[6] The influential Beveridge Report on social insurance, published in 1942, was implemented by the newly elected Labour government in 1945. A state system of care was set up via the National Health Service and National Insurance Acts of 1946, while The Education Act of 1944 ensured that every child received compulsory tuition until the age of fifteen. The government 'had hopes of a new and better age in which values would be transformed... and pursued a programme designed

Figure 15.1 Approaching the Bull Ring from the East.
Source: Image reference JLP01/08/076229: 'External view taken at night showing the Bull Ring Shopping Centre in Birmingham', John Laing Collection, Historic England Archive.

---

[6]Alan Sked and Chris Cook, Post-war Britain: A Political History (Harmondsworth: Penguin, 1979), 27.

to consolidate and strengthen the social cohesion engendered by the war'.[7] This consolidation extended to the physical environment, and national controls on new building development were established through the Town and Country Planning Act of 1947, creating green belts around the major cities and ensuring division of land use within the city centre.

By 1951 and the election of a Conservative government, the welfare state had been accepted by all parties and full employment was a common aim. With austerity arguably over by 1957, Britain was set to embrace the 'white hot heat of technological revolution', with politicians predicting that the next decades would witness a greater period of technical change than the preceding 250 years of industrial revolution.[8] Prosperity could be planned for, and Labour's 1964 election campaign 'The New Britain', with its focus on modernizing through science and technology, epitomized positivistic contemporary attitudes as innovative technical developments continued to revolutionize the working day, reducing the price of consumer goods while increasing wages.[9] A newly affluent society, that had a higher relative standard of living than ten years earlier, now had both the time and the money to consume a greater range of goods and leisure activities. As Prime Minister Harold Macmillan said, in 1957, Britons 'have never had it so good'.[10]

Advertising and television played an important part in mediating positive images of consumerism. By the early 1950s there were five million TV viewers in Britain, while cinemas screening imported movies from the United States propagated aspirational images of an advanced, and economically and technologically sophisticated, society.[11] The country was receptive to new retail typologies, for example the self-service supermarket, and to the packaging and branding techniques which stimulated discretionary shopping in a competitive marketplace. Running hand-in-hand with this new freedom to consume was the idea of mobility. The price of motorcars fell steadily whilst relative earning power rose, and the expansion of car ownership in the 1950s accelerated sharply in the 1960s as the status of the car evolved from the preserve of the wealthy to an accepted means of transport for the wider population. In short, this was a new era within which social idealism, optimism, technical innovation and mobility were to play an important role in the physical regeneration of Britain, where change was perceived as future change for the better.

Birmingham's Inner Ring Road

The opportunities afforded through private car ownership, of an aspirational suburban lifestyle and the convenience to come and go at will, signified increasing social, as well as physical, mobility. Yet these consumer choices were not without consequence for a British road infrastructure ill-suited to the growing volume of traffic and in need of improvement. By the early 1960s it was apparent that 'The Motor

---

[7]Ibid., 112.
[8]The Rt. Hon. Harold Wilson, *Purpose in Politics* (London: Weidenfeld and Nicolson, 1964), 14–15.
[9]Marwick, *British Society*, 114.
[10]Macmillan made this statement at a Conservative Party rally in 1957.
[11]Marwick, *British Society*, 100, 125.

Age' was 'a problem which must surely be one of the most extraordinary facing modern society'.[12] As Colin Buchanan identified in the 1963 *Traffic in Towns* report, public demand had made the motorcar indispensable, with congestion in urban areas increasingly problematic as drivers sought to use their cars for a myriad of local journeys.[13] The changing structure of urban to suburban living and a decline in public transport services contributed to increasing private road traffic. Thus, road transport was an important issue for planners and architects of the period and *The Architects' Journal* dedicated an entire issue to the motorcar in 1959. It predicted that there would be 16 million vehicles by 1967 and 24 million by 1974. With the then number of cars at 8,500,000, or one vehicle for every ten people and 42 vehicles per mile of road, Britain was the most crowded country in the world.[14] The journal queried how the modern city could accommodate the car and recommended that 'completely new physical forms, new planning and architectural solutions are required for any plan that attempts to provide a complete solution for a highly motorised city'.[15] It recommended that the solution of an exciting city would have to be constructed on several levels following the principle of segregation. *Traffic in Towns* took a similar view, advising that city centres be fed by primary distributors of an urban motorway standard, creating segregated environmental areas that would be pedestrian-only zones except for servicing.[16]

In Birmingham, the Corporation quickly adopted a pro-car approach after the war, planning a road network to create easy access into the city centre that removed through-traffic from the central streets via an inner ring road. The city had a tradition of embracing new architectural concepts with enthusiasm, stemming from a history of civic ambition within the city,[17] and as Birmingham was the hub of the industrial heartland of the Midlands, and the base for many new light industrial manufacturers and the motor trade, the Corporation was aware of the need to modernize the city centre to maintain economic stability and prosperity. In fact it had recognized as early as 1917 that it had a transport problem, when initial plans for a ring road were first discussed to create a befitting transport system for this commercial and industrial city. The number of vehicles licensed in the city increased by 60 per cent between 1934 and 1950 and there was concern that once the rationing of petrol was abolished, a sharp increase in both the number and use of vehicles within the city centre would follow.[18] A further factor was the growing significance of the vehicle assembly industry in the city after 1945 which led to demands for overt recognition of the distribution and use of vehicles: Birmingham was after all gaining a reputation as the 'Motown of Britain' and concentrated its efforts on road building to an unparalleled extent.[19]

Detailed plans were laid out by Herbert Manzoni, the Chief Engineer, during the war period so that upon the declaration of peace the city was ready to implement its road improvement scheme – the Inner

---

[12]*The Estates Gazette*, 188 (30 November 1963): 815.
[13]Ministry of Transport, *Traffic in Towns: A Study of the Long-Term Problems of Traffic in Urban Areas: Reports of the Steering Group and Working Group Appointed by the Minister of Transport* (London: HMSO, 1963).
[14]This was an overprediction with car ownership in the 1970s reaching around 12 million.
[15]'MOTROPOLIS', *The Architects' Journal* (1 October 1959): 269.
[16]Ministry of Transport, *Traffic in Towns*.
[17]The development of Corporation Street is a good example. No one campaigned to prevent Birmingham's modernization programme; criticism came later.
[18]*The Development Plan for the City of Birmingham 1951* (Birmingham: Birmingham Library Collections), 67.
[19]Sutcliffe and Smith, *The History of Birmingham,* 399–404.

Ring Road. The scheme (constructed between 1957 and 1971) comprised a ring about half a mile in diameter surrounding the city core, with three lane carriageways each way, punctuated by roundabouts that picked up the radial routes entering the centre.[20] A connecting spine road for bus – but not through-traffic – enabled passengers coming into the centre to be dropped off at a maximum of 300 yards from their final destination. Car parking was proposed at intervals along the ring road in multi-storey blocks as part of 'the intention that motorists should not bring their cars into the city centre'.[21]

The scheme fulfilled a twofold purpose. The first was to enable through-traffic to bypass the city centre while providing motorists, who needed to enter the core area, easy access around the Ring.[22] The second was to extend the commercial and shopping centre by encouraging private investors to develop adjacent the Ring. The Corporation, influenced by *Conurbation*, a report produced by the 'West Midland Group on Post-war Reconstruction' in 1948 with input from Manzoni, recognized that the city lacked the cultural and leisure facilities present in cities of a similar size. At a strategic planning level, the report suggested that there was

> a deficiency in amenity and in opportunities for enjoyment within the area. The deficiency applies to Birmingham as well as the Black Country areas. Since lack of services, amenities and cultural life keeps or drives away possible customers for goods [it is recommended] that shopping centres, hotels, restaurants, theatres, concert halls and assembly rooms should be developed throughout the Conurbation.[23]

The Inner Ring Road was therefore perceived as an opportunity to create a much-improved commercial centre, thus altering the physical and social structure of the city.

Through an Act of Parliament granting compulsory purchase powers immediately after the war, the Corporation was able to finance its road programme by leasing plots to interested parties, and, as ground landlords and local planning authority, exercise some control over their development. As the Lord Mayor said: 'Once we had started on the physical work of the road, I saw quite clearly that if our vision of the new Birmingham was to take shape, it would have to be made as commercially successful as possible.'[24] The Bull Ring shopping centre, built between 1961 and 1964 and designed by architects Sydney Greenwood and T. J. Hirst, was one such scheme that contributed significantly to this programme of commercial and cultural expansion.[25] The three acre site identified for development as part of the

---

[20] *The Architects' Journal* (1 October 1959): 288.

[21] Sir Herbert Manzoni, *The Development of Town Planning in Birmingham: A Seminar Given on 22 February 1968 at School of History, University of Birmingham* (Birmingham: Birmingham Library Collections).

[22] Sir Herbert Manzoni, 'The Inner Ring Road, Birmingham', *The Institute of Civil Engineering Proceedings* (March 1961), 268.

[23] West Midland Group on Post-war Reconstruction and Planning, *Conurbation, A Planning Survey of Birmingham and the Black Country* (London: The Architectural Press, 1948), 135.

[24] Oliver Marriot, *The Property Boom* (London: Hamish Hamilton, 1967), 223.

[25] The ring road plan as published in the *Architect's Journal* (1 October 1959), shows a band of proposed retail and commercial developments to its southeast section (Smallbrook Street) including J.A. Roberts' Ringway Centre, the Bull Ring Centre site and Roberts' Rotunda. To the west, a Civic Centre Scheme had been approved post-war but not executed. Within this zoned area, a new Repertory Theatre and the Central Library building were latterly built in the 1970s. J.A. Robert's Ringway Centre was critical of the expedient approach to town planning by the Corporation and the practice of its Estates Department to negotiate individual schemes with private owners and developers.

Inner Ring Road was to the south of the centre and housed the city's traditional retail markets, including the bomb-damaged nineteenth-century market hall. Overlooked by St Martin's Church, a significant local landmark, the area was medieval in origin yet peripheral to the commercial heart of the city.[26] The commercial property development potential lay in the profitability of creating a scheme that increased the city's retail and office capacity overall and improved relative rental values in the immediate vicinity by their inclusion in an expanded central business district. The advantage for the Corporation was that a private developer would facilitate design and development, including costs and risk, of a modern covered shopping centre, intended to draw new customers regionally and deliver greater economic success for the city.

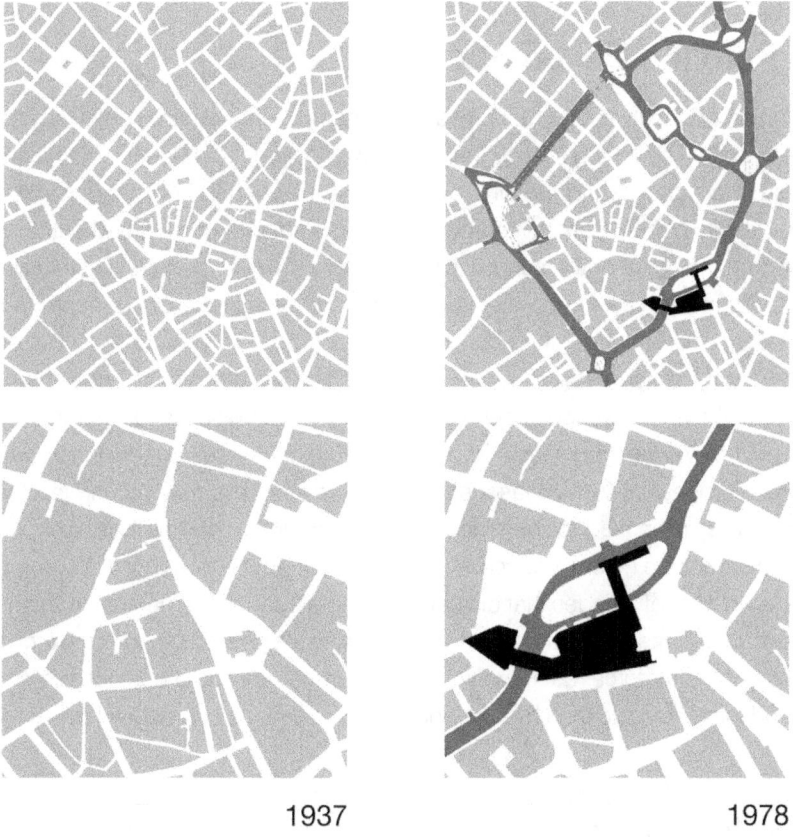

1937　　　　　　　　　　1978

Figure 15.2 Inner Ring Road and Bull Ring shopping centre site.
Source: Author's own drawing.

---

[26]The Bull Ring appears as a place name on the late eighteenth-century map of the town, but has a presumed longer association with the beast market and butchers' Shambles that occupied the area. St Martin's, rebuilt in the nineteenth century, was the medieval parish church for Birmingham.

This mix of pragmatism and belief in future prosperity delivered on the Corporation's ambition to a degree:

> By 1970 modernity was the striking feature of Birmingham... new buildings and roads made a striking contrast with many less prosperous cities. It was modern in its outlook too... was worthy of its place amongst the rebuilt cities of Europe, but an even more striking parallel was with the industrial cities of the United States. Its expressways, sprawling suburbs, tall buildings and its air of bustle and enterprise made it Britain's most transatlantic city.[27]

Moreover, the allusion to the United States also reflected precedent work undertaken in developing design requirements for the car, and specifically in research into new typologies conducted by the Corporation and others in the development programme for the Inner Ring Road and the Bull Ring scheme.

Learning from the United States

Critical thinking around the motorcar had prevailed in the post-war period, particularly in relation to the safety and conviviality of shopping streets. *Traffic in Towns* pointed to a deterioration of the environment and an increase in accidents, and the aim to protect the pedestrian from the car very much shaped approaches to design in the urban environment.[28] As Jane Jacobs has pointed out, this was part of a rhetoric focused on the 'ideal of the suburbanised anti-city... developed architecturally, sociologically, legislatively and financially' as the problem was not significantly different to conflicts between vehicles and people that had affected the nineteenth-century city.[29] At its core were the development of pedestrian areas and the segregation of people and traffic. The creation of pedestrian-only shopping districts to replace conventional high streets had previously been discussed in the *Architectural Review* of September 1941 by William and Aileen Tatton Brown. Exploring three-dimensional town planning and the twentieth-century ideal city, they reasoned that the creation of a new ground level for pedestrians was necessary.[30] They proposed for buildings to bridge roadways serving basement car parking and bus stations, with 'separate means of access for pedestrians to the buildings lining the street'.[31] These would provide 'a network of arcades that distributed people throughout the area' with shops looking inwards onto the arcade,[32] making pedestrian areas filled with life and activity through architectural variety and the absence of the motorcar as 'there would be room to come into contact with architecture on a more human and intimate scale than has ever been possible in the centre of a huge city'.[33]

---

[27] Sutcliffe and Smith, *The History of Birmingham*, 479.

[28] Ministry of Transport, *Traffic in Towns*, 19.

[29] Jane Jacobs, *The Death and Life of Great American Cities* (Harmondsworth: Penguin, 1964), 356.

[30] A. Tatton Brown and W. Tatton Brown, 'Three-Dimensional Town Planning Part 1', *The Architectural Review* 90, no. 537 (January 1941): 82–88.

[31] Ibid.

[32] Ibid.

[33] A. Tatton Brown and W. Tatton Brown, 'Three Dimensional Town Planning Part 2', *The Architectural Review* 91, no. 541 (January 1942): 17–20.

The United States, twenty years ahead of Britain, had developed its own solution to the adaptation of the shopping street for the motorcar. It had moved away from the congestion of downtown districts and established new purpose-built shopping centres located according to supply and demand and accessibility by car. The process of siting a new suburban mall was predominantly pragmatic and economic, and the Americans had spent two decades developing techniques for attracting shoppers. The commercial aspect is illustrated well in *Shopping Towns USA*; its content a planning guide to achieving 'the successful mall' and taking the reader through successive issues of siting, size, layout, methods for generating the most retail activity on plan, financing, advertising and planning for growth. Its authors, Victor Gruen and Larry Smith, advocated a simple low-level physical structure with a big-named store, visible from the road with easy access and good parking, providing protection from the weather and additional facilities to shops 'to meet other needs which are inherent in the psychological climate peculiar to suburbia'.[34] In short, a social life and recreation in a protected environment, incorporating civic and social facilities, would enhance shoppers' lives and generate a good commercial environment.

In Birmingham, the Corporation was interested in learning more about the American suburban shopping mall and the opportunities to enhance the city through such a novel shopping concept. A council delegation was sent in 1956, comprising five members of the Public Works Committee including Herbert Manzoni, 'to investigate highway and car parking development and the manner in which traffic problems were dealt with'.[35] Their itinerary included Chicago, Pittsburgh, Philadelphia and New York, with a visit in Washington to 'one of the neighbourhood shopping centres which are becoming a feature of the larger towns of the US'.[36] The subsequent report described it as 'a complete and compact shopping area including a multiple store of the type of Marks and Spencer … [where] … specialised shops surround a car parking area within a five-storey car park to hold over 600 cars'.[37] Of further interest was the Port of New York Authority bus terminal. Here 'there were two levels for bus traffic … [with] spacious and comfortable pedestrian concourses … intermediate levels provide … shops, stores and other services for the convenience of bus passengers and the general public … [and] on one floor a cafeteria refreshment bar and twelve-skittle alley produce a substantial income'.[38] This visit was influential both in terms of the ring road design (with expressways and flyovers incorporated into its layout) and in the shape of discussions with developers tendering for the several ring road frontage sites – particularly the Bull Ring site where the Corporation had earmarked the long distance bus station to go.[39]

A second visit by Sydney Greenwood, on behalf of Laing Development Company Ltd., studied in more detail the economic development of the out-of-town mall and included a visit to Victor Gruen in Los Angeles.[40] Subsequently Laing investigated the consumer market around Birmingham, considering journey times, distance, population distribution and the availability of public transport systems into the

---

[34]Gruen and Smith, *Shopping Towns USA*, 23.
[35]Public Works Committee, *Report of the Delegation Appointed by the Public Works Committee to Visit America* (Birmingham: Library of Birmingham Collections, 1956), 9.
[36]Ibid., 10.
[37]Ibid.
[38]Ibid., 18.
[39]Manzoni, 'The Inner Ring Road, Birmingham'.
[40]'Bull Ring, Birmingham', *Shop Review* (July 1961).

city centre. Comfort was a major feature in the publicity material for the scheme in which 'passengers are under cover from the time they board their bus for the Bull Ring until they step off the bus at their home destination'[41] and air conditioning, piped music, an attendant-served car park, mothers' rest room and staffed play area, restaurants, licensed premises and a ballroom suite were all proposed to contribute to the shopping and leisure experience.[42] Laing was clearly offering a revolutionary change of scene to the shopper informed by their analysis of the US-developed typology and the general marketing policy advised by Gruen and Smith's seminal book.

The Bull Ring shopping centre

If the adoption of a covered shopping centre, influenced by the transatlantic experience, was promoted by the Corporation for Birmingham strategically, the translation of an essentially suburban form into an urban context was less well-informed in terms of overarching vision or brief. A major design constraint was its relationship with the ring road, but there was little co-ordination by the Corporation in determining a specific architectural vision in the early planning stages of the Bull Ring scheme other than brief requirements 'for the intensive development of the area for retail shopping with provision for the rehousing of the traditional retail markets, provision for a central bus terminus and car parking facilities for at

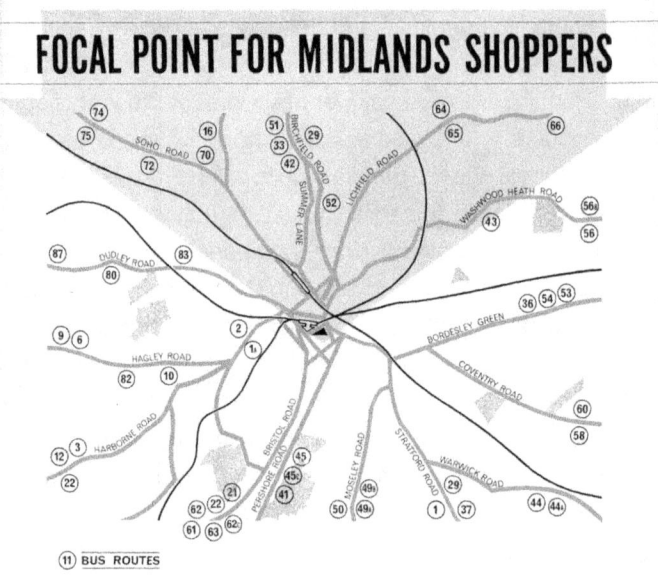

Figure 15.3 Bull Ring marketing literature advertising accessibility by bus, train and car.
Source: From Laing Development Co. Ltd., *The Bull Ring Centre Birmingham,* c.1964.

---

[41]Laing Development Co. Ltd., *The Bull Ring Centre, Birmingham*, 1960 (Birmingham: Birmingham Library Collections).
[42]Ibid.; Laing Development Co. Ltd., *The Bull Ring Shopping Centre*, c.1964 (London: British Library).

least 500 cars'.[43] Contemporary criticism levelled at the Corporation by Leslie Ginsberg, Head of the Birmingham School of Planning, was that, for ring road developments, the pace was being set by the commercial developers, and that it was by chance rather than design that already proposed schemes 'may result in a more integrated design than the City deserves'.[44] The Corporation's approach was to parcel off sometimes awkward but expensive sites on seventy-five year leases and to encourage developers in giving them a relatively free hand.[45] A degree of *laissez-faire* was apparent in the approach of the Public Works Committee for the Bull Ring site, advertised at the time 'for developers to plan this area, either as a whole or in bits and pieces'.[46] Much early work and visioning was instead done by James A Roberts, architect of the (now listed) Rotunda building adjacent the Bull Ring site, for an earlier project put forward by Property and General Investment Ltd., 'which had all but been approved by the Public Works Committee when negotiations broke down on financial grounds'.[47] This proposal, involving protracted dialogue with British Railways, Midland Red Omnibus Co. and other interests in the site including Woolworths, significantly shaped the architectural approach to both the site and the mix of functions included in the as-built Bull Ring shopping centre scheme.[48]

Roberts' aborted design straddled the ring road's multi-lane carriageways to occupy three discrete development sites, and, by pushing the open-air market into part of the new traffic island, created an entirely enclosed shopping centre accommodating multiple levels of shops, a multi-storey office development, the new store for Woolworths, restaurants, the Midland Red Bus terminal and a public garden contained by the ring road roundabout.[49] The development responded to the local topography which dropped from its highest point at New Street down towards St Martin's Church, and to the various entrance levels determined by both existing streets and proposed ring road levels. When the Public Works Committee re-advertised the site with revised terms of reference, eleven competing tenders were received, from which Laing's scheme was selected. Their scheme followed similar principles to Roberts', providing approximately 32,500 square metres of retail trading space with provision for two supermarkets, one of the largest Woolworths in Europe, departmental stores and 100 individual shop units. There was multi-storey parking for 560 cars, accessed from the south carriageway of the ring road; the new bus station entered from Dudley Street to the South, a nine-storey office block and the Midland's largest banqueting suite for up to 2000 people operated by Mecca Ltd. New indoor markets fronted the East Court adjacent the Church from where Woolworths was also accessed, serviced from a level below. One supermarket bridged across the ring road to 'Manzoni Gardens'. A second bridge with retail shops connected to accommodation to the west, planned as a department store with the banqueting suite above. This connected back to the New Street Railway Station redevelopment at higher level, with subways elsewhere breaching the 'concrete collar' of the ring road. The focal point

---

[43] Laing, *The Bull Ring Shopping Centre*, c.1964.
[44] *The Architects' Journal* (1 October 1959): 293.
[45] Ibid., 291.
[46] Ibid., 293.
[47] 'Birmingham's Bull Ring Centre', *The Architects' Journal* (4 February 1960): 187–189.
[48] Ibid.
[49] Ibid.

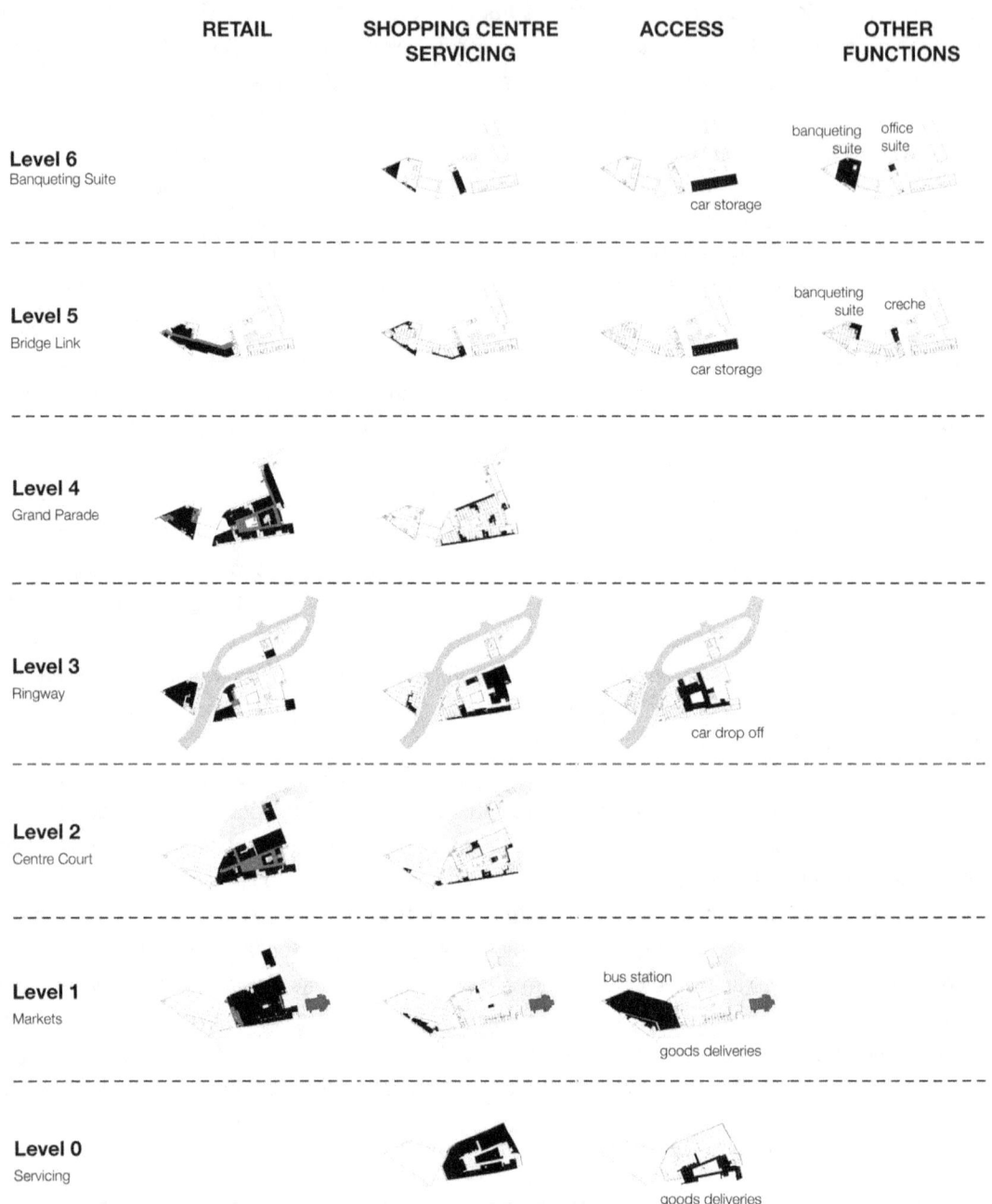

Figure 15.4 Spatial layout of the Bull Ring shopping centre, showing the interior layout from the ground level up to level six; levels seven and eight contain car storage, while levels seven up to thirteen house offices.
Source: Author's own drawing.

of the scheme was Centre Court located in the main block, an enclosed piazza where two banks of escalators carried shoppers to the upper floors.[50]

Constructed predominately from reinforced concrete with marble, quartz and reconstituted stone cladding and aluminium curtain walling, the centre was opened on 29 May 1964 by the Duke of Edinburgh who announced that 'there can be nothing wrong with the virility of civic government if it can bring about a development like this…there cannot be much wrong with architectural imagination either'.[51] Progressive and modern, with the convenience, comfort and leisure of shopping under one roof away from traffic, the scheme was pioneering for the UK but also distinct from its American cousin due to its location, complexity and relationship to the existing city centre. As Pevsner observed: 'It should be considered how this design will influence shopping centres, because the Bull Ring depends

Figure 15.5 Centre Court in the Bull Ring shopping centre.
Source: Image reference JLP01/12/001: 'Interior view Bull Ring Shopping Centre', John Laing Collection, Historic England Archive.

---

[50] Laing, *The Bull Ring Shopping Centre*, c.1964.
[51] Tim Adams, 'Elegy to the Bull Ring', *The Observer (Life)*, 5 March 1995, 27.

on some basic conceptions which make it unique... [and]... these aspects are of probably more far-reaching importance than its architecture.'[52]

Firstly, this was not the suburban prime site with surface parking that typified the American planning experience, identified to ensure good traffic flow and quick access off the highway. While Gruen illustrates more complex multi-level covered parking arrangements, most American examples were single site schemes with retail shops confined to two storeys. Birmingham's ring road defined the scheme, but here the shopper was faced with two issues. Those arriving by car and bus had easy access to the centre but their shopping experience was distributed over five levels, with connections across the road only at specific levels dictated by its engineering and the lie of the land. For those arriving by foot, the centre was dislocated from established shopping streets by the ring road, and the primary arrival points were via subways, crossing intermediately into Manzoni Gardens, or by entering the west end of the shopping centre at a higher level and bridging across. The American type was an independent self-contained shopping experience. The Bull Ring's design had to address capturing footfall from existing city shoppers as well as attracting a car-commuting destination shopper, yet in borrowing from the American model, it overemphasized accessibility by car in its approach and its marketing.

Secondly, the organization of the centre spatially stratified the retail mix inside, with the lower levels primarily serving the public markets. While Gruen's vision for the shopping centre was to serve the neighbourhood as a whole, the American model was nevertheless commercially driven in that the constraints of site, form, construction and merchandising had to be proven viable to deliver an economically profitable community shopping centre. The Bull Ring scheme was simultaneously accommodating and supplanting an existing market culture on site, with one set of design objectives serving an existing clientele, and the other creating a high-calibre destination shopping centre that, in meeting the aspirational needs of the increasingly affluent, was intended to surpass their experience of high street shopping. The commercial and civic aspirations for the site were thus at odds, with a civic ideal of a shopping centre that benefited the community as a whole, set against the developer's need to attract the tenants and trade to maintain economic viability for the construction outlay of a multi-levelled, fully enclosed and difficult to build shopping complex.

A reality check

Initial criticism directed towards Birmingham and Laing in the architectural press focused on the execution of architectural detail and disappointment that Birmingham had not seized the opportunity to make a better modern statement. Owen Luder, for example, thought that the centre worked well as a machine for receiving and distributing goods, but that its multiple levels were untested and that overall it was at best 'the champagne without the bubbles'.[53] Criticism was subsequently levelled at the Bull

---

[52]Nikolaus Pevsner and Alexandra Wedgewood, *The Buildings of England: Warwickshire* (Harmondsworth: Penguin Books, 1979), 122–123.
[53]Owen Luder, 'Birmingham's Bull Ring', *The Architect and Building News*, 26 August 1984, 400–410.

Ring shopping centre as its impact on the area began to be felt, relating to the planning theory adopted and implemented by the Corporation and the design principles applied by Laing and their architects.

There was genuine belief within the Corporation that, through the ring road and its modern developments, Birmingham was progressing. What was not questioned was for which section of society benefits accrued and conversely who might suffer at the expense of this 'progress'. Undoubtedly, Birmingham stood to gain financially from higher ground rents and the rateable values arising from redevelopment, with the intention being that this capital could be used elsewhere, especially inner city social housing provision. Other beneficiaries were the development companies that profited from commercial redevelopment, local and regional businesses and more affluent suburban residents, whose car travel into the city centre was ameliorated. That progress meant universal improvement was part and parcel of the idealistic optimism prevalent post-war. As Gordon Cherry points out, 'the control of development and planned relocation within the urban system ... all too often have served to improve options for one group of urban dweller and limit the possibilities of another'.[54]

The ring road, although successful in moving traffic, had a major impact on the social fabric of Birmingham. At six lanes, its presence was a visual and physical barrier that dislocated inner city residential pockets from the central core. This was apparent around the markets, the natural shopping area for the inner city working-class population whose access was predominately via the sequence of underpasses. The *Birmingham Mail* commented that, 'where separation has been provided around the Bull Ring, the pedestrian is treated like a second-class citizen, driven down steps and ramps into subterranean passages', with the segregation of the pedestrian 'carried out so harshly as to become a form of apartheid'.[55] Inner city residents were also overlooked in negotiations between Laing, the Corporation and Midland Bus. Only long distance bus passengers commuting from the suburbs could disembark at the Bull Ring shopping centre: there was no provision made for the Corporation bus service for central Birmingham, and no adjacent bus stops: 'indeed the new Ring Road system re-routed them far away from the Bull Ring'.[56]

The ring road also had a dramatic effect on the market itself, a lively thriving place and 'a spot well-loved and often frequented by generations of Birmingham people'.[57] The site was famed locally for its speakers' corner, but by isolating the open-air market inside the traffic island, the life, vibrancy and visual excitement of the original market was decimated. This was caused, not by the dissolution of the stalls, as the pitches remained more or less unchanged, but because of the reduced visibility of the site and cross-flow of passers-by from the market to the main shopping streets and back. As the *Birmingham Post* commented, 'perhaps the orators' corner will return, but at the moment this very human aspect is lacking, not because provision has not been made for it but because the cast seems to have dispersed, like birds before the cat next door ... [as] ... the way to Nelson's Column leads nowhere, and virtually nobody goes there'.[58] Yet the basis for the transformation of the market

---

[54]Gordon Cherry (ed.), *Urban Planning Problems* (London: Leonard Hill Books, 1974), 245.
[55]*Birmingham Mail*, 8 April 1965.
[56]*Birmingham Post*, 6 April 1991.
[57]City of Birmingham Information Department, *The Bull Ring, Birmingham*, Publication No. 27, August 1964.
[58]*Birmingham Post*, 11 February 1963.

was a belief in regeneration and improvement, and this had the support of some local traders who figured that despite increased ground rents, 'we shall attract a better class of trade...after all, this move is progress'.[59] The realization that the market thrived because of the class of people it already attracted and their economic contribution was not accepted until after comprehensive redevelopment had taken place.

Decline

Laing's promotion of a new up-market venue that complied with the Corporation's vision of extending the high street did not translate into practice. Labyrinthine, with multiple entrances and levels, artificially lit and lacking ambience due to its muted rubberized flooring, the shopping centre struggled to attract trade and it was quickly noted that pedestrians leaving the bus station exited through the market, into the subways and away to the centre of Birmingham.[60] They did not venture upstairs, either because the new shops were not of sufficient draw or because shoppers did not realize the full extent of the scheme. As a private property with opening hours (initially 11.30 pm but revised to 8.30 pm), the Centre offered few uses in the evening for anything other than window shopping, limiting casual footfall from the city centre. Ancillary leisure functions failed due to lack of economic viability with the ballroom suite and banqueting hall quickly closed after opening because the tenants pulled out. The mechanized parking was inefficient, and access to the car drop-off point designed without a filter lane caused traffic congestion, forcing the car park to close after thirty days.[61] A major problem was that the shopping centre never generated sufficient through flow. Plans in the marketing brochure for a department store did not come to fruition, and the sole anchor store was Woolworths. As early as 1965, market traders suggested that lack of variety and the presence at the far end of the scheme of a 'dead building', the Rotunda – hit by the property crash and mostly unlet – caused lack of trade.[62] By 1967 there were dozens of reports of vandalism, out-of-order escalators and 'undesirables'.[63]

The limited success that Laing had in attracting tenants led eventually to a reduction in the price of leases and a gradual re-infiltration by local shopkeepers originally kept out by the tenancy costs. In this way the Bull Ring again became the embodiment of the lower end of the retail market, in many ways similar to the retail character of the area before Laing started construction in 1961. This 'decline' mirrored the post-industrial decline of Birmingham in the latter part of the twentieth century, a popular rejection of modern architecture and growth of interest in heritage and conservation values. The material qualities of the Bull Ring shopping centre and the entire rationale of the ring road were challenged locally by a campaigning group in the 1980s, who produced an alternative development

---

[59]BCC Development Department, *Developing Birmingham, 100 Years of City Planning, 1889–1989* (Birmingham: Birmingham Library Collections, 1989), 91.
[60]Marriot, *The Property Boom*, 230.
[61]Adams, 'Elegy to the Bull Ring', 28.
[62]*Birmingham Mail*, 3 December 1965.
[63]*Birmingham Mail*, 21 April 1967.

proposal, the 'People's Plan for the Bull Ring'.[64] This aimed to repair damage done to the civic structure of the city through sensible urban design principles. Other historians have argued that 'without redevelopment Birmingham would have retained a cramped, dirty, over-crowded, inconvenient and ugly centre ... recognised as totally inadequate long before the war'.[65] While this may be true, Manzoni's modern legacy was a second comprehensive redevelopment organized around a new post-modern orthodoxy by commercial developer Hammerson, with the bulldozers moving in to clear space for a shiny new Bullring Centre opened in 2003.

---

[64]Liam Kennedy (ed.), *Remaking Birmingham: The Visual Culture of Urban Regeneration* (London: Routledge, 2004), 15.
[65]Sutcliffe and Smith, *The History of Birmingham,* 448.

Chapter 16

Malls and commercial planning policies in a compact city: The case of Barcelona
Nadia Fava and Manuel Guàrdia

In Spain commercial distribution has always trailed behind the most advanced European countries. Although from the end of the 1950s the technocratic team of Franco's regime promoted initiatives to modernize the country's retail system, these were met with only limited success. Only from the 1980s on, after the fall of Franco's regime, democratic Spanish governments adopted a policy of modernization. They liberalized commercial activity and offered assistance to small and medium enterprises. However, also then the adoption of new commercial typologies was much less intense than in other European countries. Even today, Spain trails behind the European average when it comes to shopping centre development.[1]

This chapter iterates the circumstances that informed the late arrival of new retail typologies in Spain and unravels the close relationship between commercial development and urban planning that grew in the country. After Franco's dictatorship, Barcelona in particular became a laboratory of 'commercial renewal', as many of the city's commercial structures were designed according to urban models that popularized in the 1980s, when ideas regarding public space, infrastructure and the 'compact city' governed the discourse on urban renewal. In Barcelona shopping centres thus became new points of centrality; destinations for leisure and shopping, even landmarks. This chapter places these urban commercial initiatives within international retail history and argues that in Barcelona the development of shopping centres contributed to the formation of a metropolitan city, while the typology was cleverly adapted to the culture of public space in the Mediterranean city.

Supermarkets and the public market system in a latecomer city

In the wake of the Spanish Civil War[2] (1936–1939), after a seemingly endless economic crisis and in spite of the complete isolation imposed by Franco's regime, Spain succeeded in gaining access to

---

This chapter is an outcome of the research project: *Los mercados alimentarios de Barcelona. El mercado del Born y la renovación de los mercados municipales durante el siglo XX*. (HAR2012-35387). This project was financed by the Spanish Ministry of Economy and Competitiveness.

[1] Joanna Tano, *European Shopping Centre Development Report* (London: Cushman & Wakefield Research Publication, 2015), http://www.cushmanwakefield.com/~/media/global-reports/European%20Shopping%20Centre%20Development%20Report%20Nov%202015.pdf, accessed 7 December 2015.

[2] The post-Spanish Civil War period was marked by extreme scarcity. One of the first measures taken was to regulate the retail trade in food; as a result, basic products continued to be rationed until 1952.

economic aid, thanks to the agreements reached with the United States in the context of the Cold War. Starting from the end of the 1950s, a less interventionist economic model was promoted by Franco's technocratic team, which gave retailing in the country a first thrust towards modernity. At this time, the United States became an important point of reference. In November 1956 a group of Spanish industrialists, merchants and politicians travelled to the United States to study American retailing. Their report entitled 'The Retail Market in the United States'[3] focused predominantly on supermarkets, while shopping centres were barely mentioned. Of course, when this visit took place, shopping centres in United States had only just started their conquest of the American territory.[4] Furthermore, when the report was drafted, significant social and economic disparities existed between Spain and the United States. A rapid proliferation of shopping centres in Spain must therefore have seemed unlikely to the authors of the report.[5] What the report did highlight was the specific changes that the Spanish food retail system should make to improve profits, including 'product concentration and freedom of service' and more efficient manufacturing and supply. It also recommended that greater attention be paid to creating an appropriate atmosphere for buying through the careful presentation of merchandise, adjusted lighting and qualitative packaging. Still, after years of shortages, Spain was far removed from the American lifestyle; a discrepancy that was pointed to in the report, which described America's more advanced motorization, higher female employment rate and greater ownership of electrical household appliances, including refrigerators – all prerequisites for the supermarket's economic success.

Following this report, the General Office of Supplies and Transport (Comisaría General de Abastecimientos y Transportes) launched 'Operation Supermarket' in 1958.[6] This operation, which received economic and logistic support from the state, promoted the establishment of the public Compañía Auxiliar de Abastecimientos, S.A. (CABSA, or Auxiliary Company of Supplies Corporation), which supported the opening of sixty public supermarkets in the country's leading cities. These supermarkets[7] were to offer a model that would encourage private enterprise in the sector. On 24 December 1958,[8] the first publicly financed supermarket opened in Barcelona, closed to the Passeig de Gràcia.[9] Over the next two years another five public supermarkets[10] opened in other well-to-do districts of the city, following the same location strategies as the *grandes dames* of retailing, the department

---

[3]Spanish Ministry of Industry, National Commission for Industrial Productivity, *El mercado detallista en Estados Unidos: memoria del viaje de intercambio técnico realizado por un grupo de industriales y comerciantes españoles a los Estados Unidos de Norteamérica* (Madrid: Ministerio de Industria. Comisión Nacional de Productividad Industrial, 1957).

[4]Although the first mall was built in the United States in 1922, malls did not begin to spread in earnest until the end of the 1950s. Rem Koolhaas (ed.), *The Harvard Design School Guide to Shopping* (Köln: Taschen, 2001).

[5]The rate of Spanish car ownership in the 1960s was, for instance, fourteen vehicles per 1,000 people, in comparison to 411 vehicles per 1,000 people in the United States at that time. See Joyce Dargay, Dermot Gately and Martin Sommer, 'Vehicle Ownership and Income Growth, Worldwide: 1960–2030', *The Energy Journal* 28, no. 4 (2007): 143–170.

[6]Daniel Venteo, *Caprabo 1959–2009* (Barcelona: Caprabo, 2009), 41.

[7]Some of these supermarkets were of mixed public and private ownership, while others were strictly private enterprises.

[8]'El ministro señor Gual Villaibí inauguró ayer el primer supermercado de Barcelona', *La Vanguardia*, 24 December 1958, 28.

[9]Passatge Domingo, Barcelona.

[10]Autoservicio Granvía (Gran Via de les Corts Catalanes, 538), Superservis (Galerías Astoria, with two entrances, one at Rambla dels Estudis, 113, and the other at Xuclà, 14), and Supermarket (Ronda Sant Antoni, 1 and Urgell, 2, right in front of the Sant Antoni public market hall).

stores.[11] However, in political and economical terms, the success of 'Operation Supermarket' did not lie in its creation of a public network of supermarkets, but rather in stimulating interest in the private sector for the new commercial formula. The General Office of Supplies and Transport provided both logistical and financial support. On the one hand, it offered information about transportation, handling and storage of goods, and on the other hand managed the inflation rate and developed financial incentives for private enterprises interested in opening a supermarket.

Other initiatives were also taken to support the country's economy. In 1956 a law was approved that laid the foundation for what became the most active period of market hall construction. It strove to locate a market hall within walking distance (or within less than one kilometre) of each home in every district of every town. Following this legislation, between 1957 and 1977, eighteen neighbourhood market halls were built in Barcelona in poorly serviced and marginal areas of the city. These complemented the public supermarkets that were constructed in more upmarket locations following 'Operation Supermarket'. Contrary to retail developments in the United States, these two initiatives did not aim to create a suburban food supply system in the city's outskirts, but sought to encourage 'proximity shopping'. The result was a new supermarket network, which aimed to

Figure 16.1 Josè Brangulì Soler, Opening of the public market Felipe II, 1966, Barcelona.
Source: Arxiu Nacional de Catalunya, Barcelona.

---

[11]Patrícia Faciabén Lacorte, 'Los grandes almacenes en Barcelona', *Scripta Nova* VII, no. 140 (2003).

introduce modernity for the elite – as it located these supermarkets almost exclusively in symbolic and central locations of the city – and a more 'low-brow' system of traditional public market halls, which was more concerned with price and social control[12] and which was indiscriminately spread over the city.

The French 'Hypermarché' in Catalonia in the final period of Franco's regime

The economic liberalization of Spain during the so-called 'developmentism' (*desarrollismo*) period (1959–1973)[13] was characterized by the progressive opening of the economy to foreign capital, which strengthened the presence of French economic activity in the country, especially in the retail sector. Some of the largest French companies, including Carrefour, Printemps and Prisunic, saw opportunities for business in the growing Spanish market. A special inducement was given by the Royer Law, which was passed in December 1973 in response to the bankruptcy of a substantial number of traditional shops following the growth of large retail chains in France during the 1960s.[14] This law placed restrictions on the opening of new hypermarkets and contributed to a policy of internationalization by targeting large French retailers.[15] The retail experience that French companies had acquired in their home country allowed them to rapidly adapt their stock management and logistics to support supply to their Spanish branches.[16] The ensuing success of French companies in Spain could be attributed to their long-standing knowledge of the local market and its consumers.[17]

In the 1960s Spain entered the age of mass consumption. The relative improvement of income levels went hand in hand with the modernization of retail distribution channels and the establishment of large numbers of new businesses.[18] The introduction of the so-called 'hypermarket' in Spain by French companies was, just as in other Southern European countries such as Portugal and Italy, the first step towards the shopping centre. It introduced modern distribution techniques and new economic formulas to reduce sales prices. The first hypermarket in Spain opened in 1973 during the oil crisis, when the control of food prices was one of the government's main concerns. In 1973 the Minister of Economy Agustín Cotorruelo proclaimed hypermarkets a 'novelty...which appears to be able to

---

[12]Luis Moreno and Sebastià Sarra, 'The Spanish "Via Media" to the Development of the Welfare State', in *Working Paper* 92-13 (Madrid: IESA-CSIC, 1992); Carles Carrera, 'Tradition and Modernity. Competition among Retail Location in Contemporary Barcelona', *Belgeo* 1–2 (2006): 41–51.

[13]In 1959 the Stabilization Plan (*Plan de Estabilización*) was approved by the government of Spain, the objective of which was the stabilization and liberalization of the Spanish economy.

[14]Loi Royer, 27/12/1973, is a part of the *Code du Commerce de la France*, 1974.

[15]Rafael Castro Balaguer, *Génesis y transformación de un modelo de inversión internacional: el capital francés en la España del siglo xx*, doctoral thesis (Madrid: Universidad Complutense de Madrid; Director: Nuria Puig Raposo, 2011), 238.

[16]Ibid.

[17]France had bilateral economic relations with Spain since the eighteenth century. While during the nineteenth century the French mainly invested in banking and the railways, during the 1960s, it expanded to other, new sectors. In 1960, in Madrid, SIMAGO, the first Spanish supermarket chain, was founded with capital from Hispanic-Cuban families (Simó, Mayorga and Gómez) with the stock holding from the French companies Printemps and PRISUNIC.

[18]Balaguer, *Génesis y transformación de un modelo de inversión internacional*, 202.

offer better prices in exchange for the purchase of products in large amounts, now that cars and refrigerators are widespread'.[19]

On 19 July 1973,[20] the first Spanish hypermarket was opened in the town of El Prat de Llobregat, close to Barcelona's airport and cargo port, near the new Mediterranean Motorway. This initiative of the Iberian Hypermarkets company and the French Euromarché was presented as a revolutionary new formula that would radically transform the way people shopped by making it 'easy, pleasant and fast'.[21] Located in Barcelona's densifying hinterland, in close proximity of a major road intersection

Figure 16.2 Advertising of the 'Hiper', 1973.
Source: Advertising of the 'Hiper', *La Avanguardia*, 28 June 1973, 31.

---

[19]'novedad …, los cuales parecen estar en condiciones de ofrecer mejores precios a cambio de adquirir grandes cantidades, cosa que la popularizados de los coches y las neveras hace hoy perfectamente posible?' Source: 'Comercialización y alzas de precios', *La Vanguardia*, 4 October 1973, 5.
[20]'Inauguración del "Hipermercado"', *La Vanguardia,* 18 July 1973, 26.
[21]'El hiper de Barcelona, Una nueva raza de almacenes', *La Vanguardia*, 12 July 1973, 29.

that connected the city to the coastline in an area in which every one in two families owned a car,[22] it had a stable number of one million potential customers, to which the French tourists could be added during the summer season. The single storey building had 13,000 m^2 of sales area, a bar-restaurant for 500 people, a day care centre and parking for 2000 cars. The 300 employees working in this *hypermarché* sold furniture, carpets, electrical devices, photographic and sound equipment, hardware, textiles, clothing, footwear and a wide range of processed food. The press welcomed this modern store, reflecting that 'new criteria and techniques already proven in Europe [are] now implemented in our country... Its main goal is to allow quick and economical purchases, solving the shopping problems in big cities on the basis of time, not distance'.[23] Also politicians hailed the *hypermarché* as a development that 'would promote social advancement and help to raise the standard of living of low- and middle-income Spaniards, who would benefit from the cheaper prices'.[24]

That same year another French company, Hyper-Carrefour, opened the 'Hyper' in the same area. Although both supermarkets were initially well received, they soon encountered difficulties. The new, labour-intensive system of distribution, packaging and selling did not, for instance, immediately result in profits. The economic crisis of the seventies strongly affected the middle classes, which was the main target group of the new shopping centres, while well-to-do Spaniards who were accustomed to shopping in a more traditional way resisted this new development. Finally, the powerful system of public market halls, of which nearly forty were located nearby (in Barcelona) and which had controlled food prices, formed an important economic rival to the hypermarkets.

The advent of regional suburban shopping centres

Between 1973 and 1985 Spain, just like most other European countries, experienced a severe economic and social crisis, which was characterized by steep inflation, high unemployment rates and a slow growth in the gross domestic product. In Spain this crisis coincided with a shift from an authoritarian to a democratic political regime, which was more welcoming of international influences, and accompanied by citizens and workers' demand for improved living and working conditions. The stage was set for political and social transformation as a welfare system comparable to that of other European states was introduced to the country.

In Catalonia this process was accompanied by a renewed nationalistic spirit.[25] If the Spanish government saw the development of the retail system as a key component of the country's internationalization policies, which were to ensure Spain's entry into the European Community, the

---

[22]Balaguer, *Génesis y transformación de un modelo de inversión internacional*, 239.

[23]'a nuevos criterios y técnicas ya probados en Europa y que ahora se ponen en práctica en nuestro país. Los objetivos principales están en línea con los criterios da una compra rápida y económica, planteando la solución de los problemas de compras de las grandes ciudades en términos de tiempo, no de distancia.' Source: 'Inauguración del "Hipermercado"', *La Vanguardia*, 18 July 1973, 26.

[24]'"Romper los precios", gran labor social del nuevo Hiper de Barcelona', *La Vanguardia*, 19 July 1973, 31.

[25]The Spanish general election took place on 15 June 1977. The first election of the Parliament of Catalonia was celebrated on 20 March 1980.

Catalan Parliament favoured a different approach and supported local, traditional small- and medium-sized enterprises. These ambiguous political circumstances led to the modernization of commercial policies in two partially conflicting areas: market deregulation,[26] supported by the state, and assistance for local enterprises, promoted by local government. While across Europe large retail centres rapidly emerged, the Catalan government attempted to impose restraints on the proliferation of foreign companies in the local urban context. Beyond the city limits, however, and as a result of national policies aimed at deregulation, large shopping centres did manifest themselves.

Since 1976, Barcelona was governed by the General Metropolitan Plan of Barcelona.[27] This plan envisioned a greater metropolitan Barcelona connected by highways, along which the development of regional shopping centres was projected. There, it was thought, these structures would not compete with the traditional retail stores in the inner city. The Baricentro (1980), Centro Comercial Montigalà (1991) and Centro Comercial Barnasud (1995) were developed as a result. These were located at crucial points of the mobility network and in the vicinity of high-density public housing estates. Built in the second suburban belt, Centro Comercial Montigalà in the north, Baricentro in the west and Centro Comercial Barnasud[28] in the south divided the catchment area into equal parts. If Baricentro compensated for the lack of commercial services in the nearby districts, Centro Comercial Montigalà and Centro Comercial Barnasud, which were built more than ten years later, became new nodes of centrality[29] in the region and catalysed further development.[30]

Baricentro is located in Cerdanyola del Vallès close to the large housing estates of Ciutat Badia (1972), Can Serraperrera (1973) and Fontetes (1972),[31] along the external ring road connecting Barcelona to the second-belt periphery. In the 1980s Baricentro was the only suburban shopping centre in Catalonia. Its location strategy echoed that of the first *hypermarché*: at a crossroads of the Barcelona-Terrassa and Mollet-Papiol motorways for easy accessibility. It also followed the strategy of the French shopping centres in other ways:[32] located outside the urban area, it offered a broad range of shops as well other services such as a bar, a restaurant and a nursery to 'make shopping easier for ladies and

---

[26] Helena Villarejo Galende, 'Balance de una década de regulación de los grandes establecimientos comerciales en España', *Ciudades* 10 (2007): 49–66 and Guy M. Clifford, 'Controlling New Retailing Space: the Impress of Planning Policies in Western Europe', *Urban Studies* 34, no. 5–6 (1998): 953–979.

[27] The General Metropolitan Plan of Barcelona (1976) was the result of a long development process for a regional planning project that involved twenty-seven municipalities connected by fast road and public transport facilities and safeguarded Barcelona's role as central city.

[28] 'Nuevo gran centro comercial al sur de Barcelona', *La Vanguardia,* 18 December 1993, 57.

[29] Juan Mendoza Sans, Fernando de Galán, José Ignacio, 'Los nuevos espacios comerciales en la Región Metropolitana de Barcelona', *Papers: Regió Metropolitana de Barcelona: Territori, estratègies, planejament* no. 22 (1995): 69–80.

[30] The territorial system of Barcelona's regional shopping centres can to a certain extent be compared to Victor Gruen's plan for the decentralization of shopping centres (funded by the Hudson Company) around Detroit. However, despite its appearance and the final result, this development around Barcelona was not the result of a large-scale (territorial) plan for commercial distribution; it merely resulted from the desire to create optimal catchment areas. See Victor Gruen, *The Heart of Our Cities. The Urban Crisis: Diagnosis and Cure* (New York: Simon and Schuster, 1964). Victor Gruen and Larry Smith, *Shopping Towns USA: The Planning of Shopping Centers* (New York, Amsterdam, London: Reinhold Publishing Corporation, 1960), 36.

[31] Josep Maria Carreras i Quilis (ed.), *50 anys de transformacions territorials: 1956–2006. Àrea i regió metropolitana de Barcelona* (Barcelona: Àrea Metropolitana de Barcelona, 2013).

[32] In France, Sweden and the UK, the shopping centre assumed a central role in new town planning.

Figure 16.3 Baricentro, under construction, 1980.
Source: 'L35 Arquitectos' office, Barcelona (www.l35.com/).

families'.[33] Clearly the rapidly changing and pivotal role of women for the success of shopping centres was – just as in most other Western countries – well understood. In 1979 the press announced the construction of Baricentro as the first regional shopping centre in Spain.[34] It was hailed as one of the few outstanding facilities under construction in the region, featuring '54,100 square meters of floor space with over one hundred stores in different specialties, a large hypermarket operated by the French-Spanish chain Continent, three cinemas, restaurants, gardens and parking facilities for four thousand vehicles'.[35] In its advertising Baricentro explicated it aspired to become a 'big shopping city'.[36] If supermarkets relied on their advantageous prices to draw people to the supermarket, Baricentro banked on the sense of urbanity and centrality it offered to the growing low-density suburbs for its survival.

Urban and commercial policies: Towards a compact Mediterranean city

If the Plan General Metropolitano had a strong influence on the location strategies of the first suburban regional commercial centres, Barcelona's municipal urban policies of the 1980s determined to a

---

[33]'Baricentro 34 años de una experiencia de compra única', *La Vanguardia,* 3 November 2014, 2.
[34]The project began in 1972, but it was only completed in 1980.
[35]'El "Shopping" comprende 54.100 metros cuadrados de superficie en los que se albergarán más de un centenar de tiendas de distintas especialidades, unos grandes almacenes un hipermercado explotado por la cadena franco-española Continente, tres cines, restaurantes, jardines y "parking" para cuatro mil vehículos'. Source: 'Sismograma económico', *La Vanguardia*, 27 May 1979, 37.
[36]*La Vanguardia*, 15 April 1980, 54.

great extent the emergence of inner city retailing. After Franco's death in 1975, democracy returned to Spain; Catalonia recuperated its autonomous government, the Generalitat de Catalunya, and Barcelona elected a socialist city government. Between 1980 and 1984, when architect Oriol Bohigas was urban designer of the city council, he launched a plan to 'reconstruct' the city. This plan was carried forward by Joan Busquets when he took over the position from Bohigas in 1984; an appointment he retained until 1989. In this period, Barcelona, like many other European cities, experienced demographic decline. There was thus no need to expand the city and Barcelona's planning policies accordingly came to favour the development of shopping centres within the existing urban fabric. In his 'reconstruction' of the historical city, Bohigas conceived of Barcelona as a set of neighbourhoods rather than one grand metropolis. He regarded public spaces as carriers of collective identity and therefore proposed targeted actions to consolidate public spaces in the central city and stimulate the development of such spaces in the periphery. In his book *Plans and Projects in Barcelona*, Bohigas explains that at the time the key goal of the city's urban policy was to 'modernize the historic centre and monumentalize the periphery'.[37]

During his mandate, Busquets suggested a more structured model, and identified twelve 'new centrality' areas within the city, which were connected to the metropolitan inner road system. His plan was more extensive and also better embedded within the territory. It was based on the image of a poly-nuclear city with a ramified structure, in which new commercial centres were to reinforce the existing fabric or add a new point of centrality. Montjuic, Vall d'Hebron, the Olympic Village and Port Vell were such 'new centralities' designed to accommodate the tourists attending the 1992 Summer Olympic Games. Although the Olympic Games strengthened Barcelona as a city, the metropolitan area benefited from these improvements only marginally, as they increased the dichotomy between the centre and the periphery. At this time, municipal policies attributed a strategic role to the public markets; they were deemed essential for the development of a fine-grained commercial structure. The Special Plan for Food Retailing Facilities of the City of Barcelona, approved in 1985, for instance, pinpointed municipal market halls as the main vehicle for updating the retail system as a whole. Market halls were thought of as lively commercial hubs able to encourage commerce not only inside the market, but also in the surrounding area. Public markets were thus considered 'basic polarities' for the renovation of the spatial structure of commercial activities within the city. The Special Plan accordingly concentrated on the renovation of the existing network of market halls and on preserving the local retail shops in the nearby areas, rather than on fostering new sales systems. In 1991 the Municipal Institute of Markets of Barcelona was established to administer and modernize the municipal market halls, and to maintain their social, civic and cultural centrality, while promoting traditional food retailing.

During the 1990s processes of globalization and deindustrialization informed developments in Barcelona as cities across the globe increasingly competed through 'urban marketing'. In Barcelona new cultural and service programmes were introduced to redress the city's image and economy. The introduction of shopping centres played an important role in this process and was characterized

---

[37] Oriol Bohigas, *Plans i projectes per a Barcelona 1981–1982* (Barcelona: Ajuntament de Barcelona, 1983), 65.

by two distinct phases: the first (1989–1996) with interventions in the central, most consolidated and prosperous part of the city, and the second (1997–2011) with projects in the eastern part of the city where renovation was needed.[38]

Between 1989 and 1996, seven shopping centres were opened within Barcelona's first ring road. Almost all of them were inscribed in the 'new centrality areas', which were developed for the Olympic Games. Located in the central-western and most prosperous areas of the city, close to touristic attractions, they could easily be reached by both public and private transport. The first facility, designed by the well-known architects Manuel de Solà Morales and Rafael Moneo, was the shopping mall L'Illa Diagonal.[39] It proposed an architectural and urban space that echoed the expectations of tourists and well-to-do Barcelonans. Located next to the small commercial Pedralbes Center[40] (1989) on the 'Golden Block', it fostered commercial activity on the Avinguda Diagonal. The mall opened on 2 December 1993, during a time of retail crisis,[41] in the wake of the Summer Olympics. The press, however, described its opening as the 'last event of the 1992 Olympics'.

Two other commercial centres were inaugurated in the same period along the coastline: Maremagnum[42] (1995) and El Centre de la Vila (1995). Similarly to Maremagnum,[43] which oscillated between success and disaster 'with a brilliant start by recreational and leisure activities, and about

Figure 16.4 L'Illa Diagonal shopping centre 1988–2007: before and after construction, Barcelona.
Source: Paisajes Españoles, S.A., Madrid.

---

[38]The centre commercial Las Arenas, located in Plaça d'Espanya, is an exception.

[39]The symbol of the mall carried a message: it showed a circle that attracted other smaller circles, creating voids on the rest of the paper.

[40]Pedralbes Center only measured 5400 square metres.

[41]'Las ventas del comercio minorista en Cataluña se reducen un 15% hasta mayo', *La Vanguardia*, 18 June 1993, 63.

[42]The Maremagnum complex (1995), designed by Helio Piñón and Albert Viaplana, is situated on the seafront in a former loading bay in the Port of Barcelona. It was extensively renovated in 2005 by Ricard Marcadè; L35 Arquitectos refurbished the third floor in 2012.

[43]'El Port Vell abre definitivamente un Moll d'Espanya lúdico y comercial para Barcelona', *La Vanguardia*, 8 May 1995, 36; 'El Maremàgnum les viene grande', *El País*, 1 February 2002; 'Cara y cruz en el Maremàgnum', *El Periódico*, 9 January 2014.

to collapse precisely because of nocturnal excesses',[44] 'El Centre de la Vila' never became a true success. Located in the Port Olympic district, it is a well-established cinema complex but the commercial activities never took off. Its relative failure has several reasons, ranging from its location, dimensions and commercial strategy to the capacity to manage the demands of the consumers and enterprises.

The shopping centre, Les Glòries,[45] which opened in the same year, was not inscribed in the Olympic area. It announced an important change in the role of private investments in the construction of the city. The City Council planned to renovate the neighbourhoods around the Les Glòries mall, which was characterized by aging and degraded spaces. This renovation encompassed the enlargement of Avinguda Diagonal to the sea, the construction of 5000 apartments, the completion of the waterfront and the renewal of the Glòries – Sagrera – Sant Andreu axis with the future TGV station.[46] Les Glòries was designed to boost private investments in the eastern part of the city. Today the shopping centres along Avinguda Diagonal – L'Illa Diagonal and Les Glòries – are considered important elements of the city.[47] They have consolidated the long-standing commercial role of the Avinguda Diagonal, with an extensive retail offer that is easily accessible from both the surrounding neighbourhoods and from the inner city. Maremagnum and Centre de la Vila shopping centres were planned as tourist and district commercial centres, but did not fully achieve these goals.

The economical and political crisis following the Summer Olympics, the impact of the first shopping malls on local stores and the enactment of the Planning of Retail Commerce Law in 1996 had an impact on the locational strategy of the shopping centres. Similar to the Royer Law in France and in line with the law of 1987, the 1996 law limited the construction of shopping centres larger than 2500 m² within the city. Once again, it implicitly favoured small retail outlets such as supermarkets, public market halls and local and traditional shops in the central area of the city. The goal of this law was to foster and shape an image of the compact, walkable Mediterranean city while strengthening Barcelona's reputation as an international tourist destination. In the second phase, between 1996 and 2011, the malls were thought of as 'anchors' or 'new urban cores' for peripheral districts that were in need of monumentalization and new facilities. Regional shopping centres in the Eastern part of Barcelona like La Maquinista (2000), Heron City (2001) and Diagonal Mar (2002) easily connected with metropolitan Barcelona and the inner city. They were believed to introduce new centralities of public space through private initiative.

---

[44]'La trayectoria del Maremàgnum ha oscilado varias veces entre el éxito y el desastre, con un inicio fulgurante gracias a las actividades lúdicas y de ocio, y a punto de hundirse precisamente por los desmanes nocturnos.' Source: 'Cara y cruz en el Maremàgnum', El Periodico, 9 January 2014.

[45]This complex was designed by Cristian Cirici Associates S.A. & D. José Galán and was financed by a consortium of Spanish and French investors, which was composed of Zona Franca, SCIC España and a French firm Caisse des Dépôts.

[46]'Las grandes áreas comerciales ganan terreno en la región metropolitana Barcelona Glories abre mañana sus puertas con una inversión de 40.000 millones', La Vanguardia, 18 April 1995, 32.

[47]In 2014, L35 Arquitectos, for instance, extensively restored the Les Glòries mall, and enlarged its sales area to 13,700 m²; this in a sector of the city where retailing is in a deep crisis.

Figure 16.5 Diagonal Mar shopping centre under construction in Barcelona, 2001.
Source: Manuel Guàrdia, courtesy Arxiu Nacional de Catalunya, Barcelona.

Conclusion: A balanced balance?

The 1990s, which ironically announced the start of the 'demalling' process in the United States, marked Barcelona's most important phase of shopping centre construction. An under-saturated market in combination with national policies favouring large corporations encouraged construction until long after the year 2000. Contrary to the situation in most Western countries, shopping centres in Barcelona increased in number well into the twenty-first century. Twelve shopping centres opened between 2000 and 2014 in the Barcelona metropolitan area. In 2011, in the middle of the important economic and social recessions, the last shopping centre was inaugurated: Les Arenes, by architect Norman Foster, was located in one of the most strategic public spaces of Barcelona, Plaça d'Espanya. This project, which was ostensibly born old, follows a model that does not respond to present needs and struggles to survive.

The public policy of protecting and strengthening the commercial fabric that gives shape to the consolidated city has not ceased in Barcelona. Within the city, malls are now obtaining permits to increase their volume, especially in less prosperous areas. In 2014, an article in the national newspaper *El País*, for instance, announced that 'Barcelona expands malls in the districts with the largest number of vacant business premises'.[48] A lack of expertise on commercial renewal, limited knowledge on negative experiences in countries such as France, together with electoral interests in the case of Catalonia, have resulted in an excess of large stores. The ambitious renewal of the public market halls and their surroundings, which was launched in 1990 to bolster proximity commerce, is thus still continuing today. The constant concern for public space has contributed to this process. Highly significant in this respect are the recent reforms of the city's principal thoroughfares, Passeig de Gràcia and Avinguda Diagonal. These reforms are meant to boost the competitiveness of Barcelona's tourist-oriented and high-quality commercial fabric. At the same time, an alternative economy of sustainable open-air markets, second-hand markets, farmers' markets and festival food vans is gradually emerging, which contributes to a new urban sociability and novel urban centralities. They promote a different kind of shopping experience that is more rooted in the city's history and culture, and competes with the anonymous experience of the 1990s shopping centres.

---

[48]'Barcelona amplía centros comerciales en los distritos con más locales vacíos', *El País*, 19 October 2014.

Index

Abraham & Strauss 185
Abraham Elzas 185
Adenauer, Konrad 96–7, 99, 100, 108, 109
Adorno, Theodor W. 12, 98
advertising 77, 112, 132, 147, 148, 151, 159, 164, 189, 224, 230, 242, 245
Albini, Franco 174, 175, 177
Americanization 26
Anderlecht (Belgium) 29, 53, 54, 56, 59, 60, 61, 62
Aplin, Sue 148
Aronson, Albert 122, 126, 127, 132, 133, 136
Arsovski, Tihomir 84, 86, 89, 90
Association of Large Enterprise of Distribution (AGED), Belgium 53
Auchan (France) 29, 112–13
Auderghem (Belgium) 29, 52, 56
Auxiliary Company of Supplies Corporation, Spain 239
Avermaete, Tom 1, 11, 12, 110–21

Babić, Boris 164–5
Bakema, Jaap 8, 9, 16, 65, 70, 71, 72, 74, 75, 76, 77, 80, 84, 161, 199
Baker, Geoffrey 15
Bakker, Herman 70
Banham, Reyner 173, 174
Barcelona (Spain)
    Baricentro 244–5
    Centro Comercial Barnasud 244
    Centro Comercial Montigalà 244
    Diagonal Mar 248–9
    El Centre de la Vila 247–8
    Felipe II 240
    Heron City 248
    Hyper-Carrefour 243
    Hypermarket (*hipermercado*) 238–40, 242–3
    La Maquinista 248
    Les Arenes 249
    Les Glòries 248
    L'Illa Diagonal 247–8
    Maremagnum 247–8
    Olympic Games 246–8
    Operation Supermarket 239, 240
    Pedralbes Center 247
    Summer Olympics 247–8
Barčot, Sanja Matijević 13, 14, 155–67
Bartels, Fin 215–16
Basic plan (*basisplan*) 65, 68, 72, 74, 184, 194. *See also* van Traa, Cornelis
Baudrillard, Jean 20, 31
Beaudouin, Eugène 114
Behrens, Peter 217
Belgrade Institute of Town Planning 80
Bengtzon, Olle 132
Bennet Group 196
Bernardi, Bernardo 163
Bernhard Engle & Partners 217–18
Beveridge Report 223
Beveridge, William 139, 223
Birmingham (UK)
    Bullring Centre 237
    Inner Ring Road 224–30
    St Martin's Church 227, 231
Blomme, Marcel 56, 58
Bo Bardi, Lina 179
Bocconi brothers 168, 170
Bohigas, Oriol 246
Boijsen & Efvergren 126, 131
Bombardelli, Vuko 164
Borletti, Senatore 170
Brent Cross Shopping Centre (Britain) 16–18
Breuer, Marcel 16, 70, 183, 185–95
Brezovski, Slavko 80
Brussels (Belgium)
    Amelinckx (real estate company) 60
    Anderlecht shopping centre 52–4, 56, 59–62
    Auderghem hyper market 52, 54, 56
    Devimo (real estate company) 53, 56, 58, 60–2
    Etrimo (real estate company) 58–60
    Westland shopping centre 8, 53–5, 59, 61–3
    Woluwe shopping centre 8, 53–61, 64
Buchanan, Colin 225
Bull Ring Shopping Centre (Birmingham) 18, 222–3, 226–36

Burchard, John Ely 107–8
Burton, Frederik 196

Calandra, Roberto 168, 176, 177, 178
Candilis, Georges 95
capitalism 10, 12–13, 21, 31, 96–8, 103, 123, 138, 157
Carandente, Giovanni 179
Carrefour 28–30, 32, 52, 112–13, 121, 241, 243
Cauwe, Maurice 53, 55, 56
Centre Pompidou 174
Cergy-Pointoise (France) 31–2
Chaban-Delmas, Jacques 32
Cherry, Gordon 235
Childs, Marquis W. 123
Churchill, Winston 139
Ciborowski, Adolf 79, 81, 83, 88
civic education 3, 141, 147
civic identity 16, 191–3
Cold War 27, 109, 158, 239
Colenbrander, Bernard 73
communism 96, 156–7
Communist Information Bureau 78
Congrès International d'Architecture Moderne (CIAM) 34, 65, 67, 75–6, 95, 101, 126, 160, 161, 192
consumer-citizens 3, 9–15
consumerism 5, 10, 13, 97–8, 106–7, 123, 131–2, 136–7, 148, 155, 157–8, 166–7, 194, 201, 209, 224
Copeland, Novak & Israël 58
corporate identity 172, 193
Crimson Architectural Historians 67, 71
Croatia 3, 13, 80, 155–6, 159, 160–7
Croatian Institute of Town Planning 80
Cronache della Rinascente 171, 173
Crossick, Geoffrey 193
Crossmann, Richard 140
Cumbernauld (UK) 13, 140–1
Cupers, Kenny 7, 8, 16, 25, 27

Dal Co, Francesco 67, 179
de Balkany, Robert 30
De Bodt, Jean-Pierre 55–6, 58
de Gaulle, Charles 7, 26
De Grazia, Victoria 9–10, 26, 111, 139, 158
de Rudder, Steffen 16, 17, 196
de Solà Morales, Manuel 247
Djordjevic, Aleksandar 80
Douglass, Lathrop 30
Doxiadis Associates 79
Dudok, Willem 183–5

Eiermann, Egon 98, 205, 211, 212
Elephant and Castle scheme 18

Elias, Norbert 97, 98
Elzas, Abraham 185
Erhard, Ludwig 10, 96–7
Erskine, Ralph 5, 6
Ervi, Aarne 41, 47–9
Essel, André 113
Euromarché 29, 242
Évry (France) 8, 16, 26–7, 31–5, 37

Farrell, Terry 150–1
Farsta (Sweden) 13, 40, 45
Fava, Nadia 20, 238
Feher, Ferenc 155
Feldt, Kjell-Olof 134
Finland 3, 8, 16, 38–40, 42, 44–6, 48–50
First World War 217
Fledderus, Rein 72
Flodin, Otto 41, 42
Foster, Norman 249
Fournier, Marcel 28–30, 113
Franchini, Gianfranco 174
Franco, Francisco 20, 238–9, 241, 246
Frankfurt (Germany)
    Candilis–Josic–Woods' project 16, 96, 98, 99–107, 109
    Dom (cathedral) 100
    Frankfurt-Römerberg 10, 11, 16, 19, 96, 100, 101, 102, 104–6, 109
    Old St Nicholas Church 10, 100
    Römer (town hall) 100
Franzén, Lars-Olof 131, 132, 134
Franzén, Mats 124, 131
Freie Universität Berlin 109
Freisleben, Hans Ulrich 213
Frisch, Max 100
Frölunda Torg shopping centre 217
Funaro, Bruno 15
Furman, S. 81

Gabo, Naum 190, 195
Gardella, Ignazio 177–9
GB group 52–3, 55–6, 63
Gelevski, Živko 84
General Office of Supplies and Transport 239–40
Germany. *See also* Frankfurt; Main-Taunus-Zentrum (MTZ) in Frankfurt
    Bikini tower block 211
    Born market 215
    Europa-Center 211–12, 220
    Forum Steglitz 215–17
    Hamburg-Langenhorn shopping centre 215
    Leverkusen shopping centre 215

Index

Mannheim-Vogelsang centre 215
Ruhrpark shopping centre 17, 196 211, 213, 214
Schwaben-Center 219–20
Ulm-Böfingen shopping centre 215
Wolfsburg-Detmerode shopping centre 215
Giedion, Sigfied 192
Ginsberg, Leslie 231
Gisbertz, Olaf 18, 210–21
Globke, Hans 97
Godard, Jean-Luc 10, 167
Gosseye, Janina 1, 13, 16, 138–54
Goulet, Jean 114, 115, 118, 119
Goulet-Turpin 11, 112, 114–15, 118–19
Granfelt, Bertel 128
Greenwood, Sydney 18, 226, 229
Grgić, Ana 13–14, 155–67
Gropius, Walter 98, 100, 199
Groupe Tekhné 56–8
Gruen, Victor 1, 3–6, 15, 21, 30, 40, 42, 56, 77, 142, 161, 193–5, 203, 209–10, 219, 222, 229–30, 234, 244. *See also* Southdale; *Shopping Towns USA*
Guàrdia, Manuel 20, 238–49

Habermas, Jürgen 98, 109
Hård af Segerstad, Ulf 122, 125–6, 131–2, 135
Harlow (UK) 1, 13
Haukkavaara, Ahti 42
Heinrichs, Georg 215–16
Helg, Franca 174, 175, 177
Heller, Agnes 155
Helsinki (Finland)
Building Act 38
Chamber of Commerce 38–44, 46, 184, 194
Elanto 43, 45
Heikintori 43, 48–50
Kesko 43, 45
Ministry of Interior 38, 124, 125
Munkkivuori 8, 16, 43–5, 49
OTK 43
Puotinharju (Puhos) 8, 16, 43, 45–6
Regional Planning Association 8, 38–9, 41–2, 49
Regional Planning Committee 38, 41–3, 45, 48, 50
SOK 43, 45
Tapiola 8, 16, 42–3, 47–50
Town Planning Act 38
Tukkukauppojen Oy 44
Helsinki-Kannelmäki shopping centre 217
Hentrich, Helmut 199, 211–12
Hirst, T.J. 18, 226
Hondermarcq, Henry 62
Hoog Catharijne (the Netherlands) 18–19, 21
Horkheimer, Max 12, 98

Howick, Gwen 151
Huber, Max 172–3
Hypermarket (*hypermarché*)
Anderlech 29, 52–4, 56, 59, 60–2
Auderghem 29, 52, 54, 56
French 27–9, 30–2, 52, 238, 243
GB group 29, 52–3, 55–6
Parent, Claude 118–21
Spanish hypermarket 242

Intermarché 112
Italy 10, 14–15, 78, 142, 168–73, 177, 180, 241. *See also* La Rinascente Upim; Unico Prezzo Italiano (Italy)

Jacobs, Jane 204, 228
Jacoby, Helmut 143–4
Jankovic, Živorad 165
Janson, Alvar 137
Janssens, Jozef 60–1
Jaumain, Serge 193
Jerde, Jon 67
Jobst Siedler, Wolf 204
Josic, Alexis 95
Jowett, Bill 148

Kalogjera, Berislav 161, 163
Kardelj, Edvard 79, 156
Karvinen, Erkki 42, 45, 47, 50, 217
Ketchum, Morris 40–2
Kidrič, Boris 156
Kitchen, Roger 148
Kivikoski, Juhani 44
Klemming, Hijalmar 217
Konstantinovski, Gjorgji 82–4
Koteks shopping centre 165–6
Kraemer, Friedrich Wilhelm 199
Krijgsman, Arie 70
Kučan, Ninoslav 164–5
Kučan, Vjera 164–5

La Rinascente Upim
in Catania 176, 177, 179
in Messina 176, 180
in Milan 171
in Rome 174–5, 177
Lahti, Juhana 8, 16, 38
Laing, John 223
Laing Development Company Ltd. 229
Larry Smith &Co 34
Le Corbusier 80, 95
Le Couteur, Jean 34
Leclerc, Edouard 29

Lederman, Martin 185
Leloutre, Géry 8, 51–64
Lijn, Liliane 146–7
Lintonbon, Jo 18, 222–37
Loebermann, Harald 205
Lord Campbell of Eskan 138, 141, 146
Luckmann, Charles 200
Luder, Owen 234
Luleå shopping centre 5–6

Maaskant, Hugh 70
Mack, Jennifer 12, 16, 122–37
Macmillan, Harold 224
Main-Taunus-Zentrum (MTZ) in Frankfurt 16, 17, 196–209, 213
Makedonija-proekt 80, 84
Maki, Fuhimiko 71
Maldonado, Tomàs 172
Manzoni Gardens 231, 234
Manzoni, Herbert 225–6, 229, 237
Mariotti, Jasna 9, 78–91
Markova, Lidija 84
Markus, Gyorgy 155
Marly (France) 26
Marshall Plan 96, 112, 200
Marwick, Arthur 222
mass consumption 3, 11–12, 15, 18, 31, 105, 110–15, 117–18, 120–1, 127, 129, 140, 196, 210–12, 241
Mattsson, Helena 122, 125 126, 131
Mendelsohn, Erich 205
Merrion shopping centre 18
Messel, Alfred 205, 212
Meurman, Otto-Iivari 40, 47
Midland Red Omnibus Co., UK 231
Million Programme 12, 122, 125–6, 135, 136
Milton Keynes' Centre 13, 138–54
    Milton Keynes Development Corporation (MKDC) 138–9, 141–53
Miscevic, Radovan 9, 80–1
Mitscherlich, Alexander 105, 106, 204
Mitscherlich, Margarete 105
Moneo, Rafael 247
Mosscrop, Stuart 142, 153
Mulliez, Gérard 113
Mumford, Lewis 9, 55, 65, 76
Munari, Bruno 172

National Cash Register Company (NCRC), Dayton 113
National Health Service and National Insurance Acts (UK, 1946) 223
neighbourhood unit 40, 126, 139–41, 177

new town 1, 6–8, 11–13, 16, 20–1, 26–7, 31–4, 47–8, 50, 55, 67–9, 115, 122, 125, 132, 136, 138–42, 145–6, 154
New Towns Act (UK, 1946) 13, 139
Niggemeyer, Elisabeth 204
Non-Aligned Movement 13, 78, 87, 157
Norman, Ann-Marie 133–5
Nuremberg Race Laws 97

Old George Mall 217–18
open-air markets 137, 231, 235, 250
Otto, Frei 199

Palme, Olof 134
Parent, Claude
    Commercial centres; for Epernay-Pierry 115, 120; for Ris-Orangis 115–16, 119–20; for Sens 111, 115, 118, 120–1; for Tinqueux 115, 120
    oblique architecture/ oblique function (*fonction oblique*) 11, 12, 115–21
Paris (France)
    housing estates (*grands ensembles*) 26–7, 30–1, 34
    Parly 25–6, 30–3
    Rosny 31
    Vélizy 31
parking facilities 3–5, 8, 10, 16, 26, 28–9, 33–5, 45
    in Barcelona 245
    in Brussels 5, 8, 52, 58, 60–1
    in Croatia 3, 164–5
    in Frankfurt 16, 101, 199, 201, 208
    in German shopping centres 207, 208, 213–15, 218, 220
    in Helsinki 8, 45–6, 49
    in Main-Taunus-Zentrum 201, 203 205, 207
    in Milton Keynes' Centre 16, 151
    in Parent's design 113, 118–19
    in Rinascente-Upim 174
    in Skärholmen centre 126, 131–2
    in Skopje 86
Patterson, Patrick Hyder 156
Pepper-Center 212
Perec, Georges 110
Pernaja, Antero 44
Pernaja, Pertti 44
Perry, Clarence 126
Persson, Lars 130
Petri, J. 19
Petschnigg, Hubert 199, 211–12
Pevsner, Nikolaus 151, 222, 233
Piano, Renzo 174
Piccinato, Luigi 80
Pictet, Jacques 29

Index

Planning of Retail Commerce Law (Spain, 1996) 248
Polservice (Warsaw) 79
Ponti, Gio 118
Popovski, Živko 9, 83–6, 89
Printemps 25, 32, 241
Prisunic 241
Promodès 112
Provoost, Michelle 69
public market 234, 238, 243, 246, 248, 250

Ravnikar, Eduard 80
Redslob, Edwin 212
RER *(Réseau Express Régional)*, France 34
Revell, Viljo 44, 50
Rhode, Helmut 205
Riar, Inderbir Singh 10, 16, 95–109
Roberts, Edward 196
Roberts, James A. 226, 231
Robinson, Kenneth 147
Rogers, Ernesto Nathan 107, 173, 174
Rogers, Richard 174
Roivola, Antero 45
Ross, Kristin 110
Rotival, Maurice 80
Rotterdam (The Netherlands)
    ASRO (Adviesburo Stadsplan Rotterdam), 74
    Basisplan 65, 68, 72, 74
    Bijenkorf 16, 70, 183–7, 193–5
    Lijnbaan 1, 9, 16, 19, 41, 65–77, 84, 184, 189, 192, 193, 199
    Magazijn de Bijenkorf 183
    OPRO (Architectenwerkgroep Opbouw Rotterdam) 74
    reconstruction plan 184
    Stadsvest 68
Royal Institute of British Architects (RIBA) 141
Royer Law (France) 241, 248
Rožic, Slaven 165–6

Saarelainen, Jussi 45
Sandstedt, Eva 124, 131
Scarpa, Carlo 177, 179, 180
Schein, Ionel 113
Schmid-Ott, Christoph 215–16
Schöffer, Nicolas 113, 114
Schoszberger, Hans 200–1, 203, 211
Schwartzman, Daniel 185
Schwebes, Paul 200, 201, 203, 211
Schwippert, Hans 98
Sears, Roebuck & Co 58, 185
Second World War 1, 5, 8–9, 16, 26, 29, 40–2, 65, 68, 84, 90, 139, 169, 171, 220, 223

self-service 27, 29, 52, 105, 112–14, 120, 124, 129, 140, 158, 202, 224
Sert, Josep-Lluís 58
Shapely, Peter 139, 146, 150
Shopping Towns USA 1, 6, 15, 30, 40, 77, 222, 229. *See also* Victor Gruen
Sidenbladh, Göran 132, 136
Sjöberg, Arne 40–1
Skärholmen Centrum (Sweden) 12, 122–37
    Skärholmen Committee 133–4
Skopje (Macedonia)
    City Trade Centre 9, 79, 82–91
    earthquake 78–81, 83, 87, 89–91
    Institute of Town Planning and Architecture of Skopje (ITPA) 79, 80, 81
    International Board of Consultants 79
    master plan 79, 81, 83
    reconstruction 9, 78–84, 87, 89–90
Smith, Larry 1, 30, 34, 229
Smith, Peter 151
socialism 78, 96, 123, 155–6
Solal, Jean-Louis 30–1
Southard, Tony 144
Southdale shopping centre 4–6, 30, 203. *See also* Victor Gruen
Soziale Marktwirtschaft (social market economy) 10, 96–7, 109
Spanish Civil War 238
Stalin, Joseph 156–7
Stevenage (UK) 13–14
Studio Scimemi 80
suburbanization 8, 26, 28, 34, 52, 55, 64, 199, 203, 204, 209, 210
supermarkets 2, 27–8, 30, 51–2, 86, 112, 114, 140, 158, 160, 202, 231, 236–8, 240, 243, 245, 248
Svenska Bostäder 122, 126, 131
Swinfield, John 150

Tafuri, Manfredo 67, 174
Tange, Kenzo 9, 80, 81
Tassiot, Gerald 119
Tatton Brown, Aileen 228
Tatton Brown, William 228
Taylor, David 151
Team 10 76, 95, 101, 107–8
television 75, 123–4, 129, 132, 150, 224
Tentori, Francesco 174
Thatcher, Margaret 21, 138, 149
Thelaus, Erik 217
Tito, Josip Broz 13
Tito–Stalin Split (or Yugoslav–Soviet Split) 78, 156
Toulouse-le-Mirail (France) 11, 107

tourists 243, 246–7
Town and Country Planning Act (UK, 1947) 224
Trujillo, Bernard 29–30, 34, 53, 113
Tsilika, Evangelia 16, 183–95

Unico Prezzo Italiano (Italy). See also La Rinascente Upim
  in Messina 177
  in Rome 177
United Nations 79–81, 82, 87
United Nations Development Programme 80–1
Urbanism and Trade International Association (URBANICOM) 53

Vadala', Daniele 14–15, 168–80
Vällingby (Sweden) 1, 6–7, 13, 40–1, 45, 55, 60, 64, 136, 199, 203
van den Broek, Jo 8, 9, 16, 65, 70, 71, 72, 74, 77, 80, 83–4, 199
van den Heuvel, Dirk 9, 16, 65
van der Rohe, Mies 98, 199
van Gool, Frans 69, 70, 73
Vanhaelen, Yannick 8, 51–63

Vanstiphout, Wouter 72
van Traa, Cornelis 65, 68, 72, 74, 184, 194. See also specific entries

Wagenaar, Cor 65
Walker, Derek 67, 141, 142, 143, 144, 145, 153
Weiß, Erhard 203, 204
Weissmann, Ernest 79, 80
welfare state 1–3, 8, 21, 75, 77, 95–6, 102–3, 109, 122, 128, 132, 137, 139, 150, 153, 168, 180, 186, 224
Wenzler, Fedor 80–1
Werner, Bruno E. 95
Wigforss, Ernst 5
Witteveen, W.G. 194
Woods, Shadrach 95
Woodward, Christopher 142, 153

Yugoslav Architects Association 80–1
Yugoslav Town Planning Federation 80–1
Yugoslavia 13–14, 78–9, 83, 87, 89, 91, 156–8, 161, 163, 165–7

Zagreb Fair 158, 159

www.ingramcontent.com/pod-product-compliance
Lightning Source LLC
Chambersburg PA
CBHW082033300426
44117CB00015B/2466